The Age of Revolutions in Global Context, *c*.1760–1840

Edited by

DAVID ARMITAGE

and

SANJAY SUBRAHMANYAM

palgrave
macmillan

First published 2010 by
PALGRAVE MACMILLAN

Palgrave Macmillan in the UK is an imprint of Macmillan Publishers Limited, registered in England, company number 785998, of Houndmills, Basingstoke, Hampshire RG21 6XS.

Palgrave Macmillan in the US is a division of St Martin's Press LLC, 175 Fifth Avenue, New York, NY 10010.

Palgrave Macmillan is the global academic imprint of the above companies and has companies and representatives throughout the world.

Palgrave® and Macmillan® are registered trademarks in the United States, the United Kingdom, Europe and other countries

ISBN 978-0-230-58047-3   ISBN 978-1-137-01415-3 (eBook)

DOI 10.1007/978-1-137-01415-3

This book is printed on paper suitable for recycling and made from fully managed and sustained forest sources. Logging, pulping and manufacturing processes are expected to conform to the environmental regulations of the country of origin.

A catalogue record for this book is available from the British Library.

A catalog record for this book is available from the Library of Congress.

10 9 8 7 6 5 4 3 2 1
19 18 17 16 15 14 13 12 11 10

Contents

List of Maps	vii
Acknowledgements	viii
Notes on the Contributors	ix

Introduction: The Age of Revolutions, *c*.1760–1840 –
Global Causation, Connection, and Comparison — xii
David Armitage and Sanjay Subrahmanyam

1 Sparks from the Altar of '76: International Repercussions
and Reconsiderations of the American Revolution — 1
Gary B. Nash

2 The French Revolution in Global Context — 20
Lynn Hunt

3 Revolutionary Exiles: The American Loyalist and
French Émigré Diasporas — 37
Maya Jasanoff

4 Iberian Passages: Continuity and Change in the
South Atlantic — 59
Jeremy Adelman

5 The Caribbean in the Age of Revolution — 83
David Geggus

6 The Dynamics of History in Africa and the Atlantic
'Age of Revolutions' — 101
Joseph C. Miller

7 Playing Muslim: Bonaparte's Army of the Orient
and Euro-Muslim Creolization — 125
Juan Cole

8 Imperial Revolutions and Global Repercussions:
South Asia and the World, *c*.1750–1850 — 144
Robert Travers

9 Revolutionary Europe and the Destruction of Java's
   Old Order, 1808–1830   167
   Peter Carey

10 Their Own Path to Crisis? Social Change, State-Building
   and the Limits of Qing Expansion, *c.*1770–1840   189
   Kenneth Pomeranz

   The Age of Revolutions in Global Context:
   An Afterword   209
   C. A. Bayly

   Notes   218

   Further Reading   273

   Index   288

List of Maps

1 The world in the Age of Revolutions   xx
2 The Americas in the late eighteenth century   67
3 The Caribbean in the Age of Revolutions   90
4 China in the eighteenth century   198

Acknowledgements

This volume emerged in large part from a conference entitled '"Age of Revolutions" or "World Crisis"? Global Causation, Connection, and Comparison, *c*.1760–1840', held at the William Andrews Clark Memorial Library in Los Angeles on 16 and 17 May 2008. For making that event possible, we owe special thanks to the Director of UCLA's Center for Seventeenth- and Eighteenth-Century Studies, Peter Reill, who supported the conception from the start and worked hard to ensure its realization. The moral and intellectual support of two of UCLA's senior historians, Lynn Hunt and Gary Nash, was crucial as the project took shape. We are also grateful to the Center's staff, especially Candis Snoddy and Camie Howard-Rock, for making the conference as pleasant as it was memorable. And our thanks go to Björn Wittrock, the Principal of the Swedish Collegium for Advanced Study in Uppsala, for co-sponsoring the conference. We were fortunate that Max Edling and Marie-Christine Skuncke could represent SCAS in Los Angeles, not least because Max first planted the seed for this project with a different collaboration in mind.

At Palgrave Macmillan, Kate Haines has been a notably supportive editor and Jenni Burnell, Felicity Noble and Cecily Wilson have propelled every stage of the publishing process. Palgrave's referees offered acute comments on the manuscript and Joyce Chaplin kindly read the Introduction. Lex Berman, Joshua Hill, and Gabriel Paquette offered much help with the maps. The contributors produced ambitious and original chapters with great enthusiasm and then revised them to rather strict editorial deadlines. Without their remarkable commitment and professionalism, this volume would not have been possible. Finally, we must thank Chris Bayly, who was unable to attend the conference in Los Angeles, but whose inspiration has been vital to the project throughout.

Notes on the Contributors

Jeremy Adelman is the Walter Samuel Carpenter III Professor of History and Director of the Council for International Teaching and Research at Princeton University. Among his many publications, the most recent are *Sovereignty and Revolution in the Iberian Atlantic* (2006) and (as co-author) *Worlds Together, Worlds Apart: A History of the World from the Origins of Humankind to the Present*, 2nd edn (2008). He is currently working on a biography of Albert O. Hirschman.

David Armitage is the Lloyd C. Blankfein Professor of History at Harvard University. Among his publications are *The Ideological Origins of the British Empire* (2000), *The Declaration of Independence: A Global History* (2007) and *The British Atlantic World, 1500–1800*, 2nd edn (2009), co-edited with Michael J. Braddick. He is currently working on a history of ideas of civil war from Rome to Iraq.

C. A. Bayly is the Vere Harmsworth Professor of Imperial and Naval History at the University of Cambridge. Among his publications are *Imperial Meridian: The British Empire and the World 1780–1830* (1989), *Empire and Information: Intelligence Gathering and Social Communication in India, 1780–1870* (1996) and *The Birth of the Modern World, 1780–1914: Global Connections and Comparisons* (2004). He is currently working on the history of Indian liberalism in the nineteenth and twentieth centuries.

Peter Carey is Fellow Emeritus of Trinity College, Oxford. Among his publications are (as editor) *The British in Java, 1811–1816: A Javanese Account* (1992) and *The Power of Prophecy: Prince Dipanagara and the End of an Old Order in Java, 1785–1855* (2007). He is currently based in Jakarta as Country Director for the Cambodia Trust, a British disability charity that has established Indonesia's first internationally accredited School of Prosthetics and Orthotics.

Juan Cole is the Richard P. Mitchell Collegiate Professor of History at the University of Michigan. He is author most recently of *Sacred Space and Holy War: The Politics, Culture and History of Shi'ite Islam* (2002), *Napoleon's Egypt: Invading the Middle East* (2007) and *Engaging the Muslim World* (2009). His weblog is 'Informed Comment' (www.juancole.com).

David Geggus is Professor of History at the University of Florida, Gainesville. His publications include *Slavery, War and Revolution: The British Occupation of Saint Domingue, 1793–1798* (1982), *Haitian Revolutionary Studies* (2002) and *The World of the Haitian Revolution* (2009), co-edited with Norman Fiering.

Lynn Hunt is the Eugen Weber Professor of Modern European History at the University of California, Los Angeles. She is the author of *Politics, Culture, and Class in the French Revolution* (1984), *The Family Romance of the French Revolution* (1992), *Inventing Human Rights* (2007) and various works on the methods of cultural history and historical epistemology.

Maya Jasanoff is Associate Professor of History at Harvard University. Among her publications are *Edge of Empire: Lives, Culture, and Conquest in the East, 1750–1850* (2005) and articles in *Past and Present* and the *William and Mary Quarterly*. She is currently completing a global history of the American loyalist diaspora.

Joseph C. Miller is the T. Cary Johnson, Jr. Professor of History at the University of Virginia. Among his publications is *Way of Death: Merchant Capitalism and the Angolan Slave Trade, 1730–1830* (1988). He is currently working on a world history of slaving.

Gary B. Nash is Professor of History Emeritus at the University of California, Los Angeles, and Director of the National Center for History in the Schools. Among his recent publications are *The Unknown American Revolution: The Unruly Birth of Democracy and the Struggle to Create America* (2005), *The Forgotten Fifth: African Americans in the Age of Revolution* (2006) and (with Graham Hodges) *Friends of Liberty: Thomas Jefferson, Tadeusz Kosciuszko, and Agrippa Hull: Three Patriots, Two Revolutions and a Tragic Betrayal in the New Nation* (2008). *The Liberty Bell: An American Icon* will be published in 2010.

Kenneth Pomeranz is Chancellor's Professor of History and Professor of East Asian Languages at the University of California, Irvine. His two best known books are *The Making of a Hinterland: State, Society, and Economy in Inland North China, 1853–1937* (1993) and *The Great Divergence: China, Europe, and the Making of the Modern World Economy* (2000). His current projects include work on environmental history, comparative political economy and the history of popular religion.

Sanjay Subrahmanyam is Professor and Doshi Chair of Indian History at the University of California, Los Angeles, where he also directs the Center for India and South Asia. Among his publications are *The Political Economy of Commerce: Southern India, 1500–1650* (1990), *Penumbral Visions: Making Polities in Early Modern South Asia* (2001), *Explorations in Connected History*, 2 vols (2005) and, most recently, *Indo-Persian Travels in the Age of Discoveries, 1400–1800* (2007), written jointly with Muzaffar Alam.

Robert Travers is Associate Professor of History at Cornell University. He is the author of *Ideology and Empire in Eighteenth-Century India: The British in Bengal* (2007).

Introduction: The Age of Revolutions, c.1760–1840 – Global Causation, Connection, and Comparison

David Armitage and Sanjay Subrahmanyam

The decades on either side of the turn of the nineteenth century have long been known as the 'Age of Revolutions'. The term is one of the most enduring period markers known to modern historians and has often been used by other scholars invested in identifying pivotal moments in the emergence of a putatively modern world. The revolutionary elements traditionally identified as most characteristic of the period and ripest with promise for the future included the popular sovereignty, natural rights language, and secessionist independence of the American Revolution, the anti-monarchical and anti-aristocratic decapitation of the Old Regime effected in the French Revolution, and the apparent explosion of productivity and prosperity associated with the Industrial Revolution. To these key features might be added the first formal efforts to abolish the slave trade (and, later, slavery itself), the proliferation of written constitutions as novel instruments for the distribution of political power, and an upsurge of nationalisms both within Europe and amid the first stirrings of decolonization in the Americas. The very heterogeneity of these developments defied easy causal integration but that did not prevent later historians from connecting many of them into a single epochal nexus. The combinations differed but the designation varied little, whether as a singular Age of Revolution or as a plural Age of Revolutions that were complex in their forms but cumulatively reinforcing in their long-term, world-historical effects.

The term 'Age of Revolutions' originated during the period it describes; however, its contemporary usages do not map exactly onto the geography, the chronology, or the morphology of change later associated with it. 'The "age of revolutions" arrived early in India', one historian has recently noted of the 1750s and 1760s: 'nowhere more so than in Bengal. Contemporary Britons frequently used the term "revolutions" in describing the East India Company's rise to military and political pre-eminence in Eastern India, and Indo-Persian sources used a similar term, *inqilab*.[1] Writing in this vein in August 1757, the East India Company commander Robert Clive told his father that 'a revolution has been effected . . . scarcely to be paralleled in history' after the defeat of the young nawab of Bengal, Siraj-ud-daula, at the battle of Plassey.[2] Fifteen years later in Patna, the Persian chronicler Ghulam Husain Khan Tabataba'i Husaini documented 'the revolutions of Bengal and Azimabad, as far down as the year 1194 of the Hedjra [1774 CE]' in his *Sair al-Muta'akhkhirin* ('An Overview of Modern Times') (*c*.1783).[3] Back in Europe, Jean-Jacques Rousseau had proclaimed in his *Émile* (1762) that 'we are approaching the state of crisis and the century of revolutions'.[4] By 1791, after both the American and French Revolutions, Thomas Paine thought it had finally arrived: 'It is an age of Revolutions, in which every thing may be looked for.'[5] And in 1815, John Adams assimilated the American Revolution, the French Revolution, and the Spanish-American revolutions into a single transformative moment: 'The last twenty-five years of the last century, and the first fifteen years of this, may be called the age of revolutions and constitutions.'[6]

In this book, our chronological definition of the Age of Revolutions is more expansive still, and covers the roughly eighty years from the Seven Years War (1756–63) to the beginning of the Anglo-Chinese Opium War (1839–42). By starting some years before the American Revolution and ending after the climax of the wars that shattered the Iberian empires of the Atlantic world, and by framing its concerns within such global conflicts, the book aims to envisage the Age of Revolutions in terms of the connections, both long-term and long-range, experienced by contemporaries. However, it excludes earlier significant political shifts, such as those produced by 'the Persian Napoleon' Nadir Shah (r. 1736–47) in his expansive conquests of the 1730s and 1740s, which most historians today see not as the start of something new but as closing a pattern that harked back to the great Turkic conqueror Tamerlane in the fourteenth century; it also chooses not to look ahead to Europe in 1848, to the Taiping Rebellion of the 1850s and 1860s, or to the Great Indian Rebellion of 1857–8, which seem to us to foreshadow in important ways other momentous changes beyond those most definitive of the Age of Revolutions treated in this volume.

The Age of Revolutions as defined here ranges geographically widely to encompass almost all the period's major regions and polities, from the North Atlantic World, South America, and the

Caribbean, via Africa and the Middle East, to South and South-east Asia and China. While the scope of the book has been designed to be extensive in space, it is quite intensive in time, in order to map the dimensions of change – and, indeed, of stability and the resistance to change – around the world more precisely than would be possible on a much broader timescale. It is also what might be called a 'transitive' global history: that is, a history that takes an object – in this case, the various changes subsumed under the flexible category of 'revolution' – and places it in global perspective. It does not attempt to be an 'intransitive' global history, an account of globalization or globality itself in the late eighteenth and early nineteenth centuries, though it contains much material that might contribute to a world history focused on the Age of Revolutions.

The Age of Revolutions in Global Context brings together historical specialists in most of the major areas of the world to examine the relevance and implications of models of an 'Age of Revolutions' or a 'World Crisis' to the regions they know best. On the basis of their contributions, it should be possible to begin crafting an account of the chains of causation, modes of connection, and means of comparison that might allow the decades on either side of the turn of the nineteenth century to be seen as a whole and on a global scale. The various authors have chosen different modes in which to tackle these dimensions of explanation as they apply to their own fields. Some offer integrated narratives that stress transregional and global connections. Others, in fields where the current state of research does not permit such a synthesis, emphasize instead historiographical prospects and possibilities. And, while some look outward from their particular regions to the wider world beyond them, others reverse the perspective to examine the convergence of global forces in specific regions. A fully integrated account will only be possible when all the historiographies touched by our subject have reached similar levels of development, both empirical and methodological. For the moment, a diversity of approaches is still needed. We have tried to represent that variety in the chapters, and in the accompanying guides to further reading, that follow.

To better define the book's object, it is worth beginning by asking: what were the meanings of 'revolution' in the Age of Revolutions? The period was one in which traditional ideas of 'revolution' still coexisted with newly defined conceptions generated out of the two political upheavals that have usually been seen as key to its character, the American, in the 1770s, and the French, in the late 1780s and early 1790s. Other political transformations that were seen in terms of revolutionary changes were in Haiti and Spanish America. However, it is evident that even the American and French Revolutions were so vastly different in character that only a capacious concept of 'revolution' could contain them both. The first was an instance of a regional rebellion of some scale led largely by a slave-owning creole elite, resulting in the secession of part of the territory of an empire while leaving most of the rest of that empire along with the imperial centre itself intact in terms of its dynastic logic and institutions of rule: as Gary Nash shows in his contribution to this volume, its revolutionary promises were imperfectly fulfilled, especially for the enslaved population of the infant United States and their abolitionist sympathizers in Europe.[7] The French Revolution was a more thoroughgoing instance of change being effected at an imperial centre, even if that change was eventually reversed in part, first by Bonaparte, and then by a variety of monarchical regimes in the nineteenth century. The key feature that these two somewhat disparate processes had in common was the imagining and construction of a type of notionally 'acephalous', non-monarchical polity for the first time in the North Atlantic world since the experiments at the end of the English Civil War in 1649, with the formation of the short-lived English Commonwealth. To many people in about 1800, the political language of 'revolution' thus came to imply at the very least the overthrow of monarchy.

But clearly this had not always been the case, and one needs to be careful in employing a term of this complexity. As the conceptual historian Reinhart Koselleck has reminded us, with a warning against expanding the term revolution 'to include every last element on our globe', 'our concept of "revolution" cannot be defined save as a flexible general concept [*Allgemeinbegriff*], which may find a general, *a priori*, consensus everywhere but whose precise meaning is subject to considerable variations from one country to another and one political field to another'.[8] To come to grips with what 'revolution' usually meant, it is worth turning for a moment to early modern thinkers in Western Europe before the American and French Revolutions. In 1661, the ageing French intellectual Jean Chapelain addressed a letter to his younger acquaintance, the physician and traveller François Bernier, then in the Mughal Empire ruled over by Aurangzeb. It was essential, he wrote, that the traveller should inform himself 'of the history and the revolutions of that kingdom [*l'histoire et les révolutions de ce royaume*], not merely since Tamerlane and his successors, but *ab ovo* and since Alexander'.[9] Chapelain apparently did not mean the word 'revolution' to represent just any kind of political change. Rather he meant the word to signify political changes accompanied by military struggles and civil wars, even if they did not call into question the monarchical institution itself. For this reason, Bernier was able to treat the struggle between the four sons of the emperor Shahjahan in the 1650s under the title *Histoire de la dernière révolution des États du Grand Mogol* (1670).[10]

In a similar vein, roughly a century later, the French priest Louis Bazin would write from Iran of the confusion that attended the death of Nadir Shah in a public letter with a title that spoke of 'the revolutions that followed the death of Thamas-Kouli Khan [Nadir Shah]' (*les révolutions qui suivirent la mort de Thamas-Kouli Khan*).[11] In the two instances, the usage was further facilitated by a convergence between Indo-Persian and European political terminology, for in the former too the idea that political change could be produced as a form of 'revolution' (*inqilab*) was common enough. It would be in this sense that both Robert Clive and Ghulam Husain's translator, Haji Mustafa, used the term 'revolution' of events in Bengal in the 1760s and 1770s. Between that time and the years in which Paine wrote his celebrated missive to the Abbé Raynal on the subject of the American Revolution in 1782 and then celebrated the 'Age of Revolutions' in 1791, it is possible that a partial shift took place in the meaning of the term, placing it less in the sphere of cyclical movement and more within a definite teleology, or sense of historical irreversibility. But it seems that it was still the older usage that informed a text such as Jucherau de Saint-Denys's *Révolutions de Constantinople en 1807 et 1808* (1818), regarding the tumultuous replacement of the Ottoman sultan Selim III by Mustafa IV, and then the latter's rapid replacement by Mahmud II.[12]

★ ★ ★

With this variety of overlapping, backward-looking and forward-tending, conceptions of revolution in mind, we can see some of the limitations of the two classic surveys of the Age of Revolutions from the late twentieth century. Fifty years ago, R. R. Palmer's monumental two-volume study *The Age of the Democratic Revolution* (1959–64) portrayed a series of assaults on aristocracy in the name of democracy from the Appalachians almost to the Urals. Yet for the American Palmer, as for his French collaborator Jacques Godechot, this cosmopolitan movement of political liberation took place within a unitary Western Civilization whose Mediterranean was the Atlantic Ocean.[13] In this regard, his conception was recognizably a product of the Cold War. It was also congruent with the contemporaneous assessment made in 1957 by the American modernization theorists Max Millikan and W. W. Rostow 'that we are in the midst of a great world revolution' in human aspirations, economic development, and social integration.[14]

The promise of the Age of the Democratic Revolution might have been similarly universal and teleological but its immediate historical effects were more tightly bounded. Palmer's study halted in 1799 on the threshold of the nineteenth century, just ahead of the Haitian Revolution of 1804 and decades before the Latin American revolutions had run their course.[15] On Palmer's account, the Caribbean and South America had to wait for liberation along with much of the rest of the world: 'The eighteenth century saw the Revolution of the Western world; the twentieth century, the Revolution of the non-Western.'[16] The democratic revolution was thus a gift from the North Atlantic world to other peoples who had apparently contributed nothing to its original emancipatory potential. The late eighteenth-century 'world revolution of the West', as Palmer rather oxymoronically called it, spread outward from the mostly metropolitan centres of the Atlantic world to the rest of the globe over the next century and a half. 'All revolutions since 1800, in Europe, Latin America, Asia, and Africa', Palmer concluded, 'have learned from the eighteenth-century Revolution of Western Civilization.'[17]

The other great synthetic survey of the period, Eric Hobsbawm's *The Age of Revolution, 1789–1848* (1962), bracketed out the American Revolution and described instead the combined effects of the French Revolution and the British Industrial Revolution as 'the twin crater of a . . . regional volcano' located in north-western Europe. As described by Hobsbawm, its initial eruption was regional but the consequences were global: 'since the world revolution spread outwards from the double crater of England and France it initially took the form of a European expansion in and conquest of the rest of the world'. This was a triumph of industrial capitalism and bourgeois liberalism whose effects would decisively shape the world's history right up to the moment at which Hobsbawm wrote. Industry had stoked empire but, as Hobsbawm argued, empire exported its own gravediggers. By the early 1960s, 'the worldwide revolt against the west', inspired in part by 'the revolutionary socialist and communist ideology born out of reaction against the dual revolution', was in full swing. For Hobsbawm, at least, what the West had taught the rest was how to roll back the European hegemony that had been the long-term legacy of the revolutionary era.[18] However, as Robert Travers argues in his contribution to this volume, Hobsbawm's narrative of Europeans' global hegemony in the late eighteenth century 'appears to have been conjured up by a number of historical sleights of hand'. It compressed into a few decades processes of political, military, and commercial insinuation into the world beyond Europe that had taken a century or more. It assimilated indigenous scholarship and political reflection to European categories rather than the specific traditions from which they sprang. And it overestimated the technological differences between Europeans and their allies and adversaries, especially in South Asia.[19]

In retrospect, for all their grand ambitions and real historical achievements, both Palmer's and Hobsbawm's visions of the revolutionary era now appear strikingly Eurotropic, if not quite Eurocentric, because rather narrowly focused in their conceptions of just what was revolutionary about the Age of Revolutions: the expansion of 'democracy' for Palmer, the diffusion of industry, ideology, and empire for Hobsbawm. Both gestured towards a global setting for the epochal transformations they traced, but neither attempted an integrated account of developments outside the North Atlantic world and each gave primacy to Europe as the matrix of revolution. Insofar as both the American and French Revolutions became enmeshed in the geopolitics of Franco-British imperial rivalry in the half-century after the Seven Years War, they could not but have repercussions for the Caribbean, the Middle East, and South Asia, as well as for Australasia and the Pacific basin, as Hobsbawm, at least, recognized.

In many respects, the origins of narratives like Palmer's and Hobsbawm's can be traced back to accounts of world history generated in Europe during the Age of Revolutions itself, culminating in the lectures on the subject that G. W. F. Hegel delivered at the University of Berlin between 1822 and 1830, in which he notoriously concluded that 'history is in fact out of the question' in large parts of the world, specifically Africa.[20] Such narratives remain tenacious but they are not ineradicable. As Joseph Miller argues in his chapter in this volume, the era experienced by northern European monarchies and their colonial extensions as an 'Age of (Political) Revolutions' was but one phase in a longer cycle of militarization and commercialization in the greater Atlantic world that becomes visible when the dynamics of African, rather than Euro-American, history are used to define and calibrate the dimensions of transformation.[21] World history seen from Africa – rather than African history viewed from Europe, and within European categories – shows longer and more complex rhythms of transformation than reigning cataclysmic models of revolution have generally allowed. In a similar fashion, David Geggus shows in his chapter that the pace of change in the Caribbean was not synchronous with that in Europe, North America, or Spanish and Portuguese America, and indeed that 'the changes the period witnessed [in the Caribbean] were extremely uneven and contradictory' in the effects of anticolonial revolt, slave emancipation, and definitions of freedom.[22]

Only recently have historians begun to seek such novel ways to analyse the developments of this period on a global, rather than simply regional, scale. In particular, the juxtaposition of the rise of European powers to pre-eminence within Eurasia with the fiscal-military upheavals in the great agrarian empires of Asia has suggested a new picture of an era of 'convergent revolutions'. Causation as well as connection have now returned to the agenda of historians treating this era. Developments within and beyond Europe are being brought into a single frame, not to show the diffusion of change from one (usually Euro-Atlantic) region to another, but rather to show that similar developments were taking place across the world: for example, empire-making and empire-breaking; a thickening of commercial ties leading to greater interpenetration of empires and of collaborations as well as collisions among their agents; a ramping-up of pressures to extract profit from both labour and commodities independent of any supposed industrial take-off in north-western Europe; and an expansion of plantation agriculture on islands and in littoral regions from the Americas and Africa to the Indian Ocean and Asia. These various but interconnected phenomena occurred within a fundamental shift in the relations between the major European powers and the rest of the world to create a 'World Crisis' of truly global proportions. As C. A. Bayly has recently put it, 'It is the global interconnectedness of the economic and political turbulences of this era which is so striking.' John Darwin has concurred: 'the really astonishing feature of this revolutionary age was the geopolitical earthquakes that occurred not just in Eurasia but all over the world'.[23] On Bayly's account this World Crisis had fiscal, ideological, and political dimensions that together accelerated 'the growth of uniformity between societies and the growth of complexity within them' around the world. Darwin modifies this slightly by arguing that 'The Eurasian Revolution was in fact three revolutions: in geopolitics, in culture and in economics.'[24]

Such a sweeping, nearly all-encompassing, vision is one symptom of a turn away from pointillisme among historians and a return to broad-brush painting. We say 'return' because the model for a world crisis in the revolutionary era is surely the so-called general crisis of the seventeenth century first posited more than half a century ago, also by Eric Hobsbawm.[25] Like Hobsbawm's later conception of an Age of Revolution, this periodization marked a stage in Europe's

Map 1   The world in the Age of Revolutions (adapted from C.A. Bayly, *The Birth of the Modern World, 1780-1914*, Oxford, 2004, pp. 84–5).

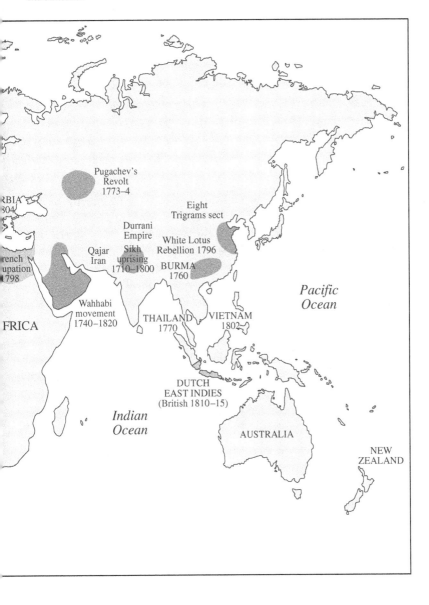

Pugachev's
Revolt
1773–4

Eight
Trigrams sect

ÞBIA
304

Durrani
Empire

White Lotus
Rebellion 1796

ench
upation
798

Qajar
Iran

Sikh
uprising
1710–1800

BURMA
1760

Wahhabi
movement
1740–1820

FRICA

THAILAND
1770

VIETNAM
1802

Pacific
Ocean

DUTCH
EAST INDIES
(British 1810–15)

*Indian
Ocean*

AUSTRALIA

NEW
ZEALAND

emergence into modernity. 'As transition itself has come to seem a
more elusive phenomenon', one recent anatomist of the earlier debate
on the general crisis has noted, 'the usefulness of crisis as an explanation for it has tended to evaporate.'[26] This has not discouraged historians' efforts to analyse various forms of instability – most conspicuous
among them, popular revolts, warfare and subsistence crises – within
a common frame. However, the relative contingency and paucity of
truly worldwide connections in the seventeenth century – compared
to the period under examination in this volume, at least – has made
global descriptions, let alone explanations, of the general crisis
implausible. Even the most expansive analyses have concluded that
seventeenth-century disorders from the Spanish Monarchy to the
Ming Empire were parallel rather than convergent, with climate
change the only possible independent variable that could have operated on a global scale to link them.[27]

The model of crisis has become somewhat moot for interpretations of the seventeenth century.[28] However, it now seems to have
migrated to the late eighteenth century, a period when thickening
interregional connections could render changes that were apparently
simultaneous genuinely synchronous. European powers – the French,
British, Spanish, and Dutch especially – had long possessed the capacity to project themselves politically, militarily, and commercially on a
truly global scale. Since the opening decades of the eighteenth
century, they had been doing so with increasing regularity and ferocity in a cycle of world wars that would continue almost unabated until
1815: as both Jeremy Adelman and David Geggus imply in their chapters in this volume, the military and geopolitical origins of this key
aspect of the Age of Revolutions can be found in the War of the
Spanish Succession (1701–14), the first of the series of world wars that
cast the interactions of European powers on a global screen for more
than a century.[29]

This was in large part because the major political units of the era
(and for long beyond) were not states, national or otherwise, but
empires. A common theme of many of the volume's chapters is that
this was 'an age of imperial revolutions'.[30] In the world beyond
Europe, the backwash of war, revolution, and imperial reorganization
collided with endogenous forces to cause parallel transformations in
the Middle East, South Asia, and beyond. European and neo-
European polities not only consolidated but also expanded their
power through conquest, commerce, and co-optation in Northern
and Southern Africa, in South and South-east Asia, and, for the first
time, into the Pacific during the decades after 1760. It was also in this

period that new regions like the North Pacific were drawn irreversibly into larger circuits of commercial exchange for the first time, joining the polities and economies ranged at the fringes of the China Seas, and new commercial agents, such as the newly independent Americans, entered into global trade demanding freedom of access to commodities, entrepôts, and markets formally ring-fenced by imperial powers and their proxy companies.[31]

★ ★ ★

The conception of a 'World Crisis' in the period *c.*1760–1840 has rapidly gained the status of a testable thesis capable of standing alongside more durable conceptions of an age of Atlantic or democratic revolutions. Proponents of the new paradigm have deliberately absorbed and built upon the earlier literature on revolutions in the late eighteenth and early nineteenth centuries. Yet what still remains a fundamentally synthetic account of these global upheavals has not been systematically tested against specific regional historiographies. Nor have many of the existing traditions of revolutionary historiography been placed into a supraregional, comparative, or global context.

The precise balance between a stress on connection and one on comparison is often quite hard to calibrate.[32] Further, connection itself is often expressed precisely in terms of comparison, even during the revolutionary era itself. For example, one of the most significant effects of the American and more particularly the French Revolutions was to create the sentiment in elites elsewhere that they had somehow failed or fallen behind if they had not been able to emulate a properly revolutionary trajectory. Phrases such as 'our country is sleeping' became common, for example, in the writings of Hungarian aristocrats of the 1810s and 1820s. Even before this, and as early as 1791, the Hungarian guardsman István Batsányi wrote the following poem 'On the Changes in France':

> O you still in the slave's collar, that yoke
> which drags you down to the grave!
> And you too! Holy consecrated kings, who
> – though the very earth demands your blood – still
> slay your hapless subjects: turn your eyes to Paris!
> Let France set out the fate of both king and shackled slave.[33]

Three decades later, two Central European aristocratic travellers were to express similar sentiments of inferiority or backwardness, but this time with respect to England. One of them wrote of how, while in England, he felt 'like a small-town tradesman in his Sunday suit, ludicrously stiff and unable to move', and also noted the enormous industrial vigour he found everywhere in the early 1820s, 'with one glass factory, coal mine and ironworks next to the other [and] the entire area . . . covered with fire and smoke like the scenery of the last judgment. . . . The steam-engines are used everywhere, and they are exquisite.'[34] A gap was opening up, in terms of both realities and perceptions, between living standards and modes of living in England and Continental Western Europe on the one hand, and many other parts of the world on the other hand. This 'great divergence' – to use Kenneth Pomeranz's well known formulation[35] – was not merely a contrast between India and China on the one hand and Western Europe on the other, but between the far closer worlds of Western and Eastern/Central Europe where the voices we have cited emanate.

What causal or other links were there between these divergences, great or otherwise, and the political revolutions of the period? The celebrated admission by Friedrich Engels of a striking lack of fit between France's political trajectory and England's economic one, leading to the invention of a sort of hybrid ideal-type in terms of political economy, may be a reasonable starting-point in relation to this issue, not least because it was clearly an inspiration behind Hobsbawm's conception of a dual, economic-cum-political, 'world revolution spread[ing] outward from the double crater of England and France'.[36] Besides, and further complicating matters, is the fact that the notion of the 'Industrial Revolution' is not a category that would have been comprehensible to actors at the time but a later imposition that itself remains the object of much debate among economic historians.[37] If such a 'revolution' did occur, when can it be located? If we attempt to locate it in the period after 1760, how does one account for the surprisingly low rates of growth of per capita income in England itself until about 1800? Should this process not then be seen as a regional and local, rather than a national, one, and if so, should we not uncouple it from the questions of the characterization of national and imperial political regimes?[38]

Three distinct lines of approach can be discerned with regard to the appropriate manner in which economic and political questions might be linked causally. The first, the origins of which may be found in the work of Thomas Malthus as early as 1820, would argue that the long-term political outcomes of the Age of Revolutions on a world scale derived from economic and technological changes, and that the triumph of Britain over France and the ascendancy of the Pax

Britannica were (as Malthus put it) 'powerfully assisted by our steam-engines'.[39] A second view is one we may associate with the doyen of modern French economic historians, François Crouzet, who famously argued that if 'war was neither a stimulus to, nor a powerful retardative factor of British growth', the political triumph of England could not simply be attributed to her 'advanced' economic status either. If we interpret Crouzet's reasoning correctly, and choose to generalize it, it would seem to lead us in a direction where long-term economic and political outcomes in the Age of Revolutions might be seen as relatively autonomous. The economy did not drive the polity, but nor was 'opulence the reward of successful aggression'.[40] A third view can also be identified, and would subordinate both political and economic questions to the determining influence of cultural factors, in particular religion. This view has been a particular favourite with 'institutionally' inclined economic historians of the last generation, who have argued, for example, that the very different outcomes in the face of similar problems faced by the Ottomans and the French Bourbons can be understood in relation to the determining influence of culture.[41]

The chapters in this volume have not been forced into any single narrow framework of interpretation but tend broadly to follow the second of these three views. They are thus at some remove from a certain number of grand sociological models of revolution, of which one of the most recent is that of Jack Goldstone from the early 1990s.[42] Goldstone tended to link early modern rebellions and revolutions (including the French Revolution) to two types of causal reasoning. One of these tied the rhythms of old regime demographic expansion to the pressure on resources and thus on the fiscal viability of states. This was an internal process, peculiar to each of the societies that were analysed by him in a comparative framing. They might thus lead to divergences but also to 'strange parallels', as another global historian has put the matter.[43] The second form of reasoning was more connective and conjunctural, and linked these societies together using such mechanisms as the flow of silver (and bullion more generally) and the attendant monetary crises they may have provoked. Taken together, Goldstone argued, these two forms of reasoning could be used to show why mere rebellions occurred in some societies and veritable revolutions in others, while still others managed to prevent resistance or instability from occurring. Ideology for him was a mere facilitating factor, though it could also at times act as a constraint on the production of revolution. In contrast, the chapters in this volume generally stress the field of the 'political', but not in any narrow sense: the political for them is an opening into a field of interdisciplinary exploration. If some of them focus on political institutions in places as far apart as China, Spanish America, and Indonesia, still others focus on the realm of political ideas, while a third group detail the actions of political agents whether within a national or in a transnational or transimperial context. This emphasis on the 'political' is, it seems to us, really an underlining of the contingent nature of processes in the period under consideration.[44]

A global approach to the Age of Revolutions clearly demonstrates that the dimensions even of political change in the period under study were markedly heterogeneous. In some parts of the world, formal political structures came crashing down, often with much shedding of blood and significant displacement of people (as Maya Jasanoff shows in her chapter on the loyalist diaspora after the American Revolution and the flight of the émigrés from Revolutionary France);[45] while in others, the same state-actors or their direct descendants remained firmly in place. One area subject to conquest from without in this period, Egypt during Napoleon's French invasion, experienced creolization rather than rupture in an encounter that produced 'more irony than binaries', as Juan Cole argues in his chapter.[46] Another locale, Java, subject first to Dutch then to British colonial rule in the period, underwent a much more wrenching transition in which Europe's revolutionary languages (such as discourses of antifeudalism) and practices proved entirely inassimilable, as Peter Carey shows in his chapter.[47]

If political revolutions produced dramatic changes in regimes in many parts of Western Europe, the Mediterranean, South Asia, and a great swathe of the Atlantic world, vast areas such as Qing China, Tokugawa Japan, Tsarist Russia, and even Habsburg Central Europe were less directly affected, as, for example, Kenneth Pomeranz's chapter on China proposes.[48] Along similar lines, a recent study of comparative experiences in East and South-east Asia in this period stresses the notion of 'crisis' rather than 'revolution', noting the existence of demographic expansion, floods, and rebellions at the time of the Qianlong and Jiaqing emperors, and 'similar phenomena' in Japan in the 1780s at the time of the Tenmei Famine (1782–7) and the death of Tokugawa Ieharu in 1786. Changes in maritime trade in the region, driven by piracy, commercial interloping, and the competition between European trading companies, among other factors, ensured that 'the turn of the eighteenth into the nineteenth century was a period of global transition and changing overseas entanglements to which the regimes of China, Japan, and Java were forced to respond'.[49]

★ ★ ★

Any global account of the period must account for stability as well as turbulence in the face of such challenges. The Ottoman Empire (not otherwise treated at length below) offers one striking illustration of the dynamics of resilience in the revolutionary era. On 6 April 1789, just three weeks before the so-called Réveillon Riot that shook Paris and led – in the charged words of one aristocratic contemporary writer – to a situation where 'blood was flowing in the Faubourg Saint-Antoine in Paris, [with] five or six thousand workers, stirred up by a diabolical cabal that aimed to destroy the [Necker] ministry and prevent the Estates from meeting', the Ottoman Sultan Selim III had ascended the throne some 1,400 miles to the south-east in Istanbul.[50] The situation he confronted was a rather delicate one, but not entirely dissimilar to that facing the ill-fated Louis XVI. A significant fiscal gap between imperial receipts and expenditures had opened up in the course of the eighteenth century, growing more acute in its second half. The same broad period saw the emergence of regional magnates, or *a'yan*, who became indispensable intermediaries and power-brokers, and impeded any simple process of fiscal reconsolidation or centralization.[51] Military pressure was mounting inexorably from the exterior, in particular from the Russia of Catherine II, specifically in the Black Sea region. In the late 1780s, Russian forces had captured a number of forts on the Dniester and a Russo-Austrian alliance seemed now to threaten not merely the Crimea and the Balkans but even the very Rumelian and Anatolian heartland of the empire itself. The Ottoman state, long considered to be the 'Sick Man of Europe', seemed once more to be in a state of terminal illness, not simply in military but in broadly political terms. The early years of Selim's rule saw further military setbacks at Fokshani and Rimnik, and the loss of Belgrade.

However, we know that the worst eventually did not come to pass for the Ottomans, and that they managed to survive in some form as late as the First World War. Deft diplomatic manoeuvrings and separate treaties in 1791 and 1792 with the Habsburgs and Russians enabled them to hold on to some of the older frontiers at the Danube and Dnieper, and also to retain control over Bosnia and Serbia. In the eighteen difficult years of the Sultan's rule, until his deposition in 1807 in favour of his cousin Mustafa IV, it was even possible for Selim III to attempt some limited reform, notably in terms of the so-called Nizam-i Cedid corps of the army, which has been termed 'the example, the lesson, the model, and the nucleus for the military reforms that were to follow' later in the nineteenth century.[52] Further, in all of this, it is easy to lose sight of the fact that the Sultan himself (usually portrayed as something of a weakling if not a *roi fainéant*) was an interesting mix in terms of his disposition and tastes. Among his friends and fellow members of the Mevlevi order of Sufis was the brilliant and somewhat iconoclastic poet Sheyh Galib (1757–99), no friend of the hidebound old imperial bureaucracy and its scribal elite. Galib even wrote somewhat irreverently of the royal house, as follows.

> The sagas of kings are but a painted rose
> nothing more
> on a fragile Chinese cup,
> made for the ruler's hand
> not my own.[53]

How did the Ottomans as a dynasty and a broad political regime survive the difficult years from 1760 to 1840, which laid low so many of their contemporary dynasties and ruling dispensations? There is clearly no simple answer to this question but there are some obvious elements of a response that we know. Various ingenious arguments can no doubt be found to explain the absence of a revolution in the Ottoman Empire at the time. We would, however, stress political arguments both from the realm of institutions and from that of ideas. The principal reason for Ottoman stability, we would argue, was scale and flexibility, an advantage that France – in view of the reversal of its imperial plans in both India and the Atlantic by 1763 – simply did not possess. The Ottomans were thus able to deploy even the rather decentralized state apparatus at their disposal to deal with crises in the Balkans as well as face the challenges of the Wahhabis, who took and held the holy cities of Mecca and Medina for nearly a decade from 1805 to 1813. The eventual destruction of Ottoman power was only possible after the scale and extent of the Ottoman state had been progressively whittled down over the course of the nineteenth century and during the First World War.

A second argument stems from the realm of ideas. Ottoman political thought in the years from 1760 to 1840, like that of Qing intellectuals in the same period, refused for the most part to contemplate the idea of a kingless polity. Even in India at the time, one of the few resources that were available to reflect on this question derived from the exegetical tradition on the epic *Ramayana*, where (in the so-called *ayodhya kanda*) one finds a reflection on the disastrous consequences of *arajaka*, or a kingless state.[54] The only viable solution, and one that was followed to the letter in Istanbul in 1807–8, was to replace a less convenient Sultan with a preferable one, while holding firm to the logic of dynasty. Even in 1840, then, at the very end of the period studied by the chapters in this volume, the central political proposition of the American and French Revolutions – namely the replacement of monarchical government with some other, 'popular' form – remained broadly unacceptable in the greater part of the world.

The Ottoman state, like the Mughals further east, was the object of the expansionary ambitions of a European power of the time – namely, Revolutionary France (rather than – as with the Mughals – the English East India Company). But they were also beneficiaries of the Anglo-French rivalry that cut short Bonaparte's expedition to the eastern Mediterranean, whereas the Mughals were never able in the final analysis to play off one European power against another after 1740. As a dynasty that had ruled in a more or less coherent manner from the 1320s, the Ottomans were also far more strongly rooted in terms of cultural capital than many others that did not have the advantage of almost five centuries of a royal past. Their 'saga of kings' was finally made not only for the ruler's hand but was a shared cultural resource for many of the elites in the eastern Mediterranean. In any event, to explain the fate of the Ottomans over these years, we must have recourse to at least three modes of historical reasoning, having to do with connection, comparison, and causation. If the history of the Ottomans is tightly connected with that of France, and to an extent that of imperial Britain, it is through comparison between the outcomes there as distinct from, say, Mughal India or Qing China that we may gain a firmer grasp of the multiple logics of transformation in this period.

★ ★ ★

That we can pose the problem of explanation in this way reflects the fact that the Age of Revolutions was a period in which the local and the global were rearticulated in radical ways. Neither the American Revolution nor the French Revolution was a local affair; both had global or at least pan-regional repercussions and receptions. This much the traditional historiography, such as that represented by Palmer and Hobsbawm, had always been willing to admit. But, as we have seen, the broad tendency of that historiography was inevitably diffusionist in character. This has meant that a typical sequence of causal reasoning might run as follows. The French Revolution occurred on account of purely internal causal mechanisms within the 'hexagon' of metropolitan France, whether these were fiscal, social, or cultural. Then the story might continue that this Revolution and its aftermath next produced an aggressively expansionist and militaristic wave that led to a variety of wars on the European continent and beyond, including eventually the toppling of the Bourbon ruler of Spain, Charles IV, and his replacement in 1808 by Joseph Bonaparte. The eventual repercussions of this process would then include the rebellion of the Spanish American colonies from about 1809 and their eventual independence after the Bourbon restoration, in which the revolutionary language learnt from the American and French examples would play a crucial role.[55]

Yet, as Lynn Hunt correctly comments in her contribution to this volume, the possibility that the French Revolution itself might be placed in a global context of causal movements, rather than seen as an exogenous independent variable causing changes on a global scale, has rarely been considered.[56] Indeed, insofar as historians have set the French Revolution in any international context, it has been either within the framework of a traditional diplomatic history or as an account of the Revolution's repercussions beyond France itself.[57] This is somewhat puzzling, because the available evidence of some form of global causal context for the late eighteenth-century revolutions in both America and France has been strong enough for some time. The fiscal problems of the French treasury have often been traced to the substantial debts incurred by the end of the global conflict which was the Seven Years War, and which were never entirely recouped thereafter, as interest payments mounted. The loss of substantial overseas territories and the imperial retreat in which France found itself in the years from 1763 to 1789 surely reduced the margin for manoeuvre that the Bourbon state possessed in relation to its competitor across the channel. In contrast, the problems of the House of Hanover from the mid-eighteenth century can be traced to an embarrassment of overseas riches rather than a lack thereof: one may even discern a certain carelessness in the management of the American continental colonies from the period (between 1757 and 1765) when the fiscal riches of Bengal become available with a disconcerting degree of ease.[58]

While a truly connected history of these rebellions and revolutionary movements is yet to be achieved, we may legitimately ask ourselves whether the flow of causal reasoning from Europe to the overseas colonial territories might not at times be usefully reversed. Indeed, such a reversal of perspectives suggests one of the major interpretive rewards of the approach taken in this volume. Diffusionist models of revolutionary change, like Palmer's and Hobsbawm's, occluded the various forms of connection and comparison that Travers calls the 'different forms of global early modernity', which did not tend in a single direction or exhibit parallel dynamics.[59] Those earlier models could not accommodate multiple centres of change, nor could they properly account for the fact that the era was one of counter-revolutions as well as revolutions, of local disturbances (like those in China that Pomeranz has mapped in this volume) that did not lead even to regional transformations, and of more diffuse processes of cultural and political hybridity, such as those Juan Cole and Peter Carey examine in their chapters on Egypt and Java. The very heterogeneity of change and the forms of resistance to it are fundamental features of the Age of Revolutions. That they are now visible to historians is not the least of the benefits of placing the Age of Revolutions in a global context.

This volume thus continues to stress the virtues of comparison between the fates of different polities in the Age of Revolutions, but insists that it must fruitfully be combined with forms of reasoning that stress the importance of connection.[60] There are of course at least two possible ways of conceptualizing such connected histories of revolution. A first would suggest that connections did exist and were known to past actors, but have for some reason been forgotten or laid aside. The task of the historian would then be to rediscover these lost traces. A second view would instead posit that historians might act as electricians, connecting circuits by acts of imaginative reconstitution rather than simple restitution. Here, the advantages of conceiving of these processes on a global scale become manifest rather quickly. Even if a certain number of individual cases – notably those of Russia, Japan, and mainland South-east Asia – have been set aside here for reasons of economy, it should be clear that they too could very easily be brought into the analysis, through either a primary emphasis on connection or one on comparison. The fate of the French polity obviously depended, for example, on the disastrous failure of Bonaparte's campaign in Russia, to such an extent that it is impossible to conceive of French history in the years from 1800 to 1820 independently of Russian history.[61]

As we move forward from the period examined in this book – the 1760s to the 1840s – to the latter half of the nineteenth century, the deeper impact of the revolutions (as well as the non-revolutions) of these years becomes plainer. However, this impact is not in terms of the production of a simple dichotomy, another great divergence as it were between societies that had undergone revolution and those that had not. Rather, influences continued to be exchanged and transmitted between post-revolutionary societies and others that remained within the framework of agrarian and sea-borne imperial polities. Rousseau and Voltaire were read in late nineteenth-century Bengal, while ideas from America provided at least a part of the spur for the Taiping Rebellion that rocked the late Qing polity. It is in this sense that the history of the Age of Revolutions must be understood in global context, both in its own time and in terms of the mark it left in the longer term.

To conclude, a common enough perception of the Age of Revolutions is that it freed the genie of revolutionary republicanism from its imprisoning bottle, to which it could never be returned. On this view, then, an uncomplicated line can be drawn – for better or for worse – from the French Revolution of 1789 to the Bolshevik Revolution of 1917, and that was not only because (as François Furet once put it) 'the Bolsheviks always had their minds fixed on the example of the French Revolution'.[62] In reality, however, the decades from 1840 to the early twentieth century saw very few successful revolutions, with the concrete results of even 1848 being quite limited and short-lived. Neither the Indian Rebellion of the 1850s nor the Taiping and Boxer Rebellions succeeded in their objectives, and in any event these objectives were in many instances less than revolutionary by any definition. The revolutionary tradition thus had in large measure to be reinvented for use after 1900, whether in Iran, Armenia, or Mexico, for example. To be sure, it may be argued, the revolutions and even the later anticolonial political movements of the twentieth century had the memory and traditions of the Age of Revolutions available to them as a resource, but they also had been overgrown in the intervening years by layers of myth and confusion that would prove difficult to scrape away. Among these was the pervasive view that these were essentially revolutions that had to be understood and analysed in a national (and nationalistic) framework. It is to the task of reinterpreting them that this volume contributes by viewing the Age of Revolutions as a complex, broad, interconnected, and even global phenomenon.

1

Sparks from the Altar of '76: International Repercussions and Reconsiderations of the American Revolution

Gary B. Nash

A half-century has passed since the first volume of R. R. Palmer's *Age of the Democratic Revolution* (1959, followed by a second in 1964) offered a stunning treatment of the geographic reach of the American Revolution. More than any other historian of his generation, Palmer initiated the move towards an Atlantic-wide consideration of political ideology and political practice in the second half of the eighteenth century. In Palmer's view the American Revolution, suffused with enlightened ideological energy, 'dethroned England and set up America as a model for those seeking a better world'. In particular, he explained how Europeans cast their eyes in wonderment upon the state constitutions cobbled together during the long war with Great Britain, seeing these expressions of fundamental law as 'the liberal ideas of the Enlightenment . . . put into practice' and 'made the actual fabric of public life among real people, in this world, now'.[1] Palmer showed how key elements of American Revolutionary ideology spread – very unevenly to be sure – across the breadth of Europe and, eventually, in paler forms, to Latin America in the first half of the nineteenth century. Among the key elements of 'the new order of the ages' were freedom of religion, popular sovereignty, the rights of man as unalienable and universal, and that all government should flow from written constitutions constructed by the people themselves.[2] The American Revolution, with the lofty goals of its early years for recreating government and society, set off a wave of radical, even utopian, thinking wherever the waters of the Atlantic tumbled ashore. Though he never quoted it, Thomas Paine's prediction in his

1

thunderous *Common Sense*, published half a year before the Declaration of Independence, expressed the heart of Palmer's almost reverential consideration of America's mission in the world as the founders of liberal democracy: 'The cause of America is in a great measure the cause of all mankind. . . . 'Tis not the concern of a day, a year, or an age; posterity are virtually involved in the contest, and will be more or less affected, even to the end of time, by the proceedings now.'[3]

In recent decades, the ascent of Atlantic history, and more broadly global history, has brought certain advances in our understanding of the international impact of the American Revolution. David Armitage's The *Declaration of Independence: A Global History* (2007) shows how the American scripture drafted by Thomas Jefferson has inspired people around the world to mount revolts against colonial masters and fashion blood-drenched movements of national liberation and self-determination.[4] But these movements, central to the break-up of empires, have usually not been accompanied by concurrent rights movements stressing individual freedom, the end of slavery and other forms of bound labour, the enlargement of the franchise, the democratization of law-making and political practice, the advent of public education, the expansion of woman's rights, or the redistribution of wealth – all of which were part of the radical agenda of American revolutionists. Similarly, P. J. Marshall's *The Making and Unmaking of Empires: Britain, India, and America c. 1750–1783* (2005) rightly argues that the loss of the American colonies did not diminish Great Britain's commitment to empire or even change its strategies for managing its ever-expanding overseas appendages.[5] The notion of empire itself and the pursuit of dominance of lands and peoples outside of Europe continued and even accelerated. Nor in their new empire in India were the names of Paine, Franklin, Mason, Jefferson, or Madison raised in the name of popular sovereignty, religious toleration, or any other plank in the platform of revolutionary reform in North America. In another case, an expansive study, attempting to combine the American Revolution with Latin American independence movements, reads similarly. In Lester Langley's *The Americas in the Age of Revolution* (1996) social upheaval in the years from 1810 to 1850 was the work of indigenous and exploited people who did not speak the language of universal and unalienable rights but, as John Coatsworth has put it, came from 'diverse strata of the rural population, each with its own needs and goals' and each unfolding 'in particular institutional settings'.[6] The American War for Independence, in sum, considered as an overthrow of colonial masters, would have much more influence – though haltingly – than the American

Revolution, an internal struggle to remake America along very different lines than had previously existed. Moreover, where the American Revolutionary universalistic and reformist goals had the quickest and greatest reach was in the parts of Europe that Palmer studied half a century ago.

Thus, we need to be cautious about overstating the aftershocks of the American Revolution, particularly about its internal struggles to restitch the social fabric of its peoples – a process which itself proceeded spasmodically and incompletely. For all the work on the Haitian Revolution of 1791–1804, occurring only several hundred miles from the new United States, the summary judgement is that the enormous upheaval of slaves owed far more to the French Revolution and to the slaves themselves (sometimes operating out of African values and African methods of attacking their enemies) than to the American Revolution. And the Haitian revolutionaries received support from only slender elements of American society, in particular from abolition-minded northerners who hoped black rebellion would aid the dismantling of racial slavery in the new American republic. In fact, even after becoming a free black republic in 1804, Haiti could not gain recognition from the American government until the 1860s.[7] A recent study of the American Revolution and the British Caribbean concludes with a null thesis – that white planters resisted the American Revolutionary ideas about natural rights, as well they might, since they lived in a sea of exploited and enslaved agricultural labourers. More surprising is that the massive slave rebellion in North America occasioned by the British offer of freedom to slaves (and indentured white servants) escaping their masters inspired little rebellion among the several million Caribbean slaves. Even the Jamaica slave rebellion of 1776 sprang not from ideological fever but from hunger that spread when the provisions from North America – fish and grain – were halted by the war.[8] The major slave revolts came later without much reference to American revolutionary ideas – in Barbados in 1816, Demerara in 1823, and Jamaica in 1831–2.[9]

That the American Revolution did not fulfil Thomas Paine's hopes outside of Europe seems to be the implicit conclusion of historians who have constructed arguments of a world crisis and 'converging revolutions' from 1760 to 1820. For example, C. A. Bayly's *The Birth of the Modern World, 1780–1914* (2004), which incorporates Asia, Africa, the Middle East, and Latin America into his study of world empires from the late eighteenth century to the First World War, shrivels the American Revolution into insignificance. Jefferson, Madison, Paine, and other revolutionary political theoreticians make

cameo appearances; the revolutionary era constitution-making that
figured so importantly in Palmer's thesis warrants no mention at all;
levelling tendencies and communitarian leanings are associated with
the French Revolution but not the American Revolution; and abolitionism merits only brief mention.[10]

Except for his neglect of abolitionism, which at least some important American revolutionary leaders promoted fervently, Bayly may be
justified in giving a back seat to the American Revolution in a globe-
encircling metahistory. In terms of the rise and fall and transformation
of European empires in the modern age, the best study of the Seven
Years War argues cogently that this prolonged global conflict of the
major European powers was 'far more significant than the War of
American Independence' (not to be conflated with the American
Revolution).[11]

One reason why the American Revolution did not reverberate
much beyond the parts of Europe where Palmer's work provided rich
detail, is that the Americans themselves did not wish to export their
revolution insofar as it spoke of universal and unalienable rights of
life, liberty, and the pursuit of happiness, particularly to slave-holding
regimes, where it was feared that the spark of rebellion might return
to enflame the fast-growing slave society in the American South. In
fact, the spark travelled in the opposite direction after 1790. It was
black rebellion in Haiti, which neither the Directory nor Napoleon
could contain, that inspired black insurrectionists in the United States,
and it was the loss of Haiti that made Louisiana so dispensable to
France and so cheap for the United States to purchase. Black
Americans aspiring for the universal rights promised in the
Declaration of Independence, as they and abolitionists understood it,
had a long struggle ahead of them, and that struggle was made all the
more difficult by the departure of some of the most talented, ideo-
logically charged black men of the revolutionary generation, who
flocked to the British to gain their freedom and then became part of
the reverse diaspora carrying them after the war to Nova Scotia, Sierra
Leone, Liberia, and even Australia.[12]

Another reason for the muted resonance of the American
Revolution in the broad Atlantic world and beyond is that at the time
the most ardent enthusiasts of the Americans' 'glorious cause' became
sorely disillusioned at the sight of the new American republic beating
a retreat from antislavery inclinations that had been a part of the New
World forward-looking agenda. Yet, as we will see, the American
Revolution allowed already well-formed antislavery sentiment to
blossom into an antislavery programme of action.[13] Had the

Founding Fathers grasped the nettle of slavery at a time when a number of factors were converging to make this seem possible, as it did to many leaders even in Virginia, the worldwide effects of the American Revolution would have been enormously different.[14] This chapter follows the travails of several Founding Fathers, urged on by European Friends of Liberty, in wrestling with the cancer of slavery that they knew must be cut from the American body politic if the revolution was to be true to its founding principles and was to usher in a new age of universal freedom.

★ ★ ★

Dr Richard Price, London's dissenting minister, tribune of religious toleration, and friend of Benjamin Franklin, yielded to no Englishman in his support of the American revolutionists' struggle for independence. For this disloyalty, by his own account, he was subjected 'to much abuse and some danger'. And hardly any writer of the post-war period was more fervent in believing that the American Revolution 'in favour of universal liberty' had opened 'a new prospect in human affairs' and ushered in 'a new aera in the history of mankind' by 'disseminating just sentiments of the rights of mankind and the nature of legitimate government, by exciting a spirit of resistance to tyranny . . . and by occasioning the establishment in America of forms of government more equitable and more liberal than any that the world has yet known'. Writing in 1784 – when the ink was hardly dry on the Peace of Paris treaty that ended the American war for independence – in his *Observations of the Importance of the American Revolution and the Means of Making It a Benefit to the World*, Price exulted that the Americans, in their 'sequestered continent', were now providing 'a place of refuge for opprest men in every region of the world' and 'laying the foundation . . . of an empire which may be the seat of liberty, science and virtue and from whence there is reason to hope these sacred blessings will spread till they become universal and the time arrives when kings and priests shall have no more power to oppress and that ignominious slavery which has hitherto debased the world exterminated.'[15]

Yet Price saw an ominous cloud hovering over North America that compromised and would surely doom the American revolutionaries' gift to humankind. With one-fifth of its population still in chains at the end of the war, the Americans were living out an atrocious contradiction. 'Till they have [abolished slavery]', lamented Price, 'it will not appear they deserve the liberty for which they have been contending. For it is self-evident that if there are any men whom they have a right to hold in slavery, there may be others who have had a right to hold them in slavery. . . . Nothing can excuse the United States if it [the abolition of slavery] is not done with as much speed, and at the same time with as much effect, as their particular circumstances and situation will allow.'[16]

Price's abolitionism had been influenced by John Lind, whose *Three Letters to Dr Price* in 1776 challenged Price's defence of the American revolutionaries. An internationalist at heart and adviser to King Stanislaus, the reform-minded Polish monarch, Lind collaborated with the young philosopher Jeremy Bentham on the Ministry-sponsored *An Answer to the Declaration of the American Congress* (1776), replying to the Declaration of Independence. Lind and Bentham laced their pamphlet with sardonic comments about American hypocrisy in proclaiming universal freedom while keeping half a million Africans in chains. Referring to Lord Dunmore's proclamation of November 1775, which offered freedom to all slaves and indentured servants who escaped their masters and reached British lines, Lind trumpeted that 'It is their boast that they have taken up arms in support of these their own *self-evident truths* – "that all men are *equal*" – "that all men are endowed with the *unalienable* rights of life, *liberty*, and the *pursuit of happiness*". Is it for them to complain *of the offer of freedom* held out to these wretched beings? of the offer of reinstating them in that *equality*, which, in this very paper, is declared to be the *gift of God to all*; in those *unalienable rights*, with which, in this very paper, God is declared to have *endowed all* mankind?'[17]

Price's comments remind us of how many of his contemporaries acknowledged the American Revolution as an audacious, breathtaking explosion of freedom unknown, as Thomas Paine put it, since the days of Noah's ark. His comments also remind us that the American Revolution was also a major disappointment, most tragically to the enslaved African Americans who hoped the moment of their deliverance was at hand, but also to the Continental Friends of Liberty who believed the Founding Fathers had betrayed the Enlightenment principles from which their revolution derived its ideological justifications. 'In Britain', wrote Richard Price, 'a negro becomes a freeman the moment he sets his foot on British ground.'[18] Why not in the new centre of Enlightenment ideas and enlightened programmes?

Price's comments on slavery in the new United States, though brief and appearing at the end of his *Observations*, provided fodder for abolitionists on both sides of the Atlantic, who jumped to put copies into the hands of American leaders. After receiving a number of

Price's *Observations*, Virginia's Richard Henry Lee, delegate to the Continental Congress, distributed copies among other delegates to the national legislature and put one in Washington's hands. Price had already packed off copies to Jefferson, John Adams, Benjamin Rush, and John Jay, Chief Justice of the newly formed Supreme Court. To the latter, he later delivered the acid comment that if it was true that his comments had offended South Carolina leaders and that they spoke for most Americans, then it appeared 'that the people who have struggled so bravely against being enslaved themselves are ready enough to enslave others. . . . The friends of liberty and virtue in Europe will be sadly disappointed and mortified' if the American Revolution 'will prove only an introduction to a new scene of aristocratical tyranny and human debasement.'[19]

Appearing almost simultaneously was Thomas Day's philippic mocking American pretensions to be tribunes of liberty. Like Price, Day had supported the American's 'glorious cause' but found nothing glorious about their perpetuation of slavery. 'If there be an object truly ridiculous in nature, it is an American patriot, signing resolutions of independency with one hand, and with the other brandishing a whip over his affrighted slaves. . . . YES, GENTLEMEN, AS YOU ARE NO LONGER Englishmen, I hope you will please to be men; and, as such, admit the whole human species to a participation of your unalienable rights.'[20]

Working loosely with English abolitionists such as Granville Sharp, Thomas Day, and John Cartwright, Price became one of the cross-English Channel reformers who pushed the American self-liberators hard in the crucial years just after the American Revolution to complete the freedom project upon which they had embarked. In particular, they zeroed in on Washington, Jefferson, and Franklin, the internationally famous trio that was best positioned to trade on the moral capital they had accumulated in the course of founding their nation. In this effort, the French and English reformers only loosely coordinated their efforts; but they were keenly aware of the common cause they were pushing and indeed were better coordinated than most historians have allowed.

With Franklin, the cross-channel ideologues had some success. Franklin the Philadelphia slave-owner of the 1740s and 1750s had responded step by step to the passionate teachings of John Woolman and Anthony Benezet, who were making the immorality of slavery a topic of general concern on both sides of the Atlantic.[21] In England from 1757 to 1762, Franklin's antislavery sentiment grew, partly as a result of the flight of King, his son William Franklin's slave, who had taken up service as a free man in the household of a gentlewoman outside London. Franklin was also nudged towards an antislavery position by the unconscious black agency of another Franklin family slave, a male child named Othello, who, according to reports from Franklin's wife, was making excellent progress in a new school for Philadelphia blacks, thus disproving notions of inherent African inferiority. When Franklin returned to London in 1764, he began to express himself publicly against slavery, most famously in 1772, by which time he was in touch with early English abolitionists such as Thomas Day and Richard Price.[22]

Though the war interrupted all discourse with English friends, Franklin became more ardently antislavery when he became an American in Paris from 1778 to 1785. While in the thick of diplomatic negotiations – first to bring France into an alliance with the Americans in the war for independence and then in the extended negotiations in Paris over a treaty of peace with Great Britain – it was convenient and even prudent to remain on the sidelines of the growing transatlantic debate over slavery. Yet Franklin was learning to buckle on his armour amidst the company of the Enlightenment figures with whom he so happily mingled – the reformer-lawyer de Beaumont, the jurist Malesherbes, the economist Turgot, and, especially, the Abbé Raynal, Voltaire, and Condorcet. Franklin was particularly taken with Condorcet's *Reflections on Negro Slavery*, published in 1781 when Franklin was at the height of his salon popularity. He bonded with the passionate Condorcet, a man half his age, more than with any other titan of the Enlightenment.[23] Where John Adams looked down his nose at the *philosophes*, thinking them naive romantic revolutionaries and not moving an inch towards forthright abolitionism, Franklin took the French intellectuals seriously and veered towards using his political capital in the interest of antislavery efforts.[24]

In the summer of 1782, when the peace negotiations with England were fully in play, Franklin took a semi-public stance in quietly circulating 'A Thought Concerning the Sugar Islands'. In it, he railed against 'the Wars made in Africa for Prisoners to raise Sugar in America, the Numbers slain in those Wars, the Number that being crowded in Ships perish in the Transportation, & the Numbers that die under the Severities of Slavery'. Given all this cruelty and violence, a devotee of sweetness 'could scarce look on a Morsel of Sugar without conceiving it spotted with Human Blood' if not 'thoroughly died red'. Franklin circulated the brief essay among Benjamin Vaughan, David Hartley, and Richard Oswald, all but making his antislavery position public. Indeed, he intended his remarks to be shown to the British government, for Oswald was a key English peace commissioner, Vaughan was Franklin's old friend and English publisher of his work, and Hartley was a Member of Parliament long involved in the peace talks. Though the essay was not published until just before his death, Franklin by this time was not chary of speaking firmly about the execrable system of coerced labour.[25]

A year later, Franklin again enlisted for duty in the ranks of the antislavery soldiers. In a letter that he probably received in July 1783, Anthony Benezet implored him to speak to the king of France about the continuing Atlantic slave trade and press the argument that 'what an honour it would be to him [the king] & his country if he would take the lead in putting an end to that unreasonable, inhuman & dreadful traffick'.[26] No evidence remains that Franklin made such an intercession with the French king, but by now he surely understood how important his support was for the friends of the enslaved. By the time he returned to Philadelphia in September 1785, Benezet was dead, though it may not have been lost on Franklin that at the funeral, the largest known in Philadelphia until then, one of the speakers vowed that 'I would rather be Anthony Benezet in that coffin than George Washington, with all his fame.'[27]

The Philadelphia to which Franklin returned had been trans-formed not only by the return of peace and the painful adjustments to a still roiled post-war economy but by the emergence of North America's largest free black community.[28] Out of the shadows to lead the emerging free black community were spirited and determined figures such as Richard Allen and Absalom Jones. Both had recently purchased their own freedom and stepped forward, their lowly posi-tions and lack of any formal education notwithstanding, to create a Free African Society, which pushed for the right of blacks to control their own burial ground and to sow the seeds for the creation of inde-pendent black churches and schools. Franklin never acknowledged in his correspondence his reaction to black accomplishment and activism, but it is reasonable to assume that he knew of the opinion of his friend Benjamin Rush, ablaze with zeal for the cause of black Philadelphians, that 'such is their integrity and quiet deportment that they [black Philadelphians] are universally preferred to white people of similar occupations'.[29]

Amidst such signs of black success, so at odds with Jefferson's musings about black inferiority, Franklin, now an old and pain-racked man, aligned himself with that to which he had contributed only halt-ingly. By his eighty-first birthday, in the year the Constitutional

Convention met in Philadelphia, he was speaking against slavery with an open heart. After accepting the ceremonial presidency of the Pennsylvania Abolition Society on 23 April 1787, just a few weeks before the arrival of delegates to the Constitutional Convention, the Old Revolutionist signed a public antislavery exhortation that declared that 'the Creator of the world' had made 'of one flesh, all the children of men'.[30]

Just before Franklin died on 17 April 1790, he signed his last public documents, a strongly worded 'Address to the Public' from the reorganized Pennsylvania Abolition Society and a petition to Congress to cut the cancer of slavery out of the American body politic. Then he had his last say on slavery: a biting parody aimed at a Georgia congressman who had attacked the Quakers for introducing a petition before the first federal congress for ending the slave trade.[31] In the end, Franklin heeded one of Poor Richard's pieces of advice: 'Search others for their virtues, thy self for thy vices.'[32] In his sojourn from slave-holder to critic of slavery, he had been moved deeply by the transatlantic friends of universal liberty with whom he had mingled in Philadelphia, London, and Paris.

While English and French antislavery activists could take satisfaction with Franklin's conversion to abolitionism, the chances for success in the new United States rested more with those who were younger, and particularly those who were Virginians. With Washington, the prospects of gaining an indispensable ally, at least for a short time, seemed bright. Washington had been troubled ever since seeing black soldiers fighting valiantly for the American cause in the battles of Newport, Monmouth Courthouse, and, most memorably, Yorktown, where the Rhode Island Black Regiment had removed any lingering doubts that black men under arms would fight tenaciously. As the war drew to an end, Washington contemplated whether he might be the key figure in securing the unalienable rights of man.

Pushing him hard was the dashing young Marquis de Lafayette, who amidst the din of war had become far more to Washington than a comrade-in-arms. From the time Washington sent the nineteen-year-old Lafayette into battle at Brandywine in September 1777, they became surrogate father and son.[33] Lafayette had not come to the rebelling American colonies with antislavery sentiments or even much acquaintance with the *philosophes* of his day.[34] Then, what we might term an unprogrammatic black agency came into play. Lafayette's transformation into a stalwart abolitionist owed much to his battlefield experiences with African Americans, most poignantly with James Armistead, the Virginia slave who served at his side and played a crucial role in the victory at Yorktown after infiltrating the British lines posing as a runaway slave and returning with crucial knowledge of the British deployments. Even before he left to return to France before the end of the war, Lafayette had become convinced that the flight of slaves by shoals to the British to gain their freedom showed that a revolution that left the edifice of slavery in place was a deeply flawed 'glorious cause'.

After returning to France following the epic victory at Yorktown in October 1781, the French nobleman acted on what apparently were earlier talks with Washington about rooting slavery out of America. When word reached Lafayette in Cadiz, Spain, that American and British negotiators had signed a preliminary treaty of peace on 20 January 1783, he dispatched a letter of congratulations to 'our beloved matchless Washington'. Lafayette proposed that the nation's conquering hero join him in a grand experiment to free their slaves. Lafayette would purchase an estate on the coast of French Guiana, and there their slaves would be settled in preparation for freedom. 'Such an example as yours might render it a general prac- tice', wrote Lafayette, and he even imagined that 'if we succeed in America', he would devote himself to spreading the experiment to the West Indies. 'If it be a wild scheme', Lafayette concluded, 'I had rather be mad that way than to be thought wise on the other tack.'[35]

Washington did not dismiss the idea. He knew he might be the exemplar whom others would follow. 'I shall be happy to join you in so laudable a work', he wrote to Lafayette, and would welcome seeing his adoptive son to discuss the details 'of the business'.[36] Lafayette indeed came to Mount Vernon the next summer – in August 1784 – where the two compatriots discussed the experiment over a period of eleven days. William Gordon, the antislavery Boston minister who would write one of the first histories of the American Revolution, recalled after visiting Mount Vernon when Lafayette was there that Washington 'wished to get rid of his Negroes, and the Marquis wisht that an end might be put to the slavery of all of them'.[37] Gordon also played on Washington's enormous clout, urging that, teamed with Lafayette, 'your joint counsels and influence' might accomplish eman- cipation, 'and thereby give the finishing stroke and the last polish to your political characters'.[38]

In the end, Washington withdrew from the project, though one planter, Joseph Mayo, had freed more than 150 slaves in the hope of encouraging other Virginia planters.[39] Yet slave-holding gnawed at Washington, all the more intensely as he became the nation's first president in 1790. If Henry Wiencek is correct, Washington drafted a public statement in which he would announce as he assumed the presidency that he was freeing some of his slaves and preparing others for eventual emancipation. Had this occurred, it would have established the precedent that the man elected to the highest office in the new republic should disavow slavery before taking office. The ripple effect was incalculable.[40]

Washington drew back from this breathtaking action, but early in his second presidential term, he told his private secretary, Tobias Lear, of his hope 'to liberate a certain species of property which I possess, very repugnantly to my own feelings'. Wiencek explains that Washington had 'experienced a moral epiphany' and did not, in the early 1790s, believe that the obstacles to emancipation set forth by Lower South politicians were 'insuperable to him at all'.[41] Disappointed at Washington's retreat from the grand experiment, Lafayette wrote to Washington with uncommon bitterness: 'I would never have drawn my sword in the cause of America, if I could have conceived that thereby I was founding a land of slavery.'[42] Washington would remain troubled by slavery; but his usefulness to the abolitionists on both sides of the Atlantic from this point forward was limited. It bears remembering, however, that Lafayette's scheme remained in Washington's mind, finally bearing fruit when the first American president's will revealed after his death in 1799 that he had provided for the freedom of his slaves. The will was published in many newspapers and his words – 'All my Negroes are to be free' – were featured in eulogies up and down the eastern seaboard.[43]

Of all the Americans that European abolitionists wished to enlist in the cause, Jefferson was undoubtedly the most important, both because of his enormous reputation on both sides of the Atlantic and because, as one of Virginia's major slave-owners (and the largest in Albemarle County), the precedent he would set if he were to take a lead in purging himself of slave-holding would almost certainly have global repercussions. As William Lloyd Garrison would say many years later, 'What an all-conquering influence must have attended his illustrious example' if he had seized the moment.[44]

Once in Paris in late 1784, Jefferson embraced French reformers. Renewing their relationship established late in the American Revolution, Lafayette became one of Jefferson's closest and most important friends in Paris.[45] At Lafayette's home and in his social circle, Jefferson communed with other French intellectuals, fellow leaders of the Enlightenment, including Chastellux, Condorcet, Buffon, La Rochefoucauld, Volney, Raynal, and the Abbé Gregoire. Most important among them were the Abbé Raynal, fierce campaigner against slavery, and the Marquis de Condorcet. Born in the same year as Condorcet, Jefferson was especially close to the man who stood as informal heir to Voltaire and was revising the monumental *Encyclopédie*. Dubbed the 'snowy volcano' for his calm exterior but passionate views, Condorcet topped his reform agenda with the abolition of slavery and the conferring of equal rights on women. As early as 1776 he had called slavery a 'horrible violation of human rights', and in 1781 he had written a widely circulated treatise that labelled slavery as a criminal act. Jefferson translated Condorcet's essay himself, rendering one sentence as even if 'the human race unanimously voted approval [of slavery], the crime would remain a crime'.[46]

Meanwhile, Jefferson learned of the efforts of the English abolitionists Granville Sharp and William Wilberforce, who were seeking the end of the slave trade and the amelioration, if not the extinction, of slavery. The fiercely determined Sharp was also concerned about the fate of the black poor in England, some of whom were African American veterans of the British army in America who had fallen on hard times in the English capital. Sharp helped to implement a plan in 1786, with which Afro-Britons concurred, by which they would settle in an area to be called Sierra Leone on Africa's west coast. That the English had no title to this land bothered nobody except the Mende people who lived there. Later, Sharp's scheme to populate Sierra Leone embraced over one thousand Black Loyalists then living unhappily in Nova Scotia.[47]

The influence of French and English abolitionists on Jefferson during his first several years in Paris was palpable. Prizing his inclusion among the intelligentsia, relishing their admiration of his *Notes on the State of Virginia*, and far away from his Virginia plantations, he found no discomfort in aligning himself with a circle of cosmopolitan intellectuals who were decidedly antislavery and prepared to do something about it. None of his French friends seem to have challenged him about the black inferiority he had alleged in the *Notes*; they were simply inclined to believe that the degradation of blacks could be lifted along with the chains of slavery.

It speaks to Jefferson's inner turmoil that while he was telling American friends that the time was not ripe for floating an emancipation scheme, he was eager to redeem the Americans' reputation in Europe by telling European friends that the time *was* right for this. In response to Richard Price's finger-wagging letter of July 1785, Jefferson replied that in the northern states 'you may find here and there an opponent to your doctrine [of ending slavery] as you may find here and there a robber and a murderer, but in no greater number'. Southward of the Chesapeake, he continued, most would oppose all emancipationist schemes, but in Virginia, 'from the mouth to the head of the Chesapeake with some degree of certainty, . . . the bulk of the people will approve it in theory, and it will find a respectable minority ready to adopt it in practice, a minority which for weight and worth of character preponderates against the greater number who have not the courage to divest their families of a property which however keeps their consciences inquiet'. Marylanders, he explained, were not as ready 'to begin the redress of this enormity', but here too the 'spectacle of justice in conflict with avarice and oppression' was tilting towards abolitionism because of 'the influx into office of young men grown and growing up' who 'have sucked in the principles of liberty as it were with their mother's milk'.[48]

With these words, Jefferson all but said that leading men of conscience who wanted to abolish slavery, supported by 'the bulk of the people', needed only courage to place the 'weight and worth of [their] character' behind an emancipation scheme. Yet Jefferson was not ready to display that courage. Part of his reluctance was concern about his political aspirations, and linked to this was the fear of offending friends and fellow planters ready to charge him with betraying his class. He had heard early in 1786 that the Virginia legislature had taken up the revised constitution he had drafted in 1783 and had scornfully rejected a petition calling for a general manumission of Virginia's slaves. This, reported Madison, 'was rejected without dissent, but not without an avowed patronage of its principle by sundry respectable members'.[49] In this situation, those sympathetic to Jefferson's proposal to free all slaves born after the passage of the law once they reached adulthood held back the measure, reasoning that since the legislature had rejected the petition for a general emancipation they would scorn and revile proponents of such a weighty attempt to change the course of Virginia's history – and that of the nation.

This was much on Jefferson's mind in 1786 when he was mingling with French intellectuals who yearned to see America wash its hands of slavery and bring its laws into conformity with its revolutionary principles. His friend Lafayette kept up his fusillade against the weak-kneed American leaders, writing to John Adams, now the American minister to England, that 'in the cause of my black brethren, I feel myself warmly interested and most decidedly side, so far as respects them, against the white part of mankind. . . . It is to me a matter of great anxiety and concern, to find that this [slave] trade is sometimes perpetuated under the flag of liberty, our dear and noble stripes to which virtue and glory have been constant standard bearers.'[50] Also pressing Jefferson hard was Jean Nicolas Démeunier, the young French thinker and devotee of the Abbé Raynal who was charged with preparing a long essay on the United States for Condorcet's revised *Encyclopédie méthodique*. Why, asked Démeunier, in a series of queries to Jefferson in 1786, had Virginia passed a revised legal code without some promise of emancipation? Eager to have Virginia's reputation saved from opprobrious comments in a book that was sure to reach an international audience, Jefferson waffled in his reply. Though he and the abolition-minded George Wythe were unable to participate in the debate, he said, 'men of virtue' were not lacking to press cogent arguments for ending slavery; but 'they saw that the moment of doing it with success was not yet arrived, and that an unsuccessful effort, as too often happens, would only rivet still closer the chains of bondage, and retard the moment of delivery to this oppressed description of men.'[51]

Continuing to avow his disgust with slavery, Jefferson scourged the man who 'inflicts on his fellow men a bondage, one hour of which is fraught with more misery than ages of that which he rose in rebellion to oppose'. But from this unequivocal position Jefferson retreated to a position that would soon steer the course he maintained for the next four decades of his life. If he and his friends could not do what they knew must be done, they must patiently await God's intervention – 'the workings of an overruling providence'. When the slaves' 'groans shall have involved heaven itself in darkness', he assured Démeunier, 'doubtless a god of justice will awaken to their distress, and by diffusing light and liberality among their oppressors, or at length by his exterminating thunder', slavery would come to an end. Jefferson was experimenting, to use David Brion Davis's phrasing, 'with the locutions which for the rest of his life would characterize his response to such questions' about slavery. 'We do not ordinarily associate Jeffersonian democracy with a quietistic surrender to fate', Davis writes. 'And what would the younger generation whom he trusted to solve the slavery problem think when they heard their intellectual mentor recommending faith in providence as a substitute for social action?'[52]

Shortly after his reply to Démeunier, Jefferson fell into a liaison that indirectly connected him with a clarion black voice becoming an important part of the English abolitionist movement. Entranced with the languorous, twenty-seven-year-old Maria Cosway, the loneliness of the Monticello widower converged with Cosway's marital unhappiness in a summer and autumn of passion. Meanwhile, across the Channel in London, the black servant of the Cosway family was writing the fieriest – and longest – abolitionist pamphlet of the late eighteenth century. Ottobah Cugoano, enslaved at age thirteen in West Africa in 1770, had gained his freedom in England in 1772, was baptized at St James's Church the next year, and had entered the service of Richard Cosway in about 1784. By this time, he was becoming a leader of London's Committee for the Relief of the Black Poor and a friend of the reformer Scipione Piattoli, adviser to Poland's King Stanislaus and drafter of the Third of May Constitution. One of those remarkable Africans who gained literacy and put it to use, the twenty-six-year-old black Londoner was at work on his *Thoughts and Sentiments on the Evil and Wicked Traffic of the Slavery and Commerce of the Human Species* at just the time the woman of the household in which he served, away from her foppish husband, described as 'a preposterous little Dresden china manikin', was consorting with Jefferson in Paris in 1786. Cugoano's *Thoughts and Sentiments* came off the press in 1787, one of the first antislavery pamphlets to flow from the pen of an African-born ex-slave. A friend of Olaudah Equiano and Thomas Clarkson, Cugoano became part of the growing international campaign to end the slave trade and slavery.[53]

Did Jefferson read Cugoano's *Thoughts and Sentiments* while playing cat and mouse with the wife of Cugoano's master? Jefferson could have read either the first edition of 1787 or a French translation published in Paris the next year. The Cosways certainly knew of the publication, for it was extraordinary for a person serving in the household of the court painter to publish a book on a touchy subject. Maria Cosway was fascinated with music, art, and Jefferson, so she may have found the muscular attack on slavery by her servant an inconvenient topic of discussion with her paramour. But Jefferson's head, if not his heart, must have caught the poignancy that the woman who had aroused passion in him as never before also held in her employ a former slave who had gained a public platform in London through his attack on slavery.

The year 1788 marked a turn, if only briefly, in Jefferson's thinking about his role as slave master. With Cugoano's attack on slavery circulating widely, Jefferson's friend Brissot de Warville took the lead in founding the Société des Amis des Noirs as a political lobby to end France's involvement in slavery and the slave trade. Lafayette, Condorcet, and other of Jefferson's friends quickly joined and implored the Master of Monticello to add his name. Dodging behind diplomatic protocol, Jefferson argued that he could not join for fear of charges that he was meddling in French politics (though he soon became involved in the intricate politics of the French Revolution). Yet Jefferson was caught up in the vibrant salon discussions that typically turned from gardens, literature, science, and philosophy to the universal rights of man. Amidst this, after receiving a letter from Edward Bancroft asking his views on an experiment in Virginia, where Joseph Mayo, a Quaker, had freed his scores of slaves and then hired them as tenant farmers, Jefferson announced an astounding change of position. Though he had only fragmentary reports that the Quaker experiment had not gone well, perhaps because freed slaves without title to their own property would not work hard, Jefferson vowed that 'I am decided on my . . . return to America to . . . import as many Germans as I have grown slaves.' He would allot fifty acres to each family, slave and German intermingled, and 'place all on the footing of the Metayers [leaseholders] of Europe. Their children shall be brought up as others are in habits of property and foresight, and I have no doubt but that they will be good citizens.' He would retain from the marketable commodities they harvested 'a moderate portion of it as may be a just equivalent for the use of the lands they labour and the stocks and other necessary advances'.[54]

Jefferson's plan to intermingle freed slaves and German immigrants on his Virginia land sharply reversed the conviction he so firmly expressed in his *Notes on Virginia* that emancipated slaves would have to be sent to some distant land because admixing with whites would never work peacefully. Is it possible that he had changed his mind not only because of his ardent friendship with his Enlightenment friends in Paris and his amorous connection with Cugoano's employer but also because of another warmth that was developing, at just this moment, with a beautiful young woman barely beyond adolescence in his own Paris household – the charming teenager Sally Hemings?[55]

★ ★ ★

For all the comments above regarding the limits of the American Revolution's ramifications outside of Europe, R. R. Palmer's focus on the reverberations of the revolution within Europe bears amendment, as the discussion above suggests, in the matter of race, slavery, and the claims of enslaved Africans in the Americas to the universal rights asserted in the Declaration of Independence. In the half-century after independence, the United States made its descent into the unenviable and contradictory status of slave-holding republic. Though the slave trade had ended in 1808, an illegal slave trade still flourished and, through natural increase, the slave population had quadrupled from half a million when the American Revolution began to nearly two million in 1820. Jefferson's Friends of Liberty on the other side of the Atlantic, understanding that the United States had descended into a 'racial Thermidor', would not leave the Sage of Monticello alone.[56] Coming to remind him of the overdue universal freedom promised in his Declaration of Independence was the Marquis de Lafayette, who visited Monticello in 1824 and 1825.

For eleven days Lafayette stayed at Monticello, sharing meals and earnest conversation with the mansion's master. Brushing aside the fervent idolatry he had encountered in scores of villages and cities, Lafayette did not hide his bitterness at the growth of slavery and the vast racial gulf that now yawned between whites and blacks. Speaking openly in the presence of Israel, Jefferson's slave, who waited on their tables and stood postillion on his master's carriage, Lafayette told Jefferson 'that the slaves ought to be free; no man could rightfully hold ownership to his brother man'; and that 'he gave his best services to and spent his money on behalf of the Americans freely because he felt that they were fighting for a great and noble principle: the freedom of mankind, that instead of all being free a portion were held in bondage', which made him grieve. Israel later related how he 'treasured [the conversation] up in [my] heart'. But Jefferson demurred. He contended that slavery should be extinguished, but that the proper time had not yet arrived, not indicating, Israel recalled, 'when or in what manner'.[57]

In what amounted to a last-ditch effort to rescue Jefferson from his own demons, Lafayette did not soften his displeasure with slavery after Jefferson adopted a defensive posture. The French hero 'never missed an opportunity to defend the right *which all men without exception* have to liberty', wrote his secretary, who accompanied him throughout the thirteen-month American pilgrimage.[58] Such forthrightness soon led Virginians to cordon off slaves as the French hero passed through the state from town to town. This became apparent after his travelling party left Monticello. After four days at James Madison's Montpelier estate, Lafayette proceeded to Fredericksburg. Slave owners there were asked to keep their slaves out of sight when the procession made its way through the town, while 'all colored people are warned that they are not to appear on any of the streets through which the procession will pass'.[59] In Savannah, Georgia, white authorities similarly banned blacks from all celebrations, but that did not stop Lafayette from searching out – after the parade – an old slave he had known nearly half a century before. Once again, the universalistic principles of the

American Revolution were emanating from the eastern rather than western rim of the Atlantic world.

By this time, African Americans were looking to England and its Canadian province in the hope that 'the cause of America', as Paine had phrased it, 'is in a great measure the cause of all mankind'. Indeed, black Americans had been embracing Great Britain, not the United States, as the avatar of freedom since the War of 1812 when thousands of Chesapeake area slaves claimed their freedom, as they had done in the American Revolution, by fleeing to the arms of the British army where freedom awaited them. Moreover, they knew as well as everyone else that, after the British and American abolition of the slave trade beginning in 1808, it was the British Royal Navy that more strenuously enforced the ban than the republican American government.[60] America, it was widely thought among those who were black, had betrayed their revolution. It would take some time to express this in the starkest terms, but by the 1840s Frederick Douglass would say of the United States: 'It is not a true democracy, but a bastard republicanism that enslaves one-sixth of the population.'[61]

Mastering the art of dramatic pronouncements, Thomas Paine was not far from the mark in 1776 by opining that the American Revolution would affect posterity 'even to the end of time'. At that time, only a few months after arriving in America, he was hopeful for both American independence and a radical cleansing of colonial society. Years later, returning to the United States in 1802 after a tumultuous experience in revolutionary France, he choked at what he found. In a series of letters 'To the Citizens of the United States', the threadbare Paine held to account the Americans in whom he had invested so much hope. Calling his missives 'sparks from the altar of Seventy-Six', he lamented the retreat in America from 'a *new system* of government in which the rights of *all* men should be preserved'.[62] Paine would carry such disappointments to his grave. Among them was the growth of slavery in the American South. What Jefferson imagined would blossom into an 'empire of liberty' in North America was turning into an empire of slavery, in part because the Sage of Monticello had held himself in bondage to the southern patrician slaveocracy rather than heeding the supplications of his transatlantic friends, who had argued for a quarter-century before he died that Jefferson could secure his place in history by stepping forward on the 'boisterous sea of liberty' to lead the abolitionist crusade.

2

The French Revolution in Global Context

Lynn Hunt

Until the past ten years or so, historians have given largely internalist accounts of the French Revolution. Most scholarly attention has focused on causes such as food shortages and on major mechanisms, e.g., the push for popular democracy or the resistance to women's rights, that were internal to the history of metropolitan or 'hexagonal' France. Few denied that the French Revolution had a global dimension, but that global dimension was usually seen either as an effect of the geopolitical ambitions of the revolutionary leadership or as an overseas echo of radical revolutionary ideology at home. The arrow of influence always pointed outward, from mainland France, and especially from Paris, to other places, including the French colonies. Mainland French historians were only too happy to note the far distant reverberations of *their* French Revolution, but by and large they rejected efforts to make the French Revolution part of a broader Atlantic movement, as R. R. Palmer had argued it should be. Indeed, those most favourable to Palmer's argument tended to come from outside of France or from the periphery of the French mainland.[1]

Hardly anyone or any country was exempt from the impact of French revolutionary ideas and wars. Radicals in the United States, Great Britain, the western German states, and various Italian cities embraced revolutionary ideals and tried to apply them at home, with mixed results. Between 1792 and 1796, citizens of the new United States witnessed more celebrations of the French Revolution than of Washington's birthday or even Independence Day.[2] Four Scottish radicals were transported to Australia in 1794 for sedition because they participated in pro-revolutionary organizations such as the Scottish Association of the Friends of the People (an echo of Jean-Paul Marat's notorious newspaper, *The Friend of the People*).[3] Their fates paled next to the nearly one hundred republicans, including leading intellectuals, who were executed in Naples in 1799 when royalists supported by the British and Russian navies forced the French to withdraw their support.[4]

Echoes of 1789 in the French colonies were even louder, as free men of colour demanded equal political rights with their white counterparts, who in turn insisted that the national French government should let the colonial assemblies, exclusively white, decide on all questions of status. In August 1791 a slave insurrection broke out in the largest and richest French colony, Saint Domingue, and after repeated turns and twists, the French National Convention abolished slavery in February 1794. The abolition and the insurrection that prompted it rocked the world of slave-holding all over the Americas. When Napoleon failed to retake Saint Domingue in 1802, where he intended to reintroduce slavery, he gave up on his ambition to gain lands across the globe and sold 'Louisiana', recently acquired from the Spanish, to the United States. The Louisiana territory of nearly a million square miles included the land of what is now fourteen states in the United States.

The French revolutionary armies often brought their ideals with them and tried to impose them, for better or worse. 'Sister republics' were set up under French direction in the Swiss cantons (Helvetic and Lemanic republics), the Rhineland (Cisrhenian, Mainz), the Netherlands (Batavian), and especially the Italian states (as many as fifteen different ones, including the ill-fated Republic in Naples). Venturing even further afield, Napoleon Bonaparte invaded Egypt, a province of the Ottoman Empire, in 1798 in order to cut British access to India. He defeated local armies, set up new assemblies, and tried to establish individual ownership of property, but mainly succeeded in arousing resistance to French intrusion. His efforts to block the British in India failed, but not before one important Indian ruler sent out an explicit call for help in fighting the British. Tipu Sultan, the ruler of the south Indian kingdom of Mysore, curried the support of a ragtag band of French soldiers and freebooters who set up a Jacobin Club in his capital of Seringapatam and helped 'citizen' Tipu fight the British in 1799, to no avail.[5] Tipu died in the climactic battle, but clearly French revolutionary ideas did not, for the French tricolour and Napoleonic eagle would appear again and again, and not just in France. When he declared the independence of Vietnam in 1945, Ho Chi Minh opened with the statement of what he termed an undeniable truth, drawn from the American Declaration of Independence – 'All men are created equal; they are endowed by their Creator with certain unalienable Rights; among these are Life,

Liberty, and the pursuit of Happiness' – which he immediately followed with the opening article of the French Declaration of the Rights of Man and Citizen of 1789: 'All men are born free and with equal rights, and must always remain free and have equal rights.'[6]

Historians of the French Revolution have begun to pay more attention to these kinds of connections to the broader world. The most intense focus of interest has been the Haitian Revolution (Saint Domingue became Haiti in 1804) and its links to the French Revolution. This work has shown not only that the events in France's richest colony Saint Domingue were influenced by what transpired in France but also the reverse, that events in France were influenced by what transpired in the colonies. To what extent and to what end remains up for debate, as David Geggus's chapter in this volume demonstrates very forcefully. Work on the colonies has not entirely dislodged the internalist account, however; often it serves to simply enlarge what is considered internal, that is, what is part of France itself. What is needed now is not an exclusively externalist account, in which external causes and influences replace the internal ones. More attention to those external causes and influences would be most welcome, but in the end we need an account that can persuasively link external and internal causes, effects, and processes.

Many questions remain to be answered if a truly global account is to gain credibility. Can popular violence and the aspiration for popular sovereignty, for example, be best understood in a global context, a national one, or a local one? How should a global contextualization be undertaken, that is, what is the relevant frame of reference for determining external causes and influences: the European powers, the rivalry with Great Britain, the Atlantic world, or a truly global context? Is the aim to show parallel developments or converging ones (as C. A. Bayly calls them) or interconnected ones?[7] And what is the larger metanarrative that results from global contextualization? Finally, and not least, can such an account incorporate, rather than efface, the many contributions made by local studies and by examinations of gender relations and other cultural processes, which have often been most fruitfully studied on the local, or at least nation-state, level? These are the questions that I hope to consider in admittedly schematic fashion.[8]

The staying power of the internalist account

The internalist account enjoyed such staying power because historians of opposing political stripes all operated from the same presupposition that the mainland nation-state was the relevant frame of reference for the French Revolution. It is perhaps surprising that the colonial aspect would disappear so much from view, since in the nineteenth and twentieth centuries the French officially considered at least some colonies as integral parts of the nation-state, but disappear it did. In France, colonial history became a separate subject, and it figured little in the interpretations of the French Revolution. Anglophone scholars followed their lead, including even R. R. Palmer, who devoted only one page to the Haitian Revolution in the second volume of his work on the Atlantic revolutions. He had ten pages on the failed Polish revolution of 1794.[9]

As far as I can determine, there is no real political difference on this subject. In the many thousands of pages in Jean Jaurès's socialist history of France, 1789–1900 (published in 1901–8), there is one page devoted to slavery under the Old Regime and one to projects for its abolition. François Furet does not mention slavery or the colonies in his influential *Interpreting the French Revolution* (1989). Simon Schama gives one sentence in his 950 pages of *Citizens* (1989) to the slave uprising of 1791 and then only to explain the high price of sugar in Paris in 1792. The blurb for the 2004 reprinting of Yves Benot's pioneering book of 1988 on *La Révolution française et la fin des colonies (1789–1794)* shows just how little had changed even then. This is, he says, a 'little studied question because, with the exception of Jaurès', though I might dispute him there, 'for the principal historians of the Revolution – Michelet, Mathiez, Lefebvre, Soboul – one might say that the colonies, the slave trade, slavery, all that is but a negligible aspect in comparison to the great French and European problems. In the same way, the hexagonal collective memory seems to have forgotten these events for a long time.'[10]

The example of Tocqueville shows just how thoroughly the blinders kept this subject from view. The colonies and slavery are never directly discussed in his classic treatment *The Old Regime and the French Revolution*, published in 1856. Indeed, the only time the colonies are mentioned is in a passage about the French peasants: people believe that the peasants only work because they are threatened with starvation, Tocqueville observes, which is much the same argument that is used about the Negroes in our colonies. Yet this oversight cannot be explained by lack of knowledge or even interest, since in 1839 Tocqueville was named to be spokesman for a parliamentary commission established to consider the abolition of slavery in the French colonies. His report was subsequently published by an abolitionist society. Moreover, Tocqueville had discussed slavery time and again in his 1835 essay *Democracy in America*. So it is not ideology, politics, or racism that prompts historians to neglect the colonial dimension of the French Revolution. It is the working of what came to seem self-evident: that the Revolution has to do with France defined as the traditional 'hexagon'.[11]

Needless to say, the internalist account was never exclusively internalist. Tocqueville's analysis of France's social and political structure rested on explicit comparisons with Germany and England because the three had such similar institutions originally but then developed in such different directions. Moreover, Tocqueville's underlying aim was the development of a metanarrative about the rise of egalitarianism, which was hardly exclusively French and was in many important respects derived from his prior study of democracy in America. Still, the struggle over the remnants of feudalism and the rise of egalitarianism in France took place for Tocqueville within the metropolitan borders. Although many nineteenth- and twentieth-century historians of the French Revolution might not have pursued Tocqueville's aggressive comparative programme, they almost always gave some weight to competition with Great Britain as an ultimate cause. The bankruptcy of the crown in 1787, from which all else followed, had to be traced back to the losses in the Seven Years War and the desire for revenge that animated the expensive support of American independence. Yet this recognition of great power rivalry did not necessarily point in a truly global direction. Indeed, it almost never did.

Two examples will have to suffice to make this point. Even in Theda Skocpol's theoretically acute attempt to take into account what she calls 'the international and world-historical contexts' of the French, Russian, and Chinese Revolutions, these contexts only supply causes for social revolution. The revolutions that result are viewed as events of the metropole alone. Even more telling is the example of Bailey Stone, who published a 'global-historical perspective' on the French Revolution in 2002. While he gives great prominence to the Seven Years War, the War of American Independence, and the general diplomatic context in Europe, he fails to mention slavery, Saint Domingue, or the Haitian Revolution. In other words, acknowledging the influence of diplomatic, military, and international financial factors does not necessarily translate into a 'global' account. It has proved very difficult to treat the Revolution itself (as distinguished from its causes or effects) in other than an internalist fashion.[12]

New efforts at internationalization

The international influence of the French Revolution has long been recognized, especially by historians working in places other than France. Revolutionary ideas and institutions travelled far and wide, whether under the coercive impact of Republican and Napoleonic armies or by the gentler but often no less momentous means of example and inspiration. The ideological and institutional maps of the nineteenth century were redrawn: slaves successfully revolted and set up an independent state in Haiti; many other new nations appeared as well (most of Latin America gained its independence from Spain in the 1820s after the Spanish had been weakened by Napoleonic domination); nationalism took shape in reaction against the French; serfdom, legal torture, and official religious intolerance were abolished in some places; the techniques of the incipient police state were perfected, to name just a few examples.

Edmund Burke sensed the magnitude of the event already in 1790, and he is worth quoting at some length because he instantly grasped what was at stake:

> It appears to me as if I were in a great crisis, not of the affairs of France alone, but of all Europe, perhaps of more than Europe. All circumstances taken together, the French Revolution is the most astonishing that has hitherto happened in the world. The most wonderful things are brought about in many instances by means the most absurd and ridiculous; in the most ridiculous modes; and, apparently, by the most contemptible instruments. Everything seems out of nature in this strange chaos of levity and ferocity, and of all sorts of crimes jumbled together with all sorts of follies. In viewing this monstrous tragi-comic scene, the most opposite passions necessarily succeed, and sometimes mix with each other in the mind; alternate contempt and indignation; alternate laughter and tears; alternate scorn and horror.

Striking in Burke's rendition is not just the magnitude of the break he detects and its potential worldwide significance but also the difficulty he has in pinning down the modes of transformation: 'everything seems out of nature'. Though Burke himself followed events in the British Empire closely – he played a key role in the impeachment of Warren Hastings, Governor of Bengal – he treated the French Revolution as an entirely internal affair, except for its example to the rest of the world. If he had put the Revolution in the global context that he himself suggests is relevant, he might have been able to make more sense of those 'most ridiculous modes' of transformation.[13]

In recent years, the most fruitful area for new research on the international dimension of the French Revolution has been the Haitian Revolution. The mulattos of Saint Domingue (as Haiti was known before independence) rose first in October 1790 but were defeated by a combined force of planter militias and French troops. Then in August 1791 the slaves began their massive uprising that eventually forced the French to agree to abolish slavery in 1794. When Napoleon tried to re-establish slavery in the Caribbean in 1802, the former slaves on Saint Domingue fought his expeditionary force and eventually made them withdraw, opening the way to the declaration of the independence of Haiti. The history of these events and the structural conditions and political processes that made them possible had long been ignored, despite the best efforts of C. L. R. James to draw attention to them in his pioneering book of 1938, *The Black Jacobins*. The trickle of work that appeared on this subject in the 1980s and early 1990s has now, however, swelled into a veritable flood as younger scholars and even older ones who made their reputations in other fields (Elizabeth Colwill in women's history and Jeremy Popkin in the history of the press, for example) have turned their attention in this direction. It is perhaps not surprising that though British and Caribbean scholars first got the ball rolling (James was Trinidadian, Michel-Rolphe Trouillot was Haitian, and Robin Blackburn was British), American historians of the French Revolution have now picked it up, because the Haitian story is so clearly related to that of slavery in the Americas more generally. French scholars too are now joining in, as can be seen by the recent book (2007) by Florence Gauthier on the mulatto Julien Raimond and his activism against a growing 'aristocracy of the epidermis'.[14]

There are many good reasons why the Haitian Revolution should be at the forefront of efforts to put the French Revolution in a global context. Saint Domingue was the richest single colony in the Americas by all accounts, thanks to its role in sugar production, and home in 1789 to 500,000 slaves, most of them born in Africa. Slaves made up 89 per cent of the colony's population, which had more than tripled since 1750. The entire United States had 700,000 slaves, and in the state with the highest proportion of them, South Carolina, slaves made up 60 per cent of the population. The global circulation of people (slaves, merchants, sailors, immigrants), commodities (sugar, tobacco, coffee, cotton, indigo), and ideas (independence, rights, racism) combined with an exceptionally complex diplomatic and military situation to make Saint Domingue an international hot spot, especially after the slave uprising began to make gains.

It has been easier to show the influence of the Haitian Revolution in the Americas than back in mainland France. As planters and their families began to flee Saint Domingue in great numbers, often for the USA, an original distrust of the refugees, who were for the most part monarchists after all, turned into growing alarm about the slave revolt. In 1793 some 6,000 colonists came to US port towns along with thousands more servants and slaves. Thomas Jefferson wrote to James Monroe on 14 July 1793: 'I become daily more and more convinced that all the West India islands will remain in the hands of the people of colour, and a total expulsion of the whites sooner or later take place. It is high time we should foresee the bloody scenes which our children certainly, and possibly ourselves (South of Patowmac) have to wade through, and try to avert them.' Jefferson, like the British but for different reasons, encouraged Napoleon to retake the colony, but once he saw the size of the expeditionary forces sent to accomplish the task, he changed tack and allowed US merchants to supply those resisting Napoleon. He ended up with Louisiana, which Napoleon sold after his soldiers became bogged down.[15]

The other Caribbean islands and South American countries also felt the impact, in some cases immediately. Within a month of the initial uprising in 1791, Jamaican slaves were singing songs about it. Since 350,000 slaves lived on Cuba and Jamaica, a canoe-ride away from Saint Domingue, the threat must have been palpable. Rumours of slave resistance and revolt spread far and wide, despite the unwillingness of the new Haitian government to explicitly encourage them in the face of continuing diplomatic isolation. The United States, France, and Great Britain refused to recognize Haiti even after they had recognized the independence of the many South American countries. In 1816, Haiti's President Pétion helped arm Simon Bolívar and allowed hundreds of Haitian fighters to sail with him to contest Spanish domination. In return Bolívar promised to try to abolish slavery wherever he succeeded. Many men of colour and slaves joined his army of liberation, and all the new Spanish American republics abolished the slave trade. They abolished slavery itself between 1829 (Mexico) and 1853. Slavery continued in colonial Cuba and imperial Brazil, as well as in the southern United States, but the Haitian example inspired abolitionists on both sides of the Atlantic.[16]

Much of my account of this international influence is taken from Robin Blackburn, whose work shows how the broader, that is, global, view is more easily taken by those offering a synthesis or comparative analysis based on available research rather than original research in often recalcitrant archives. With the exception of the magnificent transatlantic slave trade database, which was decades in the making out of bits and pieces found here and there, historians have very few sets of data that allow systematic comparison between countries, much less the tracing of global patterns. The kind of work done by Laurent Dubois, John Garrigus, and Elizabeth Colwill in notarial archives has revolutionized our understanding of the life of slaves and free blacks in Guadeloupe and Saint Domingue, but it is work that requires great patience, care, and a steady building up of information before new generalizations can be hazarded. What they and others have shown, nonetheless, is the way slaves and people of colour shaped the events in the Caribbean. In this way, the perspective laid out by James – and long before him, by Marcus Rainsford in his history of Haiti of 1805 – has steadily gained ground. No one would now deny the significance of the Haitian Revolution or its close links to the revolution in mainland France, though in his chapter in this volume David Geggus offers an important reinterpretation of some of the current orthodoxy.[17]

Less systematically investigated to date has been the influence of events in the Caribbean on 'internal' French politics. The basic outlines of the story are well known: the influence of the Abbé Raynal's *Histoire des deux Indes*, with its fiery denunciation of European colonialism and prediction of the appearance of a Black Spartacus; the emergence of French abolitionism in the 1780s and especially the founding of the Society of the Friends of Blacks in 1788 with its prominent members, including Condorcet, Lafayette, Grégoire, and Mirabeau; and the intense and evolving debates over the place of the colonies within the new constitution and especially the status of free blacks and ultimately, under pressure, slaves, the slave trade, and slavery itself. While it is probably true that most deputies to the Estates General and then the National Assembly did not want to even think about the abolition of the slave trade or slavery (slavery was nonetheless abolished in 1794), it was much harder to dismiss the rights of free blacks after 1789. The 27,000 free blacks and mulattos of Saint Domingue owned one-third of the land and one-quarter of the slaves in the colony and by their own account offered a bulwark against disintegration of the slave economy. On what grounds, other than racism, could they be denied political participation in the new order?

What is missing in this story of the French reaction to events in the colonies is a broader view, both of the place of France within the global frame and of the colonies' impact on revolutionary events themselves. French historians have yet to produce an analogue to David Armitage's study *The Ideological Origins of the British Empire*

(2000), though Emma Rothschild is in a sense in the midst of preparing one with her various studies from different vantage points of the French empire.[18] Much much more needs to done on the way the French conceptualized – or did not conceptualize – their empire, both its parts and as a whole. Too often the desire for revenge against the English seems to be the only global cause cited for the outbreak of the French Revolution. Similarly, much more needs to be done to uncover the ways in which events in the colonies after 1789 forced the French to rethink their imperial ambitions. Napoleon's efforts to re-establish slavery – successful in all but Saint Domingue – have made it seem that no rethinking took place and moreover that all the real innovation was taking place in French relations with Europe and the Middle East. I suspect that we just haven't looked closely enough. at the evolutions of imperial policy.

Finally, no systematic study has been undertaken into the influence of procolonial and anticolonial lobbies on other issues before the various legislatures. Did alignments formed over the rights of free blacks and the status of slavery and the slave trade carry over into other areas, or not? Did the Jacobin dislike for luxury and conspicuous consumption include an inherently anti-imperial position? John Shovlin has recently reminded us that the number of works in 'political economy' (a term coming into fashion in the 1760s in France) skyrocketed between 1750 and 1789 – 668 in the 1770s, 756 between 1780 and 1788 and 804 in the year 1789 alone – but he says nothing about the relative weight of discussion in this literature of the colonies and empire. Indeed, the colonies and the slave trade appear only in passing in this book on political economy and the origins of the French Revolution. I am not blaming this absence on him. As his book shows, the French romance with the rural extended from the physiocrats through the Jacobins and on to the government of Vichy and its opponents. When any of them said 'rural' or 'land' or 'soil', they did not mean the lands of plantations tilled by slave labourers.[19] A deep suspicion of the deceptions of financial speculation and the corruptions of luxury always seemed to go hand in hand with discussions of colonial trade in France. Time and again, from the John Law affair in the early 1720s to its fraudulent liquidation in fall 1793, the Compagnie des Indes would become the flashpoint for worries about the moral fibre of the nation. The murky affair of 1793 proved to be arguably the biggest turning point in the entire French Revolution: it brought down Fabre d'Eglantine, and by association, Georges Danton and his closest supporters. The Terror itself, then, is intimately tied up with the Indies Company, but just how and to what extent?[20]

If we still know so little about how events in the colonies shaped opinion within France, then it is perhaps not surprising that it is difficult to determine just what role the global framework had in precipitating the events known as the French Revolution. Bayly offers the now conventional externalist argument: 'The problem for European states, then, was that although they were increasingly being forced into warfare worldwide, most of them did not have the resources to prosecute wars, which were so costly in terms of men and treasure.' The French were the particular victims of this dilemma, it appears. 'The large financial burden taken on by the French Crown in order to help the Americans pushed royal ministers into risky, but incoherent, programmes of reform. These gradually undermined the basis of the monarchy itself.'[21] Needless to say, however, the programmes of reform only seemed incoherent once they failed and the French only seem to be the victims of the war they supposedly won because they had a successful revolution afterward. Although I doubt that Bayly wants to view revolution as a sign of failure, that seems to be the implication of his argument.

The point is not so much to criticize Bayly, who at least tries to provide a global framework for the events of the French Revolution, as to suggest that a thorough rethinking of the international situation is required. A rethinking would entail not just describing the international context, as Bayly does, but also examining more closely the links between domestic politics and the international situation. Few European states, in fact, were 'being forced into warfare worldwide', contrary to Bayly's argument. Only Britain and France were repeatedly fighting on a worldwide scale in the second half of the eighteenth century. Did they do so deliberately or inadvertently? That is, was colonial competition the source of the worldwide conflict or was worldwide conflict the unanticipated result of powers with colonies going to war against each other? While it is true that the British ability to finance war borrowing at a lower cost was a significant advantage, other factors need to be brought into the equation: the size and expense of the navies, the cost of policing the colonies, and the shifting attitudes of governments and elites towards the imperial enterprise. The French ministers fought bitterly among themselves over these issues.[22]

Revolutionary politics in a global context

So far I have concentrated on the issue of the causes of the French Revolution. Can the formative political processes of the Revolution be better understood if placed in a global context? They can, as I have tried to show in a limited way for one of these processes, the human rights revolution. The French Revolutionary preoccupation with 'the Rights of Man' has to be seen as part of the circulation of ideas and cultural practices between and within Europe and the Americas (and of course, ultimately, on a global scale – though the global scale becomes more relevant after the Declaration of the Rights of Man and Citizen than before it). New notions and practices concerning individual autonomy and the inviolability of the body took shape from the 1760s onward in the Atlantic world. They did not radiate from a single intellectual centre such as Paris. Instead, they truly circulated among leading thinkers in disparate places (think of Rousseau, Voltaire, Beccaria, Price, and Jefferson), between thinkers and a general public on at least two continents (a public that read novels, dramatic lawyers' briefs, and reforming tracts), between artists and their growing public for portraits (keeping in mind that many American portraits were painted by itinerant British painters), and among the public, the reformers, and government ministers who abolished torture, moderated cruel punishments, and instituted or refused to institute a previously unimaginable list of human rights.[23]

How do such new attitudes arise? In many different ways no doubt, but almost all of them transcend one nation's borders, as the case of human rights demonstrates. The universalism of the Declaration of the Rights of Man and Citizen resonated in a particular French political context, to be sure, but it had sources in Anglo-America and in the writings of German, Dutch, Swiss, and Italian thinkers, and it had repercussions around the world. One of the many interesting questions that might be examined is why Dutch (Hugo Grotius), Swiss (Jean-Jacques Burlamaqui), Prussian (Samuel Pufendorf), and Italian (Cesare Beccaria) thinkers had such influence on the development of universalist conceptions of natural law and human rights. Did the small countries and states on the periphery of the Great Powers have a disproportionate impact on universalism precisely because of their small size and peripheral standing?[24]

Like human rights, independence, placed in a global context by David Armitage, circulated as an idea and as a set of political practices. Bayly has written that '[i]t was in the realm of ideas that the impact of the revolutions was most obvious to contemporaries.' Yet ideas are never just ideas; they are cultural constructs that call forth actions. Human rights and independence were certainly not just ideas; they were claims that grew out of actions and produced other actions in their wake. They were such powerful ideas because they posited new capacities for autonomous action where such autonomy had not been granted in the past.[25]

While the aspiration for popular or national sovereignty clearly crossed borders, popular violence seems especially rooted to local contexts. The fall of the Bastille on 14 July 1789 or the attack on the Tuileries on 10 August 1792 appear to be very much internal French affairs, even Parisian ones, at least in terms of their causes and their unfolding. Yet revolutionary political practices circulated just as surely as did the Declaration of the Rights of Man and Citizen. It was this kind of circulation that most alarmed Burke when he railed against 'this strange chaos of levity and ferocity'. Did French villagers set up maypoles in 1789 because of their association with traditional village festivity or because as liberty poles they had attracted considerable attention in the American colonies? What did Tipu Sultan think of his liberty pole? When Roman revolutionaries burnt cardinals' hats at their 'altar of liberty' did they see themselves as followers or innovators?

The global influence of the French Revolution is usually attributed to the depth of the transformation wrought by the revolution within France and the turmoil created by the nearly unceasing revolutionary wars that continued until 1815. The revolutionaries proceeded to politicize just about every imaginable aspect of daily life, from the names of children to the measures of time (the revolutionary calendar) and space (the metric system). They killed the king and queen, abolished noble titles, eliminated the remnants of feudalism, confiscated most of the property of the Catholic Church, opened careers to merit, and proceeded to elect not just deputies and local officials but also judges, justices of the peace, bishops of the Catholic Church, and even for a time military officers. Protestants, Jews, actors, executioners, free blacks, and ultimately even slaves gained the right to vote. Who could remain unmoved by such a spectacle?

An important element in the circulation of these ideas and practices has been little examined: the materialization and as a consequence the commercialization of politics. This process had taken shape in a particularly dramatic and influential way during the agitation surrounding John Wilkes in Britain in the 1760s. Because issue number 45 of Wilkes's weekly *The North Briton* had precipitated a conflict with the British crown, the number 45 soon took on talismanic significance. It appeared on sleeve buttons and breast buckles, mugs and punchbowls, snuffboxes and brooches. Wilkes himself appeared in cartoons and on signposts and as china and bronze figurines sitting on the top of the mantelpiece. Pamphlets, broadsheets, and newspapers carried the stories of his struggles far and wide.[26]

The influence of this kind of political material culture has been
studied to some extent within France – most notoriously an entre-
preneur got a licence to demolish the Bastille prison and promptly
sold off its stones to patriots around the country – but the story has
not been traced across the boundaries of the hexagon to the colonies,
to other countries in Europe, or elsewhere. One striking, albeit para-
doxical, result of the intense politicization created by the Revolution
was the commercialization of everyday items as political souvenirs.
Playing cards, dishware, curtains, wigs, stationery – almost any item of
daily life could carry revolutionary insignia and be sold as signs of
patriotic belonging. Considerable profits could be made selling the
tokens of republican virtue. Napoleon took these developments to a
new level. In 1796 Jean-Charles Pellerin developed a technique for
printing cheap coloured wood engravings – called *imagerie d'Epinal*
after the town in eastern France where he had his business – and
before long Napoleon was the prime subject of the prints. Napoleon's
enduring fame within France – and no doubt to some extent across
the borders – rested in some considerable measure on this kind of
cultural dissemination and reproduction.[27]

And where does that leave metanarratives?

Bayly argues that 'The age of revolutions had quite dramatically
speeded up' the two changes in human life that he considers crucial:
'the growth of uniformity between societies and the growth of
complexity within them'. Three revolutions had coincided, according
to Bayly: the moral rearmament of the state to incorporate new
demands, new forms of national identity, and an industrious revolution of the middle classes. In a sense, then, Bayly combines Tocqueville
and Marx but with a global twist. Like Tocqueville he emphasizes the
ways in which people became more alike, which ironically made it
possible for the state to exercise even more power; and like Marx he
emphasizes the rise of the middle class, though not because of industry per se, and not with the implication of an inevitable class struggle.
These developments apparently fostered 'the growth of European and
American dominance over the world's economies and peoples'. I say
apparently because just how European and American dominance
follows remains opaque to me, especially since the USA in 1820
hardly seems like much of a world power and even France was relatively weak.[28]
    My metanarrative ambitions are much more modest than Bayly's.
Rather than trying to explain everything that happens in the entire

world between 1780 and 1820, I would be satisfied with explaining what happens in France and its significance for a broader world. The global turn comes at a propitious moment in the historiography of the French Revolution, for that historiography has been languishing in a kind of explanatory cul de sac. The Marxist interpretation has been effectively undermined (the French Revolution did not foster the triumph of capitalism over feudalism), and now the dominance of its 'revisionist' or Furetian (so called after the leading French historian, François Furet) challenger has come into question too: the French Revolution cannot be reduced to a semiotic circuit in which speaking for the people occupies the vacuum left by the collapse of monarchical power. Historians do not want to be forced to choose between a social revolution with political consequences and a political revolution with social ones. Can the global turn offer a way out of this dead end?

It only will, I maintain, if we can hold on to all the things we have been able to learn from local and national studies. The global turn should not just offer a broader or bigger view; it has to offer a better one. Here I think that Bayly's emphasis on dress and bodily deportment offers a promising angle of approach. But he does not really grasp the crucial gender dimension of these developments, and as a consequence, he passes by a wonderful opportunity to sharpen his analysis. After all, we did not need to wait for Bayly to recognize the importance of what he calls 'the growth of uniformity between societies and the growth of complexity within them'. Adam Smith and Jean-Jacques Rousseau and, later, Emile Durkheim and Max Weber put these developments at the heart of their diagnoses of the discontents of modernity. Bayly remarks that 'the idea of the domestic was in itself a product of public uniformity', but is it right to conclude that 'Women's clothes remained ornamental and impractical'? Only if you entirely neglect all the class dimensions of women's clothing: laundresses and fishwives did not wear ornamental and impractical dresses.[29]

The question of dress is indisputably important, however, and it is perhaps not surprising that the French Revolution has served as the *locus classicus* for this question too. As long ago as 1930, J. C. Flügel called attention to what he termed 'the Great Masculine Renunciation', which occurred during and just after the French Revolution. As Flügel put it, 'Man abandoned his claim to be considered beautiful.' Middle- and upper-class men gave up their knee-breeches for the trousers previously worn only by the working class, and they now wore their own hair rather than wigs. In 1793–4 the French revolutionary government even considered introducing a national civic uniform for all men. Sartorial display had been a privilege of social class; it became one of gender, which meant that women now expressed social class in their dress. Men's dress emphasized sameness, while women's dress emphasized difference. The art historian Kaja Silverman derives from this shift nothing less than the modern regime of the gaze; women became objects to be looked at by men, whereas in the past men were as much the object of looking as women.[30]

Bayly's reference to 'the growth of uniformity between societies and the growth of complexity within them' does not quite capture this development because he overlooks the new ways of relating cultural forms to political legitimation. The displacement of the ruler by the nation required the building of a citizenry in which individuals, at least adult male white ones, identified with each other as part of a nation of active, autonomous participators in politics. Sartorial differences between men did not disappear, of course, but they were to some extent downplayed. Similarly, Benedict Anderson has examined the role that newspapers and novels played in creating the sense of simultaneity required for the imagined community of nationalism. The new forms of collective political experience – whether of rights, independence, democracy, or nationalism, all of them products of this period – rested on new cultural forms that transformed the experience of time, space, and the apprehension of individuality. Such developments did not necessarily take place on a conscious level, and though they occurred to some extent in individual state contexts they were also deeply affected by the circulation of cultural and political forms across national and even continental borders. Participation in the global market for commodities helped to shape this process of building new citizens. The spread of tea, coffee, sugar, and cotton clothing drew attention to commonalities within and across borders and reinforced the impact of newspapers, novels, portraits, exhibitions, public concerts, and eventually museums. The new public, without which political revolution was unthinkable, was French, British, American, etc., but it was also more international than that, in ways we have just begun to examine.[31]

A better interpretation of the French Revolution will bring the global back in but it will not lose sight of the local and national. It will be a political, economic, social, and cultural interpretation. It will not take for granted that the French wanted to compete with the British for colonial domination but ask why and under which constraints. It may turn out that France's religious policy, by which neither Jews nor Protestants could own slaves, had more of a long-term impact on French colonial ventures and consequently on government finances than the rates of interest paid to government creditors. Having relatively few settlers in their colonies compared to the British saved them from independence movements but may have led them instead to revolution, both white and slave. Similarly, on the other end, the end of consequences as opposed to causes, the universalism of the French Revolution not only drew its energy from new cultural forms – from coffee-houses to art exhibitions – but also fostered yet new ones in turn. The universalistic claims of the Declaration of the Rights of Man and Citizen excited an international debate about human rights, and their very universalism virtually ensured an international audience. That audience turned to new cultural forms to make sense of the experience, whether in a positive mode, as in the wildfire spread of melodrama after 1800, or in more negative ones, such as the development of nationalist gymnastics in the German states eager to establish their difference from France. To make sense of these developments, it is not enough to invoke the global, as I have for the most part done: one must trace specific lineages where they lead. Who had melodrama and when, for instance? Were its roots just European? What the global turn has done most productively is to force us to challenge our usual categories, not to assume where the lines lead, but to actually follow them. It reminds us that we have much yet to discover, which is always an exciting prospect.

3

Revolutionary Exiles: The American Loyalist and French Émigré Diasporas

Maya Jasanoff

Two revolutions

One March day in 1794, a keen-eyed Frenchman with a pug nose limped into an inn at Falmouth, on the dark, stony coast of Cornwall. Chatting with the innkeeper over his meal, the man mentioned that he was bound for the United States as soon as his storm-damaged ship was repaired. Oh, said the innkeeper, there was an American lodger at the inn, an old general. The Frenchman asked to meet the American, and promptly started up a conversation about the United States, though he found his interlocutor awkwardly reticent. Eventually the Frenchman asked his new acquaintance for letters of introduction to friends in the United States. 'No', answered the American, abruptly; then added, 'I am perhaps the only American who cannot give you letters for his country. All my ties there are broken . . . I must never go back.' His name was Benedict Arnold. Once one of George Washington's best generals, Arnold transferred his loyalty to Britain at the height of the American Revolution. In the United States, his name stood as a synonym for treachery. He lived now in Britain, an exile, chased by stress and debt. 'I must admit that he made me feel very sorry for him', the Frenchman remarked. 'Political puritans may blame me, but I am not ashamed, for I was witness to his torment.'[1]

Well might he have felt compassion for the infamous turncoat. For the Frenchman – the diplomat Charles-Maurice de Talleyrand-Périgord – turned his own coat so many times it may as well have been made of patchwork. Talleyrand not only witnessed Arnold's punishment, he shared it. Banished from revolutionary France because of his deep connections to the royal house, Talleyrand had just been expelled from his temporary asylum in Britain because of his suspected sympathies with the Jacobins. Perhaps it was no wonder that when Talleyrand's ship approached the Delaware River many weeks later, he immediately tried to take passage again, for India: he felt most comfortable, he said, at sea.[2]

Accident put them in the same room together, but it was more than accident that cast these two notorious exiles adrift in Britain. Together they presented two faces of interconnected revolutions, and of those revolutions' international effects. Separated by only six years, the American and French Revolutions have always been understood as linked, the keystones in an 'Age of Revolutions' arching around the Atlantic and deep into Europe. They shared characters and incidents – a link neatly epitomized by the Marquis de Lafayette deciding to send George Washington a key to the Bastille, via Thomas Paine. The revolutions shared a commitment to equality and republican government, and a scepticism of organized religion. They recorded their values in documents that have been seen as laying the foundations of a concept of universal human rights. Both nations have developed powerful origin myths hinging on iconic revolutionary moments (1776, 1789).[3]

Yet one feature common to these revolutions has received less attention. Both revolutions were also civil wars, and like all such conflicts, they triggered substantial migrations of refugees and exiles. At least 60,000 Americans loyal to the British cause left the United States during and after the American Revolution – bringing 15,000 slaves with them. Resettling across the British world, in Canada, the Caribbean, West Africa, and beyond, loyalists created the most wide-ranging refugee diaspora the British Empire had ever confronted. Yet within a decade this American exodus would be numerically superseded by a French migration double the size. After 1789, between 130,000 and 150,000 people fled from revolutionary France, seeking asylum throughout Europe and across the Atlantic in the United States. While French revolutionary ideals swept across a world in flux, these French émigrés presented living evidence of the revolution's internal disruption, and added human weight to the cause of counter-revolution.

The last two decades of the eighteenth century thus saw approximately two hundred thousand loyalists and royalists on the move, ranging from Philadelphia to Freetown, St Petersburg to Sydney, the Bay of Fundy to the Bay of Bengal. They made an age of revolutions into an age of refugees – and their international resettlement patterns reflected the imperial dimensions of those revolutions. What do the contrasts between these refugee diasporas reveal about the events that triggered them, and the world in which they unfolded? Several attributes common to both migrations usefully bear comparison: their relative numerical strength, the pressures encouraging individuals to leave, their geographical distribution, and the conditions they encountered abroad. Investigating these migrations side by side also holds larger implications for interpreting the turbulent Age of Revolutions in which they took place.

At the beginning of his magisterial study of England in the Age of Revolutions, E. P. Thompson opined that too often 'the blind alleys, the lost causes, and the losers themselves are forgotten' by historians.[4] His complaint aptly describes the historiographical fate of loyalists and émigrés. Neither group has earned much place within the sprawling literatures on the American and French revolutions, and for analogous reasons. Within United States historiography, the relative absence of loyalists serves as an illustration of what happens when history is written by the victors. Loyalists are at best fringe players in canonical narratives of the nation's founding. Though several scholars have studied loyalist ideology and profiled leading loyalists, the social extent and diversity of loyalism remain less well understood, and the individual experiences of ordinary loyalists have been little explored. As a result, loyalists are often stereotyped in America as socially elite, politically reactionary, and essentially 'un-American' – conservatives who stubbornly failed to recognize that the future lay with the republic, not the British Empire. (They are still widely referred to as 'Tories', a label pejoratively applied to them by American patriots, though their political opinions ranged more widely than that term suggests.) It has become a commonplace to acknowledge certain contradictions embedded in the new republic: its self-contradictory commitment to slavery, and its hostility towards American Indians. But the flight of the loyalists calls attention to a form of exclusion that has yet to be incorporated into US national self-understandings, an exclusion rooted in political belief.[5]

The French Revolution has generated an altogether more contested and varied scholarship, as historians have tried to make sense of its transformative radicalism, its spectacular violence, and, not least, its ultimate failure. Even historians inclined to celebrate French republicanism must grapple with the fact that the Jacobins turned universal principles into mass executions; while the rebellion in the Vendée offered unforgettable evidence that revolutions double as civil wars. (Contemporaries widely perceived the American Revolution as a civil war, though the intense partisan conflict it involved gets little attention now.) But émigrés appear as little-studied and unsympathetic figures in a historiography primarily interested in probing the revolution's internal structures and socially equalizing aims. Cast as 'the white and the black' – the nobility and the clergy – the émigrés (like the loyalists) were traditionally but misleadingly assumed to have come overwhelmingly from the upper tiers of society.[6] Just as loyalist refugees appeared to be 'backward' by choosing to remain subjects of the British Empire, émigrés tended to be strongly identified with the armed forces of counter-revolution. Their eventual victory, with the Restoration, only helped to consolidate the sense that émigrés were elite reactionaries, as some old émigrés became new 'ultras', self-consciously dedicated to the values of the Old Regime. This may well be one reason why the Restoration remains a little-studied period in modern French history.[7]

These politicized historiographical traditions mean that examining loyalists and émigrés can seem, even now, to smack of conservatism. So it is not altogether surprising, considering how much the revolutions continue to resonate in France and the United States, that few academic historians have been drawn to this topic. Yet – as Thompson and historians of the French Revolution such as Richard Cobb so marvellously demonstrated – marginal figures offer valuable perspectives on big events. Bringing dissenters and outcasts into the frame provides a fuller picture of these revolutions' political, social, and cultural effects. Most of all, loyalists and émigrés illuminate the global consequences of these self-evidently international events. Rejecting or rejected by revolution, the exiles ventured out into a world reshaped by war and imperial expansion. Where did they go and what did they find?

Two diasporas

As Britain, the United States, and France shuffled towards peace in the early days of 1815, ex-president John Adams composed a long letter to a colleague, reflecting on the fissures that threatened his country. Thinking back to 1774, when he attended the first Continental Congress, Adams mused: 'If I were called upon to calculate the divisions among the people of America . . . I should say that a full third were averse to the revolution.' He contrasted their 'overweening fondness . . . for the English' with the opinions of 'an opposite third' who 'conceived a hatred of the English, and gave themselves up to an enthusiastic gratitude to France. The middle third, composed principally of the yeomanry, the soundest part of the nation, and always averse to war, were rather lukewarm to both England and France.'[8] Adams's off-the-cuff estimate (echoed in other letters) that one-third of the American population was 'averse to the revolution' has often been cited as a benchmark for the strength of loyalism in the thirteen colonies.[9] Ironically, others have interpreted this passage as a reference not to American loyalists and patriots but to American opinions about the *French* Revolution.[10]

The ambiguity of Adams's statement – or at least, the divergent readings it has invited – indicates how interconnected these revolutions were in the minds of people who lived through both. It also highlights the difficulty of gauging the extent of loyalism in the first place, let alone the number of loyalists who left.[11] The estimate of 60,000 loyalist migrants can be supported by piecing together impressionistic estimates provided by colonial governors, incomplete musters of refugees, and returns of evacuations.[12] Together, these refugees cut across the ethnic spectrum of early America. The emigration included several hundred Mohawk Indians, long-time allies of the British, who settled on land grants around Lake Ontario. At least 8,000 black loyalists, former slaves who received freedom in exchange for taking up arms in British forces, also traded in the United States for the British Empire. This mass emancipation, the largest in American history up to that time, has rightly been hailed as a key moment in the development of British abolitionism. In numerical extent, however, it must be offset by the still larger number of blacks, at least 15,000, who were carried away from the colonies as slaves by white loyalists.[13]

Counting the number of French émigrés proves considerably more straightforward, thanks to the relative centralization of the French state. Beginning in 1792, different localities registered the names of émigrés; and departments kept records of émigré names, ranks, professions, and property until the end of 1799, when the lists were officially closed. These documents not only fix the scale of the exodus reliably at between 130,000 and 150,000 individuals, they provide a degree of demographic detail about the émigrés that is simply not matched by the available records on loyalist refugees. While loyalist refugees reflected America's ethnic diversity, the French émigrés represented a genuine cross-section of society, ranging from princes and priests to bakers and blacksmiths. Though it is relatively difficult to map the strength of loyalism or trace internal American migration before the evacuations of 1782–3, available data on France paint a clear geographical picture of plebeian migration, showing it to be strongest in those regions most directly affected by invasion, civil war, or the intensity of the Terror.[14]

Bernard Bailyn once observed that the American Revolution was not a 'great social shock', like the French and Russian revolutions, blasting apart existing institutions and hierarchies.[15] Loyalists lost property in the United States, of course, but privilege and land ownership would not be reconfigured to anything like the same extent unleashed by the French abolition of feudalism and sale of *biens nationaux*. Similarly, the principles of tolerance and secularism espoused by Jefferson and his peers had fewer destructive consequences for devout Anglicans than did the Civil Constitution of the Clergy in the eyes of some French priests. For all that loyalists were prosecuted and persecuted – even, according to one etymology, becoming the victims of America's first lynchings – there was no American equivalent of the guillotine.[16] And yet, as a proportion of the population, far more loyalists left the United States than did émigrés from France. The émigrés represented about one in two hundred French citizens; while the 75,000 loyalists and slaves who left the United States comprised one in forty members of the population. Furthermore, while almost all (around 90 per cent) surviving French émigrés seem to have found their way back to France, far fewer American loyalist refugees would resettle in the independent United States.[17]

How can this proportional discrepancy be explained? Much of the answer lies in the different kinds of pressures that loyalists and émigrés encountered. The 'push' factors confronted by French émigrés, including highly punitive, nationwide legal measures and government-sponsored violence, were by and large more intense than the popular harassment and state-specific legal sanctions faced by American loyalists. But these reasons to flee were counterbalanced for émigrés by uncertain prospects abroad, where they had to find asylum in foreign countries in many cases at war with France, and open to invasion. Loyalists did not have the 'push' of the guillotine or invasion by large foreign armies to send them running. On the other hand, the combination of definitive defeat in war, concerns about their safety in the newly established United States, and strong 'pull' factors elsewhere in the British Empire made leaving their homes appear a comparatively attractive choice.

Persecution of American 'Tories' began well before the revolution, in the tumultuous conflicts over taxes imposed by parliament. From the Stamp Act riots onward, mobs and gangs like the Sons of Liberty targeted suspected loyalists, ransacking property, burning reviled figures in effigy, and, in rare but vivid instances, pouring pitch tar on victims and sprinkling them with chicken feathers. In a chilling allusion to the English Civil War, colonies established local 'Committees of Safety', designed to monitor and enforce patriotism.[18] This would be one of several American institutions emulated in revolutionary

France; another would be loyalty oaths, which became a primary instrument for determining allegiance to the new regimes. The rising tide of violence provoked some loyalists to leave before the war even began, most conspicuously the loyalist governor of Massachusetts, Thomas Hutchinson, who sailed for England in 1774.[19] With the outbreak of war in 1775, states enacted a wide range of punitive legal measures against loyalists. Many passed bills of attainder against specific individuals. Most also indicted enemies of the state in more generic terms, and confiscated their property. Maryland went a step further, voting on 4 July 1776 that 'adherents to Great Britain' were 'to suffer death'. Anti-loyalist legislation intensified after the American victory at Saratoga in 1777. Within six months of the battle, six states had stiffened and expanded their Test Laws. In 1778, New Hampshire, Massachusetts, New York, and South Carolina all passed punitive laws allowing loyalists to be arrested or banished. Pennsylvania issued an act of attainder against 'divers traitors'; New Jersey established a committee of safety; Delaware prohibited trade with the enemy. Georgia implemented a vague but sinister law against 'the dangerous consequences that may arise from the practices of disaffected . . . persons within this state'.[20]

As this range of laws suggests, loyalism could be interpreted widely, and loyalists responded to these measures in a variety of ways. The majority of loyalists, to be sure, simply kept their heads down, riding out confrontations with their patriot neighbours. A New Hampshire farmer called Abner Sanger, for example, who had volunteered with the patriots in the thrilling spring of 1775 but become disillusioned with republican ideas, was 'taken & carried before a Violent Committee' in the town of Keene with his brother, 'Condemned & put into Close Prison cold & deark'. Sanger's brother fled a few months later, but he himself stayed on and managed to avoid further arrest; once, when a patriot captain came 'into Town with his Mob to Rob & Plunder the Toreys', Sanger escaped notice by 'cuting & splitting wood on plain by Chapmans'.[21] At least 19,000 loyalists took a more active stance by joining provincial military regiments, and fighting alongside the British to defend their vision of colonial America. The threat of sanctions and harassment caused approximately 30,000 others to leave their homes and resettle in the cities under British control, New York, Charleston, and Savannah. And about 10,000 loyalists left the United States during the war, creating a precedent for the large-scale evacuations that would come with the peace.

In much the way that loyalist migration followed the ebb and flow of British military fortunes, the pace of emigration from revolutionary France mounted in step with the radicalization of the revolution. What eventually became a broad-based exodus began at the very top of the social pyramid, when, just two nights after the storming of the Bastille, one of the first and most prominent émigrés took flight. On instructions from his brother, Louis XVI, who wanted to protect the royal line, the Comte d'Artois slipped out of Paris with his family and darted across the border to Flanders. Artois and his entourage found temporary refuge in Turin, with his father-in-law the King of Sardinia, establishing there the first of several courts in exile that he and his relatives would maintain in the years to come.[22]

The 'Great Fear' and the abolition of feudalism in the summer of 1789 induced scattered emigration, particularly among nobles; but following the march on Versailles in October 1789 larger numbers fled, including many liberal aristocrats who had initially supported the revolution. In the space of just two days after the Versailles incident, 300 people applied to the president of the assembly for passports.[23] Each new political upheaval produced fresh waves of refugees. The Civil Constitution of the Clergy in 1790 turned Catholic priests into employees of the state, and required them to swear a loyalty oath, initiating widespread disaffection among thousands of 'refractory' priests who refused to comply. (In a map that bears striking similarities to patterns of nineteenth-century French anticlericalism, non-juring priests concentrated primarily in the west, as well as on the northern and eastern frontiers, in the Massif Central, and in urban areas outside Paris.[24]) The king's own failed attempt to escape from Paris in June 1791 touched off conspiracy and fears of invasion, and signalled greater tensions ahead.[25] By this time, army officers, confronting intolerable conditions in the ranks, were leaving France by the hundreds. Many of them joined the counter-revolutionary force taking shape on the Rhine under the command of the émigré princes. The spring of 1792 brought the beginning of war, and with it, the landslide into a republic. Two weeks after the storming of the Tuileries, a new law gave non-juring priests just fifteen days to swear the loyalty oath or to leave – essentially banishing in a stroke 30,000 people. Any doubts they may have had about the seriousness of the ultimatum would be swept aside by the September massacres one week later, when hundreds of prisoners and priests were slaughtered in Paris.

By the end of 1792, with the royal family locked into the Temple prison, all those who took arms against France stood under sentence of death; all émigré land and moveable property was confiscated; and all non-juring priests were expelled. A sequence of laws passed in March and April 1793 consolidated measures against émigrés, effectively stripping them of citizenship and condemning them to death. Their family members who stayed behind lost the right to hold office and to hold property – graver penalties by far than those facing families of American loyalist refugees. This had an especially great impact on women, who composed only about 15 per cent of the total emigration (half of them from the labouring and peasant classes, in which they comprised a quarter of émigrés). While the wives of some loyalist refugees remained in the United States and pursued legal action to protect their family property, émigrés' wives were actively encouraged by the state to divorce their husbands, and thereby retain their rights and possessions.[26] Some émigrés were able to manipulate the law, however, and protect their land through sham divorces or land transfers.[27]

Spreading war and the Reign of Terror sent thousands more running from the revolution: up to twice the number who had fled before 1793. Though the majority of earlier émigrés had been clergymen or nobles, about 40,000 of the new refugees came from the Third Estate. While nobles fled more or less evenly from throughout France, the geographical distribution of Third Estate emigration reflected patterns of rebellion, invasion, and the Terror. In the west, émigrés ran from the shattered villages of a region torn apart by civil war, including large numbers of refractory priests who fled to Britain. In the north-east, ravaged by invading armies, they crossed the borders into the Rhineland and Flanders; Switzerland also hosted a large émigré community. Along the Mediterranean coast, site of strong federalist opposition to the Convention, the republican seizure of Marseille and Toulon induced thousands to escape from Terror. (Many more émigrés sheltering in nearby Nice, then part of Savoy, had been forced to flee into neighbouring Piedmontese areas when French republicans captured the city in September 1792.) The huge popular migration would only abate with the Thermidor coup of July 1794.[28]

All told, the systematic nature of legislation targeting the nobility and others, coupled after 1792 by the systematic use of the guillotine to enforce revolutionary discipline, meant that dissenters within France faced greater and graver reasons to leave than did the majority of American loyalists. Granted, in France as in America, many royalists simply stayed quiet and stayed put: the majority of French nobles eluded persecution and remained; the majority of priests did swear the oath to the republic. Staying at home, among family, friends, and one's regular surroundings, is always the unmarked choice. But a further consideration must have been equally pressing as loyalists and royalists reviewed their positions: where would they actually go and what treatment would they receive abroad? From this perspective,

Americans and Frenchmen confronted quite different choices, and maps of the loyalist and émigré diasporas accordingly reveal two quite distinct geographies of exodus.

Britain's defeat in the American Revolution hit loyalists hard; and in fact the most savage partisan fighting between loyalists and patriots took place after Yorktown, particularly in the Carolina and Georgia backcountry. The loyalists' situation was compounded by what they perceived to be a further defeat, when British peace negotiators failed to secure any meaningful guarantee from the United States to restore or provide compensation for confiscated loyalist property. Loyalists interpreted the Treaty of Paris as an overt betrayal of their interests; and enough members of parliament agreed with them to bring down the ministry that had negotiated it. But not all was lost. To make things up to the loyalists, British officials put into action an empire-wide programme of relief. The centrepiece of British aid consisted of land grants, offered to loyalists free of charge and temporarily free of rent, in sparsely populated Canada and the Bahamas. The government also offered loyalists free passage to British domains around the Atlantic. And once loyalists reached their destinations, British authorities distributed allowances and supplies, from basic food rations through to shoes, hoes, and nails. Improvised though they were, these efforts together constituted a remarkably comprehensive relief effort, spanning multiple locations across the British Atlantic world.

Thousands of loyalists, deprived of their property and unsure of their prospects in the United States, decided to take advantage of British promises. The departure of British forces from the United States at the end of the revolution doubled as the largest evacuation of refugees that had ever unfolded in the British Empire. In July 1782, at least 7,000 loyalists and slaves sailed from Savannah on British transports, bound for other British Atlantic ports. In December, more than 9,000 others set off from Charleston, many of them headed for Jamaica or St Augustine. The protracted evacuation of New York began in the spring of 1783. By the time it finished in November of that year, 30,000 loyalists had left the city for other parts of the British Empire – including approximately 3,000 black loyalists, whose names were carefully recorded in one of the only registers of the evacuation, known as 'The Book of Negroes'.[29]

The last plank of the British relief programme addressed the matter of indemnification for loyalist property losses – the subject on which loyalists had felt most betrayed by the peace treaty. In 1783, parliament took the virtually unprecedented step of setting up a panel to review loyalists' property losses and provide them with compensation directly from British treasury funds. The Loyalist Claims Commission, as it was called, received more than 2,000 claims in its first nine months alone, detailing losses of just over seven million pounds – 'an alarming sum', gasped one of the commissioners, John Eardley Wilmot. When the commission wrapped up its work six years later, it had processed 3,225 claims and awarded more than three million pounds in aid.[30] As a piece of public charity alone, the Loyalist Claims Commission stands as a landmark in British welfare schemes – undertaken at a time when pension programmes, for example, were only just beginning. No less significant, by rewarding far-flung American colonists, the commission represented an embracing assumption of responsibility by the British government towards overseas imperial subjects.

Like the British Empire to which they adhered, loyalists rebounded from the loss in America on a global stage. In some of their new settings, they made a transformative impact. So many loyalists – about 30,000 all told – came to Nova Scotia that in 1784 it was divided into two, creating the province of New Brunswick. Loyalists and their descendants would dominate politics and society in the Maritimes for generations to come. In Quebec, the arrival of 6,000 loyalists helped to tip the political culture away from French-speaking Catholics and towards Anglophone Protestants, with enduring effects for the structure of modern Canada. The Bahamas had been little more than a string of sparsely-populated rocks before 2,000 loyalists (and 4,000–6,000 of their slaves) came to settle and establish plantations. Even in places where they did not form a majority of the population – such as Jamaica and Britain, home to 10,000 loyalists between them – loyalists made a mark as printers, soldiers, painters, clergymen, and more. In perhaps the most intriguing migration, in 1792 about 1,200 black loyalists moved a second time, from Nova Scotia to the experimental free black colony of Sierra Leone.[31] Loyalists scattered as far afield as India: the East India Company army would soon be sprinkled with American-born officers, including two of Benedict Arnold's sons.[32] And some black loyalists would sail even to the end of the earth, among the first convicts transported to Australia's Botany Bay.[33] Tracing the loyalist diaspora is like drawing a map of the expanding British Empire, featuring every major site of imperial involvement after 1780.

For loyalist refugees, then, the end of the revolution marked the beginning of an imperial, international exodus. French émigrés, however, experienced almost the reverse trajectory: their migration was influenced and shaped by global war, but would come to an end with peace. Most émigrés remained in Europe, where they relied primarily on the hospitality of foreign states to shelter them in a period of enormous political turbulence. The shifting regimes of the Age of Revolutions had most immediate bearing on members of the French royal family, as they quested for international recognition and support. The Comte d'Artois moved from Turin in 1791 to Coblenz, and on to Westphalia, before settling in Holyrood House in Edinburgh, in virtual if comfortable house arrest.[34] His elder brother the Comte de Provence – styled Louis XVIII after the Dauphin's death in 1795 – set up court in Verona, Brunswick, Latvia, and at last in England. Britain, Russia, and German states directly supplied the émigré government with financial, political, and military support. (Émigrés in some instances contributed to these regimes in turn: the young Duc de Richelieu, to give one prominent example, advanced rapidly in Russian service and became governor of the newly established port of Odessa.) By 1791 the royal princes in the Rhineland commanded an émigré army more than 20,000-strong.[35] In one of the largest initiatives on the émigrés' behalf, Britain sponsored an émigré landing at Quiberon in 1795, designed to capitalize on the anti-republican uprisings in the west; as events turned out, republican forces comprehensively crushed the invaders, effectively ending émigré military hopes.

The intensity of war and revolutionary ideology meant, however, that European states also often treated émigrés with caution – if, indeed, they admitted them at all. Prussia, for instance, carefully monitored the activities of French émigrés, and after 1792 established restrictions on the number of refugees who would be allowed in.[36] In the Rhineland, where some governments sponsored the counter-revolutionary armies, other states refused to allow the refugees to plot openly against France.[37] Perhaps surprisingly, émigrés would find their warmest European welcome in the bosom of France's historic enemy: Britain. From aristocrats to artisans, Britain hosted a flourishing refugee society. Here too, émigrés attracted suspicion: the Aliens Act of 1793 required all émigrés to register with the authorities, and established a surveillance system to track their movements. Yet seen as a whole, the émigré experience in Britain reflected, and in turn helped to facilitate, a broad shift in the Anglo-French relationship from enemies to allies. The last three kings of France all spent the majority of their time in exile more or less comfortably ensconced in Britain, forging connections at the highest tiers of society. The emigration facilitated Anglo-French amity on a broader level too, as French and British citizens intermingled socially to a greater extent than at any time since the Huguenot influx a century earlier. Mixed marriages were one inevitable result, such as the happy union between the novelist Fanny Burney and General Alexandre d'Arblay, adjutant to the Marquis de Lafayette. In the words of the émigrée Adèle d'Osmond de Boigne (who met her Savoyard husband in London), 'From [the émigrés'] prolonged stay in England, dates the change in attitude of the English people in favor of the French.'[38] While the majority of émigrés remained in Europe, some inevitably ventured further afield. Research has not accurately revealed how many émigrés travelled to other parts of the French Empire, including Saint Domingue – regions that would experience their own versions of the revolution, and produce their own refugee diasporas. Such an accounting would have to include the political prisoners deported to French imperial outposts, like the group of non-juring priests and royalists sent to Guiana after the 18 Fructidor coup of 1797.[39] Anecdotal evidence exposes the presence of French émigrés in another region that would be reshaped by the revolutionary wars: India. Chevalier Antoine de l'Etang, who had supervised the royal stables at Versailles, became stable superintendent and veterinary surgeon to the Nawab of Awadh in Lucknow, and worked in the East India Company's stud department.[40] The former Assembly member Bon Albert de Beaumetz travelled to America with Talleyrand, married a daughter of patriot general and secretary of war Henry Knox, and voyaged with her to Calcutta, hoping to sell American land to East India Company nabobs.[41]

The largest number of French émigrés who left Europe, though, travelled to the United States. An old, often-repeated estimate suggests that as many as 20,000 Francophone refugees lived in America in the last years of the eighteenth century. Recent research has made clear, however, that the vast majority of these had fled not from revolutionary France, but from Saint Domingue.[42] The exiles from mainland France were perhaps more notable for their social and political prominence than for their actual number. Liberal aristocrats like the Duc de la Rochefoucauld-Liancourt established personal and intellectual ties with the Federalists, committed to similar visions of government. Talleyrand formed a strong friendship with Alexander Hamilton. The exiles' transition from one republic to another was not entirely seamless, however. Staunch royalists felt less comfortable in the United States than did their more liberal counterparts, while more radical members of the French community made Americans uneasy in turn, helping to inspire America's own anti-French backlash, in the Alien and Sedition Acts of 1798.[43]

In July 1794, members of the Committee of Public Safety deposed their most radical colleagues, and Robespierre and Saint-Just lost their heads under the same blade they had caused to fall on so many others. The Thermidor coup marked the end of the Terror, and the beginning of the end of the emigration. As the pace of exodus slowed, anti-émigré legislation softened. Late in 1799, a month before declaring that the revolution was over, Bonaparte restored full rights of citizenship to relatives of émigrés; and the Concordat of 1801, re-establishing relations with the Vatican, paved the way for the return of non-juring priests. The Peace of Amiens of 1802 included a general amnesty for émigrés as long as they swore not to plot the restoration of the monarchy. Even that, of course, would be achieved in 1814. By then, the majority of émigrés had already returned to France.

The Restoration confirmed the coming of counter-revolutionary peace to a nation traumatized by a quarter-century of conflict. Haunted by the memory of the guillotine, survivors of the Revolution spun tales of the *bals des victimes* at which aristocrats were said to have cavorted in memory of their executed peers.[44] Anxious rumours continued to suggest that lands confiscated from émigrés during the revolution and sold as *biens nationaux* would now be returned.[45] That such a redistribution did *not* take place signalled a crucial point of accommodation by the restoration government with the revolutionary legacy. But the ascent of the Comte d'Artois to the throne as King Charles X in 1824 marked a self-conscious attempt to turn back the clock: he celebrated his coronation with an archaic ceremony at Reims, even touching the sick for scrofula, as his medieval forebears had done. Not coincidentally, it was during the reign of this reactionary former émigré that a French counterpart to the Loyalist Claims Commission took shape. The Indemnity Bill of 1825, passed a generation after revolutionaries had confiscated émigré property, set aside one billion francs to be allocated in bond payments to émigré families. Over the next five years, the time allotted for all claims to be liquidated, more than 30,000 families filed under the act. In the event, the window for remuneration closed with the Restoration itself: in July 1830 Charles X would be deposed in favour of his less conservative kinsman Louis-Philippe. Through decades of revolution and counter-revolution to come, liberals continued to deride the indemnity, labelled caustically the *milliard des émigrés*, as theft from the state coffers on behalf of traitors.[46]

A counter-revolutionary empire

So were they really commensurate, these two diasporas? Some broad parallels are plain. The social diversity of both groups provides striking evidence that revolutions unsettle the small as well as the great. In both America and France, personal decisions to remain loyal to old regimes did not correlate solely with any single attribute, such as social status, religious belief, or geographical origin. As a consequence of their choices, loyalists and émigrés shared the experience of property loss, legal sanctions, and relocating under stress to unfamiliar places. Both groups took up arms by the thousands to defend their positions. And once the revolutions had ended, both groups sought compensation for their losses from the governments they had consistently supported, the British and Bourbon monarchies. Both groups, above all, were casualties of republican nation-building – and to this extent unlike earlier groups of European exiles, such as Huguenots, Palatines, and Jacobites – standing as living proof of the exclusionary policies so often allied with modern nationalism.

Despite these similarities, however, the experiences of loyalist refugees and French émigrés could just as well be interpreted as an illustration of the fundamental differences between the revolutions that cast them adrift. Both of these republican revolutions were civil wars; both civil wars triggered international ones. But where the French Revolution began as a radical domestic upheaval, the American Revolution was of course a colonial uprising – and the refugees' fates underscored that distinction. French émigrés rejected the republic and were denied membership in it in turn. As exiles, they had to make friends out of their enemy's enemies, and vest their hopes in the counter-revolution, their ultimate source of rehabilitation. Loyalists, however, began and ended their lives as subjects of the British Empire, an entity that endured and was able to embrace them despite the American rebellion. By trading the thirteen colonies for British colonies elsewhere, they found an antidote to revolution by never leaving the larger polity to which they adhered. And though loyalist refugees personified Britain's loss in America, their relative success at rebuilding their lives elsewhere attested to the empire's broader success at bouncing back from defeat.

Seen as an imperial conflict, the American Revolution seems to share little with its French counterpart. This apparent contrast may, though, be more one of quality than of kind. For the French Revolution had its own imperial dimensions, and its own colonial refugees – notably those 15,000 or more émigrés from Saint Domingue. As multiethnic refugees from a colonial revolt, the Saint Domingue émigrés present some obvious similarities with the American loyalist refugees. Whereas American loyalists could travel to neighbouring British possessions in Canada and the Caribbean, however – regions that remained neutral or loyal, despite American republican overtures – the Saint Dominguans travelled overwhelmingly to the United States and nearby British domains.[47] (Mirroring the evacuations of British-held cities in North America, thousands of refugees sailed away with British forces when they pulled out of Saint Domingue.[48]) For them, there would be little shelter in other French colonies or in France itself, all unsettled by an empire-wide revolution. As Lynn Hunt has observed, internalist explanations of the French Revolution have generally failed to address the conflict's dramatically global dimensions, while externalist accounts remain somewhat divorced from the rich historiography of the revolution within France.[49] A global study of French revolutionary émigrés, colonial as well as domestic, suggests one way of bridging that divide – and could draw out the contrasts between the American and French revolutions as imperial wars in turn.[50]

Ultimately, the greatest value in exploring the American and French diasporas side by side emerges not so much from a comparison of their national particularities, as from the insights they give into the world they shared – a world in the throes of imperial reconfiguration. Loyalists and émigrés did not only trace parallel courses. Their fates directly intersected through the entity that most prominently supported both: Britain and its empire. It was more than mere geographical proximity that made Britain the most receptive European home for the French émigrés – more, also, than Britain's resistance to French invasion, which would unsettle other émigré havens in Italy and northern Europe. For Britain had already faced revolutionary resistance, and retooled in response to defeat. Britain's success at rebounding from the loss in America placed it in a strong position to confront the challenges posed by revolutionary France, and a newly cemented combination of liberal principles and authoritarian methods allowed it to become the strongest counter-revolutionary power in Europe and the world.

Imperial historians used to interpret the American Revolution as dividing a 'first', largely Atlantic, colonial British empire from a 'second' empire, anchored in Asia, and involving direct rule over millions of manifestly alien subjects. This idea has been challenged on several fronts. Not least, the British Empire was already both Asian and Atlantic at the time of the American Revolution; indeed, as P. J. Marshall has argued, the same governing methods that led to successful empire-building in Bengal actually undermined British rule in the American colonies.[51] Then, too, as the pattern of loyalist resettlement serves to remind, the post-revolutionary British Empire retained an important western Atlantic presence, fortifying its holdings in Canada, now the largest of colony of settlement, and keeping the valuable slave-based colonies of the Caribbean. Rather than seeing the American Revolution as a defining imperial moment, historians have more recently emphasized the significance of the French Revolutionary-Napoleonic wars in consolidating a new sense of British national and imperial identity. French republicanism and global war, the argument runs, catalysed the development of a British imperial state anchored in monarchical patriotism at home, authoritarian rule abroad, and an inclusive governing approach to multiethnic subjects.[52]

What tend to get lost in such periodizations of imperial change, though, are the all-important years *between* the American and French revolutions. In less than a decade after Yorktown, the empire's administrative structures, territorial limits, and governing principles would be refashioned around the world. In 1782, Irish 'patriots' won a measure of self-government, reflecting a cautionary lesson learned from America. In 1784, the India Act brought East India Company administration under closer parliamentary supervision; a few years later the impeachment trial of Warren Hastings helped to exorcize British anxieties about corrupt rule in India. Loyalist refugees themselves played a role in the reconfiguration of imperial government in Canada, from the partition of Nova Scotia to the reorganization of Quebec under the Constitutional Act of 1791. In 1787, British abolitionism consolidated with the founding of the Society for the Abolition of the Slave Trade, highlighting a moral contrast between Britain and the slave-owning United States. In 1788, as an abolitionist-sponsored colony was taking shape in Sierra Leone, another new sphere of British imperial activity opened in the Pacific, with the arrival of the first convicts in Botany Bay.

All these changes were undergirded by a clarified sense of imperial purpose. Whether it was reforming Indian government, regulating conditions on slave ships, or granting American loyalists land and compensation, contemporaries widely invoked the concept of 'national honour' to describe such initiatives. The empire might be authoritarian, ruled more through proconsuls than parliaments; but it was also accommodating, guaranteeing protection to imperial subjects regardless of where they lived, what ethnicity they were, or what religion they espoused. National honour demanded as much. The ideology and methods characteristic of the British Empire *after* Waterloo, in short, were already very much in place at the beginning of the French revolutionary wars – refined in the aftermath of Britain's earlier revolutionary war, in America.

French émigrés to Britain experienced first-hand the imperial legacy of the American Revolution.[53] The most specific way in which Britain's experience of responding to American loyalists (and the loss in America more broadly) influenced Britain's response to the French refugees (and the French Revolution more broadly) can be seen in relief efforts undertaken on the émigrés' behalf. In the wake of the September massacres, as lurid tales poured into Britain together with fresh waves of refugees, three relief committees formed in London to provide financial assistance to the émigrés, and to Catholic priests in particular. Where American loyalists in Britain had initially depended on piecemeal handouts from the government, these organizations represented a more systematic approach to relief – and not by accident. The founder of the largest relief committee was none other than the former Loyalist Claims Commissioner John Eardley Wilmot. Together with Jean François de la Marche, bishop of St Pol de Léon and informal leader of the émigré priests, Wilmot managed to raise more than £12,000 for the exiled clergy in just two months. By the end of 1793, when the British government undertook to provide funds directly to the émigrés, the Wilmot Committee had raised a total of £26,000.[54] Wilmot himself continued serving as a distribution agent until 1802.

The loyalist and émigré relief programmes shared other figures in common. One of Wilmot's colleagues on the committee, Sir William Pepperell, was himself a prominent loyalist, and had for years acted as a spokesman for his fellow refugees in Britain. Another committee member, Brook Watson, had served as commissary-general at the time of the British evacuation from the United States, and been responsible for supplying refugees in Canada and elsewhere with provisions and supplies.[55] Back home on his well tended estate at East Sheen – his 'plantation', as one loyalist preferred to call it – Watson frequently entertained loyalist refugees he had befriended in New York.[56] Several people involved in the resettlement of the black loyalists in Sierra Leone also found their way onto the Wilmot Committee, notably the young banker and abolitionist Henry Thornton, and his Clapham housemate William Wilberforce.[57] Some of those involved in émigré relief, it must be said, were well known philanthropists who lent their support to a wide range of charitable efforts. But then, the expansion of philanthropy in this period was itself a manifestation of the strengthened sense of national honour that Britons managed to extract from the loss in America. The close correlation between the loyalist and émigré relief committees presents one tangible way in which that moral sensibility informed the British response to revolutionary France.

In a memoir he published in 1815 about the Loyalist Claims Commission, Wilmot made no reference to his later work on behalf of the French émigrés. It seems fair to surmise, though, that he would have discerned in the efforts for the French the same spirit of 'liberal compensation . . . which redounds, and must for ever redound, so highly to the honor of the British Nation' that he identified in the work of the claims commission.[58] The frontispiece to his book illustrated this humanitarian sensibility with a striking image of national and imperial inclusiveness. 'The Reception of the American Loyalists in England', drawn by the American-born president of the Royal Academy, Benjamin West, shows a looming Britannia extending her protective arm over a throng of loyalist refugees, prominently featuring an American Indian, several blacks, and widows with children.[59] The allegory makes plain Britain's preferred self-image after the American Revolution, as an imperial nation-state committed to the protection of marginal and multiethnic subjects. How well did that self-image apply to the Britain that received the French émigrés?

The French émigrés may not have represented the same ethnic range as the American loyalists, but they did feature one group of people who, a short while before, would have attracted special hostility in Britain: Catholic priests. As recently as 1780, Catholics had been targeted in the greatest explosion of public violence London had ever witnessed, the Gordon Riots; and in 1801 prime minister William Pitt failed to pass Catholic emancipation in the wake of the Act of Union with Ireland. Yet among the French émigrés none attracted more sympathy and support than the non-juring priests. In October 1793, the composer Charles Burney wrote to his daughter Fanny – the new Madame d'Arblay – of an extensive network of 'very illustrious and honourable' women engaged in raising money for the priests, 'to save the national disgrace of suffering these excellent people to die of hunger before the Parliament meets and agrees to do something for them'.[60] The Claphamite Hannah More donated the profits of one of her pamphlets to the relief of the priests.[61] And one of the most enthusiastic champions of the exiled clergy was Edmund Burke, Irish-born friend of America and opponent of France, who also helped to establish a school for émigré boys.[62]

In their open support of French Catholic priests, Britons showcased that same liberal humanitarian tolerance that had been extended towards black loyalists and others. But the French Revolution gave such attitudes a fresh twist. For as the participation of 'conservatives' like Burke and More in the cause underscores, charity towards the priests and other French refugees demonstrated Britain's own relative conservatism in contrast with revolutionary radicalism. The Catholic church looked good to the British at a time when *all* churches seemed threatened by the godless Jacobins. French princes, the personification of an absolutist tradition Britons once abhorred, earned support at a time when *all* monarchies seemed threatened by republicanism on the march. (And, to be sure, when those princes no longer commanded real power.) The principles confirmed in the British Empire after the American Revolution – granting inclusive protection in return for loyalty to the crown – now stood as the pillars of a compelling counter-revolutionary alternative to France, a middle way between absolutism and republicanism. It is no coincidence that the term 'loyalist' gained new currency during the French Revolutionary wars, as 'Loyalist Associations' pledging support to the king flourished across Britain and parts of the empire.

The Age of Revolutions that began in the American colonies thus had the effect of fortifying British imperial rule. As such, Britain provides a central example in what Jeremy Adelman has identified as a worldwide revitalization of empires in this period: an age more of imperial revolutions than of democratic ones.[63] While the American defeat encouraged Britain to clarify the limits of imperial power, the French wars quickly gave Britain compelling excuses to push forward into unsettled regions. In India, British authorities responded to the perceived threat of alliances between the French and indigenous princes to depose Tipu Sultan, the aggressive ruler of Mysore, and to bind the Nizam of Hyderabad, among others, more closely to the East India Company state. In concert with the Ottomans, Britain invaded Egypt to dislodge the quasi-republic established there by Bonaparte. The French occupation of Holland provided an incentive for British forces to seize Dutch possessions in Java and southern Africa. In Latin America, Britain engaged in a complicated manipulation of loyalties, sponsoring rebellion against the Spanish empire by Francisco de Miranda and launching its own expansionist campaign in the River Plate. Though this latter mission failed, British volunteers played a vital role in Spanish American independence movements (just as they would in Greece); only for South America's new republics promptly to be drawn into Britain's informal empire. Around the world, the effects of the Age of Revolutions proved anything but democratic for those regions that fell into the grip of Britain's rapidly growing empire. The successful establishment of republicanism in the United States stands out as an exception in a forty-year period that otherwise witnessed a massive global expansion of British rule, consolidated around liberal principles.

In relation to the British empire alone, then, tracing the loyalist and émigré diasporas demonstrates the inadequacy of nation-specific paradigms or narratives of independence in explaining the consequences of these revolutions. In truth, such accounts do not even successfully describe the effects of revolution for the United States or France, both of which promptly took imperial turns of their own. While the United States pushed steadily westward towards the Mississippi, Napoleon steered France from crusading republicanism to dictatorial imperialism. In contrast to the revolutionary regimes he had implemented in Italy and Egypt, Napoleon after 1799 worked to build an empire bound together by dynastic ties, a strong military, and a meritocratic elite. Compared to the liberal principles characteristic of British imperial rule after the 1780s, however, the French Empire under Napoleon bore the stamp of its revolutionary forebear, imprinted by centralization, universalist principles, and an emerging sense of 'civilizing mission'.[64] These distinctive British and French imperial styles persisted well into the twentieth century, and their vestiges can still be identified: about a dozen former British possessions technically retain the monarch as head of state; while one-time French colonies in the Caribbean and Indian Ocean are now fully incorporated into the nation as *départements*. For French citizens as much as for British subjects, revolution facilitated an imperial reconfiguration as sweeping as it would be enduring.

Yet the contours of great events rarely look so clear to those who live through them. If comparing loyalist and émigré diasporas points out a line of continuity through the Age of Revolutions, it also provides an insistent reminder of the sheer human confusion provoked by this period of global upheaval. After all, some of the revolutionary disruptions that imperial Britain stepped in to suppress came from its very own loyal subjects. In the thickly wooded hills of the Freetown peninsula, in Sierra Leone, resentment against British authority brewed among the black loyalists who had settled in the promised land of freedom. Charged with unexpected rent on their land, and shut out of high office, disgruntled settlers launched a revolt against their British governors. For a week in June 1800, former black loyalists had to choose again whether or not to stay loyal to the government – until the rising was comprehensively crushed with the help of some freshly imported subjects, the Jamaican Maroons, whose own rebellion against the British had recently been put down. Making a tidy link from one revolution to the next, William Wilberforce sniffed that the black loyalist rebels in Sierra Leone were 'as thorough Jacobins as if they had been trained and educated in

Paris'.[65] But he might as well have said Port-au-Prince, where former slaves invoked French revolutionary principles to lead Haiti to independence. Some of these revolutionaries had been schooled in military action by the British, fighting in the American war.

Incidents such as this draw out the human texture and transnational complexity of a world in flux, where former loyalists could become revolutionaries, and revolutionaries could become imperialists.[66] As they found asylum in the wide embrace of the British Empire and beyond, loyalist refugees and émigrés understood first-hand how widely the ripples of revolution reached. Their global exodus supports the characterization of this era as a period of 'World Crisis', from which imperial powers – and the British Empire in particular – emerged strengthened and refreshed. For in the end, to loyalists and émigrés, and to the imperial Britons who confronted both groups, the Age of Revolutions and the World Crisis must have seemed very much the same.

4

Iberian Passages: Continuity and Change in the South Atlantic

Jeremy Adelman

This chapter is about the ways in which the Spanish and Portuguese empires in the Atlantic world made the passage through an age of global confrontation between rival political systems, culminating in the dissolution of the empires and the redefinition of sovereignty in the 1820s. It makes several entwined arguments. First, the Iberian empires were part of an interlocking system of imperial competitions from which there was little to immunize themselves. Instead, faced with the compound pressures of a global system, they adapted. They did so with hitherto under-acknowledged effectiveness, and with unintended effects for the internal make-up of each empire. Still, modifications could not withstand the escalation of global competition to a crisis when it ravaged the core of the system, which leads to this chapter's second claim: the Napoleonic wars – when seen from a more global perspective – hammered the occupied or stricken empires, from the Ottomans to the Iberians. For the Iberian Atlantic, the internal structures of sovereignty collapsed in the metropoles and forced colonies to amalgamate older practices with newer ones to shore up legitimacy as politics grew increasingly polarized and social systems imploded.

Rulers devised policies in response to external and internal threats. But policies required a politics, and in the age of revolution, political debates led to questions about the fundaments of state sovereignty, which set the stage for social revolutions. But the politics of these breaks, as this chapter seeks to show, depended much more on actors' efforts to follow and adapt to rules that were themselves crumbling, which opened up a broad array of possibilities – a process which, in retrospect, appears improvised and reactive. This is more than a claim about the contingencies of macrosocial change; it speaks to the chain of disequilibrium that lies at the core of how systems of sovereignty were fashioned and consolidated – and thus the alternatives embedded within them. If we are accustomed to thinking of revolutions as events that overturn one system in favour of something different, this runs the risk of obscuring the politics, often very drawn out, that connected the crises of *anciens régimes* with successors, the very *passage* that opened alternatives along the way. What is so illuminating about the Iberian empires and their progeny is that the passage was an extended one, gathering force by the late eighteenth century, prompted by common global pressures, and giving way to wide-ranging constitutional debates and civil wars in the 1820s, which revealed the multitude of political and economic arrangements – and which expressed themselves in a variety of outcomes.[1]

The quest for models of sovereignty to resolve global pressures and local conflicts yielded to hybrid and frequently unstable systems. The approach to constitutionalism – the touted mechanism for building a post-colonial order – did not rely on any single creed or practice, but was as syncretic as the imperial system it was supposed to replace. In the end, this age of revolutions – like those that would succeed it – gave birth to a plethora of intellectual proposals and institutional practices that would compete for claims to post-imperial legitimacy. The nation as the repository of sovereignty was simply one, admittedly potent, of these claims. The emergence of 'the modern' might also be seen as the result of a passage that expanded the plurality and complexity of local orders.[2]

The concept that unites the themes of this chapter, sovereignty, needs defining. Historians have conventionally been informed by sovereignty's original conceptualizers, treating the state in almost anthropomorphic, singular terms, as *the* state, with definable and coherent powers. This has been best expressed in the widespread maxim, derived from Max Weber, that the state is the legitimate monopolizer of the legal uses of violence, from which, as Carl Schmitt later added, it was uniquely endowed with the power to declare its own exceptions. Understandably, this remains a common current, not least for those seeking to end crimes against humanity by reclaiming violence as the public authority's singularity – and making it accountable. While I am not challenging the appeals of this definition for those who are anxious to replace one order (or lack of it) with a coherent successor, this chapter invokes an approach to sovereignty that stresses the basic pluralities within any given order and the global state system that envelops each one. It points to the multitude of claims by subjects, images of rulers, and practices of governance that are bundled together in loose and not always so coherent ways. This is especially the case when dealing with the pluralist legal cultures of empires and their colonies; but as this approach seeks to illuminate, this feature did not end when empires gave way to successors, but were subsumed within them, even within 'the nation' itself. What is more, political-economic orders were much less 'bounded' units; their authority aggregated at more than one juridical level, from municipalities to transoceanic constitutions. We might treat statehood as an amalgamation of practices locked in equivocal conjunctions, and are thus more about relationships between powers – exemplified by Montesquieu and Madison's image of a 'balance' – than their natural or coherent features. This applied to the internal as well as external conditions of public authority.[3]

This is important for understanding how empires worked in the early modern period, for as Lauren Benton has shown in colonies from India to New France, colonial systems rested on practices better understood through the prism of legal pluralism. But there is more: the pluralist foundations did not dissolve with the end of empire in favour of a more homogeneous nation-state. Indeed, one of the legal and constitutional options that persisted, or reinvigorated itself during the age of revolutions discussed in this book, is the choice for empire itself. What is more, where and when European power in the Americas receded, the complex improvisations of empires under duress did not end with secession; the effort to build a successor system was no less syncretic than its predecessors. This is what lay at the heart of so many of the strains and stresses on early constitutionalism in Latin America in the 1820s, which echoed the general character of what C. A. Bayly has called the 'hybrid legitimacy' of post-Napoleonic states. The revealing difference about Iberian America was the sheer diversity that exploded from beneath the veneer of unity; no cult of royalty or religion of nationhood could reassemble the pieces of former colonies with ease, or even force. The vocabulary of national self-determination did not resolve the ambiguities and equivocations that accompanied the effort to legitimate inequality and to legalize privilege, nor in some senses was it seeking to before self-determination was elevated to a universal principle after the First World War.[4]

Rivalry among European powers was a feature of state formation, as the late Charles Tilly reminded readers with his famous observation that, in Europe's contours, wars made states and states made wars. But what has perhaps been less observed is that increasingly war-making went global; we can reframe Tilly's formulation in more expanded ways, rendering European dynamics in a context that expands the boundaries of state formation beyond Europe and that shaped the power balances within it. Doing so helps us to understand the nature of the conflagration from the 1750s to the 1820s, for nowhere did European empires displace their rivalries more than across the Americas, fuelled by the soaring 'value' of possessions on account of the lucrative bond of unfree labour to resources just as freedom developed new valences in Europe. It is often forgotten that a spark for the War of the Spanish Succession was a contest over the control of the slave trade from Africa to Spanish colonies in the Americas. And thereafter, despite the Treaty of Utrecht's provisions, the struggle for mercantilist controls and territorial claims over the disputed borderlands of the mainland and islands of the Caribbean ramped up.[5]

For the Iberian empires, this presented a particular challenge. Unlike those of the relative latecomers from London and Paris, their claims to possession in the New World dated back to a precise, if entirely unworkable, settlement proclaimed by the Pope with the Treaty of Tordesillas (1494), which claimed to have delineated Spanish and Portuguese territories and gave papal blessing to their missions to colonize them and convert their native populations. In the ensuing centuries, rivals preferred to raid and pillage; English pirates, as Francis Drake famously noted, would give the Spanish no peace beyond the line, and the French also muscled in when they could. But by the late seventeenth century, this kind of poaching activity gave way to territorial possession. That they were there first meant that Iberian powers had to defend their borders from interlopers who graduated from privateering to outright occupation, and increasingly used seized outposts as bases for contraband and settlement for their own plantations. Being defensive has often carried some baggage; it has often implied being older, more ossified, less agile and responsive to changes. Not a few contemporaries in Lisbon and Madrid used this kind of alarmist rhetoric to accentuate the urgency of the pleas for change, which many subsequently took literally. The Spanish physiocrat Pablo de Olavide argued in 1768 that Spain was a reflection of England's past: 'England, that powerful and populated kingdom, was before in the same situation in which Spain finds itself today. It was devoted to the same erroneous principles and was poor, depopulated and miserable.' This Black Legend rhetoric has had a long shelf-life; it is a view that has changed only in recent years. Without discounting the limits of Iberian feudality, more and more historians have come to see Iberians adapting their political economies precisely because they had to. Being first-comers, their models of sovereignty evolved in response to the globalization of European power; that they were first-comers meant that they had to transform inherited structures that had proven so effective in a different conjuncture. The challenge was less the inability to change, but that so much had to change.[6]

Behind the defensive positions of the Iberian empires were deep debates about how to reform them to meet the growing political and military threats as the eighteenth century unfolded. By the middle of the century, rulers and ministers wrangled over how to adapt their ways and embark on increasingly ambitious plans to modify the institutions, private and public, that held their empires together. Variously described as the Bourbon (for Spain) or Pombaline (for Portugal) reforms, these were portmanteaus for a variety of ways to pursue one broad objective: to reconstitute the empires so that private rents and public revenues flowed more effectively to support and defend the territorial contours of imperial states. Alexandre de Gusmão, the Portuguese imperial minister, likened empires to bodies, and the flow of resources with trade was their lifeblood. What was needed was an 'active' model of empire to replace the 'passive' one, a system of commercial colonization to supplant the spoils of conquest.[7]

Reform recombined important aspects of empires – and gave them enough stamina to endure the intensified scramble for the control of trade and defence of imperial frontiers. Old convoys, flotillas of specie-bearing merchantmen escorted by warships, which made easy targets for predation, were suspended in favour of licensing systems for trading ships. The annual fairs, like Portobello's, a favoured magnet for marauders, faded. What emerged was a much more decentred, network-based system of commercial exchange, which was not as easily raided, but also less easily regulated. This took place earlier in Portugal's empire, which was, in any event, never as resolutely centralized as Spain's. In both, governance adapted to an emerging autonomous and dispersed commercial system, which was not as easily targeted for revenue extraction. To some extent the administrative reforms were meant to give new centralizing powers, whether this was the formation of monopoly trading companies in the north of Brazil or the creation of powerful Intendants in Spanish America, who were supposed to reinvigorate the flow of resources to the centre. Across the colonies, viceregal habits ceded space to a multitude of new legal districts and officers, further pluralizing the layers of public power. Scarcely patrolled frontiers were militarized and fortifications built, while militias were trained, comprised of plebeian colonial populations, often free blacks and mulattos. Meanwhile, to pacify unruly grey zones, 'treaties' were signed with Indian borderlanders, even by those powers like Spain unaccustomed to this legal convention. Each empire set about to

delimit and defend the territorial reach of its domain, and within each
to promote commerce, more investment in mining, settlement of frontiers, and the surge in traffic in African slaves to create a substratum of
labourers upon whose shoulders the fate of empires would rest.[8]
There were resistances, in both the metropoles and the peripheries.
In Lisbon, the Marquês de Pombal had always faced some formidable
detractors, especially among the interests who were squeezed out by
his preference for a new breed of merchant and investor. So, when his
patron, King José I, died in 1777, the minister was soon exposed to
his many critics. He was deposed. This did not scupper reform, but
simply slowed it down. The reforms also provoked unrest in the
colonies, albeit not as much because incumbent interests easily
adapted to the new opportunities presented by commercial incentives. Still, hikes in taxes did signify a departure from the older colonial pacts, which had left so much colonial extraction outside the
purview of collectors. The foiled Tiradentes revolt in Minas Gerais
(early 1789) was one such episode, though it is worth adding that it
was more of an exception to prove a rule about the ways in which
Brazil adapted itself to new policies. Spain faced analogous, though
more alarming, reactions. In Madrid, bread riots brought an end to
experiments in free grain trade. In the Americas there was even more
unrest. In the 1780s, the Túpac Amaru revolt in the Central Andes,
Comunero uprisings further north, and seditious activity across New
Spain indicated the ways in which many local peoples, sometimes
aligned with disgruntled officials, resented some of the extractive
burdens and centralizing efforts. The resistance was enough to get
officials to back off some of their reformist zeal and restore the
elements of an imagined idea of the old colonial pact.[9]
But some of the reforms intensified, especially in domains that
motivated greater commerce as a way to spur the creation of more
rents that could then be available for taxation. In Brazil, this meant
dismantling some of the powers of Pombal's commercial monopolies
and letting local Juntas do Comércio, ruled by trading magnates, regulate and promote local trade. Old Boards of Inspection lost some of
their authority. Merchant capitalists, especially in Rio de Janeiro, prospered as never before, and their rents were redeployed into the credit
systems that tied the Brazilian staple-producing hinterlands to Atlantic
commerce. As with the deregulation of trade, this was a more gradual
and less disruptive process in the Portuguese Atlantic than in Spain's
dominions. There, the opening of trade was much more sudden with
the flurry of *comercio libre* decrees and the formation of merchant
guilds in many of the port cities of the empire. The objective was to

replace an older model that sought to direct as much as possible
through the metropole to benefit merchant capital of Spain's entre-
pôt, Cádiz, with a model that promoted greater traffic between all
Spanish and Spanish-American ports as a way to enhance infra-impe-
rial trade and its rents as a whole.[10]

Bolstering the fortunes of merchant capital ushered in a dramatic
change in the social landscape on the frontiers of the Iberian colonies.
The boom in trade inducted labour to the 'wastelands' and mines from
northern New Spain to the Pampas. For this reason the late eighteenth
century has sometimes been depicted as a second Conquest, not military but commercial, a kind of 'market revolution' that spread trading
capillaries to the backlands, though it did not exactly rely on voluntary
'market' means to brace labour to the land. Far from it; across the
colonies officials and merchant capital relied on a range of coercive
techniques, from debt servitude to outright bondage, to enlist indigenous peoples into the market for wares and workers. From textile
factories (*obrajes*) in Ecuador to tea plantations in Paraguay, native
peoples were procured – with varying devices relying mainly on provisions of commodities and credit to create webs of dependent populations – for the production of commodities. The combination of greater
investments from the pools of merchant capital into mining, with the
release of workers from Indian villages, lay behind the expansion of
specie production in New Spain and the Andes, which pumped silver
into the trading networks and revenue pockets of the Iberian Atlantic.
In some spots, the boom began to exhaust itself: in Potosí the mother
lodes were getting tapped out by 1805 and food supplies for displaced
villagers were running scarce and getting expensive. In other agrarian
regions of Mexico, there is growing evidence that here too there was
overheating, rising food prices, and increasing scarcities. In a word,
there was a limit to this model of market revolution, since it so rarely
involved any fundamental transformation in techniques of production
and productivity; but it was only being reached in a few, albeit sometimes important, provinces.[11]

Where the reform-led expansion of commodity production in the
Iberian empires expanded with fewer restraints was on the agrarian
frontiers sustained by slave labour – and emboldened by the heightened traffic in African captives. Though we have become accustomed
to thinking about the abolition of the slave trade as one of the signa-
ture components of the 'age of revolutions', it is clear that in this
domain – and in so many others – a new politics of liberty coincided
with, and in some senses was a response to, an expansion of bonded
labour. Throughout the 'age of revolutions', the traffic in African

captives rose, and did not fall. Indeed, it spiked after the insurrection that spread across St Domingue and the heightened abolitionist campaigning. It was stoked by reform within the Iberian empires, which sluiced more precious metals into the commercial networks of the South Atlantic. A decisive feature was the legal opening of the slave trade between Iberian entrepôts. By the 1770s, Madrid's Council of the Indies was receiving pleas from merchants and officials from the colonies calling upon the government to free up the slave trade. Cartagena, noted one petition, was struggling 'for lack of slaves'. The government responded by ending the practice of the old *asiento* system, which allocated the contract to import slaves to Spanish ports to a single firm (and the control of which had led to the commercial feud between France and England and the outbreak of war earlier in the century). By 1789, Madrid had issued a series of decrees allowing individual merchants to participate in the traffic, followed by exemptions on duties and then a series of concessions allowing foreign merchants to unload their cargoes of captives. Brazilian merchants had enjoyed a more liberal system for decades, and by the 1780s commanded fleets of *tumbeiros* to ship their captives from Angola to South America and the Caribbean.[12]

A South Atlantic system consolidated what one Brazilian historian has called the 'Atlântico Fluminense', which pivoted around the powerful merchant class of Rio de Janeiro and the webwork of slave trading that radiated from it, tying Lima to Luanda. Consider the following numbers: from 1781 to 1790, 754,000 Africans were imported to the Americas, of whom 319,000 were destined for Saint Domingue, which meant that 435,000 were spread across the rest of the hemisphere. The following decade saw a dip to 687,000 captives shipped, but only 66,000 bound for Saint Domingue (leaving 621,000 for the rest of the Americas to exploit). And from 1801 to 1810, no slaves went to Saint Domingue, but 609,000 went to the rest of the hemisphere. After 1808, when the sea lanes were cut off for the legal trade in slaves, shipments flowed to French and Iberian ports.[13] The result was an increasingly autonomous and lucrative business that expanded the pool of commercial rents into which imperial authorities could dip for revenues, and a puissant class of merchant capitalists in the colonies to whom monarchs and ministers could turn for loans and loyalties. An internal report to the Spanish government concluded that, by the turn of the nineteenth century, 'the opulence of America, whose influence in the Commerce and Navigation among the European nations [is great] . . . could not exist without the slave trade'.[14]

Map 2 The Americas in the late eighteenth century (adapted from J. H. Elliott, *Empires of the Atlantic World*, New Haven, CT, 2006, p. 354).

Motivated by a combination of colonial pressures from merchants and landowners seeking commercial rents and officials searching for revenues, reforms had decidedly ambiguous effects. Rapid change helped to integrate the parts of the empires closer together even as the provinces of the empire grew more heterogeneous. Heterogeneous integration also had effects on the inner balances; some degree of administrative centralization coincided with the decentring of the empires' social structures. Outposts in each empire acquired endogenous powerful elites, bordering on regional aristocracies tied to merchant classes in the major ports. The result, in sum, enabled empires to establish greater territorial footprints, with agents and enforcers reaching the fringes of the systems and operating within networks flowing with credit from an archipelago of mercantile centres. Within each of these, we can see how the relations within ruling imperial coalitions thereby recomposed. Still, for all the complexity of the reforms' effects, which pulled the empires together and apart, the Iberian Atlantic was hardly stuck in sclerotic ways, unable to adapt to changes in the world market or the advent of new business practices; this was not a case of immunity to modernization that required it to be imposed from without.

The 1790s altered the delicate balance without overturning it. The outbreak of the Revolutionary Wars, especially Spain's with France from 1793 to 1795, and then more cripplingly with England from 1796 to 1802, and then again from 1804 to 1808 after the failure of the 'Peace' of Amiens, intensified the pressures on the Iberian empires, especially Spain. Warships ravaged the imperial sea lanes, especially for cargoes destined for European ports. Less affected were the coastal routes of the South Atlantic system, and the booming trade between Africa and South America. Indeed, trade flourished *within* the empires, though not necessarily (unless there was a pause in the fighting) *between* the metropoles and their possessions. The result was a commercial blow to merchant capitalists of Spain and Portugal – which was important, because when the fighting would finally settle down at the end of a bellicose cycle in 1814, battered peninsular merchant capitalists were determined to claw back their access to commercial rents, even if it meant alienating the increasingly autonomous merchants of the outposts. As with the distribution of imperial rents, so with imperial revenues; the metropoles faced growing fiscal crises as defence costs spiked but revenues from trade dwindled, while in the colonies, there was a similar rise in expenditures, but treasury income also rose, though not always at the same pace. From the 1790s, the metropoles leaned ever more heavily on the colonies for remittances; the Indies became the single largest source of income for the imperial treasuries, but subject to wild shifts and vulnerability to attacks along the sea lanes. The result was a turn to greater borrowing, which grew increasingly coercive as warfare ravaged public accounts. This was a story about a double dependency of imperial sovereignty: the centres of empires on their peripheries, and the state upon merchant capital to buoy it through years of inter-imperial warfare.[15]

Double dependency was on the minds of political economists – for those concerned with entwined relationship between private rents and public revenues. Manuel Belgrano, a lawyer with the merchants' guild of Buenos Aires and learned in physiocratic texts, was concerned that the state was growing overly dependent on the movement of goods to sustain it; its taxes and regulations threatened to weaken the foundation of opulence. He wanted freer trade to ensure access to markets for colonial producers who could then provide the social bases for a wealthy sovereign. His ideas echoed from another corner of South America: José Ignacio de Pombo in Cartagena worried that excessive taxes and regulations might breed corruption and bad manners. In 1807, he warned that 'it is very important that the government, to avoid this terrible affliction, with respect both to customs and public morals, as well as the public treasury, as well as to honorable citizens that rely upon legitimate commerce', open the ports to active trade. The concern about the state's dependency on merchant capital, and merchants' on colonial staples, involved an acknowledgement of the new spatial relationships within empires in the age of revolutions. The Brazilian political economist José Joaquim da Cunha Azeredo Coutinho noted that 'the metropole is . . . like a mother who must give the colonies, like her sons, all the good treatment and help necessary to defend and ensure their lives and welfare'. For Portugal to be a great power in the world, it needed wealthy colonies. 'It is therefore necessary that the interests of the metropole become linked to those of the colonies, and that these be treated without rivalry. For when all the subjects are richer, the sovereign will be even more so.'[16]

★ ★ ★

The portrait above defies the common image of backward and brittle systems cracking under the pressure of global competition and confrontation. These were not empires doomed to collapse. Nor were they cracking from within, as colonial subjects and their enlightened *letrados* struggled for freedom from old ways to realize proto-nationalist aspirations. Indeed, the dominant language of political economy was not rights talk, but market talk. This does not mean that the increasing mobility of property did not provoke unease about corruption and degeneration of bonds between subjects and sovereigns. It did. But this anxiety has to be put in both a global context of instability wrought by war and the commercial integration of the Atlantic world – not the unique feature of Iberian sclerosis. Property, colonial reformers argued, respected by subjects and sovereign alike, was the basis of public wealth and private opulence – a healthy and well mannered system that did not need to break with the past for its virtuous combination to work. The overwhelming tenor of debate about public affairs was steeped in loyalism, with nothing approaching the intellectual or social conditions of revolution within the Spanish or Portuguese empires. Indeed, global pressures emboldened efforts to accommodate (or rearticulate, to use an older vintage of social theory) inherited structures of production and trade into a new political economy of empire, and a new balance between merchant capital and the state.[17]

We still face the inevitable question: if empires were not fated to collapse, what did account for their break-up without explaining revolutions as the consequence of circumstance? The answer lies in the ways in which global conflagration provoked local contestation, and the slide from negotiations over how to handle a mounting imperial crisis to a civil war, and from civil war to revolution. It is not just the causality that is in question – *how* global forces shaped local ones – but also the sequence that explains what is so revolutionary about this conjuncture. We are more often accustomed to thinking that revolutions in thought or practice detonated crises of the old regimes; the story that unfolds here suggests very different sequelae with a variety of outcomes depending on the course of the civil wars within empires, civil wars that would in turn reverberate through the 1820s as constitutionalists took up the challenge of building successors to Iberian empires. The change in sovereignty, the demise of older systems and the emergence of successors, was a *process* that has often eluded triumphalist nationalist narratives, or those which insisted that old regimes – among them, empires – were doomed because they were outmoded. This process was missing, because the shifts were explained by teleologies that hid the political choices over how – indeed whether – to defend or rebuild sovereignty.

The problems were increasingly clear in the 1790s, for the more insightful imperial analysts of the time worried about the sustainability of their regimes under duress. Should the global situation deteriorate, some worried, extreme measures had to be considered. One, the brainchild of the influential minister to the Court in Lisbon, Rodrigo de Souza Coutinho, who had handled the Treasury's growing debts with some considerable skill, involved a recognition that Brazil was as important to the future of the imperial monarchy as the metropole. Should the latter run into a serious crisis, the monarchy might have to consider relocating the centre of the empire to a new world capital, Rio de Janeiro. This was, at it turned out, a prophetic emergency plan. Most observers hoped the contest between empires would wane, and the physiocratic-inspired policies be allowed to have their felicitous effects of recombining property and politics in a way that put the empires on healthy foundations. What they did not anticipate was the effects on empires as the confrontation in Europe intensified after 1805. When the crisis finally did break out, it inspired the Spanish reformer Gaspar Melchor de Jovellanos to remark that the break-up of the Spanish empire was a civil war contained within and unleashed by a broader, global one.[18]

Governments in Lisbon and Madrid faced unenviable choices as Britain and France poised to square off once more, not only involving the empires of the Atlantic, but reaching east to the territorial empires of St Petersburg and Istanbul. Within each of the Iberian capitals there was a major debate about what to do, once it became clear that Napoleon had designs on the peninsula and the possessions beyond. Some wanted alignment with London, others with Paris, and another faction urged neutrality. The last faded away after 1804; by 1807 the alignments leaned one way when Napoleon's Iberian designs were fully unveiled. For the Portuguese it was a more straightforward matter, given the longstanding alignment with England; besides it was in no position to defend its sea lanes if the Royal Navy were to take aim at them. Still, an important circle of pro-French ministers argued that French armies would invade Portugal. This was a minority faction – but strong enough to keep the Braganza Court dithering up to the last minute. The paralysis in Madrid was worse, compounded by in-fighting at the very top, which culminated in Ferdinand VII's seizure of the throne from his father and the fall of his disreputed ministry. Indeed, the cracking at the top of Spain's government created the opportunity the French ruler sought. He saw a chance to take both countries and lay claim to their possessions overseas, thereby striking a mortal blow to Anglo-Atlantic power. Sending his armies across the Pyrenees in late 1807, he set off a crisis of sovereignty at the very core of the Iberian systems. The policy decisions varied, with decisive structural consequences. The Braganza court dusted off an old emergency plan drawn up by Souza Coutinho: it fled in a massive fleet escorted by the Royal Navy, to relocate in Rio de Janeiro. 'Americanizing' the monarchy spared it the question of what bound the colonies to *ancien régime* sovereignty. In Spain, despite some entreaties to do the same, Ferdinand was captured by the French, and a makeshift government fled southwards to Andalusia, seeking refuge from French troops, to be closer to the port of Cádiz lest an escape be unavoidable. This government would therefore struggle to preserve its enfeebled centrality in an empire that had no effective centre.[19]

What all parties agreed upon in the aftermath of the invasion is that the loss of the centres did *not* imply the end of empire. The question, at least for the ruling classes and officials, was how to preserve it – especially in the face of the new Napoleonic regime's reforms, which included the promise of a constitution, equality for colonial subjects, the abolition of the Inquisition, and freedom of the press, just the kinds of decrees that appealed to Spain's and the colonies' reformers. In a sense, 1808 was the axial year of an axial age; it was not mere coincidence that the spread of abolitionism coincided with the diffusion of constitutionalism as unstable and vulnerable regimes at war sought to prop themselves with new appeals to legitimacy. The Iberian Atlantic took part in this shift through a series of improvised practices that focused on new means to embolden the loyalty of imperial subjects to their sovereign – not least because the drawn out war on the peninsula became as costly as it was brutal. Someone had to pay, and both Spain and Portugal pleaded that the colonies and their merchants underwrite the struggle. The quid pro quo was a change in rulership, not rulers, through new practices of representation. Since the break was more decisive in Spain, with the government in shock, the alteration in the rules of the game was more abrupt. The Inquisition was abolished, censorship was lifted from the press, and when Napoleon's agents sought to encourage Spain's colonies to declare fealty to the newly imposed government in Madrid (under his brother Joseph Bonaparte) by promising colonial subjects basic equality, elections, and a constitution, the fleeing Spanish government in Andalusia responded in kind: it promised to convoke a parliament to discuss making a new constitutional monarchy. The insistence that a new legal regime would undergird the state, and the assurance that colonies would enjoy basic representation in an imperial arrangement, signified a break from ancient practices in order to preserve the regime as a whole. For the Americanized Portuguese government, it was enough that the crown, court, and ministry were now based in Rio de Janeiro and could step up the cult of regalism in the colonies, which had the additional advantage of allowing influential colonial subjects access to the corridors of power. There was less need for a *de jure* change in the rules in order to preserve *de facto* integration. But the significance of public opinion, and in Spanish America of elections, was crucial, and in some areas sprung to life with vertiginous energy. In Buenos Aires, Caracas, and Santa Fé de Bogotá, the printing presses were the engines of public debate; in Lima, Mexico, and Rio de Janeiro, under the eyes of more cautious royal authorities, the press was more polite and constrained.[20]

If public opinion was one pillar of legitimacy, formal mechanisms of representation provided others. Metropolitan governments in Spain in 1808, and Portugal in 1820, called for constitutional assemblies to draft a founding charter of imperial nationhood to reinvigorate the ties between rulers and ruled. The motive here was 'liberal' in the sense that self-described metropolitan liberals thought that the monarchies would be stronger, and governments more stable, with modern law backing them up. And the only way to accomplish this was to invite elected deputies to deliberate. The Spanish Junta issued a clarion call to the colonies in the name of 'the nation', insisting 'that the Spanish dominions in America are not colonies, but an essential and integral part of the Monarchy'. Accordingly, each part of the empire-nation was invited to elect and dispatch envoys to a new assembly charged with drafting a founding charter. Much the same obtained in Portugal, later. Electoral life in towns across both empires sprang to life (with a few exceptions). However, when American delegates arrived in the assemblies, they immediately encountered a wall of resistance to their understandings of equality of all subjects of the empire. Metropolitan delegates contrived ways to diminish the strength of colonial delegations – which did little to endear Lisbon and Madrid to colonial outposts. The burst of electoral activity was meant to bolster the legitimacy of the regimes, and to some extent it did. But it also had the effect of revealing the colonial status of American subjects, which until then could be mystified by the mechanisms of viceregal justice. The innovations could not contain the effects of the spread of world war, which began to split the seams of Iberian empires.[21]

There was a second source of friction. Improvising also created resistances. Some potentates disliked the political opening altogether, and in their efforts to damp down the enthusiasm of public opinion and deliberative political life, they thwarted officials' decrees. This was most severe in Mexico in 1808; powerful peninsular merchants and

aristocrats were shocked at the Viceroy's turn to the capital's munici-
pal council, the Cabildo, for consultation on how to handle the
collapse of the metropole. The result was a riptide of unrest, culminating in the Hidalgo Revolt, which spread quickly through the
countryside and nearly engulfed the capital. Something analogous
happened in the Andes, where in Quito a new junta governed in the
name of the people, and the Peruvian Viceroy sent his armies to crush
the pretenders outright. Around the empire, the openings coincided
with an upsurge in reaction and closures, which provoked one
Granadan publicist, Camilo Torres, to issue a famous 'Memorial de
Agravios', which catalogued the abuses committed by officials who
refused to live by the letter of new laws and their spirit and thus
threatened the moral fabric of nation in defence of old privileges. He
proclaimed that Americans were not 'strangers within the Spanish
nation', but 'descendants of those who spilled their blood to acquire
new dominions for the Spanish crown'. Nor was the violence
restricted to the Spanish. Unrest came to a head in the south and
north of Brazil, for while the Americanization of the crown had
brought it closer to its colonial subjects, it also had the effect of
bracing the capital more closely with its distant provinces, like Rio
Grande do Sul and northern Pernambuco, which disliked the new
centralizing arrangements. The friction provoked armed unrest, and in
the case of Pernambuco, a secessionist movement (not from 'Portugal'
but from Rio de Janeiro, it is worth emphasizing). Localized violence
had the effect of stigmatizing the very instruments that had been
devised to revitalize the empires. For reactionaries, it was evidence of
why these changes were so threatening. For those who pushed to
expand the scope of colonial voice within empire, violence doused
their optimism. And many fence-sitters grew alarmed as the liberal,
gentlemanly improvisations began to fail.

There was a third irritant that shook the colonial coalitions that
stood behind the idea of reconstituting empires. From the 1790s, the
scramble for revenues from taxpayers and consumers, and increasingly
for loans from merchants, challenged some of the older mercantilist
regulations governing foreign vessels entering colonial ports. Belgrano,
Pombo, Azeredo, and other lawyers and political economists argued for
greater flexibility and more openness for colonial exporters.
Sometimes viceregal officials obliged, often as a means to enlist contributions to local coffers. For the most part, they had no choice, for the
French occupation basically mooted the rules that were meant to
protect traffic with the metropole; there was no metropole with which
to trade unless the colonists were going to join Napoleon's

Continental System. This meant, in effect, that Iberian colonies were thrown open as markets to 'friendly' or 'neutral' trading partners. The Portuguese were the first to announce this as a principle for the new imperial political economy; Souza Coutinho, while still aboard the flotilla crossing the Atlantic en route from occupied Lisbon, drafted an 'Open Ports' decree, which Prince João VI announced to great fanfare when he disembarked in the tropics. That it was the ruler who announced the decree would make it hard for recalcitrants to disobey. In Spanish American ports, the openings were more halting; there was greater resistance because the agents of peninsular houses feared that this would be the death knell to Cádiz (with good reason), and the struggling government in Cádiz couldn't easily open colonial ports without alienating the merchants in the peninsular port upon whom the government was increasingly dependent for loans to sustain itself. This tussle did not materialize in the Portuguese Atlantic until after the French withdrawal, whereupon old peninsular houses clamoured to reclaim old protectionist privileges. What this meant was great friction at the top of the ruling class of the empires, unravelling the ties of dependency between merchants and monarchs.[22]

The combination of these forces crippled, but did not condemn, the efforts to keep the empires together in the midst of global war. Across the imperial landscapes, conflict was brewing, and in some places erupted in civil war; in some corners of empire, such as Mexico, the Andes, and Brazil, insurgents were crushed. Elsewhere, coalitions declared home rule within empire. Some managed to survive. This was the case in the River Plate, though even the home rule coalition slipped into internal feuding. And in Caracas, autonomists, led eventually by Simón Bolívar, who began his political career in the vacuum created by a French invasion, managed to defeat loyalists, to become the first colony to secede altogether (though technically Paraguay was adrift before). This did not last. Imperial armies, backed by colonists who disliked the ways of the new government, drove Bolívar from his homeland. Here we must appreciate the depth of the ambiguity of the situation: the outlying dominions of empire, for the most part, clung to it in spite of its troubles, while politics was becoming increasingly polarized – and thus militarized.[23]

Yet as the institutional fabric of the empires decomposed they did not fall apart when their centres were at their weakest. Portuguese and Spanish armies and guerrillas, supported by a British expeditionary force, drove the French out of the peninsula in a gruelling war; colonial armies put down rebels and insurgents. Only the fissiparous River Plate provinces had successfully defected by 1814, though still without having declared independence. In that year, Ferdinand returned to power in Madrid to assert control over his fragile empire. It was then, when the restored regime tried to restore the status quo ante, that frail systems began to go up in flames; the counter-revolution begat the revolution.

What needs to be clear at this point is that revolutions did not find their origins among brewing anticolonial sentiments waiting to seize the opportunity to break free in the name of the nation when the empires were weakest. In the passage between escalating international war between empires and its internalization within them, it was not so much separation from empire that was at stake, but how to reconstitute it on new foundations, even by giving it a new centre, or multiple centres. The debate ignited by this process led to internal discord and bloodletting over how to reassemble the stricken parts of empire into new wholes in a conjuncture of rapidly changing political ground rules. Alternatives came to the fore: declarations of village or provincial autonomy, millenarian kingdoms, home rule within empire, and defence of autocracy. They all jostled in a delicate disequilibrium. Under the carapace of decomposing empires what emerged was not the idea of a singular nation born of oppression, but a plethora of ideas about sovereignty that followed the fracturing of the political spaces once outlined by empires. For the time being, this plethora could be encompassed within empires because they lacked territorial centres.

If there was little to predict the inevitable demise of the Iberian empires, why did they crumble just as the post-revolutionary European regimes pacted to desist from the kinds of escalating frictions of the previous century? Surely, this would have been the moment to reinvent the Iberian empires, as monarchs and ministers in St Petersburg, Istanbul, London, and Vienna were doing to their respective empires. But this is not what transpired in the Iberian Atlantic. It was precisely the drive to restore that blew the fragile empires to pieces, and why the developments of the passages that preceded the restoration created legacies that were too important to reverse.[24]

The spotlight now was on how the loyalist fragments within the peninsula and scattered across the colonies, which had managed to squelch most of the plebeian unrest and more radical calls for self-rule, would handle the challenge of imperial reconstruction. Instead of a single response, there were several strategies and policies. At one end was Brazil, where the mercantile elite in alliance with the ennobled slavocracy had given new ballast to the Braganza dynasty. Rio de Janeiro had become, in the appropriate image of Kirsten Schultz, a kind of tropical Versailles. Royalist pageantry and the dispensation of noble titles to rich colonists were the symbolic cover for a recalibration of sovereignty, defined above all by the decision in 1815 to make Brazil a 'Kingdom' in its own right, to accompany Portugal and Algarve. This was no longer, therefore, a 'Portuguese' empire, but a Luso-Atlantic one – a formulation that Souza Coutinho had recognized was a fact before a decree. The shift inspired the empire's jurists, legislators, and political economists to celebrate the sagacity of the monarch. There was no one more euphoric than Edmund Burke's Portuguese translator, José da Silva Lisboa, soon to be ennobled as the Viscount of Cairú for his efforts to give intellectual and legal principles to the new regime. He celebrated the King's promotion of open trade: echoing Montesquieu's idea of *doux commerce,* he noted that 'where there is commerce there is *doçura* [softness] of customs, and where there is *doçura* of customs there is commerce'. The slave trade boomed, exports prospered, and British capitalists lined up behind the modified regime. But not everyone shared this enthusiasm. There was a major uprising in Pernambuco against Rio de Janeiro's new powers, and the conflict in the southern borderlands also accentuated localist feelings. And then there was the cost of Portuguese reconstruction after the French occupation. Combined, reconstruction and simmering civil conflict left the government hobbled with massive debts and undermined the new pact of dependency between merchants and monarchs.[25]

The same forces were at work in the Spanish Atlantic, but their confluence was more incendiary. Ferdinand, bolstered by metropolitan merchants eager to reclaim defunct privileges, was determined to reinstate Spain's centrality in an empire that had, in the meantime, reaggregated its heterogeneity. The king launched a counter-revolution to recentre the empire by tearing up the short-lived constitution of 1812 and its electoral affiliations. He reimaged himself as a benevolent absolutist, spreading a new cult of his regalism to offer a rival legitimacy to the one feebly upheld by the constitution. He sent instructions to his most reactionary officers to restore a fictive absolutism, dissolving the Cortes and ordering the mass arrest of liberal reformers at home and in the colonies. Where he ran into fierce resistance and insurgents, he dispatched tens of thousands of troops now released from the peninsular campaign. The largest army to cross the Atlantic set sail for Venezuela and Nueva Granada under General Pablo Morillo to 'pacify' the colonies. Fence-sitters were frightened. And plebeian forces that had become champions of local autonomy and the abolition of slavery were outraged. Henry Wellesley, the

British ambassador, sent a confidential memorandum to Lord Castlereagh warning that the returning king threatened to shatter the 'nation', which had finally rid itself of French occupiers: 'The King will be in difficulties if he rejects the Constitution.' The words were prophetic, not necessarily because the charter had endeared itself to citizens but because they were not prepared to slide back into vassaldom, especially if citizenship had promised to deliver them from feudal or colonial-extractive burdens.[26]

Forced reunification backfired. Militarized restoration cost money – and Ferdinand resorted to coercive measures to squeeze revenues from merchants around the empire. The old loyalist coalition, held together with the promise of a measure of home rule and regal loyalism, was smashed. The effect was to embolden a new coalition, including many who had once preferred home-rule within empire and its constitution, to opt for outright secession. Whereas Simón Bolívar had all but given up on his cause by 1815, Spanish revanchism gave him a new lease on life. As these coalitions came together, and Ferdinand's armies struck out against guerrillas, insurgencies spread; Indians, slaves, and plebeian populations mobilized into 'revolutionary' forces. Secessionists embraced the abolitionist cause to enlist footsoldiers among the ranks of colonial subjects upon whom the wealth of the Indies was based. Plantation belts and mining provinces went into a major social crisis. Spanish armies became embattled occupying forces. 'Liberating armies' evolved from secessionist phalanxes to swelling regiments that demolished the social structures that had sustained colonial extraction. Mulattos like Manuel Piar and mestizos like José Antonio Páez emerged as the popular leaders of plebeian armies, a far cry from the gentlemanly urbanites who proclaimed home rule within empire a decade earlier. José Artigas, the 'founder' of Uruguay, proclaimed in 1815 that all 'Free Blacks, Sambos of the Same Class, Indians, and Poor Creoles' were entitled to their own land at the expense of the *estancieros*. The spectre of a cross-class and interracial alliance in favour of a social revolution terrified the planters of neighbouring Brazil, who clamoured for Portuguese armies to return to the Banda Oriental to preserve order. Bolívar himself, scion of a slavocrat family, went beyond the promise of freedom for slaves who joined his side; as he fought, he promised freedom for all slaves. He pleaded to the assemblymen at Angostura in 1819 for them to lend moral credentials to the cause by putting the abolition of slavery into the charter of 'Colombia's' new regime. 'You know', he told his readers, 'that one cannot be simultaneously free and enslaved except by violating at one and the same time that natural law, the political laws, and the civil laws.

... I beg the confirmation of absolute freedom for the slaves, just as I would beg for my life and the life of the republic.'[27]

This was a vortex. Mobilization on this scale and kind left little room for missteps by those seeking to restore the *anciens régimes*. It accentuated local divisions, and in many provinces deepened the civil conflict. It also forced the Spanish armies (and to some extent Portuguese troops operating in the south of Brazil) to evolve into counter-insurgent forces, which further crippled fiscally limping states. But if there were missteps, imperial monarchs took them. Across the colonies, especially in South America where the fighting was most bitter, metropolitan centralism seemed to strip Spanish Americans of what they felt they had won in preceding years, and which was seen as an acknowledgement of their loyalty to the crown when it needed their fealty and fortunes most. One by one, provinces began to secede and declare outright independence, thereby escalating the armed confrontation. Meanwhile, in the old heartland viceroyalties of New Spain and Peru, authorities were able to wield the example of the carnage in other dominions as a deterrent to secessionist temptations – but this did not prevent even die-hard loyalists from wondering where all this was going. By 1820, the strategy of military reunion of empire kicked the legs out from the legitimating work of public opinion and representation, and thus shifted the work of integration to the armies, which governments could scarcely support, not least because colonial rents were vanishing. The cycle of civil war and violence – the machinery of imperial decomposition – therefore brought down the remnant state institutions. In January of that year, army officers in Cádiz rose up, calling for a restoration of the 1812 Constitution as a check on the King's absolutism. The virus spread to garrisons around the metropole; the civil war threatened to sweep across Spain itself. Once more without a solid metropole, and with not much left to be loyal to, the remaining viceroyalties severed their ties to Spain, this time for good. This was in 1821, a decade and a half after they had begun to improvise new means to keep the empire together.[28]

Spain's internal discord metastasized to its neighbour, where similar tensions between Lisbon and Rio de Janeiro had been brewing. Garrisons in the south of Brazil seethed with resentment, for their campaigns appeared to be fruitless; many defected. Meanwhile, in the north, in Bahia particularly, discontent in the ranks broke into the open with mutinies. This was not a comforting context for big sugar planters in a province where slave uprisings were endemic. But it was in the metropole that the fragility of the regime finally broke open.

Portuguese liberals called for their own constitutional assembly; conservatives resisted. But the one thing they could agree upon was that the metropole should reclaim its place in the empire. In this they were also encouraged by Portuguese merchants who felt – understandably – deprived of their protected access to Brazilian markets thanks to the Open Ports decree. None of this earned much endearment in Brazil, whose aristocracy saw fewer and fewer returns for their support of formal ties to Lisbon. So, when the King was forced to return to Lisbon in 1821 to restore some order, and the constitutional assembly that had been convoked turned into an occasion for Peninsular deputies to heap scorn on Brazilian counterparts (as colonials, racially inferior fraternizers with Africans, and generally less enlightened), the recentralizing drive motivated a secessionist groundswell. Freedom from Portugal, noted the *Gazeta do Rio de Janeiro*, would ensure 'the bases of the kingdom's future greatness and prosperity, and free it from all elements of disorder and anarchy'. The sentiment spread. Finally, King João's son, the Prince Regent Pedro I, announced Brazil's independence as an imperial monarchy in its own right. Some assemblymen called for an army to be raised to restore Brazil's place – though the futility of this exercise was all too evident on the Spanish side. This only served to drive the Brazilian ditherers into the arms of the independence coalition.[29]

The decomposition of Iberian empires, and the age of revolutions of which they were part, have often been seen as the unfolding of the inevitable – the outcomes of compound pressures of modernization that swept them aside ineluctably, especially if there were markets to exploit and new identities to foster; outside forces 'pulled' on the inner lives of these empires. It is clearly important to any account of large-scale history: at the heart of the global crisis was the disequilibrium of competing empires. What has been proposed here is an 'endogenous' complement, an approach that accentuates much neglected 'push' factors that explain how collective actors changed their preferences – or didn't. These are overlooked in world history because they are often treated as local residuals that explain why some societies or large numbers of individuals did not quite keep up with the pace of modernization. This chapter has argued that these factors, especially the conflicts and the militarization of politics that arose when the fundaments of sovereignty were pushed to the thresholds of their existence, posed basic questions about the shape of public power. But what is important to appreciate in retracing the steps is how the agents involved were seldom seeking radical alternatives (the staple telos for revolutionary narratives). It was the passages that changed the preferences for many people because they activated disenchantments with an older order as a condition for considering alternatives.[30]

There is more to the significance of endogenous forces than the completion of a global portrait of a world filling up with the 'hyper-active' (to borrow a captivating image by C. A. Bayly) agents of European states.[31] The politics of shifting preferences as the internal process through which Iberian-American societies passed was so revolutionary because it propagated alternative models of sovereignty. Empires of the New World contained within them an assortment of arrangements, from indigenous chieftainships to high magistrates. 'Legal pluralism' helps to describe some of the hybrid nature of these systems. But when monarchies and empires were cast aside, newly independent societies faced the challenge of how to reaggregate the diversity into a whole. And which whole?

The question of how to reassemble the fragments of former colonies into something else was a latent one as long as the main attention was the defence of, and then increasingly the toppling of, incumbent systems. The shift to the latter involved a change in 'preferences' that expressed themselves in a series of intermediate positions, from fealty to the status quo, autonomy within empire, and equality of imperial parts, and finally exit. But even the exit option was often motivated by a fear of further dissolution. Several declarations announced more than just secession, they also announced the creation of new empires, like Iturbide's in Mexico, or Pedro's 'Grito de Ipiranga', which proclaimed that Brazil was a nation because of its imperial credentials. Nor were new empires of the Americas the only form for political communities. In fact, most of Iberian America could agree much more on what it was separating from than what it was separating for. We know increasingly that independence *did not* signify that large numbers of people grew clearer about what they did want as a precondition for rejecting what they did not. If anything, the efforts to fill the vacuum created by Napoleon's invasion of 1807 yielded to a range of alternatives, including among them the Americanization of the idyll of empire and monarchy, onto which liberal precepts could be grafted. Either way, Iberian implosions brought these alternatives to the surface.[32]

It was up to constitutionalists of the 1820s to find creeds and clauses to reconcile alternatives – or at least to devise a durable legal framework for deciding how to make public choices about collective preferences. But after years of civil war and mass mobilization in Spanish America, reconstructing a ruling coalition when the social hierarchies that once sustained them were falling apart and when frayed commercial and credit networks were being forced to bankroll states with uncertain life-spans, the prospects were daunting. By contrast, with the ballast of a planter–merchant alliance, buoyed by an expanding slave trade, and spared hyperinflation, Brazilian conservative pragmatists were better poised to adapt an evolving constitutional monarchy. These contrasts point to variations in the results of a more global crisis that shook commercial empires. From the multiple origins of change came multiple outcomes, suggesting that the growing interconnectedness of the world's parts was contoured by competing options for sovereignty. It was from these public choices – and the increasing violence that surrounded them – that we can trace the traumatic origins of modern politics in the Iberian Atlantic.

5

The Caribbean in the Age of Revolution

David Geggus

According to anthropologist Sidney Mintz, two institutions have defined the Caribbean region: black slavery and colonial rule.[1] No other part of the world was ruled from Europe for so long or had such a large proportion of its population living as slaves. Slavery and colonial rule shaped an export-oriented plantation economy that dominated the region from the mid-sixteenth to the mid-twentieth centuries. The years 1760–1840 may be seen as a watershed in the unravelling of this history, but the changes the period witnessed were extremely uneven and contradictory. Although the Caribbean was home to the most transformative revolution of the age, which created Haiti out of French Saint Domingue,[2] revolution was not necessarily the most transformative force at work in the region, which also saw the peaceful abolition of slavery in all the British colonies, a generalized abandonment of legal racial discrimination, and a weakening in the Caribbean's position in the world market that were only partially connected to the political violence of the Age of Revolution.[3] Scholarly assessment of the relative importance of European and local influences in promoting change in the region has trended in recent decades toward stressing Caribbean agency, but with varied success.

Continuity, change, and revolutionary change

In marked contrast to the wave of decolonization that swept the North and South American mainlands in the half-century after 1775, only one of the Caribbean's thirty or so colonies became an independent state before the 1840s. In 1804 the black population of Saint Domingue threw off French rule to found Haiti. Neighbouring Spanish Santo Domingo briefly declared its independence in 1821 only to be immediately annexed by Haiti, and it would not break away to become the Dominican Republic until 1844. In the other colonies of France, Spain, Britain, Denmark, Sweden, and the Netherlands, imperial rule remained secure and (outside of Cuba) essentially unchallenged. To the extent that the map of the Caribbean was redrawn in this period, it was due to war rather than revolution and formed part of a trend under way since 1713 that saw imperial power shift from France to Britain.[4]

The British and Spanish West Indies did not follow the example of their mainland counterparts because they were easily blockaded islands with large slave populations and few whites. Their planter classes were less willing to risk rebellion than those of Virginia and Venezuela, especially after the royal governors of those colonies had, in 1775 and 1812, encouraged slaves to turn on their treasonous owners. It may also be that a sense of American identity developed less easily in the Caribbean. The extent of absentee ownership in the British islands meant that their wealthiest landowners simply did not live there. The Spanish islands were different but, after 1763, relatively favoured by an imperial government that was eager to develop their plantation economies.

Of the region's six colonial powers, only Britain had by 1840 ended slavery in its possessions – something all the Spanish American republics except Paraguay already had largely accomplished – and the number of enslaved people living in the Caribbean was only some 14 per cent less than it had been in 1760. It is true that the enslaved proportion of the regional population had shrunk to only one-fifth, well below the 70 per cent that characterized the eighteenth-century Caribbean, but there were still in 1840 more than 40 per cent of its residents who had lived as slaves at some time.[5] In the Spanish West Indies, the use of slavery accelerated throughout this eighty-year period, as those islands underwent belated economic development boosted by Saint Domingue's demise. Although all Western powers officially withdrew from the Atlantic slave trade between 1802 and 1820, Cuba and Puerto Rico illegally imported in the 1830s about 195,000 enslaved Africans, and in 1840 their plantation economies were still rapidly expanding.[6] Antislavery ideology attracted little support in metropolitan Spain, while plantation profits and a growing black labour force diminished desires for independence in its island colonies.

Any appraisal of the Caribbean's experience of revolution in this period has to take note of this resilience of colonialism and plantation slavery in the region. Such an assessment also cannot ignore that much of the change that came about did not flow from revolutionary causes. The Haitian Revolution freed about half a million people in 1793, and perhaps another 110,000 the following year, when the French Republic (temporarily) extended emancipation to Guadeloupe and Guyane.[7] The Haitian Revolution thus liberated one-third of the Caribbean slave population definitively, and more than 40 per cent if we include those re-enslaved by Napoleon Bonaparte in 1802.[8] The British emancipation act of 1833 freed fully half of the remaining population, some 665,000 slaves (whose numbers, moreover, had fallen from about 775,000 due to the banning of the British slave trade twenty-five years before).[9] Whether in absolute or relative terms, metropolitan abolitionism contributed at least as much as Caribbean revolution during this period to freeing slaves and to shrinking the regional slave population.[10] One might further argue that the final success of British antislavery was the more significant development in that, as precedent and example, it was more relevant to the future demise of American slavery than was the Haitian Revolution.

The revolution and the British emancipation act both helped to change the Caribbean in another way by contributing to the considerable decline in the region's economic and geopolitical importance between 1760 and 1840. The Haitian Revolution ended Saint Domingue's role as the world's major exporter of sugar and coffee, and reduced France's stake in the Caribbean from being the largest to a fairly negligible one. The 1833 emancipation act severely disrupted plantation production in most British colonies, in some of them permanently. By 1840, sugar exports from the two major producers were down by half.[11]

The Caribbean's economic decline, however, was not so much absolute as relative. Regional output was far higher in 1840 than in 1760, and it was worth far more in 1815 than in 1789. Not only did Spanish West Indian sugar production triple during the French wars, and then soar, but wartime expansion in the British and Danish colonies more than made up for the fall in French and Dutch exports, which themselves experienced substantial recovery by the late 1820s.[12] British Caribbean sugar production continued to increase until the late 1820s.[13] Though it was severely disrupted by slave emancipation in the 1830s, its losses were more than outweighed by the bigger harvests in Cuba.[14] Saint Domingue's enormous coffee output, halved in the 1790s, was less easily replaced, but by 1815 expansion in Jamaica and Cuba had gone far in making up losses. Continued expansion in Cuba and subsequent recovery in Haiti itself further reduced the shortfall down to 1840.[15]

Yet by then the Caribbean was a backwater in world affairs. This was a startling shift after being at the centre of European rivalries and a dynamo of the Atlantic economy since the seventeenth century. Although Caribbean sugar exports were increasing in volume, their share of the world market was already slipping by 1815. This was initially because of the economic revival of Brazil, and later because of the growth of competition from Louisiana, Mauritius, and India, and the emergence of a successful sugar beet industry in Europe. After a half-century of gestation, Brazil also suddenly emerged in the mid-1820s as the world's primary source of coffee. Indigo, long established in the Caribbean, quickly vanished after 1800 as India reclaimed its former place in the world market, and Caribbean cotton, which briefly flourished in the late eighteenth century, met a rapid demise following the crop's take-off in the United States.[16]

Economic growth elsewhere thus diminished the Caribbean's relative importance as a source of agricultural staples, and it helped to drive down the value of its exports. After 1815, world prices of sugar, coffee, and cotton all fell rapidly.[17] The region's significance in world trade also declined as Britain and the United States pursued new overseas markets, reducing after 1800 their long reliance on the West Indies. After 1830, the French unleashed their colonizing energies on Africa, and the Dutch intensified their involvement in Indonesia. As faster-growing populations in Britain and the United States urbanized and industrialized, the Caribbean simply mattered less as a centre of wealth creation. Raw cotton overtook sugar as Britain's principal import around 1825. Although there is a great deal wrong with the 'decline thesis' of Lowell Ragatz and Eric Williams, there is no gainsaying its basic point that the Caribbean economy had come to count for less in British politics by the time slavery was abolished in 1833.[18]

This decline in the economic importance of the Caribbean as a whole was far from being simply a product of the Age of Revolution. The shrinking of the slave population was brought about jointly by British abolitionism and the Haitian Revolution. The damage done to Saint Domingue's plantations by the revolution did stimulate competitors outside the region but it redounded largely to the benefit of other Caribbean planters. Jamaica succeeded Saint Domingue as the world's primary exporter of both sugar and coffee, until it was overtaken by Cuba and Brazil. Global economic development undercut the Caribbean's once privileged position.

Revolutionary change in the Caribbean was largely confined to the French colonies in the period 1789–1803, and chiefly to Saint Domingue. This is not to belittle the magnitude of the process, for

Saint Domingue had the strongest export economy in the Americas in the late 1780s, and nearly one in four American slaves lived in a French colony. Of all the 'Atlantic' revolutions, Saint Domingue's most fully embodied the contemporary struggles for freedom, equality, and independence, and it produced the greatest degree of social and economic change. Beginning as a home-rule movement among wealthy white colonists, it rapidly spread to militant free people of colour seeking political rights, and then gave rise to the largest slave uprising in the history of the Americas. Its narrative is a succession of major precedents: colonial representation in a metropolitan assembly, the ending of racial discrimination, the first abolition of slavery in a major slave society, and the creation of Latin America's first independent state. By 1804, colonialism and slavery, the defining institutions of the Caribbean, were annihilated precisely where, during three hundred years of unchecked growth, they had most prospered.

France's other Caribbean colonies participated in these changes to varying degrees until the Napoleonic regime restored the status quo – not of 1789, but of 1786, rejecting even the timid gesture toward representative government introduced into the Windward Isles at the close of the *Ancien Régime*.[19] Elsewhere in the Caribbean, we can find, at best, potential revolutionary change, power contested with force by slaves, free coloureds, and a handful of white colonists, who did not meet with the success of their French-ruled counterparts.[20] Such conflicts, and others involving maroons and Black Caribs, clustered thickly in the Age of Revolution, making it a particularly turbulent time in the Caribbean. The 1790s and, to a lesser degree, the following decades constituted a peak period in the incidence of slave revolts and conspiracies in the region. Free people of colour also conspired for their own ends (as in Cuba in 1795), as did whites (Masonic plots in Havana in 1810 and 1821, for example). And in 1795, the British were almost driven from the islands of Grenada and St Vincent by a multiclass alliance led by free men of colour that was suppressed only with massive military force.[21]

Though all these efforts failed, one epoch-making change affected almost all colonies in the Caribbean. That was the abolition of legal racial discrimination that the British, French, Dutch, and Danish extended to their Caribbean colonies between 1828 and 1832. This momentous turning-point has attracted curiously little research. Like abolition in 1833, it was a product of reform rather than revolution, even if it is hard to exclude the French revolutionary experiment with racial equality in the years 1792–1802 as a possible causative influence. Those who have studied this transition depict it primarily as a reaction to the rapid growth of the free non-white population, to metropolitan abolitionist pressure, to colonial whites' reluctant search for allies against the enslaved, and above all, to the persistent petitioning for reform by the free coloureds themselves.[22] Since their campaigns for reform generally date from the period 1811–13, one wonders if the simultaneous, and similarly little studied, emergence of 'racial democracy' in the new Spanish American republics also helped to inspire this free coloured activism.[23]

Europe, the Caribbean, and abolitionism

Historians have traditionally located the origins of the revolutionary crisis and of abolitionism in Europe and Anglo-America. This assumption has increasingly been challenged in recent decades. In the case of the antislavery movement, arguments have been put forward that claim resistance by Caribbean slaves as a major causative factor in the emergence, development, and eventual success of abolitionism.

The dominant Euro-centred narratives of abolitionism's emergence come in three versions. The oldest and most discredited is that of Eric Williams, which focused on economic change. Yet it is also the most global, since it incorporated Caribbean soil exhaustion and slave resistance, the growth of Asian colonies, and the imperial disruption caused by the American Revolution, alongside its main argument concerning the rise in Britain of an industrial capitalism that favoured economic liberalism. Strikingly different is David Brion Davis's idealist interpretation that emphasizes eighteenth-century changes in philosophy, religion, humanitarianism, and literature, and (in its later development) the utility of the antislavery idea in British politics. Seymour Drescher's third way systematically dismisses most of Williams's arguments and presents antislavery as a question of mobilization around libertarian values that were older than the eighteenth century.[24]

Seeking to write the slaves themselves into this predominantly metropolitan narrative, Michèle Duchet contended in 1971 that the antislavery stance adopted by French *philosophes* should be seen as a response to reports of slave resistance in the Caribbean.[25] The question of whether Europeans would ever have opposed slavery if slaves had not done so is philosophically interesting, but ultimately unanswerable, since slave resistance is as old as slavery. Yet even if Duchet was correct that maroons and rebels put slavery on the agenda of the French Enlightenment, the texts she was concerned with had little to do with British abolitionism, whose foundational texts overwhelmingly depicted the suffering slave, not the rebellious slave. More recently Gelien Matthews has sought to show how the three major uprisings in the British Caribbean between 1816 and 1831 inflected antislavery discourse in Britain, but her neglect of earlier metropolitan responses to rebellion exaggerates the apparent changes.[26] Emphasizing transatlantic interaction and accepting, unlike Michael Craton, that abolitionism inspired slave rebellion, Matthews's main point is that abolitionists engaged with rather than retreated from the issue of slave insurrection, but she avoids arguing that this engagement was important to the outcome of the antislavery campaign.[27]

As for the contribution of slave resistance to the successes of antislavery, the arguments are varied and the details complex. In Robin Blackburn's view, the Haitian Revolution and the later rebellions in Barbados, Demerara, and Jamaica inspired abolitionists, enhanced metropolitan opinion of blacks, discredited slave-owners, and made politicians progressively weary of paying to defend slavery. 'The progress of abolition', he writes, 'crucially depended on . . . slave resistance.'[28] Painting on a very broad canvas, Blackburn's approach is, rather than demonstrating precise connections, to stress the primacy of the Haitian Revolution as the first major breakthrough in the struggle against slavery, and to imply that it hovered inevitably over all subsequent developments. For the doggedly empirical Seymour Drescher, on the other hand, the Haitian Revolution was of symbolic but not substantive importance; it provided propaganda to both pro- and antislavery forces, but contributed unequivocally to neither. There is no evidence, he asserts, that it was a decisive issue in the key abolition debates in the British parliament in 1792, 1807, or 1833.[29]

It is far from certain that the Haitian Revolution did, on balance, enhance the image of blacks in the Western world. Though inspiring to some, the Haitians' military victories were easily rationalized as the product of slavish qualities: cunning, endurance, immunity to disease. The revolution's numerous atrocities were selectively reported, so that black barbarism was more prominent in the public record than white barbarism. Like so much of the revolution's legacy, the impact on racial attitudes was thus ambiguous and may have done no more than reinforce existing preconceptions.[30]

The willingness of slave-owners everywhere to go on importing slaves in huge numbers after 1791 should also make us sceptical that fear of insurrection brought the slave trade to an end.[31] Certainly, the sudden revival of the antislavery movement in 1804 can be partially attributed to Haiti's achievement of independence and the public alarm it briefly created in Britain. The proslavery *Times* newspaper abruptly espoused abolition for this reason.[32] More important to the

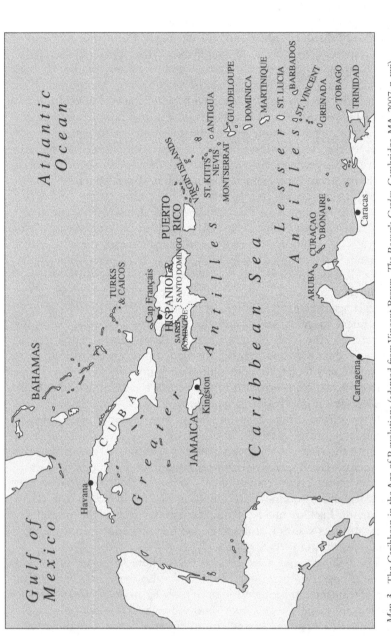

Map 3 The Caribbean in the Age of Revolutions (adapted from Vincent Brown, *The Reaper's Garden*, Cambridge, MA, 2007, p. xvi).

abolitionists' success, however, was the reconfiguration of the House of Commons earlier that year due to the incorporation of 100 Irish Members of Parliament. This changed the political landscape and, together with further changes in ministerial politics, opened the way for the successful vote of 1807.[33]

Similarly, the parliamentary reform of 1832, which decimated the West India faction, greatly facilitated the voting of slave emancipation the following year. Jamaica's 'Christmas Rebellion' of 1831 (the second largest slave revolt in the Americas) may have catalysed the process by radicalizing the demands of some leading conservative abolitionists, but the antislavery movement had already shifted from a gradualist programme to demanding immediate abolition in 1830, a development that itself had helped to set off the rebellion. Finally, as Seymour Drescher observes, the rebellion was not enough to overcome parliamentary and government opposition without another abolitionist campaign in 1833.[34]

While much of the case for slave resistance powering abolitionist success is unconvincing, one argument, applicable to both 1807 and 1833, is compelling. It is that the Haitian Revolution enabled British politicians to vote their consciences without fear that it would significantly advantage France, which the revolution had removed as a serious competitor in the tropical produce market.[35] Although this line of thinking was not brandished in public debate, it is hard to imagine Parliament ending the slave trade, or slavery, if France had remained a commercial as well as political rival. It is true that, by 1833, France's status as the traditional enemy of Great Britain was fading fast. Yet British legislators would surely have been much less likely to risk disrupting colonial production to their competitors' advantage if Saint Domingue had still been a French colony.

Europe, the Caribbean, and revolution

The simultaneity of the revolutionary crises in the Caribbean and Europe raises issues of causality and comparison. These can be largely subsumed under two questions. Could there have been a Haitian Revolution without the French Revolution? How much did the revolutions have in common?

Historians have increasingly recognized the colonial revolution as an autonomous force that helped to radicalize the French Revolution, rather than being merely a reflection of it. In the heyday of French imperialism, Léon Deschamps wrote that 'Conflicts derive from ideas and the ideas came from France'.[36] Thirty years later, the ex-colonial officer Jules Saintoyant described a colonial revolution that was parallel, not tributary, to the metropolitan revolution, but his vision extended only to the white settlers. Then the black West Indians, C. L. R. James in 1938 and Aimé Césaire in 1960, published narratives of the Haitian Revolution that made blacks its central actors and the colonial question a central issue in the French Revolution.[37] Bicentennial syntheses by Yves Benot and Robin Blackburn brought a new sophistication to integrating metropolitan and colonial developments that has led on in the past twenty years to an unprecedented burst of research on both aspects of the problem.[38]

It seems fairly easy to demonstrate how colonial affairs changed the metropolitan revolution, if only in the realm of colonial policy. At its outset, the revolution of 1789 was not generally intended to have a colonial dimension and the constitution of 1791 explicitly excluded the colonies.[39] Yet, throughout the 1790s, politicians in Paris were compelled to play catch-up with the onrush of events in the Caribbean. This began in July 1789, when wealthy colonists from Saint Domingue cajoled their way into gaining seats in the National Assembly, and it continued with the legalization of the colonial assemblies that the white colonists had elected. A small rebellion by free men of colour in 1790 won them a minor adjustment in the colonial colour bar, and then the massive slave revolt of 1791 led, first, to the granting of equal rights to all free people of colour (to win their assistance in fighting the insurgent slaves), and then to the abolition of slavery, following the invasion of Saint Domingue in 1793 by Spanish and British troops. After the Convention decided to use slave emancipation as a weapon of war in the Caribbean, the constitution of 1795 declared the colonies to be integral parts of the French Republic. Napoleon reversed this latter (and largely unimplemented) innovation as soon as he came to power, but many think it was Toussaint Louverture's decision to promulgate his own constitution in 1801 that finally precipitated Bonaparte's disastrous attempt to erase all the gains of the colonial revolution.

Although colonial policy-making in the French Revolution closely tracked the leftward trend of metropolitan politics, and then its retreat, it was predominantly reactive and the initiative generally lay with Caribbean actors. In this sense, we can speak of convergent revolutions in France and Saint Domingue. A purely metropolitan revolution, albeit with universalist pretensions, was progressively forced to take account of the claims of colonial activists, white and non-white, enslaved and free. The decree of April 1792 on racial equality in the colonies and that of February 1794 abolishing colonial slavery were milestones in American history and highpoints of the French Revolution, and primarily pragmatic responses to overseas events. This does not exactly mean, however, that the foundation of modern race-blind democracy was due to the slave insurgents of Saint Domingue, as Laurent Dubois's work appears to suggest.[40] Blacks were enfranchised, in France, at the same time as Jews, and at the same time slavery in France was outlawed, in September 1791.[41] This was a month before news of the slave uprising arrived, and at the time quite uncontroversial.

Presumably these changes owed something to the campaigning of the Société des Colons Américains, the club that Dominguan free coloureds founded in Paris in 1789, but here we know rather less about how the colonial revolution shaped the French. Benot and Blackburn, following James, and more recently Florence Gauthier and Jean-Daniel Piquet have made the case for a growing popular solidarity in France with colonial non-whites, although not always convincingly. Benot also suggested that the violence of certain revolutionary episodes might be attributed to the colonial experience of their perpetrators.[42] Jean Jaurès claimed that middle class revolutionaries became demoralized by their dishonest compromises on the race question, which in the summer of 1791 left them vulnerable to conservative reaction.[43] Seymour Drescher, taking a longer view, suggests that the early acceptance of 'scientific racism' in France was partly due to bitter memories of the Haitian Revolution.[44]

The colonial influence on the French Revolution is therefore a mixture of the obvious and the obscure. At the very least, colonial issues served to sharpen the main metropolitan conflicts, between Feuillants and Jacobins in 1791, between Jacobins and Girondins in 1793, and between radicals and conservatives in 1797.[45] Before coming to the French Revolution's impact on the colonies, we need to touch on those prerevolutionary developments on which the case for an autonomous colonial revolution is grounded. Slave resistance, free coloured activism, and white settler autonomism all had complex prehistories in the world before 1789, but historians have never agreed on their revolutionary potential.

A singular paradox of the Haitian Revolution is that the largest of all American slave insurrections took place in a colony that had seen few previous rebellions or conspiracies; in this, Saint Domingue was very unlike its neighbour Jamaica. Scholars who adopt an 'internal perspective' on the revolution and downplay French influence tend to evoke, therefore, other traditions of resistance, notably poisoning and the activities of fugitive slaves (known as maroonage), as well as the

unifying influence of Vodou, the rapid growth of the enslaved population, and a supposed worsening in its conditions of life. The critical
points in dispute concern the frequency and dimensions of resistance,
whether it should be considered apolitical or proto-revolutionary, and
how it contributed to the slave uprising of 1791, which a Haitian
nationalist tradition depicts as being spearheaded by maroons and
Vodou priests.[46]

The free coloured population of Saint Domingue was unique in
the Americas in being moderately large and moderately wealthy, and
in some respects increasingly oppressed. Some of its members were
involved with white colonists in resisting the colonial administration
in the 1760s. Only in the 1780s, however, can one speak of independent political activity. This consisted of discreet lobbying efforts by
the wealthy planter Julien Raimond to persuade the colonial minister
to reform the regime of racial discrimination, at least insofar as it
affected freeborn, light-skinned, and wealthy individuals like himself.
The fact that the free coloured population was quickly approaching
parity with the whites and played an important role in the militia
makes it reasonable to imagine that further challenges to the racial
status quo were likely, whatever happened in France.[47]

For Saint Domingue's white population, politics had a lot in
common with that of *Ancien Régime* France: the resentment of the
'ministerial despotism' of an absolutist state, law courts that posed as
popular champions, increased friction caused by vigorous attempts at
reform in the 1780s. Dominguan landowners and lawyers envied the
fiscal autonomy of the regional *pays d'état*, and the self-government
and better terms of trade of their British colonial counterparts. In the
1670s, 1720s, and 1760s, colonists had briefly rebelled against agents
of royal authority, and in the 1780s they enjoyed closer links with the
newly independent United States, as Yankee merchants opened busi-
nesses in Le Cap and Port-au-Prince. Probably only the wildest
dreamers imagined that an easily blockaded island, whose colonists
were greatly outnumbered by slaves, could emulate the mainland
colonies' secession, but to others a British protectorate may have
seemed feasible.[48]

For this white population of about 30,000, the onset of the French
Revolution rapidly changed from opportunity to threat. No sooner
had those seeking a political voice achieved their ends, than they
found the twin pillars of their society, slavery and white supremacy,
under assault from metropolitan critics, who were soon joined by free
coloured activists in Paris and in Saint Domingue who petitioned for
equal rights. The Declaration of the Rights of Man in late August

1789 seems to have had an immediate impact on the aspirations of the free men of colour. Julien Raimond went from seeking minor reforms to demanding full racial equality. For a few months, there was some doubt whether men of mixed racial descent like Raimond genuinely wished to include free blacks in their campaign, but this issue was soon resolved.[49]

The French Revolution provided the free men of colour a forum in which to campaign for change that was unimaginable under the old regime, but it also increased the hostility of their opponents, because it greatly raised the stakes. Before the revolution, racial equality meant the right to become a doctor or lawyer; now it meant access to political power. And in the context of revolutionary change, it was easier to make the charge that any concession to free non-whites would undermine the slave regime that was the basis of colonial wealth. While politicians in Paris dithered and prevaricated over the issue, Saint Domingue and Martinique went through several years of vicious conflict before white supremacy in the colonies was officially abolished.

That change came about, we have seen, in response to the slave uprising in northern Saint Domingue, which the French recognized they could not suppress without the help of the free coloureds. The relationship of the black revolution that began in 1791 with the French Revolution and with the Age of Revolution more generally is a difficult conceptual issue. Historians who integrate the slaves' epic struggle into a broader Atlantic or Western narrative are sometimes criticized for an ethnocentric misreading of the slave revolution's cultural specificity. Those who fail to make the connection seem guilty of a prejudiced analysis that denies the slaves and the state they created a place in the onward march of civilization.

Eugene Genovese, in a seminal study of slave resistance, argued that the Saint Domingue slave rebellion developed into a true revolution that sought to build a modern state under the influence of libertarian ideology from France, but then retreated into a 'tragic counter-revolution' by allowing a peasant economy to replace the plantation regime. He has been criticized for denying the slaves their own ideology and regarding their African values as archaic.[50] On the other hand, R. R. Palmer's *Age of the Democratic Revolution* and Jacques Godechot's *France and the Atlantic Revolution* have been castigated, along with any number of French Revolution histories, for omitting Haiti's revolution, whether by oversight or deliberate exclusion.[51]

It is extraordinarily difficult to know what were the expectations of those tens of thousands of slaves who took up arms in 1791.

Common sense tells us that they would not have killed and burned on such a massive scale without intending to live afterwards free from the possibility of French revenge. Yet some evidence from the first year of the revolt suggests only reformist goals, such as gaining an extra two free days per workweek, or abolishing the whip. Only two formal demands for abolishing slavery issued from the rebel camps, and one of these, in my view, was a forgery.[52] It is well known that, during negotiations with the whites in December 1791, the slaves' leaders secretly offered to force their followers back to work on the plantations if only fifty of them were freed. It is less well known that no evidence connects the future leader Toussaint Louverture to the cause of ending slavery until its actual abolition in August 1793.[53] Trying to make sense of these contradictory clues, some historians have suggested that the insurgents' aims evolved in time from reformist to revolutionary.[54] Such a formulation, however, does not fit the facts; the most radical demand – that the French leave the colony – came at the very beginning of the uprising.

Compounding this problem of goals are the contrary indications regarding the insurgents' rhetoric. Several contemporaries wrote that the slaves were demanding 'the rights of man', but these tended to be white conservatives who may have wished to discredit the French Revolution. More numerous are descriptions of the insurgents posing as defenders of the beleaguered monarch, Louis XVI, who, they claimed, had decreed they be freed (a common feature of slave revolts in the years 1790–1830).[55] The principal slave leaders, Jean-François and Biassou, would in fact maintain this 'church and king' discourse down to their deaths in the early nineteenth century. In 1793, as war broke out among the colonial powers, they allied themselves with the counter-revolutionary Spanish, who offered freedom to soldiers and their families, but they refused to join the French Republic despite its eventual adoption of emancipation for all. They also rounded up women and children on the plantations and sold them to their Spanish neighbours.[56]

Haiti's first historian, Thomas Madiou, remarked that the concept of '*la liberté générale*' was not well developed during the first two years of the slave uprising, among either the free people of colour or the insurgents themselves. Then the French *commissaire civil* (and abolitionist) Léger-Félicité Sonthonax rallied men of all colours to the cause with his proclamation of 29 August 1793.[57] Only at this point did the forces of black self-liberation and French libertarian ideology conjoin. Robin Blackburn notes that most slave revolts have been 'particularistic, seeking freedom for a given person or group'.[58]

I think this is how we should understand the slave revolt in Saint Domingue until it was transformed by its alliance with the French Republic.

Blackburn, Genovese, and Dubois acknowledge this equivocal stance of the slave insurgents of 1791 but it tends to get obscured in their interpretations. Blackburn's statement that, in the negotiations of December 1791, the slave leaders called for 'full political rights', and Dubois's suggestion that they used the term 'general will' because of an acquaintance with Enlightenment ideas, are, I believe, mistaken. They fail to take account of the way free men of colour acting as intermediaries in those negotiations were arguing their own case as well as that of the slaves' leaders.[59]

More misleading, it seems to me, is Dubois's frequent use of the word 'republican'. Assertions that 'enslaved revolutionaries . . . deploy[ed] the language of Republican rights', used 'republican symbols', or 'demanded Republican citizenship and racial equality' appear to derive from his earlier work on Guadeloupe in 1793 but do not apply to the Saint Domingue slave uprising, in which ostensibly royalist insurgents used the term '*les citoyens*' as a smearword to describe their enemies.[60] Even after Sonthonax's abolition of slavery, the few ex-slave leaders who at first joined the Republic showed little interest in republican ideology and continued in correspondence among themselves to respect the legitimist monarchical principle.[61]

Far from being driven by 'democratic ideals', the revolution that grew out of the slave uprising was authoritarian from beginning to end. If, as Dubois states, it 'created a democratic culture that was later presented as a gift from Europe', it was because the gift really did come from Europe. No doubt the gift was grudging and, as Dubois shows, subverted by what he calls the 'Republican racism' of the mid-1790s.[62] But it is perfectly clear that the succession of gifted ex-slaves who emerged from the 1791 uprising and later took Saint Domingue to independence never displayed the slightest regard for democracy. The politics of Toussaint Louverture, Jean-Jacques Dessalines, and Henry Christophe were unapologetically dictatorial. They were the heirs of the warlords Jean-François and Biassou, from whom they broke away after the French republic abolished slavery.

The Haitian Revolution, of course, was never just a slave revolution, and it is important to distinguish this authoritarian tradition from that of the free men of colour whose revolt was centred in the west and south of Saint Domingue and whose politics developed in the liberal republican mainstream of the Atlantic Revolutions. It is they who made independent Haiti a republic – but this was in 1806, not 1804. Although historians commonly refer to the foundation of the 'black republic' or Republic of Haiti in 1804, the state that Dessalines created in fact took the name État d'Haïti and was never a republic. Dessalines arrogated all power to himself – much as had Toussaint in his 1801 constitution – and took the titles 'governor-general for life', following Toussaint, and then, following Bonaparte, 'emperor'.

After Dessalines's assassination in 1806, the general and former slave Henry Christophe refused to serve as president in the new republic that his free coloured rivals constructed; its constitution was the only one of the country's first six that was not explicitly dictatorial.[63] Instead, Christophe created a secessionist state in the north that became a monarchy with an aristocratic court and its own system of tropico-medieval heraldry. Although it looked to Britain for costume and protocol, it was an absolute monarchy and African inspiration cannot be ruled out. The royal police force, recruited from slave ships, was known as the Dahomets.[64]

The political scientist David Nicholls warned against reading too much into constitutional forms in Haiti, and suggested that all Haitian governments tended to be autocratic.[65] Certainly, Alexandre Pétion, who became the first president under the constitution of 1806, ruled for several years without his Senate. However, such documents do help to situate the Haitian Revolution intellectually. The country's unique declaration of independence justified secession as an act necessary to prevent the restoration of slavery but otherwise made no mention of rights, and prudently informed the colonial powers that the new state would not seek to abolish slavery elsewhere.[66] David Armitage observes that the declaration was unusual among its nineteenth-century counterparts in not taking the US declaration of 1776 as its model, and that it replaced an earlier draft that had done so.[67]

The text distinguished between Haitians and French in terms of the latter's cruelty, colour, and vulnerability to tropical disease, and the distance that separated their countries. It called for revenge to be exacted on those French who had remained in the country. Haitian leaders were divided on this issue, and some secretly helped colonists to escape, but in the following months several thousands were systematically massacred in two waves: men first, women and children afterwards.[68] Later public documents (a proclamation of 28 April 1804 and the 1805 constitution) banned first 'Europeans', then 'white persons', from owning land in Haiti.[69] Dessalines's constitution of 1805 further mandated that all Haitians should be designated 'Noirs'. And in 1816 Pétion called on persons of African or Amerindian descent to settle in the country, where they would immediately be accepted as Haitians.

We find an echo of such bitter, quasi-genocidal tensions in Simón Bolívar's *guerra a muerte* ('war to the death') and his 1813 declaration that he would purge America of Spanish 'monsters'; perhaps, too, in the death sentence imposed on its émigrés by the French Republic.[70] However, as historian and former president Leslie Manigat observes, the Haitian Revolution had an 'ethno-national' character that made it unique. It became a symbol of racial equality, because its central issue was the subjection of black slaves by white owners. Its leaders were antislavery but not liberals.[71] This distinction, very clear to Haitian scholars, has sometimes been elided in the earnest interpretations of outsiders.

France's revolution, of course, also ended in a military dictatorship, and Latin American colonies similarly produced a monarch or two in the process of gaining independence.[72] The reality of political change in the American and Spanish American revolutions has also been hotly debated. Yet none reveals the unselfconsciously autocratic streak that ran through Haiti's revolution into the post-independence period. One is tempted to conclude that, having triumphed over slavery, the question of citizenship was something of subordinate importance to those who had made the transition from thing to person. This is doubtless why Palmer and Godechot were reluctant to incorporate the Haitian Revolution within their grand narratives of liberal republican democracy.

★ ★ ★

In the Age of Revolution, several different crises confronted the Caribbean colonies in an uneven manner that reflected the region's fragmented politics and diverse stages of economic development. Colonial rule went largely unchallenged, yet it was destroyed precisely where it had been most successful, not by a white settler elite as on the American mainland, but by the region's lowliest inhabitants. Although most of the imperial powers maintained their slave regimes, most of the regional population had by 1840 escaped from slavery, as a result of revolution or reform, and begun new lives as peasant smallholders. While the Spanish West Indies experienced exceptional economic growth throughout the period, Caribbean dominance of the international market for tropical produce peaked, then declined for good. Most colonies were compelled to abandon the principle of white supremacy that had underpinned European rule from its beginning.

The impetus for these changes was similarly diverse. In such a long colonized region, it was of course to a large degree European, but the interaction between the different crises, and between colony and metropole, was complex. Economic decline stemmed mainly from local factors (soil exhaustion, the disruption caused by revolution and slave emancipation) and from the strengthening of global competition, rather than from strictly European developments (sugar beet cultivation, the weakening of mercantilist protections). Slave emancipation in the British colonies responded primarily to metropolitan imperatives and followed a metropolitan timetable but the influence of economic decline and of slave resistance on the process warrants close examination. The legislating of racial equality owed much more to local activism and demographic change, but it also was promoted by the metropolitan antislavery movement.

The Haitian Revolution evolved in symbiosis with the French Revolution and each shaped the other, but this reciprocity was obviously uneven. The Haitian Revolution affected little more than colonial policy in the metropolitan revolution, while it is unlikely that any uprising in Saint Domingue would have developed into a revolution without the political disruption and ideological ferment caused by the revolution in France. Sharing the social and political complexity of its French counterpart, Haiti's revolution went further than the other colonial revolutions of the Americas in involving all sectors of society and in transforming economy, society, and politics. It differed from the other Atlantic revolutions, however, in that the central pursuit of freedom came to be construed in the profound but narrow sense of freedom from slavery rather than as political rights.

6

The Dynamics of History in Africa and the Atlantic 'Age of Revolutions'

Joseph C. Miller

The historical processes that European monarchies experienced at the end of the eighteenth century as an 'age of (political) revolutions' were a particular moment in a much broader, long-term global dynamic of commercialization. Africa was also very much a part of that dynamic. Europeans who went overseas to seek personal advantage in the accelerating worldwide rush towards global markets found themselves in disorienting contexts of anonymity and increasingly isolated from the smaller and more tangible families, guilds, and parishes of their parents, as well as from theoretically benevolent monarchical protectors in Europe. Both at home and abroad Europeans experienced a political crisis of confidence in royal patrons whom they saw as increasingly remote and overbearing. Feeling abandoned, they looked to themselves for salvation in civic terms, as sovereign individual citizens. While Europeans around the globe were creditors in this new world of disengaged commercial competition, Africans laboured under a burden of debt to it. They financed commercialization as debtors, with no less profoundly novel experiences of individuation and consumerism, through extraction of commodities for export and then into slaving; the overwhelming pace of commercial growth in the Atlantic left no time for them to invest in mechanized industrial productivity. Africans retained ideological frameworks and political ethics focused on collective welfare rather than embracing competitive individualism. This African 'communal ethos' judged individuation as greed rather than as opportunity. Africans thus accented the human costs of others' material gains, in ways not dissimilar to the experiences of other, former Africans enslaved in the Americas. These African historical dynamics contextualize Europe's 'age of revolutions' in broader global patterns of commercialization.

This chapter develops Africa's distinctive position in the commercializing world of the eighteenth-century Atlantic by considering Africans' equally distinctive experiences of the process. It emphasizes not such conventional and Europe-derived abstractions as the 'impact of commercialization on Africa' but the strategies with which Africans made use of the commercial resources that European merchants brought to their shores, in the form of the familiar array of textiles, metalwares, alcohol, beads and shells, and firearms to exchange for gold, ivory, dyestuffs, other extracted commodities, and ultimately – and overwhelmingly – captive people. The chapter makes no effort to provide a history of the entire continent, but instead concentrates on the sub-Saharan regions most integrated into Atlantic historical processes, from Senegambia south along the coasts that Europeans knew as Upper and Lower Guinea to the Kongo-Angola areas of western central Africa, as far as the Kalahari Desert (modern Namibia). However, the processes outlined here for Atlantic Africa did parallel those of other Africans in contact with earlier and contemporaneous commercial credit from the Sahara, the Red Sea, and the Indian Ocean.

As the Atlantic 'age of revolutions' emerged as a staple of mid- and later twentieth-century narratives of the apparent distinctiveness of 'Western civilization', Africa remained beyond even the peripheries of this progressive vision of the era.[1] And as the historical discipline moved on to begin to problematize 'the rise of the West' in the 1960s and 1970s, and recently also into efforts to construe a more balanced and inclusive 'world history', Africa has remained one of its better kept secrets, in spite of a half century of innovative scholarly inquiry into the once-dark past of 'the continent without history'.[2] This chapter elaborates an Africanist's vision of the broader historical dynamics, of which the familiar 'age of revolutions' in the northern Atlantic at the end of the eighteenth century was a part, to show Africa's alternative experience of the same historical processes of the era. It views these dynamics in terms of African historical sensibilities quite different from the surge of whiggish optimism that burst forth in the late eighteenth-century North Atlantic and coalesced philosophically in the nineteenth century as progressivism.[3] As I hope to suggest, Africans agilely incorporated historical Atlantic commercialization into a restorative historical ideology – called 'tradition' by Europeans – that flexibly absorbed novelty and hence in practice was anything but static; from their dedication to community, Africans perceived the downside of commercialization as gluttony, betrayal, and isolation.

Modern historians of Africa, generally still in recovery from the racist excesses of the first half of the twentieth century, have bent over backwards to convince sceptical professional and popular audiences that – *pace* Hegel – Africa did indeed have a history. Both Africanist and world histories have thus tended to celebrate the continent's historical past in thoroughly modern 'imperial' terms of merchant trade and military conquest. To that extent, they ignore the distinctly less militarized or commercialized historical dynamics of the vast majority of the many distinct communities there. At best, scholars have acknowledged most of Africa's history as 'societies' contrasted negatively – and hence in analytically vacuous terms – with recognizable 'states' as 'stateless'.[4] In this chapter, I intend not to indulge in this polarization, which seeks to explain Africa in terms of modern political abstractions stemming from the Europeans' 'age of democratic revolutions'. Instead, I propose to proceed from a positive and analytical characterization of what Africans in fact *did*, in the intellectual contexts in which they did it.

The humanistic and sociological foundations of western historical thought produce its familiar claims to universality, and hence logically generate thematic unity around such homogeneous and singular abstractions as 'the state' and, in the era considered here, also 'empire'. But what circum-Atlantic and Asian regions shared in the seventeenth and eighteenth centuries was not a specific institutional solution, like 'empire' or 'nation', but highly diverse ways of participating in an accelerating global process of commercialization, in its initial, particularly freebooting phases. By the very particular nation-centred standards of the modern West, from which the historical discipline grew at the end of the nineteenth century, local and regional specifics other than those of Europe appear divergent, or at best unrelated. However, historians properly view the past not through the abstractions of modern social science but through the regional particularities of how people experienced this overarching process, each in terms of their own distinct local historical heritage. These local variations – not the homogenizing sociological 'model' – constitute the historiological theme of this chapter.[5]

Arraying this modernist logic of static and homogeneous abstractions through time, as historians' commitment to tracking 'change' inclines them to do, tends to create a neo-evolutionary succession of historical stages – for example, between 'ages' of monarchical absolutism and liberal democracy, or mercantilism and free trade – construed in terms of the logic of the historian more than the experiences of their participants.[6] According to this structuralist logic, the end of the eighteenth century appears to have been transformative, and distinctive to Europeans. In terms of these same abstractions, Africa remains no less unproblematically, even paradigmatically, 'different'. But we can escape the typological contrasts implied by this schema. We can instead contextualize both regions in a very long-term global incremental historical process of managing a complex dialectical engagement of militarized political authority and commercial strategies that depended on that authority in the short run but in the longer term also undermined it. In sixteenth- and seventeenth-century Europe, and particularly on its peripheries, this millennia-long contest between militarists and merchants was passing through a phase of consolidating a distinctively singular, monarchical form of militarized authority; Atlantic Africa was significantly less militarized and characterized by a multiplicity of strategies of political integration elaborating principles of complexity and composition rather than the singularity and homogenization of 'monarchy'.

This particular African style was one of a great many contemporaneous, similarly diverse historical political strategies in play around the seventeenth- and eighteenth-century world.[7] In the conventional social science logic of modernity, which homogenizes in order to standardize human behaviour, the multiplicity and complexities of historical sorts of change appear fundamentally incoherent, even contradictory. They were incoherent also to the historical actors creating them, or attempting to resist them, since people as historical actors always confront the unfamiliar – or the as yet even inarticulable – novelties of their present moments from perspectives necessarily drawing on the familiar, that is, from their own experience, or from their pasts. By this historicized notion of change, as human actions motivated by incompletely understood and increasingly irrelevant experience, elements of innovation and conservation are always present simultaneously. Only against backgrounds of assumed typological homogeneity of the abstract sort that characterizes 'ages' do they stand out as 'contradictions'. Seen historically instead, they become intelligibly motivated human initiatives, if also significantly uncomprehending of the full historical contexts that generate them and the contextual novelties that they in turn create. Historians, if they work properly according to the distinctively historical epistemology of change, contextualize human efforts motivated by aspects of the actors' times and places, rather than trying to define abstract 'ages'. When they do, they understand change historically: incremental, partial, dialectical, unpredictable, and – since it often arises from conservative intentions – all but by definition unintended.

First the familiar: the 'Age of Revolutions' in Europe's *longue durée*

The late eighteenth-century Atlantic, viewed thus through the eyes of its creators, can be shorn of the teleology implicit in seeing in it a transformative 'age of revolutions'. Instead, the era was an intensely felt moment in which people in Europe came to terms with a long-term incremental process of monarchical consolidation of militarized power as monarchs attempted to capture other, broader processes of intensifying commercialization through ideologies of overarching, impersonal government. Africans also integrated commercialization, but in terms of the personalistic 'communal ethos' of their local communities. Commercialization is thus the integrating historical theme; the opportunity in examining alternative local and regional processings of the motivating and enabling gains from commercialization, in their European as well as in African variations, lies in appreciating the intensity and anxiety of day-to-day engagements with relative strangers that financial investments emanating from northern Europe enabled everywhere.

To contextualize and thus appreciate the intensity of these reactions in the northern Atlantic, the historian looks back three centuries before 1700 to the security of belonging to local communities and the personalism of authority in late medieval Western Europe. Europeans lived in familiar communities not unlike what in Africa I am terming a 'communal ethos'. Such intimate communities had been based on ties of residence, religion, skills, and family; often all of these had coincided in tight little worlds that felt reassuringly 'known'. On continental Europe's then-peripheries local warlords in thirteenth-century England and Scandinavia, then fourteenth-century Portugal and fifteenth-century Spain, were only beginning to assert the singularity of overarching authority that lies at the core of the later notion of monarchical rule. To assert this authority on the greater scales that they were claiming, in terms of the directness and personalism as well as affirming the mutual responsibilities of local power and loyal client at that time, aspirant monarchs had to propound ideologies of benevolent patronage for the subjects whom they were thereby also rendering more remote, weaker, poorer, and thus simultaneously in greater need of the protection of personal patronage. That is to say that 'kings', in the sense that early eighteenth-century ideologies of absolutism enshrined in subsequent political ideology, were by no means obvious solutions to anyone's problems in those earlier times; in fact, abstract absolutism was all but unthinkable. Over succeeding centuries the growing costs of maintaining so abstract a sort of rule, at first in Christian terms and then in increasingly secular sequels, and the contradiction of attempting to imagine intimacy comparable to the older experiential personalism, made sustaining the personalism of monarchical ideology an increasingly challenging – and costly – proposition.

The gunpowder revolution of the fifteenth century multiplied the costs of the dynastic conflicts accompanying the expansive strategies of these aspiring military monarchs. The monarchs' growing debts turned them to merchants and bankers for the cash and credits they needed to keep up. Traders and investors, whose wealth was not restrained by geography, threatened landed aristocracies within their military domains at home. Rather than conceding their hard- and recently won local lands and control over resident populations, and with the power claimed by the great merchant families in the 'republics' of Renaissance northern Italy as examples of the potential wealth and power of commercial challengers to mere militarism, the rulers of maritime western Europe looked off into the vast Atlantic as a field where merchant enterprise might search safely for the bullion they increasingly needed at home to presume to rule as military overlords. In the Atlantic, merchants could even be allowed to move out beyond the restrictions prevailing within Europe to transacting the products of aristocratic and ecclesiastical estates and to invest in significant productive enterprises – mines and plantations – of their own. And, as firearms made the military geography of continental Europe more and more confining, in the sixteenth and seventeenth centuries, monarchs there found these effectively empty and even hypothetical – or at best symbolic – islands and military outposts in and beyond an ocean safer and cheaper fields in which to pursue their dynastic rivalries through proxy wars rather than continuing to attempt land invasions across the increasingly defined boundaries of their consolidated continental domains.

Commercialization thus gained momentum as a historical strategy in the sixteenth century not in Europe but on the islands in the eastern Atlantic off the coast of far-western Africa: Madeira, the Canaries, and São Tomé. Unlike most of continental Europe, where military and ecclesiastical authorities held landed domains and tried to immobilize their resident peasants to the exclusion of commercial interests growing in central Europe,[8] in these uninhabited – or depopulated – oceanic places the field for commercial investment in land and labour was effectively open. But this opportune emptiness of the vast Atlantic also had its costs, multiplied several thousand-fold in the even vaster and similarly empty – or emptied – Americas. Beyond the significant windfalls of gold and silver, merchants investing in so enormous a resource had to come up with funds to develop productive enterprises, stereotypically agricultural plantations, from scratch. Theirs was the quintessential challenge of capitalism: finding financing now, against promises of repayment later, in a future imaginable as sufficiently predictable to reduce its risks to manageable proportions. In the sixteenth century, only African gold and then the serendipitous riches of American silver made much of the American continent a viable investment, only for Spain, and largely in a precociously centralized legal framework aimed at supplanting the initial and potentially uncontrollable military forms of conquest that Cortés and his successors unleashed on meso-America. Only by the end of the seventeenth century did the maritime Atlantic become a viable commercial risk. Until then, merchants and their ships were exposed to pirates and privateers, including the Dutch West India Company (1621–1640s), in the politically unregulated areas 'beyond the line', but there they were also free to pursue fortunes beyond the fiscal grasp of monarchs in distant Europe.

American silver had paid for the unprecedented costs of militarization in Habsburg Spain from the middle of the sixteenth century. Silver funded Habsburg escalation of millennium-old religiously defined conflicts with the southern and eastern Mediterranean lands under Islamic control, recently consolidated by the Ottomans, as well as against the individualist independence of Protestant merchant communities in northern Europe. All of these targets of Habsburg ambition, including England, armed themselves in response. This row of consolidating seventeenth-century military monarchies, lined up like dominoes, also tipped continental France towards territorial consolidation, and then aggrandizement on Atlantic scales at the end of the seventeenth century. In response, England and the Netherlands, lacking territories to exploit and thus increasingly minor players on a European stage dominated by land armies, turned to the growing resources of Atlantic trade, creating new financial strategies to mobilize the massive investments necessary to operate on transoceanic scales and investing also in unprecedentedly costly navies.

However, by militarizing the Atlantic, European monarchs then found themselves facing the further challenges of financing naval and other military strategies that might fill the vast, semi-defined, highly competitive political vacuum they were entering.[9] As monarchs conceded privileges and even effective autonomy to planters and traders in the remote regions of the Atlantic, the costs of developing naval capacities to seize and defend the resulting claims to distant

territories raised the fiscal ante and propelled the process of commercial investment forward at accelerating tempos.[10] Western Africa was
strategically marginal in the military sense of primary concern to
European monarchies. It was commercially capable, especially around
the sources of the gold that had originally drawn the Portuguese and
then other Europeans to trade there. It was also populous and thus a
potential market for European (but mainly, as it turned out, Asian)
wares.[11] It was not a continent where European arms were effective
or even necessary to do business. Therefore, from the perspective of
the financial strains of expansion into the Atlantic, it was the relatively
inexpensive option. As a result, with the exception of an initial
monarchical interest in Africa's gold, centred in Senegambia (the
French Compagnie des Indes) and the Gold Coast (the English Royal
African Company), Africa attracted mostly minor merchants, and only
about a tenth of European commercial investment in the Atlantic
through the end of the eighteenth century.[12]

In the seventeenth century, to marshal the personnel and generate
the funds to protect these far-flung, expensive, and increasingly
competitive enterprises, Europe's military monarchs had to assert
increasingly direct authority over individuals as 'subjects', at home and
abroad. These pressures, backed ultimately by military force, set the
stage for the crises of confidence, and also of consciousness, that
erupted at the end of the eighteenth century in the northern Atlantic.
In the Americas European merchants' successes had attracted new and
heterogeneous human collectivities of strangers, all of them lacking
the reassuring familiarity of the small communities from which they
had come – whether Europeans, Africans, or Native American
survivors of the collapse of their own local communities from slaving,
diseases, and depopulation, if not also from direct assault by European
militias. The Africans there arrived utterly isolated as slaves and
remained subject to recurrent reisolation through sales to realize their
value as collateral for debt financing from Europe.[13]

Participation in the Europe-initiated commercial economy
provoked a century-long wave of political, and eventually cultural,
adjustments on pan-Atlantic scales. These adjustments first reached
intellectual coherence in the northern Atlantic at the end of the
seventeenth century in the form of enlightened individualism. That
philosophical ideal became a political ideology in the late eighteenth-
century implementation of a civic politics of individual citizens in
North America, and then in the early nineteenth century elsewhere
throughout the Americas. This rolling wave of transoceanic commercial integration, with its ideological formulation as modern civic indi-

vidualism and national citizenship, presented critical challenges to older, territorially based, military regimes, themselves no less changing products of a preceding wave of military consolidation as 'monarchies'. And not least in Europe.

Monarchical ideologies of personalistic authority in territorially consolidated realms were all but irrelevant to Europeans thus scattered through the remote vastness of the Americas, even more so than for subjects in Europe caught in the growing political contradictions of personal monarchical authority in increasingly impersonal royal domains. At the same time, the growing costs of militarizing on the enormous scales of the Atlantic required greater and greater and unprecedentedly direct taxation by the emerging monarchies, at first at home in Europe. Monarchs styling themselves as patrons were becoming intrusive, even abusive, rather than protective as they raised the cash costs of the personal consumption that was coming to define identities in the formative world of commerce that merchants were creating in the eighteenth century. Royal 'liberties' seemed betrayed, and people had to make sense of living amidst overwhelming insecurities, by themselves, in half-formed, often disruptively transient, communities in the Americas.

In the 1760s and the 1770s these anxieties provoked a moral crisis that erupted in ideological and political forms first in North America, the region where the largest assemblages of European castaways found themselves face to face with one another. At least an initial degree of commonality they discovered in the sense of betrayal they shared. Rebellious North Americans attempted to restore the integrity of the eighteenth-century British (no longer even coherently English) monarchical polity by entrusting sovereignty to themselves, rooting increasingly civic liberties across the Atlantic, beyond the inherently limited range of the personalistic ideology of monarchy. The political crisis was, first, one of perceived perfidy of the ideally personal and protective monarch,[14] and then increasingly popular and participatory by empowered citizens in the subsequent phases that have captured the teleological imaginations of the generations of historians focused on the forward-looking aspects of the so-called 'age of democratic revolutions'. However, even the liberal political philosophies of the time rested on monarchical notions of a singular, integrated, and comprehensive 'sovereignty', the historical result of Europe's long-term process of monarchicalization. In the Atlantic the ideal of political homogeneity as benevolent, abstracted and popularized in civic terms as individual 'equality', replaced the failed personalism and paternalism of monarchy militarized on Atlantic scales.

On the broad analytical scale of these incremental historical processes of political consolidation on scales that transcended individual human experience, the so-called 'revolutions' through which the Atlantic world passed at the end of the eighteenth century were locally varied intellectual and cultural acknowledgements of the integration of monarchical authority and militarization with commercial finance, which had been gathering momentum, and momentousness, since the 1500s in the confines of far-western maritime Europe. Through three centuries, the foundations of everyone's personal security in a communal ethos of belonging in, and contributing to, companies of familiars eroded towards the individualized, mobile, material-consuming 'self' that was consistent with survival by commercialized engagements with unknown others. Mobile individuals abandoned tried-and-true ancestral integrity to commit themselves to dealing with utter strangers in the so-called 'marketplace', alone, or – to no less motivating degrees of intensity and immediacy – in increasingly civic, or public, contexts.

However, few of the Europeans adrift on the Atlantic – as distinct from the armchair political economists in Europe[15] – had personal experience of dealing, at arm's length, with utter strangers on which they might base sufficient implicit trust in such contingent commercial contacts that they might sleep soundly at night. We modern heirs to this radical anonymity of 'the market' attempt to domesticate its disconcerting implications of uncertainty and vulnerability at the level of such collective abstractions as 'society' and 'nation'. These orderly abstractions are not experienced directly but are ultimately only imagined as secure ideological spaces that somehow provide 'freedom' and 'opportunity' for individuals who are otherwise profoundly, and defiantly proudly, alone. But before so anxious an ambivalence was rationalized, violence flared everywhere along the cutting edges of the process of commercialization. Historians have seldom appreciated the parallels in the carnage experienced by Native Americans with the violence of slaving in Africa.[16] In Africa as well as in the Americas, the people dragged through capture into utter isolation, and forcibly isolated again and again through repeated sales as the human property of others, were only the most extreme among many examples of personal vulnerability to the 'invisible hand' of the market.

The historical dynamics of commercial capital in Africa

Africa faced the same challenge of domesticating the competitive chaos and individualistic resort to material consumption that

European political theorists tried to render less threatening by imagining a benevolent, if invisible, guiding hand of the market. However,
Africa had not integrated a unifying universalistic ideology like
European Christianity, and its political systems were composites of
many small components rather than the singular and homogeneous
integrated monarchies there. The historical contexts of Africans'
personal engagements with a commercializing Atlantic thus contrast
with the abstract clichés of 'empires' and 'kingdoms' that predominate
in the historical literature on the continent.[17]

Africans were not unfamiliar with trade. Two millennia before the
Portuguese contacted the western Africans living south of the Sahara,
rural communities that specialized in exploiting environmental niches
in areas capable of supporting dense populations along the upper and
middle Niger River, and also artisan families that self-ethnicized like
their agricultural and other producer counterparts, had clustered in
composite towns to provide the products of their complementing
skills to one another, directly, personally. Trade in towns like these did
not depend on specialized merchants and did not require centralized
military power, or the monumental architecture that represented it,
like that which had developed out of similar, earlier similar initiatives
in Asia, and for which the classical Mediterranean and eventually
western Europe had – for millennia – been paying the bills.[18]

Africans' alternative community, political, and economic strategies,
like these sustainable towns, were the result not of their isolation, but
of their determination to preserve the personalism of their 'communal ethos'. On the Saharan margins and Indian Ocean shores of the
continent others had engaged other maritime commercial worlds
since the Phoenicians and other traders in Mediterranean antiquity
had thrived. Their engagements with merchant capital had become
significantly more intense since the integration of the vast and highly
commercialized Islamic oecumene in the eighth and ninth centuries.
In western Africa, villagers had domesticated even the external
commercial resources that Muslim traders from North Africa introduced from the ninth or tenth centuries. To cite only one example
known well to Africanists, desert-edge farmers there developed
networking strategies to channel regional products to and from the
Saharan region, based on commercial capital provided by Muslim
merchants from the north in search of the region's gold.[19] In an
ethnicized designation characteristic of Africans' accent on culturally
self-defined communities of producers rather than on their products,
the academic literature has characterized these professional traders as
'Soninke'. But historians might understand them in terms of the

historical strategies around which they created themselves as a prominent community, capable of taking initiatives. In these terms, these
Soninke reversed Africa's producer-centred system of distribution, in
which mobile buyers tended to seek out resident producers, as patrons
to clients, by making novel commercial initiatives based on external
credit. With it, groups of Soninke traders congregated to disperse
southwards with the products of others – the bars of rock salt
emblematic of the desert trade, leather goods and textiles imported
from North Africa, and other wares they provided to consumers in
the populous agricultural region beyond the desert, on credit. Though
their dispersal involved mercantile investments in transportation and
in inventories that might have inclined them towards the sort of
commercial relationships with strangers that the communal ethos
regarded as anathema, they instead worked through familial ties to
maintain cultural coherence and a strong communal ethos of their
own in small communities scattered across hundreds of miles. From
the point of view of the Soninke, and as they are commonly described
in the literature, their dispersed, ethnically distinct villages constituted
a 'trading diaspora'.[20]

The dispersed agriculturalist communities among whom these
Soninke settled returned the compliment by using several strategies
to domesticate the merchant-strangers, effectively building permanent, personal connections with them. Notably, they allowed the alien
traders to settle their lands as invited 'guests', in villages adjacent to,
but separate from, their own, and then built intimately personal
alliances with them by offering their daughters in marriages. The
traders in turn provided bride wealth and other gifts from their inventories of imported goods. Over time, both sides, landlords and
strangers, raised the children of the other to link the two communities on a basis structured to endure (literally) through the generations.[21] The permanence and personalism of relationships maintained
through marriage alliances reflected the valuation of continuity in the
communal ethos and also, in effect, created human collateral, wives
and offspring, for the imported goods offered initially – and presumably also on an ongoing basis – on credit. Within the framework of
the communal ethos, indebted communities commonly pledged
members to creditors as collateral. Human pledges like these – known
generally in the literature as 'pawns'[22] – were not abandoned but were
offered as prized tokens of trust among neighbours, with expectations
of indefinite duration, on the condition of responsible guardianship,
enforceable through other links derived from generations of prior
engagements. Even with Muslim capital financing the Soninke – and

eventually other – trading networks in western Africa, the communal ethos thus prevailed. The tendency to domesticate foreign credit was consistent throughout the varied strategies sketched here, and in many more throughout the continent.[23]

However, external commercial capital rarely reached the remainder of the continent. There the great majority managed to produce comfortable surpluses and to distribute them widely without abandoning what one might call the domestic political economy of the 'communal ethos'.[24] Villagers along the continent's Atlantic shoreline had exploited its marine wealth in salt and fish and circulated them widely through neighbouring local communities through marriages and other human relationships without resorting to commercial contacts with utter strangers, men with goods but without connections in the small, internally oriented communities in which they lived. They built their domestic political economies around ongoing personal relationships among members of face-to-face communities. These strategies contrasted with commercial societies constructed around personally advantageous, ad hoc exchanges with strangers to acquire material goods to hoard, or 'own' personally, as well as currency tokens of value to facilitate future, similarly acquisitive, exchanges. Africa's 'communal ethos' of mutual accountability resembled life in Europe's villages, guilds, parishes, and even monarchical domains before the seventeenth century more than it depended on the competitive – not to say frequently desperate – individualism on which traders far from home, often without significant social restraints, had to depend to prosper in the Americas.[25]

Other African kin-defined communities clustered in similarly composite coastal villages and inland towns with populations numbering in the tens of thousands.[26] In the watery mazes of the delta through which the waters of the Niger River reached the Gulf of Guinea and along the Congo River system in the forests of equatorial Africa, entrepreneurial 'big men' traded extensively along the extended navigable reaches of these vast riverine systems. From the profits of their canoe ventures they assembled 'houses' of retainers, not through reproduction and kinship but by recruiting traders, artisans, warriors, and paddlers as personal clients and – as always in Africa – as participants. They muted the opportunities for personal aggrandizement inherent in commercialization by requiring the 'big men' who became wealthy to contribute much – or most – of their personal gains to obtain anonymous positions of responsibility in 'secret societies'. The ranking members of these guilds, often hiding their personal identities behind elaborate masks, distributed their revenues for the collective welfare of the communities they had assembled.[27] In agricultural areas, where kinship and reproduction prevailed, bridewealth payments linked the relatives of a reproducing couple by distributing material assets rather than concentrating them to endow a presumed autonomous pair, as did European dowries. Africans thus developed large networks capable of distributing vast quantities of the products of skilled artisanry through personal relationships rooted in the strong collective identities of their communal ethos. All of these arrangements drew on their own, local financial resources to form and perpetuate relationships with kin, clients, wives, and fellows.

Atlantic commerce

The flexibility of the communal ethos, in practice infinitely responsive to the personalities and challenges of many local moments, made it resilient, an enabling means of pursuing varied historical strategies, as long as the accessible populations – wives, clients, pawns, and other dependants – remained adequate to engage the commercial resources available. That premise failed when Atlantic commerce, growing massively from the initial modest Portuguese ventures in the 1500s, overwhelmed this balance in the eighteenth century. Africans had embraced the Atlantic opportunities they had perceived in the sixteenth and seventeenth centuries, by and large defusing their disruptively individualizing potential through the strategies that their counterparts had used successfully to absorb earlier commercial credit introduced from the Islamic mercantile economies bordering the populous sub-Saharan regions of the continent on both the east and the north.[28]

This Atlantic era, known to European merchant investors and to American planters as the era of 'the slave trade', Africans experienced as a tidal wave of commercial capital, as the gradual accumulation of American specie in Europe, and its translation there into financial capital, overflowed into Africa. In the view of Africans committed to communal reciprocities and mutual responsibilities, the Europeans took voraciously while giving as little as possible and seldom investing in enduring relationships of reciprocity. These tendencies, which Africans saw as 'cannibalistic',[29] came to prevail in the eighteenth-century North Atlantic, as the so-called 'age of democratic revolutions' there eventually recognized, and – perversely – embraced.

Africans first engaged the Portuguese on small scales, and only incidentally. They had no reason to anticipate that successors to the Portuguese and other early European merchant-strangers whom they had had little trouble containing would carry forward an incremental process of capital accumulation that acquired a momentum of its own and that would leave their successors enmeshed in immense webs of debt and violence that none of them, alone, could turn back. Since for Africans people were the primary form of 'wealth', they initially preferred to sell commodities. Beyond the gold from the part of the western African coast that Europeans designated for the glittering prospect it held for them, Africans elsewhere provided ivory, dyewoods, animal pelts, malagueta 'pepper', and other tropical exotica to attract European commercial investment. Europeans accordingly named the parts of the coast where they acquired 'grain' (Upper Guinea, modern Sierra Leone, and Liberia, after the malagueta 'grains of paradise' available there) and 'ivory' (modern Côte d'Ivoire). In all of Africa, gold alone exceeded the value of captives sold as slaves until 1700.[30] Significantly, all of these commodities were extracted rather than being products of investment in agriculture or other capitalization that might in the long run have increased supplies. Since these commodities were therefore available only in limited quantities, growing European demand rapidly exhausted supplies.

From the African perspective, however, they were readily accessible to anyone, even younger men, guests, and clients without significant stakes in local communities under the authority of village elders or in political composites headed by regional chiefs. Marginal members of the small communities of most of the continent thus found the Europeans promising lenders of imported goods to finance personal advances outside the strong and hierarchical, and thus limiting, frameworks of their lives. European credit, at least in telling part, attracted a range of new African suppliers not linked to earlier generations of African trading partners. The opportunity brought by the Europeans was more like a gold rush than the capital-intensive development of plantations in the Americas, or – as it turned out – more like plundering than production.

Older communities – around the European castles along the Gold Coast, known as Fante, to the east the Allada polity trading with Europeans at Ouidah (Whydah), on beyond the Niger Delta, where English ships dealt with villages of fishermen, and along the coast to the east and south – initially waxed in size as they grew in repute among the traders from Europe. In the process, the chiefs of these composite polities, who had exercised relatively little personal authority within them but who represented the collectivity to outsiders, obtained imports from the strangers from the Land of the Dead beyond the maritime horizons visible from the coast and deployed them internally to recruit direct political clients. The men they recruited most cheaply were not always those with the most integrated and responsible positions within their home communities, the components of the political composite. That is, the people most receptive to the lure of European commercial credit were most marginal to the African communal ethos, less invested in its complex balances of personal relationships. They were therefore not particularly reluctant to defect to chiefs aiming to stand apart from the communities in the composites they represented and to aggrandize themselves personally, at the expense of others. Nor were they particularly loath, as Europeans competed among themselves by offering more 'trust' to more ambitious potential trading partners, to take personal advantage of these further opportunities to abandon the chiefs and to advance themselves independently of the web of relationships of the communal ethos, by providing whatever the Europeans wanted, by whatever means they might find necessary, including violent ones.

Competitive individuation, supported by the Europeans' commercial credit, turned systematically violent as the growing financial capacity of the Atlantic economy continued to stimulate it. In the later decades of the seventeenth century, older political regimes along the coast, including several that had consolidated around the earlier phases of Atlantic trading, collapsed into local conflict. Examples would include Senegambia and the Gold Coast, where gold and other commodity trades had thrived earlier, and the area around Ouidah (modern Bénin) that Europeans were already counting on as their 'Slave Coast'. In western central Africa, a part of the coast that the Portuguese had claimed since the 1570s as 'Angola', major trading networks developed from four principal points along the coast, a northern one at Loango, another centred on the mouth of the Congo/Zaire River, a third at the main Portuguese military base at Luanda, and the fourth in the far south at Benguela. In the second half of the seventeenth century, in a replication of the Muslim investment that had financed the Soninke in western sub-Saharan Africa, Dutch investments at Loango financed a diaspora of traders who settled well into the interior, seeking captives. Inland from Benguela and Luanda, Brazilian traders enlisted Africans as allies in violent assaults on local communities, and the regional components of the 'Kongo' network along the lower Congo River dissolved into pervasive armed conflicts that have been termed 'civil wars'.[31]

The fires of violence, once ignited, flared ever further inland, with the considerable costs of larger and more elaborately trained and equipped armies sustained by the even more rapidly increasing capacity of European merchants to invest commercial credit in Africa. Africans' initial sixteenth-century limited extraction of ivory and other commodities had by the 1670s spawned caravans and canoes filled with men armed to protect themselves during excursions into increasingly remote, unfamiliar, and unfriendly territories, all financed at the enabling margin from the trade goods they obtained on 'trust' from Europeans. By the end of the seventeenth century the armed bands of traders were turning increasingly to fighting one another. These conflicts, and outright raiding for captives, led to a series of populist uprisings – in the Senegambian region headed by Muslim *marabouts* (Sufi clerics), inland from the Gold Coast by Akan political authorities in the forests, behind the Slave Coast by war leaders who were under pressure from both the cavalry forces of the Yoruba polity of Oyo to the north and the growing slaving near the coast for captives to sell at Ouidah.

In the same era in western central Africa east of Luanda and Benguela, the heirs to mercenaries whom the Portuguese had enlisted in the early seventeenth century had settled in by the eighteenth century. Their militarized successors as warlords concentrated in the eastern savanna grasslands at Lunda and at Ovimbundu in the highlands inland from Benguela. In terms of the African communal ethos, all of these warrior polities represented a new and violent order, assemblages of refugees of the most diverse origins, whose primary loyalties were to their warrior protectors rather than to kin in the consensual composites of the older local communities. The relatively homogeneous political identities they proclaimed accordingly became the cores of the modern ethnic identities that many of their descendants claim still today. These new ethnicized political communities emerged at the same time as the similar homogenization of common subjugation to monarchs in Europe, the neo-ethnicized bases similarly popularized in the Atlantic 'age of revolutions' as 'nations'.

As this violent frontier of Atlantic investment retreated inland in violent surges from the late sixteenth to the late eighteenth centuries, new commercially oriented communities consolidated themselves nearer the African coast by assimilating the survivors, many of them acquired through slaving. The growing financial capacity of the Atlantic economy provided the credit through which these specialized trading groups acquired their members. These were based in a string of coastal towns from St Louis near the mouth of the Senegal River in far western Africa to Benguela in what is now southern Angola, all filled with captives from increasingly remote parts of the interior, retained as the traders' profits from dealing with the Europeans. With their European sources of material wealth, external to the balanced reciprocities of the mainland communities, these coastal entrepreneurs evaded the social and cultural controls of the communal ethos and the corresponding compositional strategies of political integration.

These warily 'trusted' partners of the European slavers also tended to indebt the warrior aristocrats to whom they distributed the wares they imported, in a shadowy conceptual zone with aspects of what western economic theory distinguishes as tributes, gifts, and sales. Over time, the heirs to the generals who had founded the no longer new warrior polities a generation or two earlier faced growing costs of consolidating and sustaining the bulky military institutions they inherited. The political collectivities of isolated refugees whom war leaders had unified were proliferating into local reproducing communities built around claims to two or three generations of locally born descendants. The once-unified subject populations the founding war leaders had assembled were thereby also disintegrating. The communal ethos was arising anew, from the ashes of the violent frontier of slaving. The beleaguered heirs to the warrior-founders of these polities then turned to the coastal brokers for commercial credit to finance them. Atlantic commercial credit thus financed militarization in Africa no less than in Europe.

By the 1750s, the African merchants along the coast had become strong enough in (African) terms of the personnel they had accumulated through slaving, and their credits had indebted their warlord trading partners sufficiently in commercial Atlantic terms, that the bills began to come due. The accommodations reached, since the African warlords were effectively bankrupt, involved liquidation of the human assets they had accumulated through sales of people to Europeans and eventually provoked take-overs by the commercial suppliers on the coast. The ensuing transitions from militarism to mercantile-oriented political control proceeded, one by one, from the late eighteenth through the nineteenth centuries in many particular ways, in the many separate historical spaces on a continent that was not the unitary 'country' that it still appears to some modern observers to have been. An early example occurred in Loango, where the Dutch had financed diasporic traders in the early eighteenth century. Inland from Luanda, control of the warrior Imbangala polity at Kasanje, the main direct supplier of captives to the Portuguese at Luanda, in the 1750s fell to a representative of the principal local Angolan trading diaspora financed by Atlantic capital. As oral tradition later recalled this profound moment, in characteristically personalized and concrete images, this 'king was the first one who kept his trade goods in his compound', as opposed to distributing imports through the networks of relationships to form a composite polity, still in this era characteristic throughout Africa.[32] Similarly, African traders who were by then working through the cavalry regime at Oyo inland from the Slave Coast in the 1770s joined with royal slaves conducting the burgeoning trade to the north at the time to execute a palace coup against the last of the warrior successors of the regime's original rulers.[33] The community of Brazil-oriented merchants at Ouidah – under the famous Francisco Felix de Sousa – took advantage of withdrawal of English and French competitors after 1808, in the Atlantic age of abolition, to engineer the succession of a ruler in Dahomey, who appointed de Sousa as ambassador to the European traders of the 1830s.[34] In parts of the continent more remote from the coast, there were similar scattered moments of what can, in slightly obsolescent terms of European historiography, be called a 'bourgeois revolution'.

The historical dynamics of debt

Africa thus paralleled the experience of western Europe in substance, in sequence, and in timing along an intricate dialectical process of militarization, commercialization, and assemblage of populations of unprecedentedly diverse backgrounds in new political collectivities. However, in contrast to Europe, the African historical dynamics emanating from the Atlantic in the sixteenth to eighteenth centuries proceeded at inflationary rates, forced by the rapidity with which European commercial capacity increased. Atlantic capitalism grew faster than Africans could boost the productive capacities of their domestic economies, reliant as they were primarily on human reproduction, and production for internal consumption. These were the economic implications of the continent's 'communal ethos'. Under pressure already in the sixteenth century to keep up with commercial demand for exports, individuals in Africa turned first to extraction of commodities. In the later seventeenth century, escalating competition financed by growing European credit turned violent, and the violence became the vehicle through which African slavers extended the general strategy of extraction to capturing people. By the early eighteenth century, slaving had become the principal African means of achieving and then defending radically individuated power, primarily by acquiring and retaining people in Africa, with sales of as few as possible to European slavers as Atlantic means to African ends of accumulating dependants.

However, on Atlantic scales, the European credit that financed this African historical dynamic was not unlimited. As Africa never absorbed more than about 10 per cent of the commercial assets that European financiers invested around the Atlantic, the slaves attracted relatively little interest from the principal investors in Europe's emerging financial capitals in London, Paris, and Amsterdam, or even Bordeaux or Lisbon. Wealthy European merchants in these centres enjoyed less risky opportunities much closer to home and in the Atlantic concentrated their investments in the Americas, within increasingly dense legal frameworks created by their own monarchs. In England's mainland colonies in America, Boston, New York, and Philadelphia had bigger fish to fry, cod among them, leaving slaving there to small towns in Rhode Island.[35] This larger Atlantic context of financial strategizing consigned Africa to marginal, less well financed, often somewhat desperate merchant investors in Europe, who had limited opportunities to engage in less dirty forms of business.[36]

Nonetheless, by African scales, the hundreds of slaving captains competing each year to do business in Africa through debt-based strategies – as well, of course, as through other, more violent, tactics spurred on by rivalries among a half dozen or more European monarchs engaged in Atlantic-scale conflicts by the eighteenth century – poured commercial credit into African economies. This financing escalated competition among their African suppliers at the very time that the natural endowments of resources they were extracting as commodities dwindled. African players, marginal to begin with in their local communities, resorted to violence to cover speculative investments in shrinking supplies. Without prior elaboration of ideologies of individualism or commercial institutions and burdened by investments transcending the internal focus of their small communities, African strangers whom Atlantic commerce drew into intensifying competition with one another had few ways to resolve disputes among themselves. Further, no international law bridged the commercial economy of the Atlantic and the communal economies of Africa to guarantee repayment of the credits Europeans extended.[37] One can only speculate at the extent of the working misunderstandings that facilitated transactions along African coasts that Europeans understood as individually contracted, repayable debt, but that Africans interpreted through their ethos of communal relationality as the largesse of patron-like figures investing in relationships of obligation meant to be maintained.

Parallel historical dynamics of the eighteenth-century Atlantic

As commercialization pervaded the lives of North Atlantic consumers in the second half of the eighteenth century, Africans deploying the goods they obtained from Europeans to assemble significant and growing numbers of people, through slaving, were proceeding along lines closely parallel to the Euro-American accumulation of other Africans in the Americas, also through slaving. By the middle third of the eighteenth century, African military rulers, who sustained themselves primarily by the plunder of continuing conquests, including captives, simultaneously reached the logistical limits of political integration through violence; their costs of maintaining their military capacities exceeded the gains from capturing. The commercial enterprises that organized transportation to and from coastal entrepôts over longer and longer distances were absorbing newcomers brought in through ongoing slaving. As a result, and again in instances as many and as varied as the dozens of local historical contexts along Africa's Atlantic coasts, the merchant interests married in or otherwise gained control of the central positions in the old warrior polities.

This African 'frontier' of slaving followed a violent historical dynamic recurrent throughout the world's history, including the contemporaneous northern Atlantic. Everywhere, the initially low costs of violent military methods of seizing political control became unsustainable as they rose in the longer term. Since merchants prospered far beyond the ranges where mounted warriors could ride or troops could march, heirs to merchants who had initially sustained struggling formative military regimes tended to profit sufficiently from their investments to intrude on the power of their former sponsors. Militarists sustained themselves primarily in circumstances of renewed threat, creating enemies when necessary to do so, and (or) excluding merchants from monarchical domains. In the seventeenth and eighteenth centuries in maritime Western Europe this contested and violent dynamic of commercialization and escalating militarism gained unique momentum owing to the low entry costs of exploiting the then all but empty Atlantic and the depopulated Americas. With the late seventeenth-century 'financial revolution' in England, the bullion bought in Africa and looted and then mined from meso-America accelerated the nascent commercialization of the Atlantic to levels of capitalization in Europe that were self-sustaining. Africa, on the other hand, experienced this commercialization in compressed, indebted, and ultimately tragic ways. That is, European commercial investments in Africa stimulated in stark form, and in hardly more than a century between the descent into pervasive violence after the 1670s and the wave of commercial seizures of the military power of African polities at the end of the eighteenth century, a historical process of ebbs and flows of military initiatives and commercial integration that Eurasian regions had sustained over nearly five millennia – though at ever-escalating costs.

The initially defensive and relatively homogeneous political communities in the late seventeenth and early eighteenth centuries that the exigencies of violence in Africa enabled skilled warriors to form paralleled the unique and direct personal authority that landed lords in late-medieval Europe were then also claiming as monarchs. The most successful of these warrior-kings in Europe went on to establish this personalized and comprehensive authority as 'early-modern' monarchies. That is to say, unlike the externally oriented guardians at the cores of contemporaneous composite polities in Africa (of which Europe also earlier had had its religious equivalents), European monarchs attempted to assert direct and personal power over everyone living within territorially defined domains, claiming nominally protective roles for themselves but becoming as brutal – and ultimately as expensive – in practice as circumstances might necessitate. Africa's equivalent cohort of early eighteenth-century 'kings', the warlords who asserted unified and direct control over the refugees and slaves isolated by spreading violence, emerged at the same time as, and out of commercializing processes parallel to, the consolidation of absolute monarchy in Europe.

The parallels continue. In Africa, the merchant groups supported by European credit helped the warlords to cover the costs of their expensive military overheads to the point that these commercial interests prospered sufficiently to move into the centres of their polities. In western Europe the specie and other revenues from the remote Atlantic intensified the dynastic contests within Europe to the level of impasse in the seventeenth century. The military monarchies on the Atlantic fringes of the continent then turned to commercial resources, especially in the Atlantic, to pay for continuing pursuit of their military ambitions at home. But the initial complementing phases of these endeavours became competitive in the later eighteenth century when the consolidating military monarchies attempted to bring the growing transatlantic economy under fiscal control. Liberal ideologies of commerce, and their 'democratic' counterparts in the sphere of civic politics, provided the ideological coherence that justified revolt in the Americas, as well as in Paris.

However, Africa's 'restorative' historical vision contained the parallels to what westerners thus experienced as radical change within the conceptual framework of the 'communal ethos'. Africans saw continuity rather than change.[38] Owing to the violence-inducing rapidity with which European credit had drawn Africa into the commercializing world of the Atlantic, most Africans turned towards their communities in search of refuge and security. They tried to tap local resources of relationality to assimilate external debt, and they were trying to contain individualism at home. European merchants abroad, on the other hand, were riding a wave of commercialization rooted in centuries of incremental innovations in Asia and Europe, far from the residues of the comparable ethic of personalism and social responsibility in Europe. There, the moral terms of community integrity had troubled only a few of the people that commercialization displaced from older protections of patronage. Most, particularly in the Atlantic, saw opportunity, and in the eighteenth century they embraced individual autonomy and asserted personal 'rights' in polities construed in civic terms.

The new civic sovereignties asserted at the end of the eighteenth century became 'national' only subsequently, in the sense of a presumed, naturalized, trustworthy political community – and very, and often agonizingly, gradually.[39] The coalitions of leaders of the new republican states, initially united primarily against the kings, in Britain, France, and Spain, soon fractured in varying ways over the subsequent challenges of blending the highly diverse populations for whom they claimed responsibility into theoretically homogeneous national communities. In the *longue durée* of global historical dynamics, evident also in Africa, the era's political rhetoric of popular 'equality' before the institutions of a civic state attempted to reclaim the betrayed protections of monarchical subjects by asserting an imagined participatory consensus, a sense of direct, personal, civic belonging equivalent to the 'communal ethos' that Africans managed to maintain.

The people whom Africans had sold as slaves, however, recalled the experience we depict as 'capture', in characteristically modern terms of violated personal and bodily dignity, less optimistically. Their descendants in the southern United States recalled the stories their grandparents had told in characteristically African terms of relationality, as 'betrayal'.[40] The perpetrators who disrupted the mutually supportive communal ethos were perceived by Africans as a plague of greedy witches, as vultures picking at the bodies of the socially dead, as anyone in a communal ethos that constituted being as belonging in fact was.[41] Africans responded with increasingly desperate strategies to restore the integrity of their disintegrating communities, but through self-defeating resort to assembling outsiders through the slaving to which they had been reduced in order to keep up with the pace of commercial disintegration. Like Europeans scattered in the Americas asserting themselves as civic 'nations' to recover the security their formerly benevolent monarchs had betrayed by taxing and intruding, Africans created an approximation – however hollow – of what they had lost by covering these aggregates of strangers with the inclusive language of their communal ethos.[42]

The small communities in Africa's composite polities became contenders for the singular power of direct monarchical-style hierarchical authority rather than continuing in the modes of collaborators sustaining a form of authority in which all participated. Africans thus drew their communities ever more tightly together, in a moral climate of suspicion and latent disorder. By the logic of the communal ethos, the only perpetrators whom they could imagine within were, of course, themselves, and they thus expelled members of their own communities as 'witches', many of whom ended up sold away to Europeans, being far too dangerous for others in Africa to retain. Thus Africans looked inward rather than seeking public and political responses to the personal crises of commercialism, while Europeans looked outward, exaggerating their moment of recognition of a centuries-long series of incremental extensions of seemingly familiar ways as a transformative contrast.

The survivors of enslavement in the Americas, innocent of course, then remembered their expulsions as betrayals by those whom they had believed they could trust. Their feelings of abandonment, too, were the African counterparts of the intense resentments of American rebels who began as loyalists to monarchs in Europe stressed by the costs of the pan-Atlantic enterprises on which they had embarked. The African explicit accent on the personal isolation and social costs of commercialized – or 'capitalist' – modernity thus highlights challenges that the conventional discipline of history struggles to comprehend directly, because it is – or has been, up to now – quintessentially modernist, built on the very conceptual premises that anchor the modern abstractions of the social sciences, nationalism, and other intellectual conceits logically incapable of generating critiques of themselves. Africans' perceptions of Atlantic commercialization in terms of its costs in human relationships thus have as much to teach us about the late eighteenth-century ideological crystallization affirmed in Europe and America as 'democratic revolutions' as our understanding of commercialized encounters with strangers teaches us about Africans' intense devotion to their communities and the Atlantic historical processes that corroded them.

7

Playing Muslim: Bonaparte's Army of the Orient and Euro-Muslim Creolization

Juan Cole

Arab Muslim civilization was a multivalent cultural symbol for the French of the Enlightenment and revolutionary eras. Muslims were made to stand for both Self and Other, were deployed as both icons of enlightenment and symbols of hidebound rigidity. The most thorough experience the French of the Revolutionary era had with Muslims came during Napoleon Bonaparte's conquest and occupation of Egypt. How did the French construct this religion that was so alien to them? What differences were there among them in this regard? My question is not 'what did Islam mean to them?' in a unitary sense, but 'what were the various sorts of things they used Islam to symbolize?' More interestingly, how did they see the interplay of identity between Egyptian Muslims and French Deists? The other side of the coin is the question of how Egyptian intellectuals invoked French cultural symbols for their own, internal purposes.

The French invasion created new possibilities for cultural mixing, as both the French and Egyptians deployed key symbols of the Other for the purposes of the Self. It is this sense in which I use the term 'creolization' here. As Feo Rodrigues writes,

> The process of creolization . . . is not merely an encounter between two or more cultures that results over time in the formation of a new culture with its own internal logic and coherence. Creolization is here defined as a creative process crafted from the tensions of colonial societies, subverting the daily practice of colonialism in many social domains. It is also a process that cuts across structures of inequality, transforming both colonizer and colonized. This process is hardly ever homogeneous and pervasive through time.[1]

Just as biological mixing (*métissage*) challenged conceptions of essential races, so cultural mixing produced areas of liminality or scandal. The term as deployed here does not assume a homogeneity of either French or Egyptian culture, and is attentive to gradations of admixture, which can support or defy colonial authority.[2] Bonaparte's dalliance with Islam, so controversial with the stricter partisans of the Enlightenment, was only one such outrage. Mixing of cultural and institutional forms was typical of the late eighteenth-century renewed European onslaught on the global south. In Madras in that period, British administrator Lionel Place 'is reported to have adopted the role of an indigenous king, when . . . he was appointed the collector of the *Jagir*, the district surrounding Madras city'.[3] Anthropologist Mattison Mines remarks of this sort of institutional creolization (which he refers to as 'hybrid'):

> Acting as he did, Place conjoined British Company officer and kingly Indian big-man in his self-representation, indicating that he understood his role as the administrator of the Jagir as a dual one, playing the part of a local ruler as well as that of a Company officer. Not surprisingly, British regulations and bureaucratic procedures in Madras provided little control over the pragmatics of personal loyalties and enmities, which this opportunistic society based on personal alliances engendered.[4]

Mines thus points to another element in creolization, its ad hoc and personalistic character. Creolization is characteristic of preindustrial colonialism, before the European marginal superiority in arms, productivity, and organization permitted a more thoroughgoing imposition of cultural and institutional forms on the colonized – though new kinds of mixing emerged in later centuries. An important characteristic of creolization is that it is seen as illegitimate by the strongest representatives of the traditions it mixes together, just as mulattos had a marginal position in society.

C. A. Bayly has noted the irony that the French Revolution was experienced in Afro-Asia not as liberating but as a new Christian crusade, given that the revolution impelled colonialism in Egypt and the East Indies. The democratization of warfare through conscription allowed the deployment of bigger armies than ever before, and the industrialization of warfare gave European armies marginal advantages over Afro-Asian ones. European imperial conquests provoked Afro-Asian counter-revolutions, whether from the top by modernizing elites or from the bottom by increasingly networked clerics and by millenarian peasants and townsmen. At the level of culture and ideology, creolization, or the mixing of civilizational ideas, gave tools to European scientists, explorers, and military men thrust into a globalizing environment, as well as to Afro-Asians negotiating new roles in colonial environments.[5]

★ ★ ★

Eighteenth-century Egypt was a vassal state of the ramshackle Ottoman Empire, which had begun regularly losing wars to Austria in Europe and which had decentralized the administration of its far-flung Middle Eastern provinces as a result. The Ottomans, like many of their Muslim predecessors, maintained slave-soldiers. The Janissary infantry had its origins in a form of slavery, wherein mainly Christian boys in the Balkans were taken by the sultan and converted to Islam and trained in martial arts. The expense of bureaucratic standing armies and the importance of tribal levies in the arid Middle East contributed to the rise of slave-soldiery. In arid and semi-arid ecologies, pastoral nomads specialize in using land too dry for farming for occasional pasturage and animal husbandry, which can only be accomplished if the pastoralists are mobile. Tribal kinship organization and the skills of horsemanship and camel use made the pastoralists a formidable natural cavalry. Overdependence on tribes, however, posed dangers for rulers, since pastoralists' primary loyalty was to their own chieftains, and tribal coups against the state were frequent in Middle Eastern history.

Since slavery is a form of social death, in which slaves are cut off from their previous lives and families, they were theoretically more likely to give their complete loyalty to the ruler than were tribesmen, and rulers often packed barracks with such slaves or former slaves. In fact, Ottoman slave-soldiers in Egypt organized themselves by 'house' and established forms of fictive kinship, giving them a corporate solidarity that under some circumstances allowed them to come to power and to overshadow the weak, frequently rotated, Ottoman governor. The Egypt that Bonaparte set out to conquer was thus ruled by beys who had earlier in life been young slave-boys, owned by officers who trained them in horsemanship and sword- and gunplay. Typically the young slave-soldier would be manumitted when he grew a full beard, and would become a junior officer in the 'house' of his former master. Most slave-soldiers came from the Caucasus, but at the top one saw a shift from Circassian beys to Georgian ones in the late eighteenth century.[6] In 1798, Egypt was ruled by a duumvirate, consisting of Ibrahim Bey and Murad Bey. Although theoretically vassals of the

Ottoman sultan, Selim III, these two beys seldom sent tribute to Istanbul, and Bonaparte made the case that they were *de jure* in rebellion against their empire, such that his deposition of them was a favour to Selim III. Istanbul did not see the matter in that light.

Beneath the beys and their slave-soldiers (*kol* in Turkish, *mamluk* in Arabic) were Egyptian notables. Some were large landowners, others had managed to become administrators despite their native Egyptian rather than Caucasian heritage. More often, they were great merchants, Muslim clergymen, and Coptic Christian shopkeepers and bureaucrats. Eighteenth-century Egypt came in portions of one-tenth. It was perhaps 10 per cent urban, 10 per cent pastoralist, and 10 per cent Christian. Most Egyptians, of course, were Muslim peasants. Bonaparte's strategy was to attract to himself the Egyptian notables and middle strata, including the Muslim clergy (however unlikely that prospect), and to replace the deposed beys and slave-soldiers with them.

On his invasion of July 1798, Bonaparte vainly sought to quiet apprehensions of Egyptians with his Islam policy.[7] He sought the imprimatur of both formal Islam and Egyptian popular religion for his rule. The first portion of the proclamation he issued on arriving in Egypt went something like this, as translated from the Arabic version rather than the French:

> In the name of God, the Merciful, the Compassionate. There is no god but God, who has no son, nor any partner in His dominion. From the French Republic, which is based upon the foundation of being free and socially levelled: The great General Bonaparte, commander of the French armies, informs all the people of Egypt that for an extended period of time the regiments that dominate Egypt have acted towards the French community with scorn and contempt. Now has arrived their hour of punishment. What a pity it is! For a period of long centuries, this gang of slave-soldiers from the lands of Abaza and Georgia has been wreaking corruption in the most beautiful of climes, the like of which does not exist anywhere else on the entire earth. As for the lord of the worlds, Who is omnipotent, He has decreed the extinction of their government.
>
> Egyptians! They may say to you that I have only arrived in this region with the intention of wiping out your religion. That is a transparent lie. Do not believe it. Say to the slanderers: I only came to you in order to rescue your religion and your rights from the hand of tyrants. I am more than the slave-soldiers worshipping God, may He be praised and exalted. And I respect His prophet, Muhammad, and the glorious Qur'an. Say also that all the people are equal before God. The thing that distinguishes them one from another is only intellect, virtues, and knowledge. Among the slave-soldiers, what intellect, virtues, and knowledge distinguish them

from others, or require that they monopolize all those things that make life in this world sweet? Wherever there is fertile land, it belongs to the slave-soldiers, and likewise wherever there are beautiful slave-girls, the best horses, the most opulent dwellings, all these belong to them alone. If the land of Egypt is the fief of the slave-soldiers, let them display for all to see the title to it that God wrote out for them! He is kind and just to human beings by his succour, may he be exalted. From this day and henceforth, no one from among the people of Egypt shall be excluded from high office or from acquiring exalted rank. The wise, the virtuous, the learned shall direct affairs. Thus, the condition of the entire community will be reformed. In Egypt's past, the cities were great, the bodies of water were wide, and commerce flourished. All this would have continued had it not been for the greed of the slave-soldiers.

Judges, clerics and prayer leaders, city officials, and town notables: Say to your community that the French are also pure *muslims*. As proof of this, they descended on Rome the grand and destroyed therein the throne of the Pope, who used always to encourage Christians to make war on Islam. Then they set out for the island of Malta, and expelled from it the knights who used to assert that God requires them to make war on the Muslims. In the meantime, the French at every moment were the most sincere lovers of his majesty, the Ottoman sultan, and the enemies of his enemies, may God prolong his rule.[8]

Bonaparte's assertion that the French were Muslims seems absurd, but it is not as absurd as the English rendering makes it appear, since in Arabic the word muslim could simply mean anyone who had submitted to the one God, and non-Muslims are represented in the Qur'an as calling themselves 'muslim' in this sense. Bonaparte attempted to co-opt the Muslim clerical class as allies from the indigenous middle stratum against the Mamluks.

The prominent cleric at al-Azhar Seminary in Cairo, 'Abd al-Rahman al-Jabarti, wrote a polemical commentary on this proclamation.[9] The term 'liberty' posed a special problem for the al-Azhar cleric. In Arabic, there was at that time no conception of political liberty in the French, British, and American sense (just as there was no practical experience with the idea in most of Europe outside the North Atlantic powers). In the Middle East, absolute, divine-right monarchy was the only known political system, so that the idea of voting for members of parliament was an alien one. The word 'freedom' or *hurriya* denoted the state of being a free person as opposed to being a slave. Since Bonaparte devoted so much of his proclamation to attacking the Ottoman-Egyptians, slave-rulers, al-Jabarti wondered if he meant to boast that he, unlike them, was a freeman and had no slave origins. The chronicler inadvertently demonstrated that Bonaparte's proclamation, intended to introduce Egyptians to key political ideas of the French Republic, was using a neologism that could not easily be fathomed. Tellingly, when al-Jabarti revised his commentary in later years, he took out this speculation, since by then he had gained an understanding, at least, of what they meant by the word.

Coming to the statement that the French had destroyed the throne of the Pope, al-Jabarti wrote that in doing so, they had opposed the Christians. 'This people has opposed the Christians and the Muslims', he maintained, 'and has followed none of the religions. We see them as atheist materialists who reject the Resurrection and deny prophecy and revelation.' He added that they 'assert that the world has always existed', rather than having been created, as the scriptures taught. He bizarrely accused them of believing in astrology, such that the position of the stars dictates the rise and fall of nations, and of believing in reincarnation, using that to explain why they did not ritually sacrifice animals. These alleged French beliefs are actually just themes drawn from medieval Muslim descriptions of heresies and foreign beliefs (some of them obviously Indian), and al-Jabarti in speaking this way about the French was propagandizing against them to the other literate Muslims in the capital. His polemic enshrined a form of creolization, insofar as he assimilated the non-standard beliefs of the French revolutionaries to those of the Hindus whom Muslims had encountered in the medieval period, whose beliefs were similarly alien to the Abrahamic traditions with which most Muslim thinkers felt comfortable.

We may deduce that al-Jabarti viewed religions as composed of a theology, a prophetology, a religious Law, and a set of distinctive customs. That he saw religion as having this fourfold character made it impossible for him to accept Bonaparte's attempt to liken Enlightenment Deism to Islam. The republican French posed a puzzle to the Muslim scholar. Theologically, they were Unitarians, like Muslims; but in their social customs they resembled other Christians, and they rejected any theory of divinely inspired prophecy or the revelation of religious Law, which for al-Jabarti was the core of religion. Bonaparte made the typically Western error of thinking about Islam primarily as a doctrine, whereas for a Middle Easterner such as al-Jabarti, it was a way of life. Further, consider the five pillars of Islam. For most Muslims such as the Egyptian cleric, Islam lay in the five pillars of recognizing the uniqueness of God and the prophethood of Muhammad, praying five times a day, fasting in the month of Ramadan, giving alms to the poor, and going on pilgrimage to Mecca at least once in a lifetime. Bonaparte had nothing to say about any of these pillars except for half of the first one (monotheism). From al-Jabarti's perspective, the concordance of mere doctrine said little about how alike two religious systems might be (otherwise Judaism and Islam could easily be conflated). All this is not to say that the proclamation had no effect. Literate peasants read it differently than the Cairene patrician, apparently, for he reported that in the country-side Bonaparte's claim to be acting on behalf of the Ottoman sultan was believed by some. Although al-Jabarti in his writings about the French adopted a tone of high dudgeon, in the later of them he was covering for his years of collaboration with the French. He served on the French Diwan or Directory, helping the French to run the country. He functioned for three years in essence as a senator of the French Republic of Egypt (i.e. the hybrid government of French officers overseeing governing councils consisting of Egyptian notables, now independent of the Ottoman sultan).[10]

Pierre Amedée Jaubert, an Orientalist, compared Bonaparte's proclamation, which called on the Egyptian middle strata and little people to welcome French rule as a liberation from the grasping Ottoman-Egyptian beys, to the slogan used by the early revolutionaries, which represented them as being on the side of the ordinary folk: 'War to palaces! Peace to cottages!'[11] He implied that Bonaparte's proclamation was of a similar tenor and likely to be just as successful.

Bonaparte pursued his Islam policy vigorously. General Desvernois observed of Bonaparte in August 1798 that '[a]ssociating himself with their national festivals, appearing to interest himself in whatever they were interested in, he benevolently welcomed their shaykhs and prayer leaders, conversed frequently with them, seeking to be instructed in the needs of the country and the means of making it prosper. Sometimes, even, in order to flatter their religious prejudices, he let them entertain the expectation that the republican army was not far from embracing the faith of Muhammad.'[12] In late August, he corresponded with the prominent Muslim cleric of Alexandria, Sheikh al-Masiri, whom he had met on taking the city. 'You know the particular esteem', he wrote, 'that I conceived for you at the first instant I met you.' He expressed a hope of meeting soon with 'all the wise and learned men of the country' to establish 'a uniform regime, founded on the principles of the Quran, which are the only true ones, and which can alone ensure the wellbeing of men'.[13] These breathtaking phrases not only enticed al-Masiri with an offer of high office but also pledged to establish rule by shariah or Islamic canon law. Bonaparte may not have realized how novel the offer was within the context of Ottoman statecraft. The Ottoman Empire, despite being a

Muslim state, did not always implement Islamic canon law as it was interpreted by the clerics. The Ottoman sultans, with their Mongol and Turkish cultural background, inherited a Central Asian conception of the ruler as heaven-favoured legislator in his own right. The *kanun* or law code of Suleiman the Magnificent, and the whims of viceroys and governors, were often more important in Ottoman administration than the precise rulings of the Muslim jurists. In premodern times, Islamic law courts were only one of a number of judicial institutions in the empire. They specialized in personal status law (marriage, divorce, and inheritance). Businessmen had the option of taking disputes to the *qadi* or Islamic-law judge, but they might well prefer to have an Ottoman official decide the case on pragmatic grounds instead. Ottoman officials could be disdainful of the clerics as narrow-minded or fixated on unhelpful minutiae. Ironically, Bonaparte was more favourable to this group than their own government sometimes was.

Moiret wrote that 'the politicians' argued that speaking well of Islam and hinting that the French might convert were necessary to safeguard the army. They instanced the Roman emperors, who, they said, allowed the peoples they conquered to retain their laws and religions for the most part. 'Rather than forcing them to adopt the gods of the capital, they placed there the gods of Athens and Carthage.' The idea of the Muslim Allah as simply another idol, like Zeus in Athens or Baal in Carthage, which could be added to some deities' hall of honour in Paris along with the gods of other vanquished peoples, fails to reckon with both Muslim universalism and Muslim particularism. The Egyptian chronicler al-Jabarti makes this point when he argues that the deism of the French no more made them Muslim than the monotheism of the Jews did. Much later, on his return from his failed attempt to take Palestine, Bonaparte circulated an Arabic pamphlet in which he misrepresented the campaign as a glorious victory, 'promising to the Egyptians that he would build a mosque at Cairo that would have no equal in the entire world, and that he would adopt the Muslim religion'.[14]

If the French were sometimes willing to accommodate Islam, they hoped the ulema would take a step towards their values, as well. Moiret describes the first festival celebrating the revolution in Egypt, around September 1798, thus: 'The Diwan, the principal officials of each province, and the first magistrates of each village, were invited to the celebration and attended a dinner given by Bonaparte. This was the first time one saw the French colours united with Ottoman ones, the turban associated with the bonnet of liberty, the Declaration of the Rights of Man with the Koran, the circumcised and uncircumcised at the same banquet, with the difference that the former took sherbets and other beverages, while the other took [wines].'[15] This passage uses the technique of parallelism to suggest that the banquet was a site of creolization.

The hopes placed by some of the French in the ulema appear to have been based on analogy. They were, for all their religious trappings, the social stratum closest to the French intelligentsia themselves. Many in the officer corps had been initially schooled by local abbés and some, like Captain Moiret, had even spent time in seminary. To hope that the Egyptian clergy might take the one step towards Enlightenment deism that would be necessary to make intellectuals of them did not seem utopian in this light. Their evident interest in printing and other engines of modernity also betrayed a practical side to this group.

The militant partisans of the Enlightenment, on the other hand, tended to view Islam as a crucible of superstition. They often saw first-hand evidence of popular religious enthusiasm, involving what to them seemed like bizarre and barbarous rites. Of course, the formally trained Muslim clergy or ulema would have denied that such practices had anything to do with Islam. Ironically, bilingual Egyptians of the middle strata were probably the chief interpreters to the French of the meaning of popular religious practices, and some of their own disgust with them was probably transmitted to the Europeans. That is, the representation of one Egyptian social stratum by another as indigenous practice now becomes part of the basis for a transnational Orientalism.

An irony is that some of the more rationalist memoirists, who thought they were condemning Islam and all religion as superstition, actually reproduced the critique of popular religion common among the Muslim clerics themselves. In response to soothsayers' predictions that the French would adopt Islam, Captain Moiret remarks that the partisans of the Enlightenment either satirized these predictions or became indignant. They protested that they 'had not shaken up the superstitions of Europe so as to adopt those of the Orient, and that one should never speak anything but the truth to the people'.[16] The implication is that the secularists were primarily influential among the civilian scholars and scientists that Bonaparte had brought along to study Egypt, and their militant antireligious stance had little support among the troops, who were often hostile to the savants. (Enlisted men often blamed the savants for having dragged them to Egypt, and affectionately named their donkeys 'Savant'.)

François Bernoyer, a committed Republican in charge of design-
ing and overseeing the production of uniforms for the soldiers in
Egypt, was one such philosophically minded civilian. He described a
ceremony conducted by mystical Sufis, which he witnessed during
the celebration of the rising of the Nile. Bernoyer dismissed the Sufi
leaders as charlatans who fooled the people. He compared their dress
to that of monks, and described the prostration of disciples to the
mystic sheikh. Then he told in some horror how the sheikh spit into
the mouth of one of them, sending him into a seizure during which
he shrieked and his joints cracked. The sheikh brought the ceremony
to an end, he said, by bringing from his robe a sack of snakes and
letting them crawl all over the postulant. Bernoyer knew too much
of the particulars of what he saw to have been interpreting it solely
for himself, and it seems likely that his Egyptian translator was telling
him the significance of these various gestures. It seems likely, as well,
that his interpreter was instrumental in encouraging his disgust with
this performance. Bernoyer also reported that he witnessed the scene
of a nude old woman riding a fine mare through the streets of Cairo.
As she visited each house along the way, the residents showed her
reverence. 'They touched her buttocks with the tips of their fingers
and brought them back to their lips.'[17] In Egyptian folk Islam, blessings or *baraka* were thought to inhere in particular trees, shrines, or
persons. The reversals of the crone (nakedness, a female on a horse)
endowed her with supernatural powers in the eyes of the people. Yet
Bernoyer's puzzlement and disapproval were not French attitudes,
but those of the literate middle class, and were shared even by
Egyptian clerics.

The chronicler 'Abd al-Rahman al-Jabarti also told her story, as a
'God-intoxicated' female mystic of the people. He shared Bernoyer's
disdain for popular religious practices. Dervishes or Sufi mystics
routinely went naked in public in late eighteenth-century Egypt,
apparently to underline their achievement of a state transcending
conventional society. In his chronicle of the eighteenth century, the
historian al-Jabarti confirmed the old woman's importance in Cairo
folk culture. He reported that she had been a disciple of an ecstatic
wandering mystic or dervish, named Sheikh 'Ali al-Bakri, beginning
in the mid-1780s. He had shaved his beard and often wandered about
in the nude, though at other times he wore a long tunic and a skull-
cap. Al-Jabarti said that 'it was rumoured that the sheikh had cast a
glance at her and "attracted" her so that she became a "holy person"'.
As her flights of mystical ecstasy and feelings of unity with the
godhead increased, he reports, the Sheikha began going about

unveiled and dressing in men's clothing. The two of them attracted a following of idle young men, vagabonds, and petty thieves, and the latter began pilfering goods in the market. The two mystics provoked uproar wherever they went, with throngs jostling to get a glance of Sheikh 'Ali. Al-Jabarti recalled, 'The woman would climb onto a bench or some elevated spot, utter indecencies in Arabic or Turkish, and the people would listen to her and try to kiss her hand and so participate in something of her barakah.' The Sheikha herself attracted a loyal following among women, who gave her gifts of money and clothing. In 1786 the two mystics tried to live in Bayt al-Qadi Lane, but attracted the baleful attention of a soldier, who arrested them and their acolytes. He at length released Sheikh 'Ali, but gave his disciples a thrashing, letting them go only once they agreed to wear clothing and to 'sober up'. He then despatched the Sheikha to a hospital for the insane, having her clapped in irons. She, however, at length gained her freedom and continued her career as a female dervish or Sheikha. 'Men and women believed in her, and she became the centre of gatherings' and celebrations of the birthdays of saints.[18] Twelve years later, she was still at it, to Bernoyer's astonishment.

The story of how the Mamluk soldier intervened against the lower-class Sufis demonstrated that some upper-class Egyptians shared Bernoyer's hostility to irrational beliefs and practices. Al-Jabarti, the highly educated son of a great merchant, made it clear that Muslims of the class who attended the Sufi spectacle were 'nobody', along with the Christians. Additionally, that the Sheikha was a lower-class woman and was clearly employing mystical religion as a means of gaining power in a highly masculine society probably offended both men. Since ordinary women in both societies tended to be illiterate, magical ways of thinking, and the appeal to the supernatural to redress grievances, especially appealed to them. Muslim thinkers and French revolutionaries both stressed the value of brotherhood or fraternity, as a way both of emphasizing equality of rights among males and of excluding women from the public sphere. Bernoyer had more in common with al-Jabarti and some of his Mamluk patrons than he might have imagined, insofar as condemnation of superstition was often rooted in gender and class differences.

Al-Jabarti told the story of how, some months later, the supervisor of the pious endowment that supported the huge al-Husayn mosque near al-Azhar sponsored a celebration of the birthday of Husayn, the Prophet's grandson, and received the support of the local French officer in charge of that district. Al-Jabarti represented this festival as an innovation, perhaps disapproving of it because it sounds more like a Shi'ite than a Sunni holy day. Shi'ite Islam especially honours the immediate family of the Prophet. In Egyptian folk Islam, however, there was nothing out of the ordinary in such a celebration, since it, too, seeks blessings from holy figures related to Muhammad. Al-Jabarti said that the sponsor, Sayyid Badawi ibn Fatih, had contracted the 'European disease of love' (syphilis), but had recovered from it and so vowed to promote the festival. He paid for the clerics to recite pious verses. Then, al-Jabarti complained, things got out of hand when the Sufis showed up inside the mosque. These, he said, followed medieval mystical thinkers such as the Andalusian Muhyi al-Din Ibn al-'Arabi and others (clerics such as al-Jabarti typically considered them heretics and advocates of irrationality). They 'formed a circle' and recited mystical poetry incorrectly. Other attendees in the streets declaimed secular poetry and popular ditties. Some Sufis sat in a line reciting a famous ode in praise of the Prophet, while others sat opposite them and interjected a refrain. This practice, he said, was especially characteristic of the Isawiya Sufi order, which combined North Africans with lower-class Egyptians in its membership. 'They had in their hands drums and tambourines on which they beat loudly along with the music, and they raised their voices.' The Sufis began moving together and hyperventilating. Then the Sufi banner carriers from various districts arrived, with more celebrants, carrying lamps, candles, drums, and pipes. Al-Jabarti objected to the din they created in the grand mosque, these 'groups of poor people, each of which belonged to a different Sufi order with its own rituals that differed from the others'. The carnival festival so invaded the mosque that many common people just loitered in its corners, talking and telling stories and laughing. Yet more ordinary folk arrived, from the more distant districts of Cairo, chanting in ungrammatical Arabic what they imagined to be holy verses. (Such Sufi recitation is called 'remembrance' or *dhikr*, but al-Jabarti clearly did not approve of it.) He said that they accused anyone who disagreed with them of adhering to some medieval Muslim heresy such as that of the rationalist Mu'tazilites (who said that God must be good as humans conceive of the good), or of being a fanatical Kharijite (a sect that excommunicated other Muslims if it found them insufficiently moral in their daily lives), or of being an atheist. 'Most of them are guildsmen and practitioners of low trades, and persons who do not so much as have food for supper.'[19] Al-Jabarti's discourse about the

Sufis resembles in important ways that of Bernoyer. He disdained their ritual movements, their hyperventilation, their fanaticism, and their irrationality. Although he condemned them in the name of a more sober, more literate form of Islam, while Bernoyer disdained them in the name of Enlightenment Deism, both valued the reasoning of an educated man over the enthusiastic mysticism of the little people.

Elsewhere in his chronicle, al-Jabarti told an anecdote about high notable Yusuf Bey al-Kabir, who despised Muslim clergymen and laughed at their belief in the supernatural. He dismissed a minor clergyman, Sheikh Hasan al-Kafrawi, from his post as a religious jurist because of his beliefs. Sheikh Hasan, despite being a cleric, had followed a magician, who made phallic amulets and kept them in his house. These he sold to slave-girls in the homes of the wealthy who wished to find a means of attracting their masters' romantic interest. Yusuf Bey ordered the wizard put to death by drowning and confiscated the amulets, which he showed to the other beys. They all had a good laugh at the superstitions of the clergy.[20] Some of the attitudes here discussed, therefore, have less to do with a supposed divide between rationalist Europeans and superstitious Orientals than with occupational attitudes. Hardened, pragmatic officers on both sides often had little patience with the magical, which was about playing on the unrealistic hopes of the little people. It would be easy to tell a story of Jacobin French modernists appalled at traditional Egyptian religious practices, as a sort of clash of civilizations. But in fact, educated upper-class disapproval of folk religion was something Bernoyer, al-Jabarti, and many Mamluk officers held in common. Even anticlericalism and dislike for formal, high Islam was not unknown among the worldly Ottoman-Egyptian pashas and beys. Bernoyer's cynicism about religion, and especially about lower-class practices, had its analogues among elite Egyptians. The dichotomy here was not between West and East, but between the literate and the illiterate across cultures.

Bernoyer also ridiculed the Egyptians for their 'fanaticism' – 'the most forceful in the Orient' – in following an Ottoman-backed Mahdi or messianic figure who attempted to raise a millenarian peasant revolt against the French in the Delta.[21] The Mahdi, reports another French observer, Jean-Gabriel de Niello-Sargy, claimed to be invulnerable to French gunfire and to be able to deflect it by throwing sand in the air. When he was finally defeated and killed by the very French firearms he had disdained, his 'followers said he had ascended into heaven'.[22] The latter memoirist does not condemn Muslim superstition and fanaticism in so many words, allowing the stark reportage of the Mahdist beliefs to convey this impression to his audience. General Doguereau describes the Mahdi as a man from 'the depths of Africa', though it is possible that he meant by this that he was from the far west of the continent, i.e. Morocco. He notes that his immediate followers were '200 North Africans [*maghrebins*]' who happened to arrive a few days after he made his claim, and who ranged themselves under his banner. He describes his claim as that of being an 'angel' predicted in the Qur'an. He is said to have eschewed most nourishment, but occasionally dipped his fingers in a bowl of milk and moistened his lips with it. Doguereau describes a battle in April or May 1799, between 'the angel's fanatics' and a French unit employing artillery. He says the Mahdists kept throwing themselves against the French position, not stopping to reckon their casualties till nightfall, when they discovered a thousand dead 'and understood that God no longer performs miracles'.[23] Doguereau describes the wounded Mahdi's subsequent taking of refuge in the desert with followers as a 'bizarre scene'.

The North African messiah of the desert stands not only as an embodiment of a violent fanaticism and credulity. He is said to originate *du fond de l'Afrique*, his very origins placing him territorially and culturally even further away from Europe than Egypt. His movement also stood proof of the disjuncture in epoch between the modern French and the medieval Muslims. The revolutionary French appear to have conceived themselves as moving in a different time-stream from the Egyptians. Having superseded the age of theology, the officers of the Enlightenment and revolution know that 'God no longer performs miracles'. Their revolutionary time is one of superior firearms and human ingenuity, not of supernatural marvels. It is this superiority of the deist over the naive believer that allows on the one hand Bonaparte's instrumental use of Islam for his own purposes and on the other the destruction of religiously based uprisings by clever French tactics and by superior artillery. Ironically, of course, there is a resemblance between Bonaparte's insistence that he was sent on a divine mission to Egypt, prophesied in numerous passages in the Qur'an, and the Mahdi's own discourse about his purposes. It is often clear that in criticizing Islamic superstition, the more philosophically minded were also criticizing the religious policy of the army generals. That is, the critique of the Muslim Other, as Rebecca Joubin has shown, is very often employed by eighteenth-century French thinkers to critique the Self, which is to say reactionary tendencies among the French themselves.[24]

For their part, the Egyptian clergy used French Enlightenment rationalism to symbolize their own internal methodological debates about the permissibility of deploying Greek tools of reasoning in Muslim theology and law. Sheikh Abdullah al-Sharqawi, the president of the Cairo Diwan, later described the French in a book on Egyptian history. He wrote, 'The reality of the French who came to Egypt is that they were materialist, libertine philosophers.' He said that although to outward seeming they were Catholic Christians, in fact, 'they deny the Resurrection, and the afterlife, and God's dispatching of prophets of messengers'. Although they did believe in only one god, he complained, they had only arrived at this conclusion 'by means of argumentation' (i.e. rather than faith). They 'make reason the ruler and make some among them managers of the regulations that they legislate by using their reason, which they call "laws"'. Al-Sharqawi here underlines the difference between the revealed Law (shariah) and the civil laws (*al-ahkam*) promulgated by sultans and governors. Al-Sharqawi maintained that the French substituted civil law for the sacred. They hold, he alleged, that God's envoys, such as Muhammad, Jesus, and Moses, 'were a group of sages, and that the codes of religious law attributed to them are indirect expressions of civil law that they legislated by virtue of their reason, which was appropriate to their contemporaries'.[25]

Al-Sharqawi engaged in his own forms of creolization here, amalgamating French deism to ancient Greek philosophy, over the place of which in Muslim learning medieval clerics had waged epochal battles. The Abbasid caliph Harun al-Rashid had established a translation institute in Baghdad that rendered scientific and philosophical works of the Hellenistic world into Arabic. Other scholars brought into Arabic Persian and Sanskrit learning. Early Muslim civilization was heir to all the great preceding civilizations of the Hellenistic world, Persia, and India. A few Muslim thinkers, such as Avicenna (Ibn Sina) and Averröes (Ibn Rushd), so closely followed Greek sages such as Aristotle that they adopted into their theologies ideas that were at odds with mainstream Islam. Thus, they asserted the eternity of the world, while most Muslim theologians, like their Christian and Jewish colleagues, believed in the creation story in Genesis. Averröes argued that the prophets were actually philosophers who derived their teachings from reason, but who then turned around and expressed their conclusions with symbols such as heaven and hell, since that is what the common people would accept. Orthodox Muslim clerics viewed this theory as implying that there actually is no such thing as revelation or prophecy, and they wrote angry attempts at refuting the works of the Muslim philosophers. There were episodes of book burning and persecution.[26]

Greek learning was brought into Islam so thoroughly in the early years that an engagement with it continued to be common among most theologians, even if they rejected some of the metaphysical doctrines associated with it. Particularly in the East, in Iran and India, Greek-inspired Islamic philosophy, mixed with theology and mysticism, remained a vital tradition into the nineteenth century. In the eighteenth century, the study of Greek-inspired Islamic philosophy became a vogue among some scholars at al-Azhar Seminary, in part under the influence of visiting Indian Muslims. This group included Hasan al-Jabarti, the father of the chronicler 'Abd al-Rahman al-Jabarti. They taught philosophy (*al-hikmah*) in the evenings, outside the regular curriculum of al-Azhar, and wrote commentaries on Aristotle's *Categories*, on Porphyry's Neoplatonic version of the same work, and on a scholastic Muslim encyclopaedia of philosophy, *The Guidance of Wisdom*. Most al-Azhar clerics were more wedded to the study of the sayings and doings of the Prophet Muhammad or other strictly Islamic subjects, and many viewed the study of Graeco-Islamic philosophy with deep suspicion.[27] Al-Sharqawi was not only reacting against the actual Deism of the French, he was also painting them as having ideas similar to those of the philosophers in Islamic history. The controversy over philosophy and Greek reason had been revived among scholastics in eighteenth-century Egypt well before the Europeans invaded. The chronicler al-Jabarti, when he wrote his own father's biography, was clearly responding to charges of unorthodoxy, and defended him strongly as a 'philosopher'. Al-Sharqawi had presumably been among those who viewed the study of philosophy dimly. That is, he was lashing out both at French Deism and at rationalist approaches to metaphysics among his own colleagues, some of whom proved more genuinely interested in French science and culture than he. Ironically, despite his later critique of French rule, al-Sharqawi served as the president of the Diwan or Directory of native Egyptians established by Bonaparte, met regularly with the latter to discuss policy, and functioned for all the world like an Egyptian Talleyrand (the latter also later proved a critic of Bonaparte). His quibbles over the revival of Greek rationalism in some ways served as a screen to hide the extent of his collaboration and creolization in 1798–1801.

Conclusion

Cultural creolization in the French Republic of Egypt was not of a dialectical form, whereby culture A and culture B intermingled to produce culture C. Instead, creolization was a creative movement deployed by individuals for the purposes of bridging authority structures (as when Bonaparte intimated that he was a proto-Muslim 'great Sultan' in order to attract Egyptians' loyalties) or with the object of subverting them (as when al-Sharqawi rejected Enlightenment Deism as a mere recrudescence of heretical Greek philosophy). Bonaparte deeply feared being tagged with the essentialist tropes that Muslim thinkers had developed to characterize European aggression, especially that of the Crusades. His rhetorical strategy was to seek a creole common ground between revolutionary ideology and classical Islam, so as to obviate difference and naturalize the invaders as a form of Self. His strategy was reinvented in other ways by a cloud of European administrators in Afro-Asia during the period of imperial expansion from 1780, as when Lionel Place took on the role of the south Indian minor king in presiding over the Jagir outside Madras. Nor would al-Jabarti and al-Sharqawi be the only local notables to serve at the same time as collaborators with a colonial presence and as profound critics of its social and cultural practices. Selective creolization, in one sphere of life, appeared to allow or perhaps even enable claims of essential identity in another. Elsewhere, we see a process of convergence, whereby literate, middle strata condemnations of popular religious practices on the part of both savants and ulema are virtually indistinguishable. In Muslim cultures in particular, the long history of interaction with European texts allowed eighteenth-century thinkers to refight culture wars, as with the conflict between occasionalism and rationalism, which was fought out centuries earlier on the terrain of Athens and Baghdad, but now was refought on that of Paris and Cairo. The hard-nosed realism of some Ottoman-Egyptian administrators and the anti-Sufi, anti-superstition rationalism of some reformist clergymen approximated some of the rationalist and even clerical attitudes common in Enlightentment France. Such home-grown rationalists, or at least pragmatic realists, were a minority but not insignificant strand of eighteenth-century Egyptian culture, possibly influenced by trends in Istanbul that grew out of the impact of printing and other changing technology.

Three major attitudes to Islam emerge in the memoirs of the French officers and civilians on the invasion force. The first, associated with Bonaparte and the interests of the army, was pragmatic, instrumental, and even flattering, drawing upon a kind of Romantic view of the religion. Islam was praised, intimations were given out that the deist French Republicans were anyway crypto-Muslims, and that they might undergo a full conversion with time. A second common attitude, associated with the savants and their supporters, depicted Islam as just another religion and assumed that all religions consisted of a kind of fraud and chicanery made possible by the ignorance and superstition of people. A third point of view remained generally critical of Islam, but was willing to acknowledge virtues in Arab-Muslim civilization and in its representatives, the ulema, whom Bonaparte promoted as indigenous leaders. These three ways of thinking sometimes overlapped, of course, and all had roots in eighteenth-century French thinking on the Orient. But the first two often resulted in antithetical policy prescriptions in French Egypt, and were in severe conflict with one another.

The Corsican general's conceit of being an Enlightenment proto-Muslim is in part a purely instrumental piece of propaganda. But to say that it was instrumental is only to identify a motive. The substance of the proclamations he issued in this regard derived from his new social context as ruler of a Muslim Arab realm. He was shaped by that context just as he attempted to shape it. Just as genre in literature is a set of audience expectations, so forms of creolization play to audience expectations in Self and Other, even as they subvert simple binary oppositions.

One clear sign of creolization in the French Republic of Egypt was that it became a site of controversy and denial when the episode was over. Bonaparte and his partisans were later at pains to deny that he had become a Muslim in Egypt, while al-Jabarti and other ulema wrote virulent denunciations of the French after the Ottoman restoration to clear themselves of charges of collaboration. The varying cultural strategies used by the French and the Egyptians to make sense of their encounter produced more irony than binaries. Bonaparte played at being 'Muslim', and offered to create the first Islamic republic, but no one was more brutal in crushing the ulema when they opposed him. In sometimes snubbing and marginalizing them, Bonaparte unwittingly reproduced the social control techniques common among Ottoman and Ottoman-Egyptian lay elites. The French showed disdain for the pretensions of the Mahdi of Damanhour, but Bonaparte himself adopted the cosmic diction of the Mahdi in his own proclamations after the Cairo Revolt, drawing from al-Jabarti the same sort of rationalist disgust as Desvernois displayed towards the desert messiah who opposed the French. Bernoyer thought his litany of Muslim acts of fanaticism a condemnation of that and of all religion, but many of his more trenchant critiques were echoed by the great al-Azhar cleric 'Abd al-Rahman al-Jabarti. The French savants, with their strong sense of division between the medieval and the modern, appear to have been unaware that their discourse helped to revive controversies at al-Azhar about the permissibility of appealing to the tools of Greek rationalism, such as the syllogism and Aristotelian premises. Whether they played at each adopting the role of the other, or pretended to be utterly different, both mimesis and difference locked them in an unwilling embrace.

8

Imperial Revolutions and Global Repercussions: South Asia and the World, c.1750–1850

Robert Travers

Imperial revolutions and early modern state formation in South Asia

In Eric Hobsbawm's rendering of the *Age of Revolution* (first published in 1962), 'the world revolution spread outward from the double crater of England and France'. The dual revolution that underlay this global eruption comprised the French political revolution and the British industrial revolution, and these together launched the lava-streams of European imperialism. In this model, Europe was situated broadly speaking on the supply side of modernity, and India (as part of the non-West) on the demand side. 'Before the merchants, the steam-engines, the ships and the guns of the West – and before its ideas – the age old-civilizations and empires of the world capitulated and collapsed.'[1]

Hobsbawm's impressively sweeping and vigorous narrative contained certain counter-currents to the prevailing message of European agency and domination. His account of British industrialization, for example, emphasized not only the 'capitalist conditions' of internal regimes of property, but also the economic conjuncture between 'the cotton industry, and colonial expansion'. The growth of the British cotton industry, in this view, was a 'by-product of overseas trade, which produced its raw material, and the Indian cotton goods', which spurred domestic emulation and import substitution.[2]

Hobsbawm was also conscious that the grounds of modern history were rapidly shifting in a new age of twentieth-century revolutions, which he described as a 'world-wide revolt against the west'. It was now evident, he argued, that the European 'domination of the entire world' in the four centuries of 'the age of Vasco da Gama' was 'complete' but also 'temporary'.[3] Nonetheless, even the dialectical erosion of European domination in the twentieth century confirmed the fundamentally European origins of modernity. It was, after all, the dual revolution of Europe that eventually provided 'the non-European world with the conditions and equipment for its eventual counter-attack'.[4]

Hobsbawm's Marxist inflected account cannot be taken as representative of the state of world history in the 1960s, but its emphasis on the exclusively European motors of modernity did reflect a broader inheritance from the grand narratives of the age of European empires in the nineteenth century. Now, forty years later, his notion of four centuries of complete European 'domination of the entire world' appears to have been conjured up by a number of historical sleights of hand.

To consider his references to India, for example, Hobsbawm compressed the long drawn out, hundred-year, British conquest of the Indian subcontinent into the conquest of Bengal in the 1750s, 'a step that would lead them in our period to become ruler and administrators of all India'.[5] He tended to assume a vast technological and military superiority for the British as far back as the mid-eighteenth century, even though, as David Washbrook has recently written, British conquerors 'sailed in wooden ships and carried muzzle-loading muskets which were frequently fired back at them'.[6] Hobsbawm's narrative co-opted any signs of 'Westernization' in India into his model of the dual European revolution. Thus, he described the Bengali reformer Rammohan Roy as an Indian-style French revolutionary, ignoring Roy's intellectual training in Indo-Persian and Sanskritic forms of scholarship.[7] And by a trick of temporal displacement, Hobsbawm described popular resistance to European imperialism, for example the Indian mutiny/rebellion of 1857, as medieval or 'Homeric' if it did not conform to a 'Western' style of revolutionary nationalism.[8]

South Asia plays a different role in C. A. Bayly's recent account of the age of revolutions in his *Birth of the Modern World*. Bayly is concerned to explore the 'interconnectedness and interdependence of political and social changes across the world well before the supposed onset of the contemporary phase of globalization', and to frame this interconnectedness as polycentric rather than Eurocentric. Bayly also wants to blur the lines between the early modern and the modern; in this view, modern states that emerged from the crises of the age of revolutions were always deeply intertwined with older forms of power and order, so that 'passages to modernity' overlaid rather than simply erased 'old regimes'.[9]

According to Bayly, the first cracks in the old regimes of a connected early modern world appeared not in Europe but 'in the Middle East and South Asia', in the weakening frames of the great Islamic empires of the Ottomans, the Safavids, and the Mughals. But these cracks were less the result of enfeebled Oriental tradition than of processes of commercialization, militarization, and the crystallization of new social forms that were at least comparable, though not identical, to similar trajectories in Europe. The confluence of commercialization, social crisis, and military conflict in Asian land empires as well as in European sea-borne empires gave the age of revolutions its global character, as the force of revolutionary events 'ricocheted around the globe'.[10]

Thus, Bayly pushes the age of 'converging revolutions' back from 1776 or 1789 to the decline of the Safavids and the Mughals in the late seventeenth and early eighteenth centuries. In South Asia, the invasion and plunder of the Mughal imperial heartlands by the Persian warrior-prince Nadir Shah in 1738–9 marked a point of no return for the emperors in Delhi; further invasions followed from Afghans in the north-west, and Marathas from the south-west.[11] These shocks to the system of the Mughal empire in turn sparked a further intensification of intra-European competition for trade, land and national glory in the Indian Ocean. Armed companies of European traders, powerful at sea but chafing against military weakness on land, made strategic alliances with warring Indian states, using their impressive cash resources to recruit land-armies, and forcibly subordinating fertile and commercialized regions such as Bengal to the authority of extensive commercial bureaucracies. By invading and manipulating indigenous systems of trade, finance, and state formation, the British defeated French pretensions to a stronger foothold in South Asia, laying the initial groundwork for a new style of territorial imperialism in the East.[12]

Following Bayly, therefore, and adapting Jeremy Adelman's notion of 'imperial revolutions' from the Atlantic world, we might argue that there were two extended moments of imperial revolution in South Asia, neither of them explicable solely in terms of 'the rise of Europe'.[13] The first, dating perhaps from the death of the Emperor Aurangzeb in 1707, and the subsequent factionalism in the Mughal court, combined with provincial rebellions and external invasions, led to a broad process of political decentralization and regional state formation. At the same time, however, Mughal bureaucratic, fiscal, and military techniques, as well as the overarching prestige of Mughal imperial authority, continued to influence regional power-brokers. The second phase of imperial revolution was predicated on this earlier moment of competitive regional state formation: it followed from Anglo-French conflict in southern India in the 1740s and 1750s, proceeded through the English East India Company's conquest of Bengal in the 1750s and 1760s, and reached its culmination in the extensive 'paramountcy' claimed by the British Empire in India by the 1820s. Even then, however, the British Empire, acting through the East India Company, continued to acknowledge at least what Sudipta Sen has called 'the nominal regality' of the erstwhile Mughals.[14]

In the 'ricochet' effect described by Bayly, British expansion in India was connected not just to imperial crises and regional conflicts within South Asia, but also to the global war between Britain and post-revolutionary France. Fears of the French threat to India were used in the 1790s to justify a new assault on hostile Indian rulers such as Tipu Sultan of Mysore.[15] Tipu, the Maratha confederacy, and later Ranjit Singh of the Punjab showed that Indian regional states were not simply passive victims of European expansionism. They employed new military technologies and styles of rule, and developed more centralized systems of taxation and debt-financing to pay for growing armies. Nonetheless, over the long term such relatively confined territorial states were gradually tamed by the sheer scale of British imperialism, which drew on a unique combination of maritime and territorial strength.[16]

Contemporary observers often remarked on the 'revolutionary' character of these imperial transformations. By the early 1760s, British East India Company officials were writing memoirs about the 'revolution' in Bengal, as the Company propped up, then overturned a succession of provincial governors (nawabs), gradually appropriating the trappings of Mughal imperial sovereignty for itself.[17] The great parliamentarian Edmund Burke, reflecting on the decline of the Mughal Empire, referred to the 'stupendous revolutions that have happened in our age of wonders'; this was in 1783, six years before the revolution in France.[18] Similarly, Indian scholar-administrators trained in the Persianate idioms of Mughal and post-Mughal governance often used the Arabic/Persian term *inqilab*, implying a revolution in the literal sense of overturning, to describe the subversion of Mughal authority by regional rebels, regional pro-consuls and European traders.[19] The rise of European traders was especially bewildering to many of these Indian authors, given common assumptions about the relatively lowly political status of merchants, and also the difficulty of comprehending the distant politics of European commerce and state formation.[20]

Many Indian scholars and scribes experienced the imperial revolutions of eighteenth-century South Asia as a crisis that seemed to disturb established moral and political communities. A high official of the Mughal successor state of Arcot in south-eastern India, writing in the 1780s, looked back in amazement to the great buildings erected by earlier Indian rulers; he described his own era, when the nawabs of Arcot were reduced to virtual pensioners of the English, as 'days of dilapidation and ruin' in which 'construction of a building of equal beauty is beyond human power'.[21] Another Persian history, written also in the 1780s but by a member of the Mughal gentry from Bihar in the north-east, took a similarly melancholic view of his own age: 'the earth', he wrote, 'is totally overwhelmed by an everlasting darkness'.[22] The author, Ghulam Husain Khan Tabataba'i Husaini, diagnosed a crisis with deep roots in a Mughal imperial service corrupted by greed, bribery, and the leasing out of offices to unqualified officials. But he also laid substantial blame on the alien style of rule introduced by foreign merchants, on their habits of commercial monopoly, on their ignorance of local manners and customs, and on 'the aversion which the English openly show for the company of natives'.[23]

Perhaps surprisingly, such fears about traditional imperial virtues trampled by a potent modern mixture of commerce and conquest were also shared by many British observers of the revolutions in South Asia. The East India Company's military adventurism led to repeated financial crises and prolonged conflicts with the British state over the rights to new territorial revenues. Meanwhile, Asian conquests and massive standing armies challenged British views of their own empire as an empire of liberty by contrast with the supposedly more tyrannical empires of Spain or Portugal.[24] Edmund Burke, for example, one of the sharpest British observers of the South Asian revolutions, shared with some of the dispossessed Mughal gentry a powerful sense that British mercantile conquerors had overturned established norms and hierarchies through a combination of greed and ignorance, laying low the old princes and landlords in favour of a rampant British and Indian monied interest. He feared the revolutionary implications for Britain itself of this new accretion of military and monetary power, insidiously seeping back into the landed interest in Britain, and corrupting its wives and daughters and with them its virtue.[25] After 1789, Burke suggested that Indianism and Jacobinism were two sides of the same devalued coin of modern speculative revolutions.[26]

Even the East India Company's own high officials were concerned at the corrupting effects of their rule in South Asia. Warren Hastings, Burke's great rival and Governor of Bengal from 1772 to 1785, bemoaned the 'Exclusion of old and experienced Muttasseddies [revenue officials] from Employment and Confidence, and the trust reposed in Servants of the English gentlemen'.[27] Hastings framed many of his state-building measures as efforts to restore the glory days of an earlier period of Mughal imperial order. Invoking an 'ancient constitution' of empire in India in urgent need of repair, Hastings and others adapted the Mughal discourse of imperial corruption to their own ideological advantage.[28]

Thus, imperial revolutions led to a period of intense ideological instability, as established elites came to terms with new circumstances, and the new British conquerors cast around desperately for conceptual frames to understand their novel form of empire. By the 1790s, however, in the context of the wars with revolutionary France, a more confident and unified British imperialism in India was announcing itself as a sharp break from an imagined history of 'Asiatic despotism'. Embracing conquest as a vehicle for a new style of enlightened, regulated, and bureaucratic despotism, symbolized by the compilation, publication, and translation of elaborate codes of administrative law, the British Empire in India settled into a long complacency rooted in an increasingly racialized doctrine of corruption.[29] British imperial officials, once suspected as rapacious speculators, were now apparently rendered uncorrupt by the combined effects of rule-books, breeding, and the colour of their skin. At the same time, Indian officials were more rigorously excluded from high office in directly ruled territories.[30] Hardening racial distinctions were also linked to constructions of religious difference as a form of ethnicity, as some British orientalist scholarship valorized a newly discovered ancient Hindu civilization (with deep linguistic connections to ancient civilization in Europe), while deploring the alleged effects of Islamic conquests.[31] Meanwhile, published codes of 'Hindu' and 'Islamic' law may have encouraged more unified, classicized conceptions of religious practice as a form of social identity.[32]

The concept of imperial revolutions may help to situate South Asia within a broader global complex of revolution and world crisis in the long eighteenth century. Yet, for historians of South Asia, the imperial frame delineated by 'Mughal decline' or 'the rise of the British' has also come to seem unnecessarily confining and inadequate. Some historians of the late Mughal Empire have questioned the idea of a sudden decline in a centralized imperial bureaucracy leading to a broader social and economic malaise; they have argued instead that Mughal authority had always rested on a complex system of alliance-forming and alliance breaking with regional power-holders.[33] Similarly, a revisionist school of colonial historians questioned the idea of a colonial 'revolution' in governance and social relations, empha-sizing the limited and cautious character of early colonial rule, and its reliance on various forms of indigenous 'agency'. In a landmark essay from 1973, Eric Stokes suggested that the first century of British rule was an era of social 'stagnation' rather than social 'revolution', marked less by the onset of 'modernization' than by the colonial exploitation of pre-existing social forms.[34]

Revisionism in colonial Indian history also spawned counter-revi-sionism. As revisionists developed an argument for certain lines of continuity across the precolonial/colonial divide, they were criticized for underestimating the dramatic ruptures of colonial invasions, the unprecedented coercive force exercised by colonial armies, and the social and cultural dislocations that followed from colonial strategies of extraction and domination.[35] The dust has not yet settled on argu-ments about continuity or change, collaboration or resistance, agency or domination. Yet beneath the clouds of polemic, historical under-standings of the 'early modern' period in South Asia have been trans-formed. In particular, the concept of state formation has gradually broadened out beyond what Frank Perlin (a pioneer in the new history of state formation) called 'functionalist' or 'regime-centred' accounts focused on relatively static systems of official hierarchies, to consider the wider contexts and infrastructures in which power operated.[36]

New work on state formation has revealed forms of political culture that can be neither separated from, nor entirely subsumed within, narratives of the rise and fall of empires. Historians are increas-ingly pushing beyond, or between the lines of, the imperial archives of Persian or English administrative records, exploring the connected articulation of historical memory, political authority, and social groups within different regions and vernacular languages.[37] One of the effects of this work has been to challenge the generalizations of 'Indian' history with the varied patterns of state-making in the diverse regions of the subcontinent. Subrahmanyam writes of a 'panorama' of state forms taking shape in the 'penumbral regions' of eighteenth-century South India, with varied strategies of expansionism and survival depending on local political ecologies, and also on the chang-ing commercial relations between agrarian hinterlands and coastal regions.[38] Similarly, Frank Perlin notes the 'paradoxically decentral-ized' forms of political centralization in the western Deccan region, where great royal courts, little kings, noble households, and village level entrepreneurs interacted in sometimes symbiotic, sometimes contradictory ways.[39] Historians are also coming to grips with the varied configurations of colonialism itself, which struck different regions at different historical moments, and with widely differing institutional configurations.

If this work challenges us to think beyond the homogenizing effects of old imperial narratives, it is also crystallizing certain new themes that suggest a varied but also interconnected set of transformations. These include: monetization as a technology of both commerce and sovereignty; the growing political prominence of commercial and banking groups; the role of highly mobile cadres of scribal experts in spreading administrative technologies and terminologies; and the importance of different types of historical narratives in authenticating claims to rights, perquisites, and political authority. Prominent myths, residues of colonial 'orientalist' scholarship, such as the unchanging rigidity of caste, or the absence of any 'historical' forms of knowledge in precolonial South Asia, or the absence of corporate or intermediary groups intervening between all-powerful rulers and peasants, are now being comprehensively exploded.[40]

This work, apart from revealing layers and textures of power too often absent from older political histories, also opens up exciting possibilities for rethinking the complex effects of the imperial revolutions of the eighteenth century. For example, ideas of continuity and change need to be studied as historical categories, and not simply as historiographical or analytical ones. A regime of colonial conquest posed the issue of continuity and change in especially urgent ways for both rulers and ruled, with substantial repercussions for understandings of space, time, and the relationship between past and present.[41] Colonial conquest was often followed by a rash of documentary collections, as old forms of knowledge were gathered up and sifted within new forms of archive. Often this had the effect of freezing a particularly favoured image of, for example, land tenures, village communities, or legal norms. Prachi Deshpande has shown how historical narratives were produced by prominent Maratha lineages in the seventeenth and eighteenth centuries to record military valour or to legitimize titles to honour and land. These were then read in the nineteenth century by colonial officials and an emerging Marathi middle class to construct 'Maratha' as a social category referring to a specific (Hindu) 'people' in a particular place.[42] In a different yet related process studied by Norbert Peabody, Rajput kingship was reinvented by British overlords and their local allies, who created more fixed, territorially bounded entities in a system of indirect 'empire by treaty'; previously, the perquisites of sovereignty had been shared between a layered complex of royal and sacral authorities. At the same time, antiquarian officials such as James Todd endowed the region and its reinvented kingdoms with a colourful feudal and chivalric past.[43]

Frank Perlin has argued that colonial conquests in the western Deccan led to an 'unprecedented centralization of monetary production and control', the displacement of rural elites, a decrease in rural employment, a narrower delimitation of property right, and a consequent flattening out of the 'intermediary ground' of noble households and communal institutions that characterized the precolonial order – leading exactly to the 'climate of Asiatic despotism' that colonial histories tended to read back into a cruel Asiatic past.[44] This argument finds echoes in other versions of a 'neo-traditionalization' thesis in early colonial India, in which colonial authority is seen to have first exploited the old order political economy and then gradually, in the context of economic depression and an emerging global division of labour in the early nineteenth century, pressed it into new but supposedly 'traditional' shapes.[45]

One of the most important historiographical effects of this new work on early modern and colonial state formation is to open up points of connection and comparison between different forms of a global early modernity. In this way, global history can mean something more than imperial history writ large, and the delineation of a world crisis in the age of revolutions can extend beyond the contrasting fortunes of vast empires. Frank Perlin, again, has compared the growing power of English and Dutch merchants over textile producers in Eastern Europe to similar processes of mercantile centralization and control of artisanal labour within South Asia.[46] Jon E. Wilson, meanwhile, has suggested that one of the most important effects of colonial governance in South Asia was to draw sharper lines between 'state' and 'society', with the state constituted by abstract bureaucratic categories, and with the realm of the social taken up as a distinct space for Indian 'social reformers' in the emerging print culture of early nineteenth-century Bengal. He finds points of comparisons here with other self-consciously new and 'modern' kinds of state-building projects in post-revolutionary France and nineteenth-century Germany. As Wilson argues, such comparisons will not efface the distinctive valences of a colonial regime, but enable more closely specified accounts of what these were.[47]

Imperial repercussions: South Asia and the world of empires

While the modern historiography of South Asia continues to be largely framed by the question of the colonial impact on the Indian subcontinent, the recent revival of interest in global history has also opened up a set of new questions about the wider repercussions or side-effects of major events such as the transition to colonialism in South Asia. Recent historiography has emphasized that South Asia was already entangled with multiple forms of 'connected history' – oceanic, imperial, commercial, religious, linguistic, artistic – well before the acceleration of European imperialism in the age of revolutions.[48] Yet between 1750 and 1850 South Asia was forcibly wrestled into a new form of global connection forged by the modern British Empire. The rise of British India had wide repercussions for the British state and society in an era of global war and industrialization. From the mid-eighteenth century, Indian territories became not simply a 'bridgehead' to a new form of territorial empire in South Asia, but also a jumping off point for a new global imperialism in the Indian and Pacific Oceans. At the same time, the British conquest of India generated reactions from other European empires, notably the French and the Russians, and from other Asian empires, notably the Chinese, in an era of heightened competition over land and trade. This section attempts to sketch in some of these global repercussions of the rise of British India in the wider world of empires.

John Maynard Keynes, who began his career as an economist by studying the fluctuating fortunes of the Indian rupee, had a strong sense of the global and imperial networks supporting modern British institutions. Keynes dated the modern age to the 'accumulation of capital that began in the sixteenth century', which in turn followed from 'the treasure of gold and silver which Spain brought from the New World into the Old'. He traced Britain's foreign investments to the 'treasure which Drake stole from Spain in 1580', of which Queen Elizabeth invested £40,000 in the Levant Company; 'out of the profits of the Levant Company', he continued, 'the East India Company was founded; and the profits of this great enterprise were the foundation of England's subsequent foreign investment'. Keynes further calculated that '£40,000 accumulating at 3% compound interest' approximated nearly to the actual volume of England's foreign investments in 1930, so that every pound that Drake brought home had become £100,000 pounds.[49]

Keynes's lesson on the amazing 'power of compound interest' subtly discounted the amazing power of empire, but at the same time it suggested the centrality of overseas commerce, especially in Asia, to Britain's subsequent financial strength. Modern economic historians of Britain have in general been much more circumspect about the role of Asian commerce in Britain's economic performance. If an older Marxist tradition saw intimate connections between industry and empire, many economic historians since the 1960s have argued for the essentially internal, microeconomic processes underpinning the industrial revolution. Drawing on conceptions of 'Smithian growth' or 'institutionalist' economic theory, the new economic history focused attention on regimes of private property and internal capital accumulation, or on proto-industrialization and urbanization in creating dynamic clusters of expertise and economic organization.[50]

More recently, more 'externalist' explanations of British economic change, emphasizing the critical role of global conjunctures, have come back into vogue.[51] A new emphasis on the role of consumption has highlighted the importance of tropical, colonial products in generating new forms of mass market.[52] Attention has shifted back from industrial take-off in the late eighteenth and early nineteenth centuries, to the longer-term growth of commercial profit linked to the 'financial revolution' of the late seventeenth century; again, this tends to re-emphasize the role of colonial trades, and of the fiscal-military state in protecting Britain's terms of trade.[53]

In such arguments, the Atlantic empire tends to loom larger than the Asian sphere, given that Britain's trade with Asia, even as it grew in importance across the eighteenth century, remained much smaller than the Atlantic trades.[54] So, for example, Patrick O'Brien emphasizes the demand of fast-growing colonial markets for British manufactures in North America and the Caribbean, while Kenneth Pomeranz highlights the role of Atlantic slave colonies as a novel kind of dependent periphery that enabled some European economies to overcome Malthusian resource constraints.[55]

Yet if Asian trades were relatively small in the eighteenth century, they were also intertwined and symbiotic with the larger pattern of British commercial relations.[56] Indian cotton-piece goods stimulated emulation and import substitution in Britain, and helped to pay for slaves in Africa. China tea, paid for in large part by the profits of Indian opium exports, fed the demand for West Indian sugar.[57] In both the Netherlands and Britain, as Pomeranz has reiterated, the risks and distance involved in Asian trade catalysed institutional innovation, in the creation of permanent joint stock corporations, in which ownership was separated from management, and protection costs were internalized.[58] The English East India Company was one of the major pillars of the London stock market, and also helped to fund the growth of the British national debt and fiscal-military state through forced loans and customs revenues. Thus, when military adventurism in India led the Company close to bankruptcy in 1772 and 1783, ministers agreed that bailing out Company investors was necessary to maintaining national credit.[59]

In part, the Asian colonial trades may now seem more important to the history of British state formation because the transformations in the British economy and society in the age of revolutions appear less sudden and dramatic than they once did. The idea of a multisectoral, incremental 'industrial evolution' has encouraged a more flexible and multifaceted causal analysis. Moreover, as in Boyd Hilton's recent magisterial account, British historians are tending now to emphasize the economic and political uncertainties and instabilities attending the early industrial age. Hilton highlights the widespread contemporary sense that the endurance of the British state, facing down related threats of Malthusian overpopulation and revolutionary sentiment, was by no means assured.[60] Thus, apparently marginal gains from foreign trade and investment may seem to attain a new significance. Javier Cuenca Esteban's detailed reconstruction of British national finances during the Revolutionary and Napoleonic wars suggests that remissions of funds from India may have been crucial in sustaining national credit at a moment of severe strain.[61] Similarly, Huw Bowen's reconstruction of the tentacular presence of the East India Company in the early nineteenth-century British economy, as exporter as well as importer, and as a presence in the provinces as much as in London, also highlights the added value for Britain of the Indian empire.[62] Meanwhile, if Asian trades were still a comparatively small element in Britain's imperial trading system in the early nineteenth century, they would become increasingly important later on. By the later nineteenth century, India's export surplus, to China in particular, was vital in maintaining industrial Britain's own balance of payments.[63]

The role of British India as a political and social, rather than only financial, outwork of the British state in the age of revolutions may also need rethinking. Again, Hilton's picture of a landed and commercial oligarchy looking nervously down at a fast expanding population of 'mad, bad and dangerous people' raises the question of the role of the colonies in sustaining the domestic order. The number of poor Britons serving in the rank and file of British forces in India was quite small – less than 30,000 in 1800 – but given their extremely high mortality (conventionally estimated at 25 per cent per annum in the late eighteenth century), this flow of poor recruits may have represented a significant vent for an overstretched domestic population.[64] For the officer classes, service in the Indian armies or civil service represented a reasonable fall-back position, especially after demobilization at the end of the Napoleonic Wars. As a source of power and jobs for Scottish and Irish landowners, merchants, and soldiers, British India also helped to integrate the composite kingdom into a more cohesive national whole.[65]

Moreover, at moments of crisis in British national politics, Indian affairs played a crucial and still understudied role. In an era of expensive military conquests, the new empire in India often appeared as a source of financial and political turbulence in Britain, but it also provided a form of imperial compensation for the loss of North American colonies. The particular institutional formation of British India, in which the national state annexed but also propped up the semi-detached empire of the East India Company, enabled ministers to garner the glory of the new empire, while filtering out the less desirable 'blowback'. For example, in the immediate aftermath of the American war, the king's chosen minister, William Pitt the Younger, restabilized royal and ministerial authority in part through a carefully calibrated alliance with the East India Company. Pitt's India Act of 1784, reforming alleged abuses in India, was an important part of his self-presentation as an uncorrupted man of virtue. At the same time, the nervous and debt-ridden Company was allowed to retain a measure of autonomy and control over its patronage, and backed Pitt in the crucial 1784 elections.[66]

The alliance between nation-state and Company state after 1784 was remarkably stable through the following decades given the context of revolutionary upheaval and global war. From the ministerial point of view, this mode of informal or semi-formal empire allowed a measure of control over vital strategic and commercial interests, while at the same time limiting national liabilities. The Company funded most of British military and naval forces in Asia, the effects of imperial militarism and patronage were held at arm's length from the domestic constitution, and the Company or its governors remained useful scapegoats in the event of setbacks in India, such as Richard Wellesley's financial mismanagement, or Lord Auckland's disastrous invasion of Afghanistan in 1838. Meanwhile, the very gradual dismantling of the Company's commercial monopoly between 1793 and 1833, and the opening of India to evangelical missions, enabled ministers to quench domestic political pressures with a steady drip of colonial reforms.[67]

Meanwhile, the British-Indian 'garrison state' was an important venue and occasion for the ideological rearmament of the counter-revolutionary '*ancien régime*' in Britain and the empire.[68] What Bayly called the 'constructive conservatism' of counter-revolutionary British nationalism, and what Hilton has termed the new efflorescence of 'Church and King Toryism', found a natural home in India.[69] Scottish scholar-administrators justified enlightened despotism as a necessary stage of societal development, analogous to monarchical absolutism in late medieval Europe.[70] A revivified monarchism found Indian expressions in British sponsorship of the formal sovereignty of the Mughal emperors and other Indian 'princes', and also in Queen Victoria's emergence as an imperial monarch in the 1840s, symbolized by the establishment of special royal honours for the Indian army.[71] The official culture of British India, with its strongly militaristic, masculinist, and patriarchal ethos, also formed part of the wider regendering of British politics in the age of evangelical revival.[72] British male officials professed to guard the imagined patriarchal traditions of Indian society, even as they positioned themselves as 'protectors' of Indian women, and sought to shelter the relatively small population of European women from the supposed threats of Asiatic corruption.[73] Reforms designed to maintain the respectability of empire, specifically by regulating interracial sexual encounters and family life, generated new conceptions of Britishness as a form of ethnicity.[74] Meanwhile, a concern for protecting the perquisites of (especially male) landed aristocrats was a cornerstone of Indian governance, as it was for many of the ruling elite in England.

The large mobilization around the reform of the East India Company in the early 1830s showed that British India continued to fuel domestic reformism. As Miles Taylor has detailed, domestic merchants and radicals made strategic alliances with British settlers, Indian and Eurasian reformers, and radical newspapermen from the Indian presidencies, demanding an end to the China monopoly, freedom of the press in India, and reforms to make the authoritarian structures of Company rule more accountable to a local 'public'.[75] India was not, then, simply a useful appendage for propping up the British oligarchy, but also a rallying point for liberal critics of the 'old corruption'.

Nonetheless, demands for imperial reform were bought off with commercial concessions at relatively little cost to the domestic state, while the militaristic colonial regime largely resisted pressures for greater openness and accountability. Meanwhile, if many British radicals continued to disparage the Indian empire, other liberals tried to make the empire a vehicle for the cause of reform.[76] C. A. Bayly's recent study shows that the leading Indian liberal of the 1830s,

Rammohan Roy, was not so much (as in Hobsbawm's version) a champion of French republicanism against British industrialism; instead, he advocated a post-revolutionary or even counter-revolutionary style of constitutional liberalism, proposing a gradualist reform of imperial institutions, drawing eclectically on European and Asian ideas and institutions, so that imperial power would be made progressively more accountable to an evolving Indian public.[77] For the British Empire in general, political evolutionism underpinned the broader consolidation of imperial authority during and after the age of revolutionary scares. Whiggish constitutional history, combined with more sociological theories of 'stages of civilization' drawn from Scottish Enlightenment writers, appeared to justify authoritarian forms of rule over 'backward' peoples as a temporary expedient – an ideological move that was bolstered by a growing awareness of separate economic trajectories between industrializing regions of Europe and poorer agrarian societies.[78]

If Indian conquests became a vital adjunct to the British domestic order in the age of revolutions, they also became the launching pad for the redefinition and globalization (in a very literal sense) of Britain's overseas empire. From the point of view of 'British Indian' history, the early conquests of Bengal can be seen as the 'bridgehead' to a new style of territorial imperialism, with massive armies paid for by taxes from the land.[79] From another point of view, however, territorial conquests in India became an appendage for a global maritime empire built on the East India Company's early modern foundations.[80] Warren Hastings, the first Governor-general of British India, was interested not only in extending forms of tribute from Indian lands, but also in opening up a new commercial route to China through Tibet, and in strengthening the line of communication and trade through the Red Sea and Suez.[81] Alan Frost has argued that William Pitt and Henry Dundas formulated a consciously global strategy for imperial consolidation in the aftermath of the conquest of Bengal and the American Revolution. Partly this was driven by the need to provide extra naval protection for Indian territories, and partly by the desire to extend naval and commercial power into the Pacific. Thus, New South Wales was imagined as a reserve of naval supplies and a commercial emporium, as well as a dumping ground for transported convicts.[82]

This continued oceanic perspective on empire helps to explain why ministers like Pitt professed to renounce the aim of further territorial conquests in India.[83] In the early nineteenth century, the East India Company extended its commercial and military operations west into the so-called trucial states of the Persian Gulf region, and also east into the Straits of Malacca, the Chinese coast, and the Philippines. Some Dutch colonies seized during the wars with France, such as Java, were later returned; others, crucially the Cape Colony, were retained and used to further extend British naval, maritime, and commercial strength. Singapore and later Hong Kong emerged as new imperial cities, while forms of 'tributary alliance' with local princes were exported from India to the Gulf states and later the Malay sultanates, creating what Sugata Bose has called a 'sea-change in sovereignty' in the Indian Ocean arena.[84] Bose and Thomas Metcalf have recently detailed how the Indian empire stood as the vital springboard for British expansion in Asia and Africa during the high imperial age, sending out merchants and labourers, soldiers and policemen, law codes and theories of racial ordering into the new imperial world.[85]

Even in the late eighteenth century, other powerful European states were intensely aware that new conquests in India were shifting the balance of power in Europe. India was thus more tightly bound into European conceptions of global politics beyond the ambitions of British imperial statesmen. The fullest repercussions were felt in France, after military escalations in south India led to the humiliation and bankruptcy of the French East India Company. The American war, and the resurgence of Hyder Ali of Mysore as a military threat to the British position in south India, triggered a new flurry of French military and naval activity in the late 1770s and 1780s, catalysing an even stronger British response. Hyder's son, Tipu, continued to hope for French aid against the British (sending envoys to the court of Louis XVI in 1787), while the British feared naval actions launched from the Île-de-France.[86]

As it turned out, fortified by the fiscal windfalls of his recent territorial conquests, Napoleon would take a different route to challenging the rise of imperial Britain. 'Truly to overthrow England', he declared, 'we must occupy Egypt.'[87] As both Maya Jasanoff and Juan Cole have recently emphasized, destabilizing British India was one of major goals of his Egyptian campaigns. By invading Egypt, he could compete with Britain's growing colonial commerce, cut off the quicker overland route for communication between Britain and India, and lay the groundwork for eventually recovering France's position in India itself.[88] Napoleon sent a small expedition to India in 1802 to make alliances with Indian states, and even in the 1830s Louis Philippe was still trying to consolidate a diplomatic and military alliance with the Ranjit Singh in the Punjab.[89]

Perhaps the most quixotic example of imperial ambition towards India was the Cossack invasion force launched by Tsar Paul I of Russia in 1801. Described by one recent historian as a 'suicidal mission' launched on the 'personal whim' of Tsar Paul, this surprising turn of events has sometimes been given as evidence of the tsar's insanity and a contributory factor in his subsequent assassination.[90] Other historians have suggested the plan may have originated with Paul's new ally Napoleon, and even that it may have represented a pragmatic response to British naval superiority.[91] In the light of Napoleon's comment that 'great reputations are only made in the Orient; Europe is too small', Paul's hubristic venture might at least be taken as a sign of the way that British imperialism in South Asia was changing European conceptions of imperial prestige.[92] Russian military strategists continued to regard British India as a potential weak-point in the British world system, and in 1857, on the eve of the great mutiny/rebellion, they reconsidered the feasibility of invading India as a way of promoting a general uprising.[93] Meanwhile, the officer classes of British India's garrison state remained acutely aware of the potential for mutiny and rebellion, and obsessed with the lack of good intelligence about frontier regions. These preoccupations fed a tendency to exaggerate external threats, which itself spurred periods of renewed militarism and conquest as the British pushed their armies up towards the north-west frontier.[94]

The rise of British India, then, helped to redraw imperial ambitions and imperial frontiers across the world. If it enabled Britain to steal a march on other European rivals, it further exacerbated the vulnerabilities of imperial systems outside Europe, the Ottoman and the Chinese empires. China felt the brunt of European expansionism in a new and more brutal form thanks to the resources brought to bear on its trading ports from British India. George Bogle's mission to Tibet in the 1770s and Lord Macartney's mission to China of 1793 signalled British desires for further commercial penetration of Chinese markets, but it was Indian reserves of opium, monopolized by the East India Company and transported by British private traders, that proved most threatening to the integrity and good order of the Chinese empire in the long run. Britain's growing willingness and ability by the 1830s to coerce Chinese port authorities into unequal treaty arrangements, and the power of opium to suck silver reserves out of the Chinese economy, were a direct challenge to imperial authority in China.[95]

South Asia's global connections

The rise of British India marked and contributed to the intensification of a modern form of globalization increasingly dependent on European imperialism. Yet this picture needs qualifying in two important ways. First, the territorial conquests of the late eighteenth century were themselves predicated on a much longer trajectory of European commercial, naval, and territorial consolidation in the Indian Ocean region, which made Asian states and empires vulnerable to various forms of dependency on European shipping, and to flows of silver carried by Europeans from the Atlantic world.[96] Thanks to early victories in India, the British were in the best position to exploit these structural dependencies, while trying to dictate the terms of South Asia's global connections. Second, European imperialism in Asia in the age of revolutions remained more constrained and fitful in actuality than the ambitions of imperial statesmen or the imaginations of later imperial historians often allowed. European expansion often worked by exploiting webs of connection forged in an earlier phase of globalization, and South Asian merchants, sailors, labourers, scholars, and pilgrims continued to make their own global networks under the surface of, or even in competition with, European globalism.[97]

As Indian territories became embroiled with a global British empire, their ties to the world economy were dramatically reworked. From a situation in which (as David Washbrook has put it) Indian artisans had 'clothed the world' with high quality cotton textiles, Indian artisans lost most of their overseas markets from the 1820s to the rise of the British cotton industry.[98] If the extent of deindustrialization is still argued about, and the character and impact of colonial policies disputed, the dramatic trend from an artisanal to agricultural export economy is clear.[99] Prasannan Parthasarathi has recently added his study of weavers in southern India to an older body of literature on the coercive colonial controls on weavers, which depressed artisanal incomes even before the onslaught of Lancashire goods.[100] Despite frequent harassment by the British, other European companies, and increasingly American buyers too, continued to sustain demand for Indian textile exports into the early nineteenth century.[101] But competition over procurement led to new restrictions on weavers, backed by the colonial state, just as the colonial assault on Indian regional states undercut the demand for high-end consumables by Indian courts. David Washbrook has argued that these effects of colonial rule, added to a penal tax regime, intensified the depressive effects of the loss of export markets for Indian manufactures after 1820.[102]

The substitution of primary for industrial exports expanded cash-cropping in some regions of South Asia, but at the same time left peasant farmers increasingly vulnerable to 'hectic cycles of profitability and decline' that characterized the early nineteenth-century world economy.[103] Indian sugar, raw cotton, and indigo found growing if unsteady overseas markets; opium was the one sustained boom product of the period, its major profits flowing to the East India Company and the European merchants who managed the China trade.[104] The ruptures in South Asia's export economy signalled what Pomeranz has termed the 'great divergence' between industrializing regions of Europe and the rest of the world, but they also hampered attempts by European merchants to turn the new empire into a financial windfall. If the narrative of the China trade leading to the Opium Wars can give the impression of an irresistible force of European capitalism opening up Eastern markets, the ready resort to violence often reflected the continued insecurity and fragility of European commercial expansion.

After all, only a few years before the first Opium War, many of the major agency houses in Calcutta, the grand, neoclassical capital of British India, had gone bankrupt. The career of John Palmer, finely narrated in a recent book by Anthony Webster, illustrates both the new opportunities and the pitfalls attending British merchants in the emerging empire.[105] The son of an aide-de-camp to Governor Warren Hastings, John Palmer served in the navy and fought in the American revolutionary war, before settling in Calcutta, and rising to be a senior partner in one of the most successful Calcutta 'agency houses'. These trading firms managed funds for the official classes of British India as well as Indian investors, and engaged in banking and commodity trades throughout Asia. Palmer's firm was heavily involved in the opium and indigo trades, was linked (through Palmer's half-brother) with debt-financing to the Nizam of Hyderabad, and dealt extensively with Penang, Java, and Canton. Palmer even developed his own merchant fleet of over twenty ships, profiting from the dismantling of the Company's monopoly of the trade between India and Europe in 1813.

If close ties with the expanding Company made Palmer into a 'merchant prince', they also helped to break him. His brother became embroiled in a political scandal in Hyderabad; meanwhile the Company's war with Burma in 1825–6, and its consequent heavy borrowing, shrank the money market and drove up interest rates in Calcutta. Finally, the London corresponding firm that Palmer depended on for managing the remittance of funds for his British

Indian clients began to call in its debts at a moment of downturn in commodity prices. To make these remittances, agency houses were forced to lay out capital advances to indigo planters which they frequently did not recover, especially if prices dipped. The collapse of Palmer's business in 1830 presaged a more general run on the Calcutta houses, and showed the fragility of the circuits of foreign trade and banking in early colonial India. In part, Palmer's fall reflected a more competitive environment with the end of the Company monopoly, and the fact that London financial houses were forging links with Asia independently from the old agencies. With the rise of the steamship and later railway investments, European capital would find a more direct and secure role in Asian markets.

In the meantime, and even after this, Indian bankers and merchants continued to find significant niches within oceanic and interregional commerce. The view that European steamships and modern colonial empires fundamentally sundered older Indian Ocean trades is now being re-evaluated. Rajat Ray and Sugata Bose have argued for the endurance of an oceanic 'bazaar' economy linking Asian merchants operating at an intermediary level within a European-dominated commercial system.[106] Claude Markovits has shown how the 'global world' of Sindhi merchants survived and even thrived in the colonial period, noting that South Asian merchants in the western regions had longer to adjust to the colonial onset than those in, for example, Bengal. Some networks, like Gujarati traders in Zanzibar and East Africa, or the Shikarpur Sindhis trading in Afghanistan and Central Asia, predated European colonial expansion; some, like the Hyderabadi traders studied by Markovits, adjusted to being squeezed out of state financing by British conquerors, and inserted themselves into new colonial patterns of overseas trade.[107]

European expansion also interacted with, often conflicted with, but never entirely cut off competing forms of religious universalism, for example diverse modes of Islamic universalism.[108] Tim Harper has argued that much of the colonial world in the mid-nineteenth century existed as a 'Euro-Islamic condominium', noting the continuing salience of Ottoman suzerainty across South and South-east Asia, and the survival and dynamism of the Hadhrami diaspora of merchants, pilgrims, and scholars.[109] The British Empire itself sponsored neo-traditional forms of Islamic kingship, enabling the Shi'i rulers of Awadh to declare their regal independence from the Sunni Mughal emperors, and establishing systems of indirect rule throughout India, the Persian Gulf, and Malaya.[110] At the same time, the British continued to preserve the faded vestiges of Mughal authority in Delhi, until the mutiny/rebellion of 1857 showed that Hindustani loyalties to the old empire were too strong and too deep to be safely ignored. In deposing and desacralizing the Mughal emperor after 1857, the British thus indirectly contributed to the revival of the idea of the Ottoman caliphate as a Pan-Islamic suzerain in the late nineteenth century,[111] even while they continued to ape Islamicate imperial forms in the oriental gothic or Indo-Saracenic styles of public buildings, or in the great durbar ceremonials of the high Raj.[112]

Prior to the rise of British India, the Mughal court and other Islamicate courts in India had been vital nodes within what Juan Cole has termed a 'far-flung ecumene of Persian culture'.[113] Again, the British Empire coexisted in a tense relation to this 'Persophone world culture', initially appropriating the glamour of Persian as an imperial language, and plundering Persian treatises for vital information about revenues, laws, and other immediate concerns of imperial administration. Sir William Jones also relied on Persian scholarship during his path-breaking studies of Sanskrit and Indo-European languages.[114] The British maintenance of Persian as an administrative language until the 1830s, early experiments in printing Persian texts, and the survival in straitened means of a post-Mughal class of scholar-administrators meant that India's strong Persian connection survived into the nineteenth century.[115] But it was increasingly threatened by moves to Anglicize the high levels of administration, by the colonial sponsorship of Brahminical Hinduism as the true cultural bedrock of ancient India, and at a deeper level by the continuing vernacularization of Indian language and literature. British India's 'Persian connection' would increasingly become defined by the great power rivalries of the great game,[116] while one of the most profound long-term effects of modern globalization would be to universalize increasingly hard-edged national and religious distinctions, often under the cover of empires.

The recent vogue for global histories has underscored a broader recalibration of the field of modern history, challenging older notions of a Western 'core' of modernity and a non-Western 'periphery'. They have underscored that modern forms of globalization were layered, diverse, and entangled with earlier patterns of connection. Within these new perspectives, the 'age of revolutions' appears as a particularly unstable and confusing set of transitions, with power and wealth shifting inexorably and subtly, and regions such as South Asia becoming gradually 'reglobalized' within European imperial systems. The unevenness and ruptures within these processes give the lie to any notion of modern globalization as successive waves of connectivity become ever stronger and more widespread. When Thomas Macaulay complained in the British House of Commons that 'a broken head in Coldbath Field excites more debate in this house than three pitched battles in India', he was observing a form of forgetfulness that was as important to empire as new orientalist knowledge.[117]

Modern empires, we know, worked to divide and rule as much as to connect. Relying on its efforts 'to control labour, fix prices, and establish monopolies', the British Empire often struggled against new forms of integration unleashed within its own system of rule.[118] Thus, Thomas Munro, in a minute of 1824, justified the strict imperial controls over the press in British India, arguing that press freedoms as demanded by some British and Indian radicals would spell disaster. Crucially, a free press would undermine the implicit hierarchies of race and status on which military discipline depended; Indian soldiers would learn 'to compare their own allowances and humble rank, with those of their European officers'; the desire for a 'national government' would spread, but without the moderating effects of a mature public, leading to mutiny, general rebellion, and anarchy.[119] David Washbrook has suggested how the authoritarian style of government that Munro was defending in south India, combined with prolonged economic depression, led to 'the closure of broader lines of communication' that had characterized the region's history in a previous era of numerous competing states and commercial expansion. For him, the reduction of 'South India's links with the rest of the world' was 'perhaps one of the key meanings of colonialism in South India'.[120] This example suggests that historians may need to attend to forms of imperial 'deglobalization' alongside conventional emphases on Western imperialism as a moment in the history of 'globalization'.

The main benefits of the turn to global history may come less from the abstract formulations of types or styles of globalization than from the reframing of local, regional, imperial, national, and transnational histories. Global perspectives are currently pulling the history of colonial South Asia beyond the dichotomy of empire and nation, metropole and colony, and recovering more supple lines of connection and comparison than imperial or anti-imperial national histories allowed for. An emphasis on transregional and oceanic ties that were reshaped within the colonial world can encourage new regional histories that resist the teleology of the territorial nation state. At the same time, studies of diaspora and circulation foreground the role of 'expatriate nationalisms' and 'competing universalisms' in creating the modern world order.[121] Recognizing analogous patterns of state and social formation beyond the bounded categories of Europe, Asia, or Africa enables comparisons between modern forms of governance that can respecify rather than take for granted the notion of a 'colonial modernity'. Such studies will continue to show how networks of exchange always transcended the ties that bound metropole and colony, and that the British Empire never fully mastered the global connections it worked to create, even as its armies and navies remade the world in the age of revolutions.[122]

9

Revolutionary Europe and the Destruction of Java's Old Order, 1808–1830

Peter Carey

Introduction

At first glance, it may seem strange that Java, an island situated half a world away from Revolutionary France, should end up being one of the key battle grounds in the global conflict that followed the fateful Girondin decision to declare war on Austria in the spring of 1792. Yet, in the compass of less than a decade, Java's own *ancien régime* was violently overturned as in quick succession a Franco-Dutch regime (1808–11) under Napoleon's only non-French marshal, Herman Willem Daendels (1762–1818), and a five-year British occupation (1811–16) under the equally dictatorial Sir Thomas Stamford Raffles (1781–1826), transformed the colony. This paved the way for the restoration of Dutch rule in 1816 under the terms of the Treaty of Vienna, by which time the commercial dealings of the Company had been replaced by the beginnings of a modern colonial state, the post-January 1818 Netherlands Indies. Over the next century, this would reduce the power of the local rulers and establish Dutch authority in nearly every corner of the archipelago. The boundaries of present-day Indonesia were determined at this time.

Java's destiny had long been linked to the emerging global economy through the Dutch connection and the international business networks of the overseas Chinese. These latter were the key to the Dutch management of a complex trading system that underpinned the wealth of the failing Dutch East India Company (Vereenigde Oost Indische Compagnie, henceforth VOC) in Asia. Java's rice and textile exports sustained the Company's original trading bases in the Spice Islands (Ambon, Banda, Ternate, and Tidore), while its commodity exports – in particular coffee from West

Java, and indigo and sugar from the Bataviasche Ommelanden (Batavian hinterland) developed with overseas Chinese capital – had begun to make their mark on world markets. Java was also a major rendezvous point for Dutch trade from its factories in Surat, Malabar, and Nagasaki, as well as a potential military strongpoint in the Indian Ocean given its extensive dockyards at Pulau Onrust in the Bay of Batavia and its port and shipbuilding facilities along Java's north coast. Such assets were a tempting prize for both the French Republic and the Republic's First Coalition enemies, in particular Britain.

Despite its commercial and military importance, however, the island, whose estimated population was some 3.5 million in 1795, was not a Dutch version of the British Raj. A declining power in Europe, Holland appeared to be on its way out in Java while the south-central Javanese rulers in Yogyakarta and Surakarta enjoyed *de facto* sovereignty. The Fourth Anglo-Dutch War of 1780–4 was the turning point. Faced with mounting debts, the VOC was declared bankrupt and its assets were taken over by the Dutch state on 1 January 1800. By then control of the Dutch possessions in the east had been taken out of the hands of the Directors of the VOC and vested in the new Committee for the Affairs of East Indian Trade and Colonies, a creation of the new Batavian Republic (1796–1806) formed after Holland's incorporation in the French *Grande Nation* when General Jean-Charles Pichegru's Army of the North had crossed the Dutch Republic's frozen Maas and Waal rivers and installed a pro-French regime in The Hague (January 1795).

News of these dramatic events in Europe and their implications for Java's old order were slow to percolate through to the distant archipelago. The fact that VOC personnel, scions of the great *mestiço* Indies families who were then politically pre-eminent in Java, continued in post well beyond Daendels's administration (1808–11) meant that the local Javanese rulers had difficulty in getting a true insight into the scale of the political revolution that was then transforming Europe. Holland's weakness masked political realities. Indeed, the fact that the Dutch governor-general and Council of the Indies felt the need to appeal to the south-central Javanese rulers to help them to defend their colonial capital – Batavia – during the international crises that sped the VOC's demise reinforced the courts' suspicion that the Dutch were on their way out militarily in the Indies.

Following Holland's occupation in 1794–5, the *Stadhouder* (head of state), William V (reigned 1766–85, 1787–95), fled to London and from his place of exile in the royal palace at Kew issued the so-called 'Kew Letters', which ordered that the Republic's colonies be handed over to the British to prevent them falling into French hands. So began a twenty-year period in which the East Indies was drawn into the global conflict between Britain and France. During this period of the Revolutionary (1792–9) and Napoleonic (1799–1802, 1803–13, 1815) wars, the archipelago became a battle ground on land and sea. Between 1795 and 1797, British naval forces operating from Madras and Pulau Pinang captured most of the Dutch possessions outside Java. Although returned to Holland under the terms of the Peace of Amiens (1802), all were recaptured by the British in the seven years that followed the renewal of hostilities in Europe in May 1803. During this time the East Indies were placed under strict naval blockade, an interdiction so tight that Napoleon's younger brother, Louis Bonaparte (King of Holland, 1806–10), took care to send Daendels out to Java with a replacement governor-general following on a separate fast frigate in case he fell into British hands.

The tragedy for the Javanese was that just as all the signs seemed to point in the direction of a Dutch collapse, half a world away in Europe events were taking place that would change the Javanese 'Old Order' for ever. The twin political and industrial revolutions then tearing the *anciens régimes* of eighteenth-century Europe apart would hit Java with the force of an Asian tsunami. In the space of just four years (1808–12), the relationship between the European government and the south-central Javanese rulers was transformed. The Yogyakarta sultanate bore the brunt of these changes. In quick succession, the re-energized Franco-Dutch regime of Daendels (1808–11) and the British-Indian administration of Raffles (1811–16) forced open Yogyakarta's eastern outlying territories, plundered its court, and exiled its reigning monarch. After the fall of the *kraton* (fortified royal capital/court) in June 1812 and the imposition of new treaties, the relationship between Batavia and the princely states began to resemble post-Plassey India when the British replaced the Mughal emperors in Lower Bengal. The returned Dutch administration of Governor-general Godert Alexander Gerard Philip Baron van der Capellen (in office 1816–26) continued this process. Desperate for money but keen to protect the welfare of ordinary Javanese, van der Capellen attempted to square the circle between increased fiscal returns and his ethical principles, which ignited a powder keg in south-central Java. Adverse environmental and health conditions, in particular the May 1821 cholera epidemic and the December 1822 eruption of the central Javanese Mount Merapi volcano, combined with soaring rice prices, triggered massive popular uprisings in July and August 1825 that heralded the outbreak of the Java War (1825–30).

This conflict was a watershed in the history of Java and of what – after 1945 – would become the Republic of Indonesia. For the first time a European colonial government faced a social rebellion covering a large part of the island. Likewise, the Javanese experienced for perhaps the first time a rebellion that had at its heart social and economic grievances rather than dynastic ambitions. Most of central and east Java and many of the *pasisir* (north coast) areas were affected. Two million Javanese, nearly half the island's total population, were exposed to the ravages of war, one-quarter of the cultivated area of Java sustained damage, and about 200,000 Javanese died. In securing their pyrrhic victory, the Dutch also suffered: 7,000 Indonesian auxiliaries and 8,000 of their own troops perished. The war cost their exchequer an estimated 20 million guilders. The end of the conflict left the Dutch in undisputed control of the island and a new phase of colonial rule began with the inception of Governor-general Johannes van den Bosch's 'cultivation system' (1830–70). This turned Java into a globally linked cash crop economy, a development that proved immensely profitable for Holland, with an estimated 880 million guilders (present-day US$100 billion) accruing to the Dutch exchequer, easing the Netherlands' transition to a modern industrial economy. The war thus marked the end of a process, maturing since the Daendels administration (1808–11), that saw the change-over from the Dutch East India Company era, when contacts between Batavia and the south-central Javanese kingdoms had had the nature of ambassadorial links between sovereign states, to the 'high colonial' period when the Principalities occupied a clearly subordinate position to the European power.

For the Javanese, this five-year conflict had far-reaching implications. The emergence of a strong charismatic leader in the person of Pangéran (prince) Diponegoro (1785–1855), who took the title of the Javanese messianic *ratu adil* ('just king'), served to bring many disparate social elements under the single banner of Javanese Islam. Widespread millenarian expectations caught the imagination of the peasantry and acted as a catalyst for social and economic grievances, accumulating since the beginning of the nineteenth century. The concept of holy war (*prang sabil*), imagery from the Javanese shadow-play (*wayang*), and Javanese nativist sentiments, made up of an intense longing for the restoration of an idealized traditional order – which Diponegoro described as 'restoring the high state of the Islamic religion in Java' – all forged a common identity among the prince's followers. In this fashion, nobles, dismissed provincial officials, religious teachers, professional bandits, porters, day labourers, tax-paying farmers (*sikep*), and artisans were brought together briefly in a common cause. The Java War was thus significant for Indonesia's future. The subtle interplay of economic grievances and millenarian hopes created a movement of unique social breadth which anticipated the nationalist movement of the early twentieth century.

The cultural dislocation wrought by the new European imperialism shaped the young Diponegoro. A key transitional figure, he lived through the shift from the old order of late eighteenth-century Java to the new 'high colonial' era when steamships plied the trade routes of the Netherlands-Indies archipelago, linking Diponegoro's place of exile in Sulawesi (Celebes) to the main Javanese ports. A traditional figure steeped in the values of pre-modern Java, particularly the spirit world of the south-central Javanese courts, he also pointed to the future. One thinks here of his use of Javanese Islam, particularly its millenarian traditions, as a way of forging a new identity for Javanese Muslims in an era when the old Javanese order was crumbling.

Diponegoro inhabited a world increasingly divided between those who were prepared to accommodate themselves to the new European dispensation and those who saw the Islamic moral order (*agami Islam*) as the lodestar in a society that had lost its traditional moorings. The Java War thus gave impetus to a process still working itself out in present-day Indonesia, namely the integration of Islamic values into contemporary Javanese and Indonesian identity. Diponegoro's world view also encompassed a distinctly contemporary concern with how Javanese Muslims should live in an age of Western imperialism. For the prince, unlike most present-day Indonesian Muslims, the answer lay in the waging of holy war and the development of a clear distinction between the *wong Islam* ('people of Islam', Muslim believers), the European *kapir laknatullah* (heretics accursed by Allah), and the Javanese *kapir murtad* (apostates), namely those who had allied themselves with the Dutch. There was also a concern on the prince's part for the preservation of specifically Javanese values as expressed in language, dress, and cultural codes. This can be seen most clearly in his treatment of Dutch prisoners and his insistence that they adopt Javanese dress and speak to their captors not in the reviled language of the new colonial state – 'service Malay'[1] – but in High Javanese (*krama*), the medium of the court elite.

Despite his adoption of Ottoman dress and bestowal of Ottoman military titles – *Basah* ('Pasha') and *Ali Basah* ('The High Pasha') – on his military commanders, Diponegoro was no Islamic reformer. A traditional Javanese Muslim, he had no problem reconciling the spirit world of Java with membership of the international *ummat* (community of Muslim believers) whose religious and politico-cultural centres lay in the Hejaz (present-day Saudi Arabia) and Ottoman Turkey. Although Diponegoro did not prevail in achieving his goal of restoring the high state of the Islamic religion in Java, his wider moral vision of securing an honoured place for Islam in the life of the nation had a lasting resonance. Indeed, following Indonesia's political independence from the Dutch in 1945, it has continued to be negotiated, especially in the current post-9/11 world of global conflict between what some in the Islamic community perceive as the 'materialistic' values of the West and what many more – believers and unbelievers alike – acknowledge as the deeply fissiparous loyalties of the worldwide Muslim *ummat*.

Daendels's political revolution, 1808–1811

The 'beginning of the ruin of the Land of Java' had been the prophetic warning delivered to Diponegoro during a pilgrimage to visit Java's spirit guardians on the south coast in circa 1805. Specifically, he had been told that this destruction would start in just under three years' time. Right on cue, on 5 January 1808, Daendels arrived in Batavia to take up his post as governor-general. Lawyer, revolutionary, politician, and career soldier, he was very much a product of the new Europe forged by the French Revolution. A participant in the 'Patriot Revolt' against the *Stadhouder* in Holland (1786–7), he had helped to set up (and commanded) the Batavian Legion (1792–5), which had fought alongside French Republican forces in the 1794–5 invasion of the Dutch Netherlands. Later, as head of the pro-French Unitarian Party, he had earned himself a reputation as a 'headstrong, sentimental and obstinate' character.[2] A man of few scruples, great energy and a penchant for using force to achieve his political ends, he was destined to make a lasting mark on the history of Java.

One of the marshal's primary strategic considerations in planning Java's defence was the position of the independent courts. Their power and influence marked them out as potential rivals to the European government and as dubious allies in the event of an enemy attack. In this respect, the court of Yogyakarta was by far the more redoubtable in the light of its military resources and substantial cash reserves. Imbued with a fierce hatred of *ancien régime* monarchies, Daendels promulgated a celebrated Edict on Ceremonial and Etiquette on 28 July 1808, which did away with most of the ceremonial functions previously performed by the Residents for the rulers, which were considered degrading. Instead, Daendels's Franco-Dutch regime accorded them various privileges more in line with their positions as direct representatives of the governor-general and the royal government in The Hague.[3] Thus the First Residents now received the title of 'minister', wore new Napoleonic era uniforms (blue coats with high collars braided in gold with olives, olive branches, and flat gold buttons, white breeches with embroidered knee bands and white silk stockings, and tricorn black hats with black straps and cockade), and were allowed to carry a blue and gold state parasol or *payung* emblazoned with the arms of the King of Holland. On official occasions, they were not to remove their hats when approaching the ruler, who was to rise to greet the Dutch representative and make space for him immediately to his left on his throne, thus allowing him to sit at exactly the monarch's level. Likewise, they were no longer required to serve the ruler in a menial fashion with drink and betelnut. Various other articles regulated the new forms of greeting when saluting the ruler both inside and outside the *kraton*: the minister, for example, was now accorded a military escort of mounted dragoons on all official visits to the court and was no longer expected to stop his coach when passing that of the ruler on the high road. Such changes in ceremonial amounted to a very substantial alteration to the position of the Dutch representatives at the courts that struck at the heart of the Javanese understanding of the Dutch presence in Java.

The edicts effectively destroyed the finely balanced political structure that enabled the courts' acceptance of Dutch rule in Java. If the articles of the edicts were carried out as the marshal wished there could no longer be any pretence that the Resident was a joint servant of the European government and the ruler. Even the diplomatic skills of the former VOC officials posted to the courts could not disguise the scale of the changes now being demanded. The Yogyakarta court chronicle describes how immediately upon receipt of the edict, the sultan ordered his throne to be changed in order to maintain his more elevated position during state functions. This involved making it narrower so that only the ruler could sit on it, and having a wooden footstool placed under it so that he would always sit higher than the Resident even when he went to visit him in the Residency, a procedure that nearly resulted in an armed clash between the sultan's entourage and British officers in the Residency 'throne room' at the time of Raffles's visit to Yogyakarta on 27 December 1811.[4]

The political pressure now bearing down on the south-central Javanese rulers to accept their changed status opened up deep divisions at the courts. Those who were prepared to work with the

European government began to display their pro-Dutch views in striking sartorial and personal ways. During his May 1803 inspection tour through south-central and east Java, the governor of Java's North-east Coast, Nicolaus Engelhard (in office 1801–8), had already noticed that the Surakarta ruler's court was beginning to dress 'in European style' despite the huge debts this entailed.[5] Even in the more traditional Yogyakarta court, the value of adopting the cultural as well as political fashions of Java's foreign rulers was noted. The Crown Prince, who would rule briefly (1812–14) as sultan under the British, sought to prove his pro-Dutch sentiments by insisting that his tea should be served with milk like that of his Dutch guests,[6] and crying out at the top of his voice during a military review in honour of visiting Dutch officers that Yogyakarta courtiers and officials should speak nothing but Malay on that day 'because that was the language which the sultan's friends, the Dutch, used with their people!'[7]

Attempts by Daendels and his senior officials to make the Javanese rulers understand that the marshal's edicts were part of a pan-European republican movement to overthrow the 'feudal order' fell on deaf ears. So baffling indeed was Daendels's language about the abolition of feudalism that the official Javanese translator in Semarang had great difficulty rendering the Dutch text into Javanese when the prime ministers of the two south-central Javanese courts came to the north coast port city to present their official compliments to the newly arrived governor-general:

> I receive with much pleasure and sincerity the homage of the [Surakarta ruler] through his prime minister and further ambassadors.
> I do not consider this solemnity in the light of homage by a vassal to his lord paramount, the feudal system having been abolished in Europe, but I look upon the same as congratulations on my safe arrival on this island and on the commencement of the administration of His Majesty's possessions in India.
> The [Dutch] East India Company and the Republic of the United Provinces had lost their former influence in Europe. But the election of the Emperor's brother to the throne of Holland has caused the political influence of that country to be re-established by adopting a more ener-getic mode of administration and by a most intimate union with the mightiest empire in the world. It is the wish of King Louis to promote the happiness of his subjects on the island of Java and he offers them peace, prosperity and a benevolent government:
> And I do solemnly declare in the name of His Majesty, the friend and protector of the princes and inhabitants of Java, that I will endeavour to maintain peace and to render the island of Java as prosperous as possible.[8]

As the prime ministers and their respective parties made their way back to the south-central Javanese courts with Daendels' declaration in their hands, they must have wondered what exactly was going on. A post-feudal Java? The happiness of subjects? The mightiest empire in the world? How to make sense of all this in the context of an 'Old Order' in Java that had seemed so immutable?

Luckily, symbolic explanation was at hand. No sooner had the Yogyakarta delegation returned home than Daendels's deputy, Jacob Andries van Braam (1771–1820), came over from Surakarta on an official visit with his wife. It was usual on such occasions for the court to honour its distinguished guest with a tiger and buffalo fight on the southern *alun-alun* (open field behind the *kraton*). Van Braam was not disappointed.[9] However, the particular fight he witnessed had an interesting denouement: in the first round of the contest, the tiger severed the leg tendons of the buffalo and then refused to fight further. In the second, when a new tiger was introduced, it jumped clean out of the ring of guarding spearmen and was only caught and killed behind the elevated platform on which the sultan was sitting with his Dutch guest. 'This situation, which had never occurred before', van Braam reported to Daendels, 'caused the Javanese to make many conjectures with regard to me . . . and the sultan made me a compliment and said that it had occurred in my honour!'[10]

Some compliment; some honour! What van Braam did not realize was that these contests had a deeper meaning. Whereas for a visiting European dignitary like himself a tiger and buffalo fight might have been seen as a rather gruesome form of entertainment, the equivalent of bear-baiting or bull-fighting in Europe, for the watching Javanese the contests had a much more profound significance. They equated the Europeans with the quick and deadly tiger and themselves with the powerful wild buffalo. Although the former was ferociously aggressive, it had no staying power and was nearly always defeated by its slower, more cautious and resilient adversary. In this particular case, both rounds had shown the Dutch 'tiger' in a rather unflattering light: in the first, although able to move in for the kill with the buffalo's tendons severed, it had not done so. In the second, the tiger had jumped clean out of the ring. Did this not mean that the Javanese could expect some unusual developments in terms of their Dutch adversary? At the time of van Braam's visit, the British invasion still lay nearly three years away, but when it happened, those Yogyakarta courtiers who could recall the October 1808 tiger-and-buffalo fight on the southern *alun-alun* might have been forgiven for surmising that it presaged a time when the once mighty Dutch and their now defunct East India Company would be placed completely *hors de combat* as far as their rule in Java was concerned by a new and more formidable European enemy.

The British interregnum, 1811–1816

News that the British were planning an invasion of Java was known there soon after the fateful tiger-and-buffalo fight in Yogyakarta. In late 1810, a returned Mecca pilgrim from Java's north coast, Haji Mustapa, who appears to have witnessed the British naval build-up in Melaka and Pulau Pinang, was arrested by the Franco-Dutch authorities for spreading rumours of an imminent British attack.[11] At the same time, the future British lieutenant-governor of Java sent secret letters to various Indonesian rulers from Melaka announcing that the British would be coming to help them 'make an end' of everything associated with the Dutch and the French in Java and the eastern archipelago.[12] With the fall of the last Franco-Dutch stronghold in the Indian Ocean, Mauritius (Île-de-France) on 7 December 1810, the way was clear for a full-scale attack on Java. The Javanese elite would now experience Britain at its imperial zenith, what historian Chris Bayly has termed that island nation's 'imperial meridian' (1780–1830).[13] They would also find that they had exchanged one form of colonial tyranny for another, no longer a Napoleonic marshal this time but a 'virtual Napoleonic philosopher' and instinctive authoritarian, Thomas Stamford Raffles, a man 'who had a strong distrust of the [native] chiefs and a desire to rule autocratically'.[14]

Appearing off Batavia on 3 August 1811, the British expedition consisting of over 10,000 seasoned troops – half British line regiments and half Bengal sepoy battalions and Madras horse artillery – was an altogether more impressive army than Daendels's hastily gathered force, two-thirds of whom were raw local recruits. Despite the obvious mismatch, the British-Indian attackers appear to have conducted themselves with extreme ruthlessness. This can be seen from the name of the swamp – 'the swamp of the corpses' (Rawa Bangké, now Rawa Mangun) – into which they flung the dead after they had overrun Daendels's great redoubt at Meester Cornelis (present-day Jatinegara) on 26 August 1811. Casualty figures ran as high as 50 per cent for the European defenders and 80 per cent for the local Javanese and Madurese auxiliaries.[15] This was more a *battue* than a battle. During the six-week campaign the Franco-Dutch force lost over 10,000 men. Such behaviour, occasioned perhaps by the ideological nature of the conflict in which the British were engaged, namely the overthrow of French Republicanism and the restoration of pre-revolutionary monarchical principles in Europe, gave the lie to the enlightened and liberal ideals proclaimed by the Governor-General of India, Lord Minto (in office 1807–13), following the Meester Cornelis engagement:

> The inhabitants of Java now touch the fortunate moment when they will be placed under the protection of a power which will keep the calamities and sufferings of war far from their shores and under the guardianship of a just and beneficent government whose principle it is to combine the interests of the state with the security, prosperity and happiness of every class and denomination of the people. Let the people prove itself worthy of those blessings by a timely display of grateful zeal and obedience.[16]

Such 'shock and awe' continued when the British turned their attention to Yogyakarta, which they took by storm in a three-hour operation that began at first light on 20 June 1812. Even Raffles admitted that while British casualties were light, losses among the Javanese defenders had been 'dreadful'. The body of the Javanese commander, who was tracked down and killed in his private mosque, was intentionally mutilated.[17]

This was the first time in Javanese history that a European force had overrun a *kraton*, and the plundering went on for four whole days, an unending stream of booty being carried to the Residency on ox-carts and on the backs of porters. In India, booty was one of the major perquisites of East India Company officers and the British army in India had fought for the right to keep everything in fortresses, courts, and strong points taken by assault. Yogyakarta was no exception. Raffles referred briefly to this process in a dispatch to Lord Minto written soon after the fall of the *kraton*:

> The whole of the tangible property of Djocjocarta fell to the captors . . . but in the immediate distribution they took more upon themselves than was justifiable. . . . I had no reason to expect so hasty and hurried a measure on their part, but the mischief being once done, it was useless to object or condemn. . . . The universal opinion [has been] that in places carried by assault the army was entitled to make an immediate distribution of treasure and jewels, and the authority of Lord Cornwallis [Governor-General of India, 1786–93, 1805] as well as the precedent of Lord Lake [commander-in-chief of the Indian Army and conqueror of Scindia during the Second Mahratta War, 1803–5] were considered decisive.[18]

In vain did the lieutenant-governor cite the example of Lord Wellesley (Governor-General of India, 1797–1805), who had tried – but failed – to prevent the army helping itself to the massive booty from the treasure of Tipu Sultan of Mysore (reigned 1782–99) when his fortified capital at Seringapatam was stormed in 1799 at the end of the Fourth Anglo-Mysore War (1798–9).

The treaties signed between the British government and the courts on 1 August 1812 gave legal title to the radically altered political environment in which the south-central Javanese *kraton* were now forced to exist. The new treaties, the lieutenant-governor averred, would place the south-central Javanese courts 'on such a footing as might no longer endanger the tranquillity of the country'[19] and would open up their administrations to significant liberalization and reform. The annexation of these eastern outlying provinces, many of which had earlier been demanded by Daendels, meant that numerous – but not all – Yogyakarta and Surakarta provincial administrators (*bupati*) lost their positions and livelihood, for the British government only wanted to retain officials from the rank of sub-district head downwards.

The introduction of Raffles's land tax scheme into these annexed regions and the lieutenant-governor's over-optimistic view of their productive capacity – Kedhu in particular – resulted in great hardship for the local population. Not only were the tax demands pitched too high, but the population – particularly those with dry fields – were also required to pay in cash – preferably silver – rather than in kind. This forced them into the hands of Chinese moneylenders who charged extortionate interest, an issue we will return to shortly. At the same time, many of the previous dues and personal services expected by the local Javanese officials remained in force.[20] Raffles's land annexations in August 1812 exacerbated social problems at the courts and in Javanese society more widely, which would later manifest in the breadth of support for Diponegoro at the time of the outbreak of the Java War.

There was one further clause in the treaties that bore even harder on the local population of the princely states. This was article eight, which stipulated that all foreigners and Javanese born outside the Principalities should henceforth fall directly under European government jurisdiction and be tried according to government law.[21] Raffles stressed that the article was specifically designed to afford protection to the Chinese and to ensure that they received their legal rights. But this seemingly innocuous provision had far-reaching consequences, in particular for the inhabitants of south-central Java. After February 1814, when the Resident's courts were established, all litigation between these inhabitants and the Chinese, as well as foreigners or subjects born outside the territories of the south-central Javanese *kraton*, was tried under government law and not under Javanese-Islamic law. This meant that Javanese plaintiffs and defendants hailing from the sultan's and Sunan's dominions, who became involved in litigation with non-Javanese or those Javanese born in government territories, were forced to have their cases tried under legal norms and law codes of which they had no personal knowledge or understanding.

Raffles's 1812 treaty, his subsequent legal reforms, and the question of the sovereignty of Javanese-Islamic law in criminal cases would all prove significant in the later context of the Java War. Unlike the issue of Islamic religious practice, which tended to divide Diponegoro's court and *santri* (student of religion) supporters, the former favouring a rather less strict observance than the latter, British moves against the competence of the royal and religious courts in criminal cases united the two groups. Diponegoro's demands to be recognized as the regulator of religion with special competence over issues of criminal justice thus had widespread resonance.

The 1812 treaties were a disaster for the south-central Javanese courts. Not only did they involve a significant reduction in their territory, they also left a potentially dangerous long-term social and economic legacy, especially in Yogyakarta. Here the combination of the fall of the court, the plundering of its treasury, artefacts, and archives, and the imposition of Raffles's treaty dealt a shattering blow to the prestige and charisma of the court. Besides the financial and territorial losses, the looting of the *kraton* was undoubtedly felt at a deep psychological level by most Yogyanese. In previous Javanese history, such an event had usually signified that the court had been irredeemably defiled. The loss of magical power that such a defilement entailed usually necessitated the removal of the court site to another place. This had happened after the fall of Pléréd in June 1677 and Kartasura in June 1742. But there seems to have been no attempt to move the Yogyakarta *kraton* after June 1812, a seemingly fateful month for the fall of Javanese courts. Besides, the sultanate did not have the financial resources even if it had wished it. The sense of shame and disappointment at the events of 1812 persisted, however. There are references in the Javanese sources that even before the British attack some held the view that the court's lustre (*cahya*) had been so tarnished that a move was essential.[22] The aged Pangéran Ngabèhi, elder brother of the exiled second sultan, probably spoke for many when he referred to the surrender of his personal *kris* (stabbing dagger) at the time of the British assault as a form of castration.[23]

Later, following the second sultan's restoration (17 August 1826) and
return to the *kraton* (21 September 1826) during the Java War, some of
the letters written to him by Yogyakarta princes, who had joined
Diponegoro, dwelt on the sense of shame they had experienced in
witnessing his treatment at the hands of the British and the humiliation
of the plunder of the *kraton*.[24] These feelings of humiliation and bitterness towards the Europeans were to deepen during the fourth sultan's
reign (1814–22), when the political and economic influence of the
European government in the princely territories became ever more
pronounced. They put in perspective the attempts by Diponegoro early
in the war to bring about the final destruction of the Yogyakarta *kraton*
and to establish a new undefiled *kraton* at another site. 'All Java knows
this', the lawyer Willem van Hogendorp would later write, 'how the
Dutch allowed the kraton [of Yogyakarta] to be turned into a brothel
and how Diponegoro has sworn to destroy it to the last stone and expel
the [European] landowners who have driven out the Javanese officials.'[25] The yearning for moral regeneration under the banner of Islam
and the restoration of the sultanate's prestige became significant themes
in the years preceding the Java War and go far to explain why so many
members of the Yogyakarta court rallied to Diponegoro in 1825.

The role of the Chinese

The plight of the Chinese in south-central Java at the time of the
outbreak of the Java War in July 1825 was due in large measure to
another aspect of the British administration – continued by the
returned Dutch administration after August 1816 – which
contributed to the rising unrest in the south-central Javanese countryside. This was the working of the tollgates (*bandar*). In the space of
just twelve years (1812–24), following the British take-over in August
1812, the revenue received by the colonial government from the
bandar in the Yogyakarta territories alone nearly quadrupled.[26] These
stopping places, which were positioned a day's journey on foot from
each other, were frequented by Chinese merchants, some of whom
had bought the right from the local captain of the Chinese or *kapitan
cina* to levy tolls from other travellers for looking after their goods and
belongings overnight. Over time, a fully fledged *bandar* would be
established run by a Chinese tollgate keeper. Sometimes a market
would also develop from the wayside stalls (*warung*) serving the
overnight shelter. Then, as the Chinese *bandar* became more familiar
with the surrounding countryside and greater pressure was put on
him by his *kapitan cina* to pay higher rents, smaller tollgates (*rangkah*)

would be set up on adjacent country lanes. Observation posts (*salaran*) were also constructed on the borders of the customs districts controlled by the separate *bandar* to check that the requisite taxes had been paid before traders passed into a new zone. These developments were accelerated by the rise of regional trade in the seventy years of peace that followed the Giyanti treaty of the mid-eighteenth century. So much so that just before the outbreak of the Java War, in the words of the Dutch commissioners charged with enquiring into the administration of the principalities in 1824, 'there was a tollgate at the entrance of nearly every village and hamlet'.[27]

A senior Dutch official, Jan Isäak van Sevenhoven (1782–1841), who considered the tollgates along with the porters' guilds as the two greatest evils of pre-war Javanese peasant society, gave a depressing account of the sort of scene that became an all too familiar occurrence at tollgates throughout south-central Java in this period. He described how a Javanese on the way to market would be forced to wait for hours in a queue before his load was inspected. If his buffaloes grazed on the tollgate keeper's land during this time he was fined, and if this fine was not paid his draught animals were impounded so that at harvest time it was not uncommon for a Javanese farmer to surrender the bulk of his profits to cover the rent of his own animals from the local *bandar*.[28] When the peasant cultivator's turn came for his load to be inspected, the tollgate keeper would browbeat him and demand that he hand over a large percentage payment on his goods for right of passage. The peasant cultivator would then throw himself at the tollgate keeper's mercy: '*Ampun tuwan* [Have mercy, Sir!], my family is poor!' But if he refused payment, he ran the risk of having his entire load confiscated. During the long hours of waiting, the farmer would often be tempted to take opium, which was readily available at the *bandar* and usually retailed by the keeper as an additional income source. In the event of an overnight stay, there would be the added beguilement of *ronggèng* (dancing girls, prostitutes) and gambling parties, which would further eat into the farmer's meagre savings. If he had serious ill-luck at cards, the farmer would often be forced to part with his clothes and even the money, which many Javanese traders and peasant cultivators borrowed from their village heads to cover the cost of the toll dues. In such a situation, it was not uncommon for a peasant cultivator to take to a roving life as a bandit or porter on the roads rather than face the ignominy of returning empty-handed to his village.[29]

Appeals to local Javanese officials about abuses of power by the tollgate keepers were usually unavailing because the officials themselves were given cash gifts to ensure they overlooked extortionate practices. In addition, a journey to the court towns to put a case before the Residency court was usually beyond the means of the average farmer. The only way a 'little man' (*wong cilik*) could revenge himself on a toll-gate keeper would be by enlisting the help of local bandits and getting them to plunder the *bandar* or burn it to the ground. Such cases of burglary and arson occurred with increasing frequency in the years before the Java War, as can be seen from the rising value of goods stolen from the tollgates.[30] Many Chinese tollgate keepers also lost their lives. This situation became desperate following the outbreak of the war when all the tollgates in the vicinity of Yogyakarta were burnt to the ground.[31] But popular retribution such as this often spelled disaster for the inhabitants of neighbouring villages, which, under the terms of the Javanese criminal codes, were liable to pay an indemnity amounting to two-thirds of the value of any stolen goods or a 'blood price' (*diyat*) – which was double the amount for a dead Chinese than for a Javanese – to the family of the murdered man if the crime could not be resolved satisfactorily.[32]

Faced with the threat of constant attack, the tollgate keepers began to organize their own 'private armies' of bodyguards and thugs, some of them recruited from former sepoys, thus adding another twist to the spiral of violence in country areas as the Java War loomed.[33] Even when van Sevenhoven was first writing just before the British take-over of the tollgates in August 1812, the potential that they might develop into a serious impediment to trade in south-central Java was already evident. Twelve years later, when he served as commissioner enquiring into the administration of the principalities, the *bandar* had become so effectively sited that nothing could be transported on the roads without going through one. If a Javanese tried to evade a toll-gate by taking a cross-country route, the tollgate keeper's spies would usually report his action, resulting in the forfeiture of his goods.[34] The increase in customs posts had a significant effect on the price of food-stuffs in south-central Java. Nowhere was this more evident than in Yogyakarta, where prices of rice and other necessities were nearly double those in Surakarta, which benefited from cheap transport costs for bulk goods along the Bengawan Sala (Solo River).

The colonial government was perfectly aware of the harmful effects of the tollgates and it made some moves to restrict their influence before 1825. The British abolished the *bandar* along the Solo River in February 1814 and the Dutch followed suit in Kedhu in 1824, a move that led to an immediate increase in the number of markets and the level of trade in the province.[35] In the same year,

Governor-General van der Capellen appointed a three-man team of commissioners headed by the Residents of Yogyakarta and Surakarta and including van Sevenhoven, soon to take over as Resident of Surakarta (in office 1825–7), to enquire into the working of the toll-gates in the Principalities. The team reported back in October 1824, unequivocally recommending the abolition of all internal customs posts and suggesting that the European government should indemnify itself for the lost revenue – estimated at about a million Indies guilders – by annexing the western outlying provinces of Bagelèn and Banyumas. They also urged that all Chinese residents in villages and hamlets should be ordered to move to the royal capitals, that every unmarried Chinese who had been in the Principalities for less than two years should be expelled forthwith, along with those who were unemployed or guilty of extortion, and that no new Chinese immi-gration should be allowed.[36] As one of the commissioners, Hendrik Mauritz MacGillivray (1797–1835), later put it:

> The Chinese are our work tools and although each year we rejoice over the increased [tax revenues] which are ascribed to [increased] prosperity and welfare, we bind the iron yoke more firmly on the shoulders [of the Javanese] . . . for a million guilders a year worth of taxes we compromise the welfare and happiness of almost two million inhabitants who are not immediately under our protection . . . but whose interests are so clearly linked to ours.[37]

Only the 'good nature and peacefulness' of the Javanese, in the commissioners' opinion,[38] had enabled the oppression of the tollgate system to continue for so long. They ended with a fearful prophecy: 'We hope they [the Javanese] will not be awoken out of their slum-bering state, for we reckon it as a certainty that if the tollgates are permitted to continue, the time is not far distant when the Javanese will be aroused in a terrible fashion.'[39] Despite the dire warnings of imminent agrarian unrest from nearly every official who studied the problem, the post-1816 Dutch administration felt it could not forgo the lucrative tollgate revenues from the Principalities.[40] The nearly threefold rise in annual profits from the tollgate farms in Yogyakarta between 1816 and 1824 seems to have made the senior officials in the Finance Department in Batavia blind to the fact that the *bandar* were paralysing trade. Writing in November 1824, a mere two months after taking over the once profitable tollgates of Bantul and Jatinom to the south of Yogyakarta, the local Chinese tollgate keeper reported that he had become bankrupt.[41] A prolonged and severe drought since the beginning of the year had destroyed the cotton crop and basic food-stuffs such as castor-oil plants, soya beans, and maize were in short supply. Rice prices were soaring but little trade was being carried on in the local markets because commerce had effectively collapsed.

In these terrible months before the Java War, the south-central Javanese countryside became a place of suspicion and terror. Armed gangs operated with virtual impunity, murders were rife, and the daily activities of the local peasant cultivators took place under the ever-watchful eyes of the tollgate keepers' spies, who were positioned on every village and country road to prevent the evasion of toll dues. Even the dead on their way to burial were liable for imposts, and mere passage through a tollgate even without dutiable goods would expose the traveller to what the Javanese sarcastically came to refer to as the 'bottom tax' (*pajak bokong*).[42] Neither were high-placed Javanese offi-cials exempt. The Secretary (Assistant-Resident) of Yogyakarta, Pierre Frederic Henri Chevallier (1795–1825), remarked how the grey-haired *bupati* of Nganjuk, a district in the Surakarta eastern *mancanagara*, remarked wrily that he was less fearful of the tigers infesting the teak forests on his cross-country journeys to the Sunan's capital to attend the *Garebeg* festivals than he was of the bare-faced thugs who manned the tollgates on the Nganjuk–Surakarta highway.[43] Other Javanese offi-cials spoke with scarcely concealed contempt of the obscene way in which their wives and daughters were physically searched for items of jewellery by Chinese *bandar* newly arrived from the maritime provinces of China who were barely conversant in Malay.[44]

The Dutch now began to refer to the Chinese as 'a race of customs house keepers' in their reports echoing the common Javanese expression for them as 'tollgate people'.[45] Huibert Gerard Nahuys van Burgst (1782–1858), who served as Resident of both Surakarta (1820–2) and Yogyakarta (1816–23), noted that barely one Chinese in twenty who came to the Indies from China ever returned to the place of their birth, so rich were the pickings in Java.[46] Yet not all Chinese were by nature oppressors. Before the post-1816 Dutch administration had ratcheted up its fiscal demands to intolerable levels, there were a number of favourable reports of the behaviour of Chinese tax-farmers. During the British period, the principal Chinese land-renter in Wirasaba in east Java, Lib Sing, who controlled over 200 villages, was reported to have been 'a kind and indulgent master' under whom the *wong cilik* or common people liked to take service because 'the lands and villages in his area were better looked after than elsewhere'.[47] Similar reports were made of the Chinese land-renters of Ulujami near Pekalongan on the north coast, the 'rice granary' of Semarang.[48] Even Chinese tollgate keepers were praised. In May 1812, during his journey across Java, van Sevenhoven noted that the Chinese *bandar* at the ferry crossing at Kreteg on the Opak River to the south of Yogyakarta 'seemed the very best sort of tollgate keeper', whose subordinates 'appeared healthy and robust'.[49] What had changed in the post-1816 period was not the character of the Chinese but the character of the fiscal regime they served. And for this the post-1816 Dutch administration must take full responsibility.

Although van der Capellen's government was principally responsible for the sharp rise in tollgate and market revenues after 1816, the British were the midwives to another equally disastrous development: the rapid extension of the opium retail trade. The greater ease of opium imports from Bengal following the lifting of the British blockade of the archipelago in August and September 1811 and the financial pressures on Raffles's government were the key reasons.[50] Once again, the Chinese came to assume a prominent and invidious role as farmers and retailers, opium retail and tollgate farming often going hand in hand.

The statistics for official opium sales in the Principalities reflect the sharp increase in opium consumption that began in the British period. Between 1802 and 1814 sales doubled from forty chests of 148 pounds avoirdupois each to eighty, by which time the wholesale value of a chest had increased twofold due to the effects of inflation, the tightness of the British naval blockade (1804–11), and the more stringent British enforcement of the opium monopoly after they assumed control of Java in August 1811. During the decade 1814–24, revenue from the Yogyakarta opium farm multiplied five times. By 1820 there were 372 separate places licensed to retain opium in the sultan's territories, namely nearly every major tollgate, sub-tollgate, and market in the sultanate. The exact number of opium addicts is difficult to ascertain. On the basis of consumption figures compiled in the late nineteenth century, a Dutch official estimated that some 16 per cent of the then 20-million strong Javanese population took opium.[51] But if one counts all those who inhaled and digested 'poor men's' varieties of the drug, such as opium-soaked cigarettes, opium-seasoned coffee, and opium-laced betelnut, the incidence of narcotic consumption was almost certainly very much higher.[52] Raffles, for example, distinguished between the crude opium or *manta* 'eaten' by people in the interior of Java, particularly in the Principalities, and the prepared opium or *madat/candu* smoked extensively along the north coast.[53]

During his journey through south-central Java in May 1812, van Sevenhoven remarked on the widespread use of opium among the members of the porters' guilds and unemployed labourers in the court towns. He also noted how the tollgate opium outlets had spread the habit among Javanese in the countryside.[54] As he passed through the usually bustling market of Klathèn one morning, he noticed how full the opium dens were and how threadbare their inhabitants: some were barely clothed, others were dressed in worn-out *kain* (wrap-arounds).[55] One and a half cents was enough, on average, to purchase a small wad of opium-soaked tobacco, containing at the most 76 milligrams of opium, which represented about 15 per cent of a porter's daily wage at this time.[56] For many it offered the only release from a life of unrelieved toil and hardship. In Pacitan, in the immediate post-Java War period, a huge religious feast (*slametan*) would be held to celebrate the end of the coffee harvest when crop payments would go on 'opium eating'.[57] The drug was also used widely as a stimulant and as a valued part of the Javanese pharmacopoeia for treating various ailments.[58] During the Java War, there were reports that many of Diponegoro's troops had 'fallen sick' for want of opium, and Chinese peddlers did a brisk trade behind the prince's lines when the violent sinophobe sentiments of the first months of the war had abated somewhat.[59] Several Yogyakarta princes and high officials also acquired a taste for the opium pipe, and princely addicts were noticed among Diponegoro's followers at his headquarters at Selarong in late July and early August 1825.[60]

A pastime for the rich, opium addiction was a disaster for the poor. Even the slightest predilection for the drug would exhaust the scarce savings of the Javanese peasant and made his already difficult economic position even more precarious. The road to social degradation and crime was ever present. Nahuys recognized this during the Java War when he called for the rounding up of the thousands of landless labourers and footloose vagrants in south-central Java, 'men with no ricefields whose [thin] shoulders and smooth hands bear no marks of labour and whose eyes, lips and colour betray the habitual use of narcotics'.[61] The social consequences of opium addiction and the increasingly salient role played by the Chinese as retailers were yet another strand in the rapidly deteriorating socio-economic conditions in south-central Java in the post-1816 period. Along with the tollgates, the opium farm lay at the heart of the rise in anti-Chinese sentiments among the Javanese population in the decade before the Java War. Attacks on Chinese tollgate keepers and merchants would become an increasingly salient feature of popular movements in south-central Java as the war neared.

Conclusion

The humiliations experienced by the Yogyakarta elite at the hands of the Dutch and the British were the inevitable outcome of their inability to come to terms with the reality of the new European colonialism born of the twin industrial and bourgeois democratic revolutions that had convulsed the Atlantic world in the late eighteenth century. The changes had been introduced into Java too rapidly and in too brutal a fashion. In the space of just under four years, the south-central Javanese courts had been forced to accommodate themselves to a new form of centralized colonial government that stood in direct contradiction to their own political philosophy of divided sovereignty in Java. Given time, they might have been able to reshape their political conceptions to legitimize the changed realities, but they could not do it in the quick fire way demanded by Daendels and Raffles. The result was disaster. This was particularly the case for Yogyakarta, which had entered on this period of cataclysmic change with ostensibly the most powerful and prosperous court, but in fact hopelessly divided against itself and ruled by a vain and inflexible man. The rapid germination of intrigues within the court literally tore it apart just at the time when it needed its undivided energies to cope with the new challenges posed by a resurgent Europe. The Yogyakarta sultanate had been founded by the sword in the mid-eighteenth century. In June 1812, it could be said to have perished by the sword.

For the British colonial government in Java, there was little doubt about the significance of their victory. Raffles's exceedingly able Dutch assistant, Harman Warner Muntinghe (1773–1827), who later took British citizenship, hailed it as an event of similar significance to Robert Clive's victory at Plassey in June 1757, which had opened up the whole of northern India to British rule. Raffles echoed this in a dispatch to his patron, Lord Minto, when he stated that 'the European power is for the first time paramount in Java . . . we never till this moment could call ourselves masters of the more valuable provinces in the interior, nay, our possessions on the sea coasts would always have been precarious and, had [our] military force been materially reduced, much eventual danger was to be apprehended'.[62] Although both Yogyakarta and Surakarta would continue as dismembered states after 1812, they were never again in themselves capable of posing a threat to the position of the European government. When a new challenge did materialize under Diponegoro's Javanese-Islamic banner in July 1825, it would owe its inspiration and energies to influences outside the great court traditions. The support given to the prince by the religious communities and the Javanese peasantry, both groups who felt themselves increasingly excluded from the new colonial order and oppressed by the Chinese-run tollgate system, was more important than the traditional foci of court patronage and loyalty. In many ways, June 1812 rather than the end of the Java War should be seen as the date when the new colonial era dawned in Java. Out of this collapse and the legacy of bitterness that it left, however, a new and more potent combination of elements in Javanese society would emerge. It would bring the restored Dutch colonial regime close to destruction at the start of the Java War and lay the foundations for the future Indonesian nationalist movement of the early twentieth-century. A turning point as significant as any in the colonial era, it would set the course of Indonesian history for the next hundred and fifty years.

10

Their Own Path to Crisis? Social Change, State-Building, and the Limits of Qing Expansion, c.1770–1840

Kenneth Pomeranz

The period from about 1770 to 1840, or at least 1785 to 1840, can be seen as one of escalating crisis for the Qing empire, fitting well with the proposed 'age of revolutions' or 'world crisis'. (In the Qing case, however, the situation worsened after 1840.) The most striking indication of trouble was a series of rebellions, which revealed surprising military weaknesses and wiped out longstanding fiscal surpluses. Four of these rebellions – including by far the largest one – originated in highland areas to which many Han Chinese[1] farmers had recently migrated: in Taiwan (1787–8); Hunan and Guizhou (1794–5); Sichuan, Hubei, Henan, and Shaanxi (the White Lotus Rebellion of 1796–1805); and in Shaanxi again (1813–15). North China millenarians led two brief uprisings (1774, 1813) – the only two that could, by any stretch of the imagination, be said to have begun in a 'core' region. (The relevant area was a long-settled, easily accessible plain entirely populated by Han Chinese, but it was economically and ecologically quite fragile.) Chinese pirates off the Guangdong coast, allied with a resurgent Vietnamese state, led another. Unsuccessful Qing incursions into Burma (1770) and Vietnam (1788) and an inconclusive war with the Kokandis on the far western frontier (c.1817–35) add to this sense of accumulating problems.

But ultimately the Qing defeated all rebels, and lost no territory to invaders; they also fought successfully against Nepalese/Gurkha troops in Tibet in 1788 and 1793. Thus, though our period ended with Qing defeat in the Opium War (1839–42), this should not be seen as the inevitable culmination of a steady military decline. While the Qing could not defend their coast against *new* technologies (most notably, steamships that allowed the Anglo-Indian forces to move upriver behind coastal gun batteries),[2] they remained reasonably successful against known threats. Circa 1835 they might even have thought things were improving: certainly 1805–35 had been better than 1785–1805.

Arguments for a steadily gathering crisis must therefore begin on other levels: socio-economic, ecological, and fiscal. Here the evidence is mixed. Despite rapid population growth, core regions were reasonably prosperous, and do not show clear signs of economic decline until after 1830.[3] But there were fundamental trends that left the Qing very little room for manoeuvre.

Causation? A frankly materialist sketch of the Qing path to late eighteenth-century crisis

Coastal China from Shanghai on south was among the world's richest regions until the Industrial Revolution: in particular, Yangzi Delta living standards (population 31,000,000 plus in 1770) were probably comparable to mid-eighteenth-century England's or Holland's. Its agriculture was exceptionally productive – not only per acre, but per labour day – its handicraft industries (especially textiles) huge and solidly profitable, and at least its grain markets – the only ones for which we have thorough studies – remarkably well integrated.[4]

Estimates of real wages for unskilled Chinese workers are less positive; the most recent study suggests that even in China's richest regions they were in the mid-eighteenth century well below real wages in Amsterdam or London, and more like those in Milan.[5] However, this is not inconsistent with a general comparability in living standards. Wage labourers were a small minority in China: probably under 10 per cent of rural adults even in the highly commercialized Lower Yangzi, where one might expect widespread landlessness. By contrast, in at least England and Holland, wage labourers probably represented close to half of the working population by the late seventeenth century. And as we shall see shortly, Chinese wage labourers were far poorer than most tenants, let alone smallholders. Thus a comparison of unskilled real wages is a comparison of the bottom of the income scale in one place with something close to the middle in the other.

Land, labour, and tenancy systems

China had an unusually low rate of landlessness, even in highly commercialized and densely populated regions. In poorer areas, most farmers were smallholders, with probably little more than 15 per cent of land farmed by tenants, and 10 per cent or so by wage labourers.[6] In richer regions, tenancy was common, sometimes covering more than half the land, but most tenants had very strong cultivation rights, which were themselves a kind of property.[7] These rights seem to have emerged as matters of local custom during the fifteenth century, amidst considerable rural unrest.[8] By the middle to late seventeenth century, these rights had become widely (if often reluctantly) accepted by both landowners and officials of the new Qing dynasty; they could be legally bought, sold, mortgaged, inherited, and so on.[9] A spectrum of rights existed, varying in strength and details, depending on the time, place, and manner in which they were acquired, but the general outlines seem to have become increasingly standard over time, at least in 'advanced' areas.[10]

Having secure use rights, these tenants often behaved like owners, making land-improving investments (which strengthened their claim in cases where any doubt remained).[11] They also resembled owners of their own means of production in that they earned something closer to their average product than their marginal product. The best estimate I can currently make is that secure tenants earned 2.5 to 3 times as much as year-round wage labourers in the same region, and were almost as far ahead of insecure tenants; their net earnings were closer to those of smallholders.[12]

Political and demographic reinforcement

The Chinese state wanted an independent peasantry it could tax and rule without going through local magnates; thus, despite some misgivings, it generally supported secure tenancy arrangements.[13] Such arrangements also gave tenants strong incentives to do the very careful work needed for high-yielding wet rice cultivation, without monitoring by landlords (who increasingly lived in towns). However, some grim aspects of the social system also kept the numbers of completely dispossessed people small.

First, some women were sold, either as concubines or as servants. We know very little about the 'typical' circumstances of such sales, but some presumably involved hard-pressed families who sold a daughter rather than their land rights. The number of women thus removed from the regular marriage market was probably under 5 per cent,[14] but that was non-trivial. Second, some families (including some prosperous ones) practised sex-selective infanticide.[15] While we do not know how widespread this was either – or how it varied by time and region – the imbalance from differential infant and child mortality was probably at least 10 per cent: the same imbalance found for the (quite possibly atypical) imperial lineage.[16] In nineteenth-century Xuzhou – in a particularly poor, disaster-prone and violent region – the male:female sex ratio apparently reached 129:100.[17]

These imbalances created a permanent crunch in the marriage market; thus the poorest men – typically landless labourers – rarely married.[18] In each generation, some luckless smallholders and tenants fell into the proletariat – as one would expect in a competitive economy – but since few proletarians reproduced, their numbers did not grow. (In Europe, by contrast, proletarians may have had higher birth rates than small farmers.)[19] Having only one mouth to feed, labourers could survive on the fraction of tenant incomes that they earned. And in some sense, the non-growth of the proletariat helped to stabilize the Chinese socio-economic system.

In another sense, however, these 'bare sticks' were a major source of instability. They had little to lose, often lacked community ties, and were over-represented among bandits, rebels, and those involved in (or scapegoated for) criminal activity. Neither of the Qing standing armies – the Eight Banners and the Green Standard army – made much effort to recruit/absorb these men into the forces of order during peacetime, though local officials sometimes hired them as additional 'braves' once the standing forces had failed to suppress a conflict. Interestingly, married men temporarily away from 'their' women – whether in cities or on the frontier – were not considered similarly threatening;[20] apparently it was lacking a proper social niche, not the physical absence of a female companion, that made men seem, and sometimes be, dangerous.

Consequences for migration, regional differences, and fiscal issues

Unskilled urban workers in China earned little more than agricultural labourers – as one would expect without strong guilds – and thus much less than secure tenants or smallholders.[21] Consequently, most people had little reason to head for the cities; the urbanization rate remained low;[22] and the large agricultural surplus instead fed *rural* industrial producers who remained embedded in farm households. Individuals often specialized (in theory, men ploughed and women wove[23]), but *households* combined diverse income streams.[24] Home-based commercial handicrafts allowed women to earn money without compromising female modesty,[25] and households with some land rights plus another source of income had a stake in order. To the extent that the Qing had an 'economic development policy', it often consisted of officials helping poorer areas to imitate the combination of farming and rural handicrafts epitomized by the Yangzi Delta.[26]

These same factors also shaped migration. While per capita income differed greatly among Chinese regions – with the Yangzi Delta perhaps 50 per cent above the empire-wide average circa 1750[27] – real wages for the unskilled were apparently fairly uniform.[28] Thus people who could not pay the substantial rent deposit required for secure tenancy in long-settled areas (or the even larger sum needed to buy land), would gain little by heading for the Yangzi or Pearl River Deltas. For them, the frontier offered better opportunities: per capita incomes were lower but working to clear land often yielded ownership or cultivation rights on that land.[29] Thus, net migration was strongly *away* from the richest regions in China. That pattern, in turn, had the effect of maintaining, rather than eroding, economic gaps between regions.[30]

Richer areas paid higher taxes. The Yangzi Delta in particular paid far more than other areas, but local elites (loosely supervised) provided most of its public goods.[31] Surplus revenues extracted from the Delta went elsewhere and helped to underwrite the conditions for family farming (and Confucian morality) in more ecologically fragile areas. These measures included subsidies for well-digging in the semi-arid north and north-west, paying to control major north China rivers (while expecting southern communities to manage this themselves), placing most emergency granaries in poor areas, providing loans to help migrants to certain regions start farms, and so forth.[32] Thus interregional transfers directed part of China's surplus towards stabilization in peripheries rather than capital accumulation and possible transformation in the cores.

From stability to crisis

There were other reasons why the Qing economy, though certainly dynamic, was not moving towards Western-style modernity. The Yangzi Delta's handicraft industries were, for various reasons, probably less well positioned for technological change than at least some of their Western counterparts.[33] The Delta was particularly poorly positioned for the vital transition to much more energy-intensive kinds of production. It had never had much heavy industry, largely because it lacked metallic ores and, above all, energy sources. Wood, coal peat, and even water power (due to flat terrain) were all scarce;[34] there were also significant obstacles to importing large amounts of energy.[35] Under the circumstances, the relative price of energy was exceptionally high along the China coast, making it unlikely that people would focus on finding ways to be more productive by using more of it. (One study finds that in 1704 real wages in Canton were almost at London levels, but charcoal was almost twenty times as expensive relative to labour as it was in London.[36]) Meanwhile the Delta's light industry relied heavily on long-distance trade with other parts of China, exchanging cloth and other handicrafts for about 20 per cent of its grain supply plus raw cotton, timber, beancake fertilizer, and other primary products.[37]

In the absence of growth based on technological transformation, it was crucial for China that extensive growth continue – which it could not do forever. By the end of the eighteenth century the system outlined above was stagnating, and during the nineteenth century, it unravelled. Population growth in long-settled parts of the interior (e.g. the Middle Yangzi and North China) decreased the amount of grain, timber, etc. those areas supplied to the coast; they also developed their own handicrafts, substituting for imports from the coast. By 1840, an average piece of cloth exported from the Yangzi Delta bought half as much rice as in 1750, trade volumes probably shrank too.[38] Thus in economics, as in politics, crisis began in peripheries and eventually affected cores. The Delta found some growing markets, mostly in Manchuria, South-east Asia, and among high end domestic consumers. Moreover, the Yangzi Delta's population almost stopped growing from c.1770 to 1850, while China's almost doubled.[39] Delta living standards probably didn't fall much, but they did stagnate.

This made subsidizing other regions increasingly burdensome. Meanwhile, population growth in those poorer regions made ecological stabilization increasingly challenging: the soaring cost of Yellow River control, which absorbed 10–20 per cent of Qing spending from 1820 to 1850, is the outstanding example, but not the only one.[40] With most lowland territories becoming crowded by the mid-nineteenth century – except in Manchuria, which the Qing tried to maintain a preserve for 'traditional' Manchu lifestyles – new farms were carved from hillsides, wetlands, and other ecologically risky places.[41] Adding Western incursions and other misfortunes pushed the system beyond its limits, and environmental, political, and social crises in the poorer regions (especially ethnically mixed frontiers) reinforced each other. The resulting unrest eventually engulfed rich regions, too – most famously when the Taiping emerged from the Guangxi mountains to make the Yangzi Valley a battleground for over a decade – inaugurating a century of disunity and recurrent uprisings.

Frontiers, instability, and state capacity

Most large-scale collective violence occurred in areas that could be called frontiers. Some were 'frontiers' in the sense of being near some other polity (e.g. the Vietnamese/south China piracy crisis and war with the Kokandis). But most involved frontiers of settlement rather than of conquest, i.e., areas that were far from any border, but which had been fairly sparsely populated until a recent influx of settlers. Some cases involved violence between Han newcomers and other ethnic groups. But the biggest uprising of all – the White Lotus Rebellion of 1796–1805 – occurred in the highlands of Hubei, Sichuan, and Shaanxi, where very few non-Han lived. A combination of factors brought Han migrants to this region in the late eighteenth century: population growth, increased lowland demand for mountain products (especially timber, paper, charcoal, and iron), and increased familiarity with American maize and potatoes, which would grow at high elevations with relatively little labour (making it easier to feed loggers, paper-makers, etc.). This rugged terrain had previously had very few people and little law and order: many earlier residents were people, such as salt smugglers, who preferred inaccessible territory. White Lotus sectarian networks seem to have helped to organize immigrant society – in contrast to some other highland districts where many of the migrants were Hakka[42] and ethnic organization helped to keep order. When the Qing attempted to crack down on the illegal White Lotus sect, they touched off a defensive rebellion that they could not contain.[43]

This summary of 'frontier' problems allows at least some negative conclusions. The problem was not one of 'imperial overstretch' in the most direct military sense; the biggest problems were not in recently conquered territories. Second, though many of these uprisings occurred in areas of considerable ethnic tension, ethnic minorities were not always the rebels; nor were Han Chinese always allied with the state. The Lin Shuangwen rebellion on Taiwan, for instance, was mostly carried out by Han Chinese, and certain groups of 'cooked aborigines' (i.e. semi-civilized, from the state's perspective) played a critical role in its suppression.[44] Many East Turkestani Muslims fought for the Qing during the Kokandi invasion, despite rumours about Muslim fifth columnists and massacres of Muslims by Han militia.[45] In multiethnic Yunnan, the brief rebellion of 1817–18 did not divide people on ethnic lines, and the Qing found a variety of allies to help them suppress it. They created much more trouble for themselves in the 1830s and 1840s, when they allied themselves with Han militia, which *were* organized on ethno-religious lines, and reflexively blamed Muslims for most disturbances.[46] Neither frontier settlement nor ethnic diversity automatically bred rebellion; the biggest problems ensued when a Qing state with little grass-roots presence on the frontier nonetheless decided that it could not tolerate certain alternative systems of local authority.

Consequently, even though these uprisings often occurred in ethnically diverse peripheral regions, they do not fit into the wave of 'tribal breakouts' that C. A. Bayly sees occurring in many Asian empires between 1780 and 1830. They do, however, confirm the importance of frontiers as an outlet for migrants.[47] The problem was not necessarily that the frontier was 'disappearing' – at least not in the early part of our period. (Taiwan, for instance, still had plenty of cultivable land during and long after the Lin Shuangwen Rebellion.) The bigger issue was that periods of rapid immigration outstripped the ability of the Qing to tie the leaders of frontier society firmly to the state (and to regulate downstream environmental consequences of some new settlements). Violence could result both from the weakness of state control and from sudden, lurching, efforts to rein in non-state organizations to which frontier authorities had previously ceded a good deal of *de facto* control.

The Qing were certainly not the only empire in this period that failed to control the movement of land-hungry frontiersmen, to tax them for their own defence, or to retain their loyalty – British North America comes to mind, for instance. However, the scale of the migrations,[48] the particular importance of highland areas[49] that were both ecologically fragile and inhospitable to regular troops (especially cavalry, a Qing speciality), and the disproportionate role of young men destined to be *permanently* single all suggest a distinctive variant of more widely shared problems. The Qing civil administration was also quite thin on the ground – by 1800 a magistrate with an average staff of perhaps a few hundred would be responsible for a county averaging about 300,000 inhabitants[50] – but that in itself cannot be a full explanation: similar or higher ratios prevailed in densely populated core regions that remained fairly peaceful. Probably the bigger difference is that core regions often had large numbers of 'gentry'. These men had participated in Confucian education and the civil service exams, and were often wealthy, but were not in office; they often helped to fund and organize public projects and mediated between state and society. While a considerable literature emphasizes the role of disgruntled lower gentry in various sorts of unrest, we must remember the much larger numbers of such people who served as crucial auxiliaries of orthodoxy.[51] Frontiers often lacked such people, and government there needed to recruit lineage heads, minority chieftains, unlettered landlords, and others into functionally equivalent roles in order to operate effectively.

In this context, it is noteworthy that there were some fairly common problems that the Qing did not face. The relative absence of serious foreign threats between 1759 and 1839 is an old story, but it is equally striking that the Qing were remarkably untroubled by urban uprisings prior to 1900. A few strikes in Lower and Middle Yangzi cities turned violent during the very early Qing (though fewer than in late Ming), and there were other sorts of occasional unrest;[52] but in general Qing cities were fairly peaceful, and certainly saw very little antistate violence. While many rural uprisings eventually took control of mid-sized or even major cities, no major uprisings against the state began there. Moreover, only a tiny percentage of eighteenth- and nineteenth-century incidents of collective violence (most of it among social groups and not targeting the state) occurred in Beijing or in provincial capitals. Many did touch prefectural and county capitals, or other cities, but these cases were clustered in a few periods of exceptional instability, and rarely originated in town. The baseline of collective violence in 'ordinary' times was mostly rural; in the most disorderly periods, rural incidents would increase further above this baseline, and the number of incidents in low-level urban centres (e.g. county capitals) would jump suddenly.[53]

The contrast to the morphology of European disturbances – which often began with an urban incident and spread to the countryside only if the urban unrest incident proved unusually lasting, giving rural people a perceived opening by paralysing the state[54] – is particularly striking, but the role of urban insurgency in China seems to me (more impressionistically) to be relatively minor as compared to Ottoman and late/post-Mughal patterns. It is further worth remembering in this context that, while China's urban population was small in percentage terms, it had many of the world's largest cities in absolute terms. Moreover, because of patterns of sojourning, China's cities were probably just as male as the tumultuous frontier areas I have described (and much more male than the more restive cities of Western Europe, which often had female majorities); they may, however, have had fewer lifelong bachelors than the frontier.

Moreover, except for the two brief millenarian uprisings in north China mentioned above, China's long-settled lowland areas were also relatively peaceful until the end of our period. Even in eighteenth-century Fujian, which was notorious for its 'lawlessness', at least the

Map 4 China in the eighteenth century (adapted from Susan Naquin and Evelyn S. Rawski, *Chinese Society in the Eighteenth Century*, New Haven, CT, 1987).

MANCHURIA

Heilongjiang

Jilin

Shengjing

Rehe ●

● Beijing

Mt. *Wutai* △ ZHILI

SHANXI   SHANDONG
                △

JIANGSU

'an ●

AANXI   HENAN   Yangzhou ●
                  Nanjing

                     ● Suzhou ●
                        Shanghai
HUBEI   Hangzhou ●   ANHUI
Hankou   Ningbo ● Putuoshan
              Huizhou ●

HUNAN   JIANGXI   ZHEJIANG

HOU   FUJIAN

                Quanzhou
                Zhengzhou ●
                Xiamen ●

UANGXI   GUANGDONG ●
         Guangzhou   Chaozhou
              ●
                          ·········· Province boundary
         TAIWAN   - - - Macroregional boundary
                          ——— Qing Empire boundary

reported homicide rate was lower than in many parts of the North Atlantic world.[55] While some long-settled lowland areas suffered from endemic and violent competition between groups – lineage feuds (often tied to land reclamation) in coastal Guangdong and Fujian, banditry in impoverished, flood-prone Huaibei, etc. – antistate violence was generally rare until the more general breakdown of the mid-nineteenth century. The geography of anti-Qing uprisings, then, seems consistent with the economic, demographic, and fiscal system sketched out above, and stands in sharp contrast to various patterns that seem more typical of some other empires: cases where challenges to the state were provoked by more intensive extractive efforts in core areas (which might offend elites, plebeians, or both), new patterns of class conflict, the breakdown of arrangements between tribal military specialists and agrarian states, and various stresses related directly or indirectly to wars between states.

Connections? From political economy to politics, policy, and ideas

The heavily structural account given above should not obscure the significance of conscious policy choices. For instance, the Qing chose to keep Manchuria largely off-limits to Han settlement, though that outlet would accommodate about twelve million permanent migrants (and millions more seasonal or life-cycle migrants) once restrictions were lifted in the late nineteenth century, providing considerable relief to the North China plain – probably the most ecologically, economically, and socially strained lowland region in the empire, and the only one to generate significant antidynastic uprisings during this period.[56] Foreign trade would probably have increased faster with more liberal policies, providing some relief to coastal cores suffering from the contraction of long-distance internal trade discussed above (though it would have been small relative to the regional economies involved). More consistent policies on various internal frontiers might have done better at preventing violence than the stop-start policies on immigration, land clearance, and 'Sinicization' of non-Han populations that actually prevailed. Different policies for what was becoming a less effective bureaucracy might have allowed tax collection, flood control, military provisioning, and so on to function well somewhat longer, though in the case of flood control they probably could not have avoided crisis too much longer.[57] And to the extent that different policies might have at least postponed crises, it becomes less likely that global influences specific to this period were the crucial factors.

The strongest case for a very powerful 'global' influence in this period would probably be the opium trade. Maritime imports alone went from a level sufficient to supply 100,000–200,000 daily users in the mid-eighteenth century to enough to supply perhaps ten million addicts (in a population of about 380 million *c.*1839); the most rapid increases came after the development of Malwa opium *c.*1815.[58] Both domestic opium production and imports from Central Asia (as opposed to British India) also escaped state suppression campaigns, so that the Anglo-Indian role in this epidemic was crucial only for a few decades; but in that time, British India produced the innovations in opium processing, quality control, and methods of consumption that combined to create a much more attractive and addictive product.[59] And while this trade solved some basic revenue and control problems for the British, it exacerbated such problems in China.

In economic terms, the increasing outflow of silver that resulted caused considerable disruption to China's monetary system – especially when combined with a downturn in Latin American silver production during and immediately after the years of revolution – with particular impact on those peasants who sold their output for copper but paid taxes in silver.[60] But here, too, we should not exaggerate. First of all, the copper–silver exchange rates that were figured into tax collection were generally not market rates, but rates set by local administrative fiat. At any rate, land taxes remained quite low in comparative perspective;[61] and a century of rising grain prices and (largely) fixed nominal tax rates from 1730 onwards should have offset much of the increase caused by currency shifts in the last couple of decades of that century. The outflow of silver might have had more general effects on commerce, but these are not currently understood.

Socially, the impact was probably a good deal larger. Addiction per se no doubt took its toll, and the increased difficulty of maintaining public order in the key smuggling areas (principally the Guangdong coast) had implications for later conflicts. Moreover, opium imports may have had a role in stimulating another important kind of commerce. An interesting but largely unexplored topic in eighteenth- and nineteenth-century Chinese history is the proliferation of firearms in private hands – which is probably related both to increased smuggling and to the increased number of frontier settlements that could not count on protection from the Qing. Given that the Qing military was also relatively slow to adopt new, more powerful, firearms during the late eighteenth and early nineteenth centuries, the gap between civilian and state coercive abilities was quite likely to have been declining during this period – in contrast to many places where

military build-up was accompanied by the gradual disarming of civilians.[62] But here, too, we should remember that any strong impact
from opium trading comes late in our period and strongly affected
only some regions.

Foreign ideas were considerably less influential. The liberal democratic ideas of the Atlantic revolutions had no significant impact in
China until much later. Foreign religious ideas – specifically millenarian Protestantism – would soon have a major impact by inspiring the
Taiping Rebellion (1851–64), but not quite yet. Major Islamic revolts
– assuming one even wants to call Islam 'foreign' at this point in
Chinese history – are also mostly post-1850. Jahangir's 1826 inva-
sion/*jihad* was Muslim in inspiration, but it was successfully defeated,
and many Muslims in the area stood by the Qing; ironically the rebellion's greatest long-term impact may have been that it led to a hardening of anti-Muslim attitudes among some Han and Manchu
powerholders, thus indirectly radicalizing later generations of Muslim
subjects.[63]

In other cases, we can find politically relevant intellectual and
cultural developments in China that might possibly have been influenced by foreign contact, but were probably home-grown. Thus, for
instance, we find the Qing, in the course of an early nineteenth-
century conflict with Britain over Macao, articulating ideas of territorial sovereignty that sound increasingly 'Westphalian'.[64] But this was
not the first time they had done so – they had made similar arguments
in the course of defining their borders with Russia a century earlier.[65]
Nor was it a once and for all change: for several decades more, the
Qing continued to employ both 'territorial' and 'tributary' ideas of
sovereignty as suited them in particular cases.

The global circulation of ideas about what it meant to claim territory – including new kinds of mapping, ethnographic investigation,
and so on[66] – certainly had some impact on Qing frontier policy,
especially in the south-west. However, those influences may well have
been stronger c.1600–1760 and after 1850 than in the century in
between. The mid-eighteenth century saw not only the completion
of conquests in Central Asia, but (beginning slightly earlier) a change
in policy regarding frontiers of settlement. After the first decade or so
of the Qianlong reign (1736–96), there was a retreat from Yongzheng-
era (1723–36) attempts to expand direct rule in the south-west.[67]
Later – around the turn of the century, and especially after 1820 –
intellectuals showed a renewed interest in more direct rule, Han
immigration, and assimilationist policies on minorities. When the
Qing realized, after defeating Jahangir's invasion of Xinjiang, that they

needed to keep more troops there than they could comfortably afford, one might have expected eighteenth-century proposals to pull back from the far north-west to be heard again; but instead the regime turned to promoting more colonization of the area as a way of financing its troops there, with enthusiastic support from some of the same groups that had previously been sceptical of expansion into Central Asia.[68] Perhaps one factor behind this increased assertiveness was an increasing perception that both Muslim and European foreigners were hostile and dangerous, but this is speculative. At least explicitly, 'statecraft' thinkers drew on older Chinese thinkers and internal political debates, not foreign ones, to justify this agenda.[69] Moreover, this new aggressiveness had little impact on policy outside of Xinjiang and perhaps Yunnan. Thus while some changes in thinking about sovereignty and cultural unity may parallel trends elsewhere, this seems less firmly connected to global currents than some earlier developments, such as the interest that Kangxi (r. 1661–1722) had shown in Jesuit cartography, ethnography, etc. over a century earlier.

Back to comparisons: dilemmas of growth and statecraft

If it is hard to find strong global connections, it is much easier to find useful points for comparison, since both the Qing state and Chinese society faced many of the same basic problems as other empires. The effects of commercialization and population growth were, to some extent, experienced across much of the world; so were growing fiscal problems as various sorts of government costs grew faster than population or revenues; so were resistance to new fiscal expedients, and difficulties in controlling the agents who mobilized some of the additional revenues states sought.

In 1713, the Qing had taken the unusual step of freezing the land tax, their main source of revenue – and largely kept that promise throughout our period. The grain tribute surcharges assessed on the Lower Yangzi did rise significantly, and we think that irregular, off-the-books charges by local governments also grew. Because grain tribute surcharges not only rose sharply, but fell very unevenly on different types of households (as was probably also true of illegal local surcharges), they caused significant discontent in the Lower Yangzi during the 1830s and 1840s. But even in these prefectures, the most heavily taxed in the empire, the tax bite peaked at 10–15 per cent of agricultural output;[70] empire-wide it was under 4 per cent of agricultural output, and less still of total income.[71] By 1766, 'public' revenues,[72] which were almost 70 per cent from agricultural levies, were about 60 per cent higher than in 1682[73] – when military victories on Taiwan and in the south-west finally completed the Qing conquest – while the population had at least doubled. Under the circumstances, the Qing needed to raise revenues from non-agricultural sources to provide themselves with some flexibility and with the means to meet certain growing costs: principally those of flood control and of stipends for rapidly multiplying Manchu bannerman families, and in the years to come, of suppressing rebellions.[74] They did not, however, pursue new revenues as aggressively as European states (which faced endless war among relative equals) or probably South Asian states during the Mughal/British interregnum.

To some extent, Qing efforts to tap new revenue sources paralleled those seen in many other places: state commercial monopolies and taxes on foreign trade. This is hardly surprising – in a preindustrial society, non-agricultural revenues mostly mean commercial revenues, and monopoly rents and taxes levied at ports of entry are easier to collect than more generalized sales taxes. In fact, what stands out in comparative perspective is how small the Qing efforts were in this direction, even during the immensely expensive suppression of the White Lotus Rebellion (1796–1805). The salt tax monopoly was successfully reorganized to yield more revenue,[75] but it remained the only domestic monopoly of any importance. Compared to various other empires' measures – tobacco, alcohol, sugar, salt, and other consumer goods monopolies, licensing and royalty schemes for mines, and so on – this represents fairly modest revenue-raising.

The government-backed oligopoly on foreign trade at Canton was by no means unique, despite British efforts to paint it as highly peculiar.[76] Officials at Canton faced strong pressure in the early nineteenth century to increase customs receipts, which went directly to the imperial purse. But maximizing revenue often involved sacrificing control, as officials turned a blind eye to an increased smuggling (including that of opium) so as to draw ships to port while raising the exactions on their legal cargoes.[77] Such trade-offs between revenue and regulatory power were part of many expedients undertaken by growing but hard-pressed states around the world, including tax-farming and sales of office. The phrase 'growing but hard-pressed' is important here, pointing to at least two complexities that are well known but bear repeating. First, revenue-enhancing, control-compromising measures were often both a contributing factor to the crises of the late eighteenth century and a response to them. Second, many states became considerably larger, at least fiscally, at the same time that some of their other capacities and their legitimacy may have weakened.

What is striking, though, is how much less decisively the Qing chose revenue over other priorities. Tax farming and the sale of offices remained rare in China until the much greater crisis of the Taiping Rebellion. (Exam degrees were sold earlier, but they did not usually lead to administrative appointments.) Huge sums were raised in 'contributions' from wealthy individuals, especially during the White Lotus Rebellion; Wang Yeh-chien has estimated that the share of state revenues coming from merchants' contributions and commercial taxes soared from 17 per cent under Qianlong (1736–95) to 54 per cent under Jiaqing (1796–1820). But it then fell to 36 and 23 per cent during the next two reigns.[78]

As large-scale fund-raising from merchants was not institutionalized, neither were most favours granted in return for contributions. Contributions sometimes yielded small implicit grants of authority; the elite of Suzhou, for instance, apparently gained greater control over the designation of its local worthies and historical sites in return for massive payments to help defeat the rebels.[79] But in comparative perspective, this does not represent a particularly large compromise of the state's control of key resources. And only after 1850 did the state borrow – an expedient that often compromised control in return for cash, and was both a contributor and a response to state crises from Bengal to Boston.

Without the use of such measures, the growth in Qing revenues both leading up to and during the late eighteenth- and early nineteenth-century crisis was comparatively modest. As noted before, Qing state revenues rose less than the population did between 1682 and 1766. Between then and 1850 statutory revenues barely rose at all.[80] The real figure is somewhat higher, thanks to increased payments from sources such as the Canton customs that went directly into the Imperial Household Department; and in an emergency, the state had the capacity to raise huge though irregular revenues from 'contributions' without diluting its power. Illegal local government exactions probably rose, but not enough to change this general picture. Overall, Qing revenue-raising seems to have a modest increase compared to Ottoman trends over the same period.[81] It may have been closer to *trends* in France (where revenue as a share of GDP stagnated *c*.1800–50) though the French state started from a considerably higher base, in part because its revenues had grown significantly in the decades leading up to the Revolution.[82] It was very small compared to British efforts.[83] By contrast, Chinese government revenues (in real terms) probably grew faster from 1850 to 1937 than those in most colonies or in the Ottoman Empire, and kept up with revenue growth in at least some Western European countries,[84] despite the fact that Chinese economic growth in that period lagged increasingly far behind that in most of Europe. But that later revenue growth went along with sharper changes in the nature of Chinese state-making.

The Qing did not simply 'fail to raise enough revenue' in this period, and therefore 'fail to respond' to the crises they faced; instead, they responded differently. For example, the Jiaqing period (officially 1796–1820, but really 1799–1820) saw reforms that involved pulling back from financially unsustainable state commitments and intrusions into local society that had provoked popular resistance, while renegotiating relationships between different parts of the bureaucracy and between the state and local elites. The state's endorsement of gentry-led militia during the White Lotus Rebellion – which it had previously forbidden – should be seen not as a premonition of its loss of control over its own armed forces a century later but as a pragmatic adjustment that allowed it to defeat the rebels while causing less carnage in local society and spending less money than it had early in the rebellion.[85]

The contrast between these measures and contemporaneous European efforts at what Charles Tilly called 'nationalization'[86] is striking. In early modern Europe, the fundamental challenges of military administration involved (a) getting the state's hands on more resources and (b) gaining control of the suppliers, mercenaries, financiers, and other contractors *external to the state* who made huge profits from military mobilization (and in doing so reduced the bang the state got for its buck). It thus made sense that late eighteenth-century efforts to streamline mobilization would concentrate on bringing more of the process in-house, and would contribute to an increase in the size of state apparatuses that might well accelerate, rather than reverse itself, in times of crisis. In China, however, the principal challenge was controlling corruption and malfeasance by commanders and suppliers, who were *already* officials of the state (or sub-officials, such as yamen runners). Thus the innovation that accompanied Qing war-making was often focused on finding ways to control (or even circumvent) the state apparatus itself, and less on expanding that apparatus to incorporate new functions.[87]

Some similar points could be made about the 'campaigns' to engineer environmental stability and safety from famine. The Qing had no need to add functions such as flood control, assistance to people resettling on selected frontiers, or the creation of large buffer stocks of grain to the list of tasks that the state at least sometimes carried out. Nor, more generally, did they need to argue with elites over whether *in principle* these were tasks that properly belonged to 'state' or 'society'. As R. Bin Wong points out, there was a strong consensus that what mattered was making sure these tasks were carried out; who carried them out was less important, and could be decided on pragmatic grounds reflecting local conditions (particularly the reliability of the local gentry).[88] Instead, the larger challenge in the first half of the nineteenth century was to control the costs of what had become very large in-house programmes for environmental and social stabilization.

But while the rural-focused social and economic dynamics outlined in the first part of this chapter endured well past the crises of our period – indeed, until very recently in some ways – the distinctiveness of Chinese state-making began to change much sooner. Beginning in the 1850s, we increasingly see the Chinese state aggressively raising taxes and focusing more on commercial taxes;[89] granting more privileges to merchants in return for revenue; borrowing; modernizing its standing army; and so on. A bit later, we see it investing in infrastructure designed more to help create a modern sector in rich areas rather than focusing on stabilizing poorer ones.[90] Even for this later period, one would not want to overdo the degree of convergence in state-making strategies, but similarities to both European and colonial processes were definitely stronger in the post-Taiping period than before. Does that mean that the policies of *c.*1770–1850 should be seen as some sort of detour – a delay before China 'figured out' the 'right' policies for coping with new challenges?

From a certain highly teleological perspective, such an argument makes sense, but its limitations become clear if we think prospectively about the problems and challenges the Qing could have seen *c.*1800, and about their successes as well as their failures. The financial and other contributions from elites (both near the war zones and far away) that the Qing needed in order to withstand rebellions were successfully mobilized, without significant compromises of state autonomy; the White Lotus sect was politically neutralized (1813 proved to be its last rebellion); a gradual (as it turns out, perhaps too gradual) trimming of non-functional military units got under way; and undersized county governments in many areas both took on more staff (admittedly, mostly outside the official personnel system) and began, at least in selected areas, to develop a new division of labour with local elites.[91] Neither military units nor owners of capital nor other elites shifted support towards rival claimants of sovereignty. Though crucial socio-economic issues could not really be *resolved*, modified versions of old management techniques were at least effective enough to stave off empire-wide crisis until the outbreak of the Taiping Rebellion in

1851 – an event that certainly derived in part from the intensification of problems discussed in the first part of this chapter, but also belonged in some respects to an era of unprecedented challenges. In that period, the ways in which other parts of the world had emerged from the 'world crisis' of 1760–1840 would, of course, matter much more to China.

One could argue, then, that some basic material challenges were shared among late eighteenth-century empires. At a very high level of abstraction, all of them were coping with the effects of societies 'outgrowing' old state structures, rather than with 'collapse', 'stagnation', or 'decay'. But beyond those kinds of gross generalizations, commonalities that span the Qing and other cases become harder to develop; the fundamental institutional inheritances and reform strategies of officials dealing with late eighteenth-century crises seem very different. Under the circumstances, the effect of global flows on the Qing was also relatively muted in this period: not trivial, but quite probably smaller than in the previous 200 years, and certainly far smaller than in the 150 years to come. For the time being, global currents took a decided back seat to the working out of tensions generated by domestic social and political structures. Connections remain worth probing, but for this time, place, and set of issues, comparisons seem a more promising optic.

The Age of Revolutions in Global Context: An Afterword

C. A. Bayly

The global 'turn' in historical studies was an indirect response to the perceived decline of the nation-state, the huge flows of capital across the world, and the rise of Asia in the international economy that occurred in the 1990s. Much of the new global history consisted of comparison and analogy at world level, though analogy, as Freud once said, is the weakest form of analysis. This volume demonstrates, however, that a global perspective can be combined with significant revisions in regional and national histories. Two interconnected questions emerge from the book. First, what determined the 'age of revolutions' as a period of global historical time? Second, what were its defining characteristics and consequences?

The volume takes the Seven Years War, 1756–63, as its starting point. It is certainly true that in different ways the French, American, and even Caribbean and Latin American revolutions were indirect consequences of the enormous fiscal and military burdens placed on European states, especially Britain, France, the Netherlands, Spain, and Portugal, following their attempts to project power transnationally on the basis of limited and politically contested domestic resources. Yet a significant context for these worldwide European conflicts was set by the prior deformations of large multiethnic empires outside Europe: particularly the Ottomans, Safavids, Mughals, and Mataram in present-day Indonesia. The fragmentation, decentralization, or collapse of these powers from about 1700 created threats to world trade and also opportunities for the enrichment of the expanding European empires. In the context of mercantilist ideologies, it drew European states into worldwide warfare and the invasion of indigenous societies in the Middle East, Africa, Asia, and the Pacific. Yet the decline or transformation of these great non-European empires was itself brought about by a host of regional and local revolts. If these cannot easily be described as 'revolutions', they were certainly upsurges against intrusive state-forms, taxation systems, and official cults. They were given range and force by new ideologies that were deeply heterodox for the ruling groups and, by implication, they were socially levelling.

What were the defining characteristics of the period at a world level? While revolutionary upsurges, new concepts of the self and citizen, and the idea of popular rights were pervasive, a major actor in this volume is the growing state itself: militarized, increasingly intrusive, and, in many regions, muscle-bound by its conflict with revolution and ideological rebellion. In one important respect, the volume greatly extends the argument about the growth of the state during this period by bringing in the African continent more centrally. Previous writers have tended to see Africa as an exception to these global developments by virtue of the relative weakness of its states and the existence of the 'exit option' of flight or migration for peasants and labourers, leading to the characterization of the state as a mere 'gate-keeper'. Joseph Miller, by contrast, shows here that weapons, new ideologies of kingship, and transnational trade helped to create a new state order in Africa, at least comparable with developments in Europe or Asia.

It has long been clear, as Albert Camus once wrote, that the ultimate beneficiary of all revolutions is the state. But over recent years historians have been able to show much more clearly how the transnational dimensions of modernizing and militarizing government expanded, at the same time as its internal density grew greater. The response to the revolutions across the world created a kind of knock-on effect. In Europe, for instance, it was the searing experience of the Irish rebellion of 1798, supported by revolutionary France, that forced the British elite to try to buy middle-class Catholic support by creating the Union of Britain and Ireland, a move that rapidly backfired. The complex financial relations between revolutionary France and Algeria in the 1800s created the conditions for France's ultimate conquest of that country after 1830 and large sections of the former Napoleonic army were mobilized to accomplish this. The Revolution and Napoleon's occupation of Spain and Portugal after 1805 created the conditions for the creation of new creole states in Latin America.

The invigorated state roamed more widely even than this. Because Britain was outclassed militarily in Europe, it seized a whole range of indigenous and colonial states in the Caribbean, Asia, and Africa, ruling them through forms of more intrusive viceregal power. The new provinces included much of western and southern India, Java and

Ceylon, the Cape of Good Hope, and, for a time, Egypt. European and Indian troops, seamen, and administrators were scattered across the world in greater numbers than ever before as the size of military forces hugely increased. Distant new linkages were made, so that Maori whalers were found off the coast of Newfoundland and South Asian merchants traded in Brazil. There emerged, too, 'para-colonial' regimes, such as Tipu Sultan's Mysore, the Sikh Punjab, Thailand, Mehmet Ali's Egypt, or Qajar Iran. These drew on some of the techniques of European state-building pioneered during the wars. If not revolutionary in the European sense, they spurned or transformed existing dynastic legitimacy, becoming mini-Bonapartist regimes. Tipu Sultan raised the Cap of Liberty over his fortress in south India and rejected the authority of the Mughal Emperor, now compromised by the British. Ranjit Singh's new model army in the Punjab was officered by a number of refugees from Napoleon's armies.

Not all the older supremacies fragmented. The introduction to this volume considers the survival of the Ottoman Empire and asks the question why it did not experience a revolution itself. For the Ottomans, the European revolutions were upsurges of atheism that disrupted the God-given order of monarchies. But the Ottoman Empire did, in fact, experience a sort of revolution quite apart from the Wahhabi uprising in its fringes. The destruction of the Janissaries was in reality a revolution of the state *against* society, as was much of what followed through to the Tanzimat reforms after 1839. The Qing Empire, as Kenneth Pomeranz argues here, soldiered on through this period, despite increasing internal dissent. This was perhaps because it was a smaller and less burdensome polity, financing itself, as Pamela Crossley has suggested, by external expansion more than by increasing internal taxation.[1]

Yet across much of the world the most striking development was the internal rather than the external expansion of the state, which followed from the revolutionary and Napoleonic wars. At the close of the American Revolution, William Pitt, the British Prime Minister, had reduced the duties on tea to help bail out the East India Company, pushing forward Britain's opium and cotton trade with China. But the general picture was of the increase in internal taxation, especially on the wealthy, thus completing the story of John Brewer's 'military-fiscal' state in Britain.[2] Elsewhere, the pressure for regular revenue during time of war created, first, a new tax-paying landlord class in Bengal in 1793 and, later, a secular increase in taxation on all British Indian territories. Effectively, then, it was the Indian peasant tax-payer or revenue-payer who financed the greatly expanded

British Indian armies and created the conditions for further intervention and territorial expansion throughout the next century. This change was paralleled elsewhere across the world, though in a less dramatic form. The experience of French occupation created more integrated and intrusive bureaucracies in the German states, as T. C. W. Blanning has shown.[3] In Russia, the expansion of the purview of the state under Catherine the Great was speeded up dramatically after 1815 as demobilized soldiers were planted in military colonies adjoining the Khanates of the Crimea and in the Caucasus.

The 'conservative turn' in the global history of the revolutionary age, then, has left the state as the great winner. In the case of the revolutionary states of Latin America, the emphasis has fallen on the conservatism that preserved the rights of the Church, the corporations, and the creole elites. The revolutionary shine has even been taken off the 'black republic' of Haiti where, once again, the survival of an indigenous African and mixed-race slave-holding ruling class has attracted recent scholarly attention. Equally, many historians have commented on the fact that it was precisely at the time of the revolutionary surges, from 1780 to 1830, that the slave trade reached its apogee. The abolition of the British trade in 1807 had little effect on the institution of slavery, while the trade itself merely moved into Portuguese, Spanish, and Arab ships. Even in the British case, naval moves against the trade often provided justification for colonial expansion and invasion of the sovereignty of African and Arab rulers. It was justly remarked that William Wilberforce was as passionately in favour of British Christian domination in India as he was hostile to the slave trade.

In the recent past, historians of Great Britain were taken to task for spending their careers trying to prove that 'nothing happened'. That disease now seems to be in danger of becoming a global complaint. So was there anything revolutionary about the 'revolutionary age'? The answer remains affirmative if we turn to a field that has been somewhat unfashionable in the midst of the 'cultural turn': the history of political thought. Here the years between 1763 and 1842 did indeed witness an epochal change in the nature of popular 'claim-making' and in the wider construction of political thought. It seems to me that the concept of claim-making, put to good use by Frederick Cooper,[4] links ideas to social practice in the manner called for by Lynn Hunt in this volume. It was a change that affected liberal and conservative ideologies as much as radical ones. It transformed understandings of the role of the state and the nature of international order as much as it empowered a radical republicanism and discourse of popular rights. Indeed, this change created the very foundation of modern global politics: the dichotomy between 'right' and 'left' that replaced the antithesis between sin and goodness as the measure of Man. It was transnational in implication and it also powerfully affected people's understanding of and reaction to broader economic and social changes. The introduction correctly reminds us that change came slowly and patchily across the world, but that is no reason to deny its very existence.

One striking illustration of this point is embodied in David Armitage's own notion of the 'contagion of sovereignty', which spread globally after the American Declaration of Independence.[5] Armitage focused on the diffusion of this idea within the Americas and the Atlantic world. But one can see it reflected across the globe before the end point of this volume. Elites in the Philippines debated 'independence' and government by Filipinos before 1820. In India, even a reluctant creole empire-loyalist such as Rammohan Roy spoke of the inevitability of India's 'separation' from Great Britain if the East India Company's despotism did not abate. British radicals as well as conservatives in India and Ceylon were meanwhile using the word 'independence' itself to describe the coming dissolution of empire. The point about this, as well as other idioms in the new political language, was not that they necessarily had immediate effects, but that they could be generalized, pluralized, and appropriated to different conditions.

Another version of this new political idiom can be seen in the notion of the liberal or 'mixed' constitution. Here we see the final act of John Pocock's 'Machiavellian moment' being played out across the world and in Asia rather than the Atlantic world.[6] The idea of the republican constitution, Anglicized by British political theorists, and appropriated by American patriots, came home to Europe at the same time as it spread across the Asian world. The concept of a constitution, of course, was itself an ideological compromise between republican populism and the powers that be, compatible even with constitutional monarchy. When the European Union celebrated the fiftieth anniversary of the Treaty of Rome in the Presidential Palace in Rome in 2006, the Polish Republic sent a late nineteenth-century historical painting of the declaration of the Polish Constitution of 1791, 'the second oldest democratic constitution in the World', as its national contribution to the exhibition. That constitution was stillborn at least until the 1920s. More immediately significant across the world was the declaration of the Cádiz constitution of 1810, which resulted in stirrings across the whole Portuguese and Spanish colonial world.

Filipinos, who had already been alerted to the idea of the 'British constitution' during the British occupation of Manila in the early 1760s, took up the idea again as a way of fending off the power of Madrid. Rammohan Roy hosted dinners in the Calcutta Town Hall to celebrate the Iberian constitutions, while his British, Irish, and Portuguese friends toasted radical movements and the free press across the world, including India itself. Meanwhile he searched the Sanskrit texts, imagining his own version of a once and future Indian, or rather 'Hindu constitution'.[7]

A third major ideological change over these three generations was the hardening of ideas about the rights of peoples, states, and nations. The works of Tom Paine and Benjamin Constant were diffused across the world and translated into numerous languages by the 1850s, soon to be joined by versions of Mazzini's 'Duties of Man'.[8] These ideas of human rights 'bonded' with ideas in societies outside Europe with which they had an elective affinity. Older idioms concerning the virtue of the pioneer, who mixed his labour with the land and its produce, echoing Locke, proved hospitable to the notion of rights in the Americas. Christian notions concerning the free will of the spirit bonded with ideas of the status of Brahmins in Goa and aristocratic birth in the Philippines to give rise to early movements for native rights to be recognized alongside those of the Spanish- and Portuguese-born. In the Muslim world the particular status afforded to submission to God and Quranic piety empowered the Wahhabi movements in Arabia and related jihadist purist movements in Central West Africa, and ultimately India and China.

These movements were 'revolutionary' in a broad sense even if they do not conform to the teleology of Western political thought. The introduction and Robert Travers's chapter draw attention to the discursive battle between those who lauded the revolution of rights, those who saw merely the sudden overthrow of legitimate power (*inqilab*), and those who saw merely rebellion in the upsurges of these times. Yet most of the great rebellions of this era were infused with a sense of customary rights or of spiritual equality, as in the case of the Sikh movements of the Punjab or the neo-Buddhist and nativist revolts that scarred China in the latter part of Qianlong's reign. Rebellion in China took two forms: first, the creation of local insurrectionary states; second, networks of millenarian dissidence such as the White Lotus movement or the Three Trigrams 'conspiracy'. Arguably, the Qing regime survived because these two elements never came together in this period as their equivalents did in Europe. The Taiping Rebellion, which broke out a decade after the end date of this volume, saw local state-building empowered by a semi-Christian and neo-Buddhist ideology.

One critically important form of rights claiming that imprinted itself heavily on the 'age of revolutions' was the demand for freedom from slavery. The European and American revolutionary movements were, of course, ambivalent about freeing slaves en masse. In general a consensus, which allowed the continuation of slave-holding, persisted right through to the end of our period. But, as Christopher Brown writes, the movement to end slavery was pre-eminently an evangelical Christian ideological movement that pluralized the idea of emancipation and spilled broadly into political theory and practice. Once enunciated it changed the nature of political discourse.[9] By the 1830s, the subjection of poor Indian women to dancing and prostitution and the subjection of colonized people more generally were being denounced as 'slavery'. Shortly after, as copies of *Uncle Tom's Cabin* appeared in India, activists saw a similarity between American plantation slavery and the 'slavery' of the Bengal peasant.

Freedom extended to the idea of freedom in the market. Indeed, the longer-term consequence of Napoleon's Continental Blockade was to spur forward the British attempt to break into foreign markets under the rubric of 'free trade'. Free trade imperialism was one of the most revolutionary consequences of the 'age of revolutions', leading directly to confrontations with the Ottoman Empire, Egypt, Burma, and China. For a time, France also adopted laissez-faire policies in equal measure. Just as the antislavery movement and antipiracy policies resulted in attacks on the sovereignty of African and Arab principalities, so attacks on monopoly as 'despotism' signalled the rise of imperialism across the world.

The emergence of the nation-state from the detritus of revolutionary war absorbed the attention of historians for many generations. But the theories of Jürgen Habermas provided them with a new marker of cultural change. The 'public' as an entity, reflecting both on government and also on popular practice, emerged from the *salon*, the coffee house, and the commercial practice of the eighteenth century. But its significance was enormously expanded by the worldwide revolution. As noted, politics across the world became polarized between 'right' and 'left', transforming the language of politics. By the 1810s and 1820s Indian rogue horsemen – the Pindaris – could be called the 'Frenchmen of India', while Bishop Heber could note the Indian 'advanced Whigs' of Calcutta. More significantly, the newspaper and ephemeral pamphlet publications expanded hugely in volume and the range of critical political scrutiny the press purveyed increased vastly. Hundreds of newspapers sprang up in the United States alone between 1780 and 1830. There was an equivalent expansion of newspapers catering to the elites of the new South American republics. Meanwhile, the first newspapers, some in indigenous languages with indigenous editors, sprang up in Calcutta, Penang, Singapore, and Canton. The Istanbul and Beijing gazettes remained official publications, but they were forced to engage with information supplied by nearby colonists' newspapers and even to engage in debate with them. Newspapers deployed the idea that there existed a transnational 'public', or as we would now say a 'public sphere', which represented the common concerns of all humanity. This was a direct result of the revolutionary paradox: its elevation of both the idea of the separateness and sovereignty of peoples and the existence of a wider sphere of 'rights of man'.

A final question raised by this collection concerns the outer boundary of the 'age of revolutions' at a global level. At one end of the period there was the Seven Years War, rightly seen as the first truly transnational war in history, ranging as it did from the Americas to the East Indies. As for the end date of the 'revolutionary age', the present volume breaks with a predominantly European time-frame by taking the onset of the Anglo-Chinese Opium War as its end point. To reiterate, Kenneth Pomeranz's chapter on China helps to foster a sense of difference within global history. Nevertheless, the rapid unravelling of Qing authority after 1850 points to massive political and ideological challenges that were only just held in check over this period of apparent expansion and relative social peace. Philip Kuhn's *Soulstealers* provides some evidence for this view.[10] China was perhaps only just entering its own 'age of revolution' at the end date of this volume.

A few years after the tumultuous events in Canton, the 1848 revolutions in Europe set off further chain reactions of dissidence and conquest in Ceylon, French India, Canada, and Indochina. The rhetoric of 'the Rights of Man' was empowered once again across the world. Perhaps the true end of the 'age of revolutions' was marked by the reaction of the 1850s. The state across Europe and the Americas, now empowered by railroads and new military capacity, strengthened itself enormously, especially after the unification of Germany and Italy and the American Civil War. The colonial state over much of the rest of the world also entrenched itself violently for another two generations: in India in 1857, and through the French conquest in Indochina, for instance. One small sign of the future was the creation of a new state in Japan consequent on the Meiji restoration of 1868–72. Broadly, then, we may think of the 'age of revolutions' of the years from about 1760 to 1840 as framed in turn by a longer period that stretched from 1720 to 1850, including a phase when the state was unusually dominant stretching from about 1850 to 1914 (or 1870 to 1911 in the case of China). The expansion of the state was in turn matched by the ideological and military challenges to it. Thus the perceptive and novel essays in this volume begin a wider reconceptualization of global history.

Notes

Introduction: The Age of Revolutions, c.1760–1840 – Global Causation, Connection, and Comparison

1. Robert Travers, *Ideology and Empire in Eighteenth-Century India: The British in Bengal* (Cambridge, 2007), p. 31; see also Robert Travers, 'Imperial Revolutions and Global Repercussions: South Asia and the World, *c.*1750–1850', ch. 8 in this volume, and Rajat Kanta Ray, 'Indian Society and the Establishment of British Supremacy', in P. J. Marshall, ed., *The Oxford History of the British Empire*, II: *The Eighteenth Century* (Oxford, 1998), pp. 508–10, 519–20, 523, on Mughal responses to *inqilab*.

2. Robert Clive to Richard Clive, 19 August 1757, in *Bengal in 1756–1757*, ed. S. C. Hill, 3 vols (London, 1905), III, p. 360.

3. Ghulam Husain Khan Tabataba'i, *A Translation of the Sëir Mutaqherin; or View of Modern Times*, trans. Haji Mustafa, 3 vols (Calcutta, 1789–90), I, p. '467' (sc. 463). For a discussion of this work, see Iqbal Ghani Khan, 'A Book with Two Views – Ghulam Husain Khan's "An Overview of the Modern Times"', in Jamal Malik, ed., *Perspectives of Mutual Encounters in South Asian History, 1760–1860* (Leiden, 2000), pp. 278–97.

4. 'Nous approchons de l'état de crise et du siècle des révolutions': Jean-Jacques Rousseau, *Émile, ou de l'éducation*, 4 vols (Amsterdam, 1762), II, p. 54.

5. Thomas Paine, *Rights of Man: Being an Answer to Mr. Burke's Attack on the French Revolution* (London, 1791), p. 162.

6. John Adams to James Lloyd, 29 March 1815, in *The Works of John Adams*, ed. Charles Francis Adams, 10 vols (Boston, 1850–6), X, p. 149.

7. Gary B. Nash, 'Sparks from the Altar of '76: International Repercussions and Reconsiderations of the American Revolution', ch. 1 in this volume; compare Nash, *The Forgotten Fifth: African Americans in the Age of Revolution* (Cambridge, MA, 2006).

8. Reinhart Koselleck, 'Historische Kriterien des neuzeitlichen Revolutionsbegriff', in Koselleck, *Vergangene Zukunft. Zur Semantik geschichtlicher Zeiten* (Frankfurt, 1979), pp. 68–9; also in English as 'Historical Criteria of the Modern Concept of Revolution', in Koselleck, *Futures Past: On the Semantics of Historical Time*, trans. Keith Tribe (Cambridge, MA, 1985), pp. 39–54.

9. *Un libertin dans l'Inde moghole: Les voyages de François Bernier (1656–1669)*, ed. Frédéric Tinguely (Paris, 2008), pp. 18–19.

10. François Bernier, *Histoire de la dernière révolution des états du Grand Mogol* (Paris, 1670). On the politics of the term 'revolution' in English around the same time, see Ilan Rachum, 'The Meaning of "Revolution" in the

English Revolution (1648–1660)', *Journal of the History of Ideas* 56 (1995), 195–215.

11. Louis Bazin, SJ, 'Seconde Lettre . . . contenant les révolutions qui suivirent la mort de Thamas-Kouli-Khan' (post 1747), in *Lettres édifiantes et curieuses, écrites des missions étrangères*, 26 vols (Toulouse, 1810–11), IV, pp. 256–80.

12. Baron Antoine de Jucherau de Saint-Denys, *Révolutions de Constantinople en 1807 et 1808, précédées d'observations générales sur l'état actuel de l'empire ottoman* (Paris, 1818).

13. R. R. Palmer and Jacques Godechot, 'Le problème de l'Atlantique du XVIIIe au XXe siécle', in *Relazioni del X Congresso Internazionale di Scienze Storiche (Rome, 4–11 Settembre 1955)*, 6 vols (Florence, 1955), V, pp. 175–239; Godechot, *Les révolutions (1770–1799)* (Paris, 1963); Eng. trans., Godechot, *France and the Atlantic Revolution of the Eighteenth Century, 1770–1799*, trans. Herbert H. Rowen (New York, 1965); Palmer, *The World of the French Revolution* (New York, 1971).

14. Max F. Millikan and W. W. Rostow, *A Proposal: Key to an Effective Foreign Policy* (New York, 1957), p. 4.

15. As noted forcefully by Jaime E. Rodríguez O., 'Two Revolutions: France 1789 and Mexico 1810', *The Americas* 32 (1990), 239–56. Among accounts inspired by Palmer, Lester D. Langley, *The Americas in the Age of Revolution, 1750–1850* (New Haven, CT, 1996), is expansive and hemispheric, and Wim Klooster, *Revolutions in the Atlantic World: A Comparative History* (New York, 2009), is both hemispheric and transatlantic.

16. R. R. Palmer, *The Age of the Democratic Revolution: A Political History of Europe and America, 1760–1800*, 2 vols (Princeton, NJ, 1959–64), I, p. 13. For important reassessments of the work, see especially Palmer, 'La "Révolution atlantique" – Vingt ans après', in Eberhard Schmitt and Rolf Reichardt, eds, *Die Französische Revolution – zufälliges oder notwendiges Ereignis? Akten des internationalen Symposions an der Universität Bamberg vom 4.–7. Juni 1979*, 3 vols (Munich, 1983), I, pp. 89–104; William Pencak, 'R. R. Palmer's *The Age of the Democratic Revolution*: The View from America after Thirty Years', *Pennsylvania History* 60 (1993), 73–92; Bernard Bailyn, *Atlantic History: Concept and Contours* (Cambridge, MA, 2005), pp. 25–30; and Edoardo Tortarolo, Annie Jourdan, Jack A. Goldstone, Simone Neri Serneri and Peter Onuf, 'L'era delle rivoluzioni democratiche di Robert R. Palmer', *Contemporanea* 10 (2007), 125–55.

17. R. R. Palmer, 'The World Revolution of the West, 1763–1801', *Political Science Quarterly* 69 (1954), 1–14; Palmer, *The Age of the Democratic Revolution*, II, p. 574.

18. Eric Hobsbawm, *The Age of Revolution, 1789–1848* (London, 1962), pp. ix, 2–3, 4.

19. Travers, 'Imperial Revolutions and Global Repercussions', ch. 8 in this volume.

20. G. W. F. Hegel, *Lectures on the Philosophy of World History: Introduction*, trans. H. B. Nisbet (Cambridge, 1975), p. 176; Susan Buck-Morss, *Hegel, Haiti, and Universal History* (Pittsburgh, 2009).

21. Joseph C. Miller, 'The Dynamics of History in Africa and the Atlantic "Age of Revolutions"', ch. 6 in this volume.

22. David Geggus, 'The Caribbean in the Age of Revolution', ch. 5 in this volume.

23. C. A. Bayly, *Imperial Meridian: The British Empire and the World, 1780–1830* (London, 1989), ch. 6, 'The World Crisis, 1780–1820'; Bayly, *The Birth of the Modern World, 1780–1914: Global Connections and Comparisons* (Oxford, 2004), pp. 88–9; John Darwin, *After Tamerlane: The Rise and Fall of Global Empire* (London, 2007), p. 162.

24. Bayly, *The Birth of the Modern World*, p. 119; Darwin, *After Tamerlane*, p. 160.

25. E. J. Hobsbawm, 'The General Crisis of the European Economy in the 17th Century', *Past and Present* 5 (May 1954), 33–53; Hobsbawm, 'The Crisis of the 17th Century – II', *Past and Present* 6 (November 1954), 44–65; Trevor Aston, ed., *Crisis in Europe, 1560–1660: Essays from Past and Present* (London, 1965); Geoffrey Parker and Lesley M. Smith, eds, *The General Crisis of the Seventeenth Century*, 2nd edn (London, 1997).

26. Jonathan Dewald, 'Crisis, Chronology, and the Shape of European Social History', *American Historical Review* 113 (2008), 1047. For penetrating discussions of the concept of crisis, see Reinhart Koselleck, 'Some Questions Regarding the Conceptual History of "Crisis"', in Koselleck, *The Practice of Conceptual History: Timing History, Spacing Concepts*, trans. Todd Samuel Presner et al. (Stanford, CA, 2002), pp. 236–47; Koselleck, 'Crisis', trans. Michaela W. Richter, *Journal of the History of Ideas* 67 (2006), 357–400.

27. Geoffrey Parker, 'Crisis and Catastrophe: The Global Crisis of the Seventeenth Century Reconsidered', *American Historical Review* 113 (2008), 1053–79; Michael Marmé, 'Locating Linkages or Painting Bull's-Eyes around Bullet Holes? An East Asian Perspective on the Seventeenth-Century Crisis', *American Historical Review* 113 (2008), 1080–9.

28. For a recent survey, see J. H. Elliott, 'The General Crisis in Retrospect: A Debate without End', in Elliott, *Spain, Europe and the Wider World, 1500–1800* (New Haven, CT, 2009), pp. 52–73.

29. On which see Jeremy Adelman, 'Iberian Passages: Continuity and Change in the South Atlantic', ch. 4 in this volume; Adelman, *Sovereignty and Revolution in the Iberian Atlantic* (Princeton, NJ, 2006).

30. Jeremy Adelman, 'An Age of Imperial Revolutions', *American Historical Review* 113 (2008), 319–40.

31. Ryan T. Jones, 'Empire of Extinction: A Natural History of Russian Expansion in the Eighteenth-century North Pacific' (PhD dissertation, Columbia University, 2008); Leonard Blussé, *Visible Cities: Canton, Nagasaki, and Batavia and the Coming of the Americans* (Cambridge, MA, 2008); James Fichter, *American Enterprise, British Empire: The East Indies in the Transformation of Anglo-American Capitalism, 1773–1815* (Cambridge, MA, forthcoming).

Notes 221

32. Compare Patrick O'Brien, 'Historiographical Traditions and the Modern Imperatives for the Restoration of Global History', *Journal of Global History* 1 (2006), 3–39; Michael Adas, 'Reconsidering the Macronarrative in Global History: John Darwin's *After Tamerlane* and the Case for Comparison', *Journal of Global History* 4 (2009), 163–73.
33. István Batsányi, 'A franciaországi változásokra' (On the Changes in France) (1791), quoted in Ivan T. Berend, *History Derailed: Central and Eastern Europe in the Long Nineteenth Century* (Berkeley, CA, 2003), p. 2 (translation slightly modified).
34. The diaries of István Széchenyi and Baron Miklós Wesselényi, cited in Berend, *History Derailed*, p. 39.
35. Kenneth Pomeranz, *The Great Divergence: China, Europe, and the Making of the Modern World Economy* (Princeton, NJ, 2000).
36. 'Generally speaking, for the economical development of the bourgeoisie, England is here taken as the typical country; for its political development, France': Karl Marx and Friedrich Engels, *The Communist Manifesto*, ed. Gareth Stedman Jones (London, 2002), p. 221 (Engels's note to the 1888 English edition).
37. Anna Bezanson, 'The Early Use of the Term Industrial Revolution', *Quarterly Journal of Economics* 36 (1922), 343–9; David Cannadine, 'The Present and the Past in the English Industrial Revolution, 1880–1980', *Past and Present* 103 (May 1984), 131–72.
38. See Maxine Berg and Pat Hudson, 'Rehabilitating the Industrial Revolution', *Economic History Review* n.s. 45 (1992), 24–50, a response in large measure to the important revisionist and 'gradualist' account of N. F. R. Crafts, *British Economic Growth during the Industrial Revolution* (Oxford, 1985).
39. T. R. Malthus, *Principles of Political Economy Considered with a View to Their Practical Application* (London, 1820), p. 409.
40. François Crouzet, 'The Impact of the French Wars on the British Economy', in Crouzet, *Britain, France and International Commerce: From Louis XIV to Victoria* (Aldershot, 1996), pp. 208–9. Also see, more generally, Erik Aerts and François Crouzet, eds, *Economic Effects of the French Revolutionary and Napoleonic Wars* (Leuven, 1990); Kevin H. O'Rourke, 'The Worldwide Economic Impact of the French Revolutionary and Napoleonic Wars, 1793–1815', *Journal of Global History* 2 (2006), 123–49.
41. Eliana Balla and Noel D. Johnson, 'Fiscal Crisis and Institutional Change in the Ottoman Empire and France' (19 February 2008), SSRN Working Paper available at http://papers.ssrn.com/sol3/papers.cfm?abstract_id=1096744, accessed 12 June 2009.
42. Jack A. Goldstone, *Revolution and Rebellion in the Early Modern World* (Berkeley, CA, 1991).
43. Victor Lieberman, *Strange Parallels: Southeast Asia in Global Context, c. 800–1830* (Cambridge, 2003).
44. This stress on the political also lies behind a recent analysis of the transfer of the court from Portugal to Brazil: José Jobson de Andrade Arruda,

Uma colônia entre dois impérios: A abertura dos portos brasileiros, 1800–1808 (Bauru, 2008).

45. Maya Jasanoff, 'Revolutionary Exiles: The American Loyalist and French Émigré Diasporas', ch. 3 in this volume; see also Jasanoff, 'The Other Side of Revolution: Loyalists in the British Empire', *William and Mary Quarterly* 3rd ser. 65 (2008), 205–32.

46. Juan Cole, 'Playing Muslim: Bonaparte's Army of the Orient and Euro-Muslim Creolization', ch. 7 in this volume; see also Cole, *Napoleon's Egypt: Invading the Middle East* (Basingstoke, 2007).

47. Peter Carey, 'Revolutionary Europe and the Destruction of Java's Old Order, 1808–30', ch. 9 in this volume; see also Carey, *The Power of Prophecy: Prince Dipanagara and the End of an Old Order in Java (1825–1830)* (Leiden, 2007).

48. Kenneth Pomeranz, 'Their Own Path to Crisis? Social Change, State-Building and the Limits of Qing Expansion, *c.*1770–1840', ch. 10 in this volume.

49. Blussé, *Visible Cities*, pp. 6–8.

50. Letter from Charles Élie, Marquis de Ferrières, in Marquis de Ferrières, *Correspondance inédite, 1789, 1790, 1791*, ed. Henri Carré (Paris, 1932), pp. 37–8; also see the discussion in Paul Friedland, *Political Actors: Representative Bodies and Theatricality in the Age of the French Revolution* (Ithaca, NY, 2002), pp. 129–31.

51. Bruce McGowan, 'The Age of the Ayans, 1699–1812', in Halil İnalcık and Donald Quataert, eds, *An Economic and Social History of the Ottoman Empire*, 2 vols (Cambridge, 1997), II, pp. 637–758.

52. Stanford J. Shaw, 'The Origins of Ottoman Military Reform: The Nizam-i Cedid Army of Sultan Selim III', *Journal of Modern History* 37 (1965), 291–306.

53. Sheyh Galib, 'To Me Love Is the Flame', in *Ottoman Lyric Poetry: An Anthology*, ed. and trans. Walter G. Andrews, Najaat Black and Mehmet Kalpaklı (Austin, TX, 1997), pp. 153–4.

54. R. S. Sharma, *Early Medieval Indian Society: A Study in Feudalisation* (Hyderabad, 2001), pp. 62–4.

55. For an excellent overview of the current historiography of Spanish America in the Age of Revolutions see Gabriel Paquette, 'The Dissolution of the Spanish Monarchy', *The Historical Journal* 52 (2009), 175–212; compare José M. Portillo Valdés, *Crisis atlántica. Autonomía e independencia en la crisis de la monarquía hispana* (Madrid, 2006).

56. Lynn Hunt, 'The French Revolution in Global Context', ch. 2 in this volume.

57. For example, Albert Sorel, *L'Europe et la Révolution française*, 8 vols (Paris, 1885–1904); Jacques Godechot, *La Grande Nation: l'expansion révolution-naire de la France dans le monde de 1789 à 1799* (Paris, 1956); Joseph Klaits and Michael H. Haltzel, eds, *The Global Ramifications of the French Revolution* (Washington, DC, 1994); Bailey Stone, *The Genesis of the French Revolution: A Global-Historical Interpretation* (Cambridge, 1994);

Stone, *Reinterpeting the French Revolution: A Global-Historical Perspective* (Cambridge, 2002).
58. See generally P. J. Marshall, *The Making and Unmaking of Empires: Britain, India, and America, c. 1750–1783* (Oxford, 2005).
59. Compare the essays collected in 'Early Modernities', *Daedalus* 127, 3 (Summer 1998).
60. Sanjay Subrahmanyam, 'Connected Histories: Notes towards a Reconfiguration of Early Modern Eurasia', *Modern Asian Studies* 31 (1997), 735–62.
61. Dominic Lieven, *Russia Against Napoleon: The Battle for Europe, 1807 to 1814* (London, 2009).
62. François Furet, *Interpreting the French Revolution*, trans. Elborg Forster (Cambridge, 1981), pp. 85–6. For a classic view on the genealogy of modern revolutions, see Crane Brinton, *The Anatomy of Revolution*, expanded edn (New York, 1965).

Chapter 1: Sparks from the Altar of '76: International Repercussions and Reconsiderations of the American Revolution

1. R. R. Palmer, *The Age of the Democratic Revolution: A Political History of Europe and America, 1760–1800*, 2 vols (Princeton, NJ, 1959–64), I, pp. 239–40, 282.
2. Michael Lienesch, *New Order of the Ages: Time, the Constitution, and the Making of Modern American Political Thought* (Princeton, NJ, 1988), cit. C. A. Bayly, *The Birth of the Modern World, 1780–1914: Global Connections and Comparisons* (Oxford, 2004), pp. 86, 493 n. 1.
3. Thomas Paine, *Common Sense* (Philadelphia, 1776), 'Introduction' (unpaginated).
4. David Armitage, *The Declaration of Independence: A Global History* (Cambridge, MA, 2007). For a discussion of Armitage's book, which stresses claims of statehood more than individual rights, see *William and Mary Quarterly* 3rd ser. 65 (2008), 347–69.
5. P. J. Marshall, *The Making and Unmaking of Empires: Britain, India, and America c. 1750–1783* (Oxford, 2005).
6. John H. Coatsworth, 'Patterns of Rural Rebellion', in Friedrich Katz, ed., *Riot, Rebellion, and Revolution: Rural Social Conflict in Mexico* (Princeton, NJ, 1988), p. 30, quoted in Lester D. Langley, *The Americas in the Age of Revolution, 1750–1850* (New Haven, CT, 1996), p. 150; compare Jeremy Adelman's chapter in this volume.
7. Laurent Dubois, whose *A Colony of Citizens: Revolution and Slave Emancipation in the French Caribbean, 1787–1804* (Chapel Hill, NC, 2004) and *Avengers of the New World: The Story of the Haitian Revolution* (Cambridge, MA, 2004) are the latest of a tidal wave of recent Caribbean studies, assigns nearly zero significance to the American Revolution in the Haitian uprising against French masters. See also David Geggus's

chapter in this volume for further thoughts on the paltry influence of the Haitian Revolution in transforming the rest of the Caribbean slave regimes.

8. Andrew Jackson O'Shaughnessy, *An Empire Divided: The American Revolution and the British Caribbean* (Philadelphia, 2000); Richard B. Sheridan, 'The Crisis of Slave Subsistence in the British West Indies during and after the American Revolution', *William and Mary Quarterly* 3rd ser. 33 (1976), 615–41.

9. Gelien Matthews, *Caribbean Slave Revolts and the British Abolitionist Movement* (Baton Rouge, LA, 2006),

10. Bayly, *The Birth of the Modern World*.

11. Fred Anderson, *Crucible of War: The Seven Years' War and the Fate of Empire in British North America, 1754–1766* (New York, 2000), p. xviii. Though it goes unsaid, Anderson is surely referring to the geopolitical importance of the Seven Years War and not to its greater importance than the American Revolution in terms of political Enlightenment-based ideology.

12. I have studied Thomas Peters and others in this movement of black abolitionists out of the country in Gary B. Nash, 'Thomas Peters: Millwright and Deliverer', in David G. Sweet and Nash, eds, *Struggle and Survival in Colonial America* (Berkeley, CA, 1981), pp. 69–85; and in Nash, *The Forgotten Fifth: African Americans in the Age of Revolution* (Cambridge, MA, 2004). See also Cassandra Pybus, *Epic Journeys of Freedom: Runaway Slaves of the American Revolution and Their Global Quest for Liberty* (Boston, 2006) and Simon Schama, *Rough Crossings: Britain, the Slaves, and the American Revolution* (New York, 2006).

13. Deirdre Coleman, *Romantic Colonization and British Anti-Slavery* (Cambridge, 2005); Christopher Leslie Brown, *Moral Capital: Foundations of British Abolitionism* (Chapel Hill, NC, 2006). For the comments in 1779 of one concerned Dutch reformer regarding American slavery, see J. W. Schulte Nordholt, 'The Impact of the American Revolution on the Dutch Republic', in *The Impact of the American Revolution Abroad* (Washington, DC, 1976), p. 48; for similar dismay among Russian reformers, see N. N. Bolkhovitinov, 'The American Revolution and the Russian Empire', ibid., pp. 86, 89.

14. For an argument that the Founding Fathers had a better chance of accomplishing a gradual abolition of slavery in their own lifetimes than historians have generally been willing to allow, see Nash, *The Forgotten Fifth*, ch. 2.

15. Richard Price, *Observations on the Importance of the American Revolution*, in *Price: Political Writings*, ed. D. O. Thomas (Cambridge, 1991), pp. 117–18.

16. Ibid., p. 150.

17. [John Lind and Jeremy Bentham,] *An Answer to the Declaration of the American Congress* (London, 1776), p. 107, quoted in Brown, *Moral Capital*, p. 133.

18. Price, *Observations on the Importance of the American Revolution*, in *Price: Political Writings*, p. 150.

19. Betty Fladeland, *Men and Brothers: Anglo-American Antislavery Cooperation* (Urbana, IL, 1972), p. 42; Price to John Jay, 9 July 1785, in *The Correspondence of Richard Price*, ed. W. B. Peach and D. O. Thomas, 3 vols (Durham, NC, 1983–94), II, pp. 292–3. Price had used the same language in a letter to Jefferson, 2 July 1785, ibid., II, pp. 289–90. See also Price to Benjamin Rush, 22 July 1785, ibid., II, pp. 293–4. For distribution of pamphlets to Continental Congress members, see ibid., II, p. 271 n. 1.

20. Thomas Day, *A Letter from ***** in London, to His Friend in America, on the Subject of the Slave-Trade* (London, 1784), discussed in David Brion Davis, *The Problem of Slavery in the Age of Revolution, 1770–1823* (Ithaca, NY, 1975), pp. 398–9. Day wrote his screed in 1776, when he was twenty-five years old, but withheld publication until 1784. Quakers in Philadelphia and New York quickly republished it so that it would receive wide circulation in centres of American political power.

21. Thomas Slaughter, *The Beautiful Soul of John Woolman: Apostle of Abolition* (New York, 2008); Maurice Jackson, *Let This Voice Be Heard: Anthony Benezet, Father of Atlantic Abolitionism* (Philadelphia, 2009).

22. Gary B. Nash, 'Franklin and Slavery', *Proceedings of the American Philosophical Society* 150 (2006), 618–35.

23. Claude-Anne Lopez, *My Life with Benjamin Franklin* (New Haven, CT, 2000), pp. 200–3; in his *Runaway America: Benjamin Franklin, Slavery, and the American Revolution* (New York, 2004), David Waldstreicher sees Franklin's sea-change as more limited.

24. Adams called them 'atheists, deists, and libertines'; quoted in William Howard Adams, *The Paris Years of Thomas Jefferson* (New Haven, CT, 1997), p. 75.

25. *The Papers of Benjamin Franklin*, ed. Leonard W. Labaree et al., 39 vols to date (New Haven, CT, 1959–), XXXVII, pp. 619–20, lviii.

26. Benezet to Franklin, 8 May 1783, in *The Papers of Benjamin Franklin*, XXXIX, p. 575.

27. George S. Brookes, *Friend Anthony Benezet* (Philadelphia, 1937), p. 162.

28. For an analysis of the rapid decline of slavery in the Philadelphia area and the growth of a free black population, see Gary B. Nash and Jean R. Soderlund, *Freedom by Degrees: Emancipation in Pennsylvania and Its Aftermath* (New York, 1991), p. 18, Table 1.

29. Rush to Granville Sharp, August 1791 in *The Letters of Benjamin Rush*, ed. L. H. Butterfield, 2 vols (Princeton, NJ, 1951), I, p. 608. I have treated this era of black institution-building in Gary B. Nash, *Forging Freedom: The Formation of Philadelphia's Black Community, 1720–1840* (Cambridge, MA, 1988), chs 3–5.

30. Quoted in Nash, 'Franklin and Slavery', 635.

31. 'The Pennsylvania Abolition Society to the United States Congress' (3 February 1790); 'Sidi Mehemet Ibrahim on the Slave Trade' (23 March 1790), available at http://franklinpapers.org/franklin/ (The 'digital Franklin').

32. Benjamin Franklin, *Poor Richard, 1738. An Almanack for the Year of Christ 1738*, in *The Papers of Benjamin Franklin*, II, p. 197.

33. Henry Wiencek, *Imperfect God: George Washington, His Slaves, and the Creation of America* (New York, 2003), p. 261. Lafayette had lost his own father when he was a teenager, and Washington had no children of his own. Later, calling Washington 'my adoptive father', Lafayette named his first son George Washington Lafayette.

34. Louis Gottschalk, *Lafayette Between Two Revolutions* (Chicago, 1950), pp. 3–4.

35. Lafayette to Washington, 5 February 1783, in *Lafayette in the Age of the American Revolution: Selected Letters and Papers, 1776–1790*, ed. Stanley J. Idzerda, 5 vols (Ithaca, NY, 1977–83), V, pp. 90–3.

36. Quoted in Wiencek, *Imperfect God*, p. 262.

37. Ibid., p. 262.

38. Gordon to Washington, 30 August 1784, in *The Papers of George Washington. Confederation Series*, ed. W. W. Abbot and Dorothy Twohig, 6 vols (Charlottesville, VA, 1992), II, p. 64.

39. Paul Finkelman, *Slavery and the Founders: Race and Liberty in the Age of Jefferson* (Armonk, NY, 1996), p. 106.

40. Quoted in ibid., p. 273.

41. Ibid., pp. 274–7.

42. Quoted in Fritz Hirschfeld, *George Washington and Slavery* (Columbia, MO, 1997), p. 121.

43. François Furstenberg, *In the Name of the Father: Washington's Legacy, Slavery and the Making of a Nation* (New York, 2006), pp. 84–8.

44. Garrison is quoted in David Brion Davis, *Was Thomas Jefferson an Authentic Enemy of Slavery? An Inaugural Lecture Delivered before the University of Oxford on 18 February 1970* (Oxford, 1970), p. 4.

45. William Howard Adams, *The Paris Years of Thomas Jefferson* (New Haven, CT, 1997), pp. 11–12; the Lafayette–Jefferson relationship, along with letters between them, can be followed in Gilbert Chinard, *The Letters of Lafayette and Jefferson* (Baltimore, 1929). Many years later, Jefferson remembered that Lafayette, already an honorary citizen of several American states and cities, 'was my most powerful auxiliary and advocate', the man who paved the way for negotiating commercial and diplomatic treaties. Quoted in Jason Lane, *General and Madame de Lafayette: Partners in Liberty's Cause in the American and French Revolutions* (Lanham, MD, 2003), p. 92.

46. For Jefferson's friendship with Condorcet, see Adams, *Paris Years of Jefferson*, pp. 134–40; on Condorcet's wide influence on the slavery question, see Richard Popkin, 'Condorcet, Abolitionist', in Leonora Cohen Rosenfield, ed., *Condorcet Studies*, I (Atlantic Highlands, NJ, 1984), pp. 35–48. Jefferson's translation of Condorcet's *Réflexions sur l'esclavage des nègres* is in *Papers of Thomas Jefferson*, XIV, pp. 494–8.

47. Liliane Willens, 'Lafayette's Emancipation Experiment in French Guiana, 1786–1792', *Studies on Voltaire and the Eighteenth Century*, 242 (Oxford, 1986), pp. 345–63; Lloyd Kramer, *Lafayette in Two Worlds: Public Cultures*

and Personal Identities in an Age of Revolutions (Chapel Hill, NC, 1996), p. 164. On Sharp and the saga of the Black Loyalists, see Graham Russell Hodges, *The Black Loyalist Directory: African Americans in Exile after the American Revolution* (New York, 1996), and Pybus, *Epic Journeys of Freedom*, chs 5, 7, and 9. For a hyperdramatic portrayal of Sharp and the travails of the ex-slaves from North America in Nova Scotia and Sierra Leone, see Schama, *Rough Crossings*.

48. Price to Jefferson, 2 July 1785; Jefferson to Price, 7 August 1785, in *Papers of Jefferson*, VIII, pp. 258–9, 356–7.

49. Madison to Washington, 11 November 1785, in *Papers of George Washington, Confederation Series*, III, pp. 355–6.

50. Lafayette to Adams, 22 February 1786, quoted in Louis Gottschalk, *Lafayette Between the American and the French Revolution* (Chicago, 1950), p. 229. What Lafayette proposed and instituted was the purchase of land in French Guiana. The colony had been the site of a disastrous attempt in 1763 to populate it with French, Germans, Swiss, Belgians, Venetians, Genoans, and Maltese to create a commercial and agricultural power with the military capability to attack British holdings in the region and to offset the loss of French Canada. Few of the settlers had any farming experience. The settlement was poorly planned and, plagued by excessive heat and a hostile disease climate, over ten thousand people died in the ensuing calamity. That fiasco meant, however, that Lafayette would not have to confront suspicious plantation owners as he would in the French West Indies. Lafayette bought land, hired a manager recommended by Condorcet, and wrote to Washington eagerly of his plans. Lafayette did not anticipate immediate emancipation of slaves in French Guiana, but believed that gradual exposure to education and better working conditions would prepare them for freedom. Harder realities intruded. A yellow fever epidemic raged in Guiana at the time of launching the scheme and the disease killed Lafayette's manager. Lafayette turned his attention more to the unfolding events in France and gave charge of the project to his wife.

51. Jefferson's lengthy interchange with Démeunier is in *Papers of Jefferson*, X, pp. 3–65; the quoted sentences are on p. 63.

52. Davis, *The Problem of Slavery in the Age of Revolution*, pp. 175–6.

53. Quobna Ottobah Cugoano, *Thoughts and Sentiments on the Evil of Slavery and Other Writings*, ed. Vincent Carretta (New York, 1999). For Cugoano's prominent role in London among free blacks and abolitionists, see Stephen Braidwood, *Black Poor and White Philanthropists: London's Blacks and the Foundations of the Sierra Leone Settlement, 1786–1791* (Liverpool, 1994). Two years after the publication of Cugoano's book, Richard Cosway subscribed to Equiano's *Interesting Narrative of the Life of Olaudah Equiano*.

54. Jefferson to Bancroft, 26 January 1789, *Papers of Jefferson*, XIV, pp. 492–3. Bancroft's letter to Jefferson, 16 September 1788, is in ibid., XII, pp. 606–8. John C. Miller sees 1788 as the year when 'Jefferson's moral revulsion against slavery reached its climax': *The Wolf by the Ear: Thomas Jefferson and Slavery* (New York, 1977), p. 100.

55. In great detail and with keen insights, Annette Gordon-Reed has explored the Jefferson–Hemings relationship in *The Hemingses of Monticello: An American Family* (New York, 2008). Ten years later, Jefferson rekindled his emancipationist inclinations through the ardent friendship he forged with Tadeusz Kosciuszko, the Polish military engineer who had fought for seven years in the American Revolution and had returned to the United States in 1797, when he made Jefferson the executor and beneficiary of his American assets. For the full story of this hidden chapter of American history, which provides an illuminating example of how the rights agenda of the revolution reshaped the ideology of a European reformer, especially regarding universal individual rights, see Gary B. Nash and Graham Russell Gao Hodges, *Friends of Liberty: Thomas Jefferson, Tadeusz Kosciuszko, and Agrippa Hull, A Tale of Three Patriots, Two Revolutions, and a Tragic Betrayal of Freedom in the New Nation* (New York, 2008).

56. 'Racial Thermidor' is the term used in Patrick Rael's *Black Protest and Black Identity in the Antebellum North* (Chapel Hill, NC, 2002), p. 48.

57. Miller, *Wolf by the Ear*, pp. 273–5; for Israel's recollection of Lafayette's strictures on slavery, see Fawn M. Brodie, *Thomas Jefferson: An Intimate History* (New York, 1974), pp. 461–2; and Lucia Stanton, 'The Other End of the Telescope: Jefferson through the Eyes of His Slaves', *William and Mary Quarterly* 3rd ser. 57 (2000), 144. After gaining his freedom in the 1830s, Israel adopted Jefferson as his surname. 'The Memoirs of Israel Jefferson' are reprinted in Annette Gordon-Reed, *Thomas Jefferson and Sally Hemings: An American Controversy* (Charlottesville, VA, 1997), pp. 247–53.

58. *Virginia Herald*, 27 November 1824, quoted in J. Bennett Nolan, *Lafayette in America Day by Day* (Baltimore, 1934), p. 259.

59. Kramer, *Lafayette in Two Worlds*, p. 218; the incident was described in Lèvasseur's travelogue.

60. Don E. Fehrenbacher, *The Slaveholding Republic: An Account of the United States Government's Relations to Slavery* (New York, 2001), ch. 5. Fehrenbacher concludes that American 'enforcement tended to be episodic, rather than systematic, and the engagement of federal officials in the battle against the slave trade ranged all the way from diligence to nonfeasance, with some instances of corrupt involvement in the traffic' (p. 152). For African Americans turning to England as the best ally in the struggle to overthrow slavery, see Van Gosse, '"As a Nation, the English Are Our Friends": The Emergence of African American Politics in the British Atlantic World, 1773–1861', *American Historical Review* 113 (2008), 1003–28.

61. *The Frederick Douglass Papers, Series One: Speeches, Debates, and Interviews: I, 1841–1846*, ed. John W. Blassingame (New Haven, CT, 1979), pp. 80–1.

62. *The Complete Works of Thomas Paine*, ed. Philip S. Foner, 2 vols (New York, 1969), II, pp. 992–1007. The italics are Paine's.

Chapter 2: The French Revolution in Global Context

1. R. R. Palmer, *The Age of the Democratic Revolution: A Political History of Europe and America, 1760–1800*, 2 vols (Princeton, NJ, 1959–64). Jacques Godechot's 1963 book in the same vein, *Les révolutions (1770–1799)*, was published in English translation two years later as *France and the Atlantic Revolution of the Eighteenth Century, 1770–1799*, trans. Herbert H. Rowen (New York, 1965); Godechot taught in Toulouse. More recently, Annie Jourdan, who teaches in Amsterdam, has published an updated view: *La Révolution, une exception française?* (Paris, 2004).

2. Simon P. Newman, 'American Political Culture and the French and Haitian Revolutions', in David Patrick Geggus, ed., *The Impact of the Haitian Revolution in the Atlantic World* (Columbia, SC, 2001), p. 87 n. 29.

3. Palmer, *The Age of the Democratic Revolution*, I, pp. 472–3.

4. Palmer, *The Age of the Democratic Revolution*, II, pp. 382–91.

5. *Copy in the French Language together with a Translation of the Proceedings of a Jacobin Club formed at Seringapatam, by the French Soldiers in the Corps Commanded by M. Dompart* (Madras, 1799).

6. Ho Chi Minh, 'Declaration of Independence of the Democratic Republic of Vietnam' (2 September 1945), in Ho Chi Minh, *Selected Works*, 4 vols (Hanoi, 1960–2), III, p. 17.

7. C. A. Bayly, *The Birth of the Modern World, 1780–1914: Global Connections and Comparisons* (Oxford, 2004), ch. 3, 'Converging Revolutions'.

8. When these broader questions are not posed, the meaning of a global context remains uncertain. See, for example, Joseph Klaits and Michael H. Haltzel, eds, *The Global Ramifications of the French Revolution* (Cambridge, 1994). The excellent essays in this collection show that the French Revolution had effects around the world but it does not use that knowledge to create a new understanding of the French Revolution itself.

9. Palmer, *The Age of the Democratic Revolution*, I, pp. 146–56, II, p. 338. On the difficulties of incorporating the colonial, see Frederick Cooper, *Colonialism in Question: Theory, Knowledge, History* (Berkeley, CA, 2005), pp. 3–32.

10. Jean Jaurès, *Histoire socialiste, 1789–1900*, 13 vols (Paris, 1901–8), I, p. 50, II, p. 984; François Furet, *Interpreting the French Revolution*, trans. Elborg Forster (Cambridge, 1981); Simon Schama, *Citizens: A Chronicle of the French Revolution* (New York, 1989), p. 602; blurb for the Benot book at http://www.bibliomonde.net/livre/revolution-francaise-fin-des-colonies-1789-1794-4201.html (accessed 4 June 2009).

11. The most efficient way to see the differences in Tocqueville's treatment of France and the United States is to do a word search on Frantext available at http://humanities.uchicago.edu/orgs/ARTFL. I looked at *esclave, esclavage*, and *colonies*. For Tocqueville's interest in Algeria, see *Alexis de Tocqueville: Writings on Empire and Slavery*, ed. and trans. Jennifer Pitts (Baltimore, 2001).

12. Theda Skocpol, *States and Social Revolutions: A Comparative Analysis of France, Russia, and China* (Cambridge, 1979); Bailey Stone, *Reinterpreting the French Revolution: A Global-Historical Perspective* (Cambridge, 2002).
13. Edmund Burke, *Reflections on the Revolution in France* (London, 1790), pp. 11–12.
14. Elizabeth Colwill is preparing a book based on notarial records for Saint Domingue; *Facing Racial Revolution: Eyewitness Accounts of the Haitian Insurrection*, ed. Jeremy D. Popkin (Chicago, 2007); C. L. R. James, *The Black Jacobins: Toussaint L'Ouverture and the San Domingo Revolution* (London, 1938); Robin Blackburn, *The Overthrow of Colonial Slavery, 1776–1848* (London, 1988); Michel-Rolphe Trouillot, *Silencing the Past: Power and the Production of History* (Boston, 1995); Florence Gauthier, *L'Aristocratie de l'épiderme: Le combat de la Société des Citoyens de Couleur, 1789–1791* (Paris, 2007).
15. Robin Blackburn, 'Haiti, Slavery, and the Age of the Democratic Revolution', *William and Mary Quarterly* 3rd ser. 63 (2006), 643–73; the quotation from Jefferson appears on pp. 657–8.
16. Geggus, ed., *The Impact of the Haitian Revolution in the Atlantic World*; see also Geggus, *Haitian Revolutionary Studies* (Bloomington, 2002), esp. p. 171.
17. For the slave voyages, see http://www.slavevoyages.org/tast/index.faces; Laurent Dubois, *A Colony of Citizens: Revolution and Slave Emancipation in the French Caribbean, 1787–1804* (Chapel Hill, NC, 2004); John Garrigus, 'Blue and Brown: Contraband Indigo and the Rise of a Free Colored Planter Class in French Saint-Domingue', *The Americas* 50 (1993), 233–63; Marcus Rainsford, *An Historical Account of the Black Empire of Hayti: comprehending a view of the principal transactions in the revolution of Saint Domingo; with its ancient and modern state* (London, 1805).
18. David Armitage, *The Ideological Origins of the British Empire* (Cambridge, 2000); Emma Rothschild, 'A Horrible Tragedy in the French Atlantic', *Past and Present* 192 (August 2006), 67–108.
19. John Shovlin, *The Political Economy of Virtue: Luxury, Patriotism, and the Origins of the French Revolution* (Ithaca, NY, 2006), p. 2: his figures on political economy come from Christine Théré, 'Economic Publishing and Authors, 1566–1789', in Gilbert Faccarello, ed., *Studies in the History of French Political Economy: from Bodin to Walras* (London, 1998), pp. 1–56. More attention to the imperial dimension can be found in Paul Cheney, 'Finances, Philosophical History and the "Empire of Climate": Enlightenment Historiography and Political Economy', *Historical Reflections* 31 (2005), 141–67.
20. Compare Michel Benoit, *1793, la République de la tentation: une affaire de corruption sous la Ière République* (Précy-sous-Thil, 2008).
21. Bayly, *The Birth of the Modern World*, pp. 93, 95.
22. Michael D. Bordo and Eugene N. White, 'A Tale of Two Currencies: British and French Finance During the Napoleonic Wars', *Journal of Economic History* 51 (1991), 303–16; Jonathan R. Dull, *The French Navy*

and *American Independence: A Study of Arms and Diplomacy, 1774–1787* (Princeton, NJ, 1976).
23. Lynn Hunt, *Inventing Human Rights: A History* (New York, 2007).
24. Franco Venturi, *Utopia and Reform in the Enlightenment* (Cambridge, 1971).
25. David Armitage, *The Declaration of Independence: A Global History* (Cambridge, MA, 2007); Bayly, *The Birth of the Modern World*, p. 86.
26. The essential starting point is John Brewer, *Party Ideology and Popular Politics at the Accession of George III* (Cambridge, 1976).
27. Barbara Ann Day-Hickman, *Napoleonic Art: Nationalism and the Spirit of Rebellion in France (1815–1848)* (Newark, DE, 1999), focuses on a later period but gives some sense of the diffusion of such images.
28. Bayly, *The Birth of the Modern World*, p. 119.
29. Ibid., p. 15.
30. I have discussed these developments in Lynn Hunt, 'Freedom of Dress in Revolutionary France', in Sara E. Melzer and Kathryn Norberg, eds, *From the Royal to the Republican Body: Incorporating the Political in Seventeenth- and Eighteenth-Century France* (Berkeley, CA, 1998), pp. 224–49. See also J. C. Flügel, *The Psychology of Clothes* (London, 1930), p. iii; Kaja Silverman, 'Fragments of a Fashionable Discourse', in Tania Modleski, ed., *Studies in Entertainment: Critical Approaches to Mass Culture* (Bloomington, IN, 1986), pp. 139–52.
31. Benedict Anderson, *Imagined Communities: Reflections on the Origin and Spread of Nationalism* (London, 1983).

Chapter 3: Revolutionary Exiles: The American Loyalist and French Émigré Diasporas

I am grateful to David Armitage, François Furstenberg, Patrice Higonnet, John Merriman, and participants in the '"Age of Revolutions" or "World Crisis"?' symposium for comments on an earlier version of this chapter.

1. The episode is recounted in *Mémoires du Prince de Talleyrand*, ed. Duc de Broglie, 5 vols (Paris, 1891–2), I, p. 231; translation mine. If the story is true, then Arnold may himself have been waiting to sail: he was in Guadeloupe three months later, when the island was recaptured by the French.
2. Ibid., I, p. 232.
3. On connections between these revolutions, see R. R. Palmer, *The Age of the Democratic Revolution: A Political History of Europe and America, 1760–1800*, 2 vols (Princeton, NJ, 1959–64); Patrice L. R. Higonnet, *Sister Republics: The Origins of French and American Republicanism* (Cambridge, MA, 1988); and the numerous studies of figures common to both revolutions, such as Thomas Jefferson, Thomas Paine, and the Marquis de Lafayette. François Furet's observation that 'the history of the French

Revolution has been a story of beginnings and so a discourse about identity' could equally be applied to the United States: Furet, *Interpreting the French Revolution* trans. Elborg Forster (Cambridge, 1981), p. 6.

4. E. P. Thompson, *The Making of the English Working Class* (London, 1966), p. 12.
5. Anglo-Canadian historians, by contrast, traditionally celebrated loyalists as 'founding fathers'; but the association of United Empire Loyalists with the nineteenth-century Tory party helped to perpetuate a sense of loyalists as conservatives within Canadian historiography as well. See Norman J. Knowles, *Inventing the Loyalists: The Ontario Loyalist Tradition and the Creation of Usable Pasts* (Toronto, 1997).
6. Donald Greer contested this sterotype with a statistical demonstration that approximately half the émigrés belonged to the Third Estate: Greer, *The Incidence of the Emigration During the French Revolution* (Cambridge MA, 1951), pp. 63–5.
7. But for new perspectives on these 'reactionary' years, see Sheryl Kroen, *Politics and Theater: The Crisis of Legitimacy in Restoration France, 1815–1830* (Berkeley, CA, 2000); R. S. Alexander, *Re-Writing the French Revolutionary Tradition: Liberal Opposition and the Fall of the Bourbon Monarchy* (Cambridge, 2003); and John Merriman, *Police Stories: Building the French State, 1815–1851* (Oxford, 2006).
8. John Adams to James Lloyd, January 1815, in *The Works of John Adams*, ed. Charles Francis Adams, 10 vols (Boston, 1850–6), X, p. 110.
9. In a letter of November 1813, Adams estimated that 'about a third of the people of the colonies were against the revolution' (quoted in Thomas McKean to John Adams, January 1814, in Adams, *Works*, X, p. 87); and he later observed that British ministers had 'seduced and deluded nearly one third of the people of the colonies' into supporting them (Adams to Dr J. Morse, 22 December 1815, in Adams, *Works*, X, p. 193). Writing about the membership of the 1774 Congress, Adams stated that 'To draw the characters of them all . . . would now be considered as a caricature-print; one-third tories, another whigs, and the rest mongrels' (John Adams to Thomas Jefferson, 12 November 1813, in Adams, *Works*, X, p. 79).
10. See Paul H. Smith, 'The American Loyalists: Notes on Their Organization and Numerical Strength', *William and Mary Quarterly* 3rd ser., 25 (1968), 260.
11. The best modern estimate (based on military enrolment) suggests that one-fifth of the white colonial population sympathized with Britain during the American Revolution: Smith, 'The American Loyalists', 269.
12. A full accounting of these figures will be provided in my forthcoming book on the loyalist diaspora.
13. Christopher Leslie Brown, *Moral Capital: Foundations of British Abolitionism* (Chapel Hill, NC, 2006), ch. 4.
14. Greer's appendices provide breakdowns by region and occupation: Greer, *The Incidence of the Emigration During the French Revolution*, pp. 109–38.

15. Bernard Bailyn, *The Ideological Origins of the American Revolution*, rev. edn (Cambridge, MA, 1992), p. 19.
16. See Christopher Waldrep, *The Many Faces of Judge Lynch: Extralegal Violence and Punishment in America* (New York, 2002), pp. 15–20.
17. William Doyle, 'Introduction', in Kirsty Carpenter and Philip Mansel, eds, *The French Émigrés in Europe and the Struggle against Revolution, 1789–1814* (London, 1999), p. xix. My estimate of the loyalist migration excludes the five to seven thousand residents of East Florida who, at the time of the evacuation, 'are imagined to have gone over the Mountains to the States &c.' ('Return of Persons who Emigrated from East Florida to different parts of the British Dominions', 2 May 1786, The National Archives, Kew, CO 5/561, fo. 407).
18. On popular persecution of loyalists, see especially Robert M. Calhoon, *The Loyalists in Revolutionary America 1760–1781* (New York, 1973), chs 24–7.
19. Bernard Bailyn, *The Ordeal of Thomas Hutchinson* (Cambridge, MA, 1974).
20. These measures are summarized in Claude Halstead Van Tyne, *The Loyalists in the American Revolution* (New York, 1902), Appendices B and C, pp. 318–41.
21. Diary of Abner Sanger, 15 January 1777 and 31 May 1779. Library of Congress, Manuscript Division: Abner Sanger Diary, fos 52 and 114.
22. For a classic, elite-centred narrative of the emigration, see Ernest Daudet, *Histoire de l'émigration pendant la révolution française* . . . , 3 vols (Paris, 1905–7).
23. Greer, *The Incidence of the Emigration During the French Revolution*, pp. 22–3.
24. Timothy Tackett, *Religion, Revolution, and Regional Culture in Eighteenth-Century France* (Princeton, NJ, 1986), esp. ch. 2.
25. Timothy Tackett, *When the King Took Flight* (Cambridge, MA, 2003), ch. 6.
26. Greer, *The Incidence of the Emigration During the French Revolution*, p. 113.
27. The phases of flight are neatly summarized in Greer, ibid., pp. 21–37, and Kirsty Carpenter, *Refugees of the French Revolution: Émigrés in London, 1789–1802* (Basingstoke, 1999), Appendix 1. See also Peter McPhee, *Living the French Revolution* (Basingstoke, 2006), pp. 98–103, 154–5, 208–12.
28. Greer, *The Incidence of the Emigration During the French Revolution*, pp. 38–62. Prominent loyalist women who stayed behind to fight for property rights included Grace Galloway and Janet Smith, both of whose husbands departed for England. Confiscation of family or marital property would be the subject of numerous lawsuits in the years after the revolution.
29. Manuscript copies of this document survive in the UK and US National Archives, and it has been published as *The Black Loyalist Directory: African Americans in Exile after the American Revolution*, ed. Graham Russell Hodges (New York, 1995).

30. John Eardley Wilmot, *Historical View of the Commission for Enquiring into the Losses, Services, and Claims of the American Loyalists* . . . (1815; reprinted Boston, 1972), pp. 50, 90–1.

31. This has been most recently chronicled by Simon Schama, *Rough Crossings: Britain, the Slaves and the American Revolution* (New York, 2006), and Cassandra Pybus, *Epic Journeys of Freedom: Runaway Slaves of the American Revolution and Their Global Quest for Liberty* (Boston, 2006).

32. Arnold's son Edward went to India 'under the Patronage of Lord Cornwallis', and his son George followed three years later. 'Edward Shippen Arnold', 'George Arnold', q.v.,V. C. P. Hodson, *List of the Officers of the Bengal Army, 1758–1834*, 4 vols (London, 1927–47); Benedict Arnold to Jonathan Bliss, 19 September 1800, New Brunswick Museum, Benedict Arnold Papers.

33. See Pybus, *Epic Journeys*, passim.

34. Lord Mackenzie-Stuart, 'French Émigrés in Edinburgh', in Carpenter and Mansel, eds, *The French Émigrés in Europe*, p. 109.

35. Frédéric d'Agay, 'A European Destiny: the Armée de Condé 1792–1801', in Carpenter and Mansel, eds, *The French Émigrés in Europe*, p. 33.

36. Thomas Höpel, 'French Émigrés in Prussia', in Carpenter and Mansel, eds, *The French Émigrés in Europe*, pp. 101–7.

37. T. C. W. Blanning, *The French Revolution in Germany: Occupation and Resistance in the Rhineland, 1792–1802* (Oxford, 1983), pp. 52–3.

38. Adéle d'Osmond de Boigne, *Mémoires de la comtesse de Boigne, née d'Osmond*, ed. Jean-Claude Berchet, 2 vols (Paris, 1986), I, p. 142; translation mine.

39. Miranda Frances Spieler, 'Empire and Underworld: Guiana in the French Legal Imagination, *c*.1789–*c*.1870' (PhD dissertation, Columbia University, 2005).

40. Rosie Llewellyn-Jones, *Engaging Scoundrels: True Tales of Old Lucknow* (New Delhi, 2000), pp. 12–13.

41. Frances Sergeant Childs, *French Refugee Life in the United States, 1790–1800* (Baltimore, 1940), pp. 36–7.

42. For the estimate of 20,000: Palmer, *The Age of the Democratic Revolution*, II, p. 514; Childs, pp. 15, 63–6. Ashli White estimates that at least 15,000 Saint Dominguan refugees arrived in the USA: White, '"A Flood of Impure Lava": Saint Dominguan Refugees in the United States, 1791–1820' (PhD Dissertation, Columbia University, 2003).

43. François Furstenburg, 'US and French Atlantic Connections: The Case of the French Émigrés in America, *c*.1789–1803', unpublished paper.

44. Ronald Schechter, 'Gothic Thermidor: The Bals des Victimes, the Fantastic, and the Production of Historical Knowledge in Post-Terror France', *Representations* 61 (Winter 1998), 78–94. On the traumatic effects of the Revolution more generally, see Patrice Higonnet, 'Terror, Trauma and the "Young Marx" Explanation of Jacobin Politics', *Past and Present* 191 (May 2006), 121–64.

45. D. M. G. Sutherland, *France 1789–1815* (Oxford, 1985), pp. 386–7. Such rumours did help aristocrats to repurchase their confiscated lands from revolutionary buyers, however.

46. Almut Franke, '*Le milliard des émigrés*: The Impact of the Indemnity Bill of 1825 on French Society', in Carpenter and Mansel, eds, *The French Émigrés in Europe*, pp. 124–37. The claims and payments are thoroughly outlined in André Gain, *La Restauration et les biens des émigrés . . .*, 2 vols (Nancy, 1928).

47. John Bartlet Brebner, *The Neutral Yankees of Nova Scotia: A Marginal Colony During the Revolutionary Years* (New York, 1937); Andrew Jackson O'Shaughnessy, *An Empire Divided: The American Revolution and the British Caribbean* (Philadelphia, 2000).

48. White, '"A Flood of Impure Lava"', p. 29. Maria Nugent, the American loyalist wife of Jamaica governor George Nugent, routinely encountered Saint Domingue émigrés during her time in Jamaica. See *Lady Nugent's Journal of Her Residence in Jamaica from 1801 to 1805*, ed. Philip Wright (Kingston, 1966).

49. Lynn Hunt, 'The French Revolution in Global Context', ch. 2 in this volume.

50. For a suggestive intervention, see R. Darrell Meadows, 'Engineering Exile: Social Networks and the French Atlantic Community, 1789–1809', *French Historical Studies* 23 (2000), 67–102.

51. P. J. Marshall, *The Making and Unmaking of Empires: Britain, India, and America c. 1750–1783* (Oxford, 2005).

52. C. A. Bayly, *Imperial Meridian: The British Empire and the World, 1780–1830* (London, 1989); Bayly, 'The First Age of Global Imperialism, c.1760–1820', *Journal of Imperial and Commonwealth History* 26 (1998), 28–48; Linda Colley, *Britons: Forging the Nation, 1707–1837* (New Haven, CT, 1992). I also treated these wars as an imperial watershed in *Edge of Empire: Lives, Culture and Conquest in the East, 1750–1850* (New York, 2005).

53. British authorities even appear to have considered granting French émigrés who wished to settle in Canada the 'same Proportion of Lands, Rations, farming Utensils &c.' that American loyalists had received – a plan judged 'at least, problematical' by one suspicious Kingston loyalist. John Stuart to William White, 26 November 1798, Archives of Ontario: Stuart Family Papers, MS 606, p. 90.

54. Carpenter, *Refugees of the French Revolution*, p. 47. Robert Tombs and Isabelle Tombs state that Wilmot raised more than £400,000: Tombs and Tombs, *That Sweet Enemy: The French and the British from the Sun King to the Present* (London, 2007), p. 213.

55. Watson is perhaps best known today as the subject of 'Watson and the Shark', a large, curious canvas painted by the American loyalist John Singleton Copley. The image depicts an incident from 1749: the teenage Watson was swimming in Havana harbour when a shark attacked him and bit off his lower right leg. Watson commissioned the painting in the

mid-1770s; it now hangs in the National Gallery of Art in Washington, DC (see http://www.nga.gov/feature/watson/watsonhome.shtm), accessed 4 October 2008.

56. New York Historical Society, *Diary of Samuel Shoemaker of Philadelphia, 1783–1785*, p. 131.

57. For the committee membership see Carpenter, *Refugees of the French Revolution*, p. 45.

58. Wilmot, *Historical View of the Commission*, p. 1.

59. On this image and the later portrait of Wilmot in which it appears, see Helmut von Erffa and Alan Staley, *The Paintings of Benjamin West* (New Haven, CT, 1986), pp. 219–22, 565–7.

60. Fanny Burney, *Diary and Letters of Madame D'Arblay* . . . , 7 vols (London, 1846), VI, p. 11.

61. William Roberts, *Memoirs of the Life and Correspondence of Mrs. Hannah More*, 2 vols (New York, 1834), I, p. 420.

62. Carpenter, *Refugees of the French Revolution*, pp. 107–9; assorted letters in *The Correspondence of Edmund Burke*, gen. ed. Thomas W. Copeland, 10 vols (Chicago and Cambridge, 1958–78), vols VII–VIII.

63. Jeremy Adelman, 'An Age of Imperial Revolutions', *American Historical Review* 113 (2008), 319–40; Adelman, 'Iberian Passages: Continuity and Change in the South Atlantic', ch. 4 in this volume.

64. Despite the vast scholarship on Napoleonic Europe, there are relatively few treatments of French cultural imperialism in these years. But see Stuart Woolf, 'French Civilization and Ethnicity in the Napoleonic Empire', *Past and Present* 124 (August 1989), 96–120; Todd Porterfield, *The Allure of Empire: Art in the Service of French Imperialism, 1798–1836* (Princeton, NJ, 1998); and Michael Broers, *The Napoleonic Empire in Italy, 1796–1814: Cultural Imperialism in a European Context?* (Basingstoke, 2005).

65. Quoted in Christopher Fyfe, *A History of Sierra Leone* (Oxford, 1962), p. 87.

66. A good example of such a complex figure would be J. Hector St John de Crèvecoeur, widely hailed in the United States for his exceptionalist meditation 'What Is an American?' – but himself wrong-footed twice by revolution, first as a loyalist in revolutionary America, then as a petty nobleman in revolutionary France: Edward Larkin, 'What Is a Loyalist? The American Revolution as Civil War', *Common-Place* 8, 1 (October 2007) (http://www.common-place.org/vol-08/no-01/larkin), accessed 11 June 2009; Simon Schama, *The American Future: A History* (New York, 2009), pp. 223–38.

Chapter 4: Iberian Passages: Continuity and Change in the South Atlantic

1. Peter Gourevitch, *Politics in Hard Times: Comparative Responses to International Economic Crises* (Ithaca, NY, 1986), pp. 17–19; on Trotsky see

Charles Tilly, *From Mobilization to Revolution* (Reading, MA, 1978), pp. 190–1.

2. C. A Bayly has argued that the birth of the modern world was one that saw an increased uniformity, from practices of dress to intellectual currents. Of course, the process of global integration did facilitate kinds of isomorphism. The argument in this chapter is that (a) there were basic social and material forces that conditioned the emergence of a variety of arrangements for rule, and (b) efforts at diffusing uniformity from the centres unintentionally created greater diversity at local levels. In some fundamental ways, Latin America and the Caribbean were much more internally diverse in the 1820s than they were in the 1780s. See C. A. Bayly, *The Birth of the Modern World, 1780–1914: Global Connections and Comparisons* (Oxford, 2004).

3. James J. Sheehan, 'The Problem of Sovereignty in European History', *American Historical Review* 111 (2006), 1–15; Saskia Sassen, *Territory, Authority, Rights: From Medieval to Global Assemblages* (Princeton, NJ, 2006). Most work on sovereignty has been done by political scientists, mainly concerned with international relations. See Daniel Philpott, *Revolutions in Sovereignty: How Ideas Shaped Modern International Relations* (Princeton, NJ, 2001), and on how sovereignty rests on contradictory principles and practices, see Stephen D. Krasner, ed., *Problematic Sovereignty: Contested Rules and Political Possibilities* (New York, 2001).

4. Lauren Benton, *Law and Colonial Cultures: Legal Regimes in World History, 1400–1900* (Cambridge, 2002); Bayly, *The Birth of the Modern World*, p. 139.

5. Charles Tilly, 'War Making and State Making as Organized Crime', in Peter B. Evans, Dietrich Rueschemeyer and Theda Skocpol, eds, *Bringing the State Back In* (New York, 1985), pp. 169–91; Stanley J. Stein and Barbara H. Stein, *Silver, Trade, and War: Spain and America in the Making of Early Modern Europe* (Baltimore, 2000), pp. 120–1.

6. Gabriel B. Paquette, *Enlightenment, Governance, and Reform in Spain and Its Empire, 1759–1808* (Basingstoke, 2008), p. 39; Kenneth Maxwell, *Pombal: Paradox of the Enlightenment* (New York, 1995).

7. Jeremy Adelman, *Sovereignty and Revolution in the Iberian Atlantic* (Princeton, NJ, 2006), pp. 13–36.

8. David Weber, *Bárbaros: Spaniards and their Savages in the Age of Enlightenment* (New Haven, CT, 2005), ch. 5; John Fisher, *Commercial Relations Between Spain and Spanish America in the Era of Free Trade, 1778–1796* (Liverpool, 1985); Jorge M. Pedreira, 'From Growth to Collapse: Portugal, Brazil, and the Breakdown of the Old Colonial System (1760–1830)', *Hispanic American Historical Review* 80 (2000), 839–64; Maxwell, *Pombal*; Stanley J. Stein and Barbara H. Stein, *Apogee of Empire: Spain and New Spain in the Age of Charles III, 1759–1789* (Baltimore, 2003).

9. Kenneth Maxwell, *Conflicts and Conspiracies: Brazil and Portugal, 1750–1808* (Cambridge, 1973), pp. 23–8, 67–71; Anthony McFarlane,

'Rebellions in Late Colonial Spanish America: A Comparative Perspective', *Bulletin of Latin American Research* 14 (1983), 313–38; Eric Van Young, 'The Age of Paradox: Mexican Agriculture at the end of the Colonial Period, 1750–1810', in Nils Jacobsen and Hans-Jürgen Puhle, eds, *The Economies of Mexico and Peru During the Late Colonial Period* (Berlin, 1986), pp. 64–90.

10. Manolo Garcia Florentino, *Em Costas Negras: Uma história do tráfico Atlântico de escravos entree África e o Rio de Janeiro (séculos XVIII e XIX)* (Rio de Janeiro, 1993); Fisher, *Commercial Relations Between Spain and Spanish America*.

11. Richard L. Garner, 'Long-term Silver Mining Trends in Spanish America: A Comparative Analysis of Peru and Mexico', *American Historical Review* 93 (1988), 898–935; Matilde Souto Mantecón, *Mar abierto: La política y el comercio del Consulado de Veracruz en el ocaso del sistema imperial* (Mexico City, 2001); Enrique Tandeter, 'Forced and Free Labour in Late Colonial Potosí', *Past and Present* 93 (November 1981), 98–136.

12. Archivo General de Indias (Seville), Estado, Americas, 86A, 14, 'Dictámen leido en Consejo pleno con asistencia de su Governador'; Adelman, *Sovereignty and Revolution*, pp. 65–73.

13. David Eltis, *Economic Growth and the Ending of the Transatlantic Slave Trade* (New York, 1987), p. 247.

14. AGI, Indiferente General, Legajo 2826, 8 August 1802. The literature on the effects of the slave trade is now vast. See Jorge Gelman, *Campesinos y estancieros: una region del Rio de la Plata a fines de la época colonial* (Buenos Aires, 1998); Sheila de Castro Faria, *A Colônia em Movimento: Fortuna e Família no Cotidiano Colonial* (Rio de Janeiro, 1998).

15. Jacques A. Barbier, 'Peninsular Finance and Colonial Trade: The Dilemma of Charles IV's Spain', *Journal of Latin American Studies* 12 (1980), 21–37; Richard L. Garner, *Economic Growth and Change in Bourbon Mexico* (Gainesville, FL, 1993), pp. 230–45.

16. Manuel Belgrano, 'Memoria-3', in *Escritos económicos* (Buenos Aires, 1954), p. 99; José Ignacio de Pombo, 'Informe de Don José Ignacio de Pombo del Consulado de Cartagena sobre asuntos económicos y fiscales', in Sergio Elias Ortíz, *Escritos de dos economistas coloniales* (Bogotá, 1965), p. 157; José Joaquim da Cunha Azeredo Coutinho, *Ensaio económico sobre o comércio de Portugal e suas colónias* (Lisbon, 1992), pp. 91–102.

17. J. G. A. Pocock, 'The Mobility of Property and the Rise of Eighteenth-Century Sociology', in Pocock, *Virtue, Commerce, and History: Essays on Political Thought and History, Chiefly in the Eighteenth Century* (Cambridge, 1985), pp. 103–23; Hilton Root, *The Fountain of Privilege: Political Foundations of Markets in Old Regime France and England* (Berkeley, CA, 1994).

18. José da Silva Lisboa, *Princípios de Economia Política* (Lisbon, 1804), pp. 112–16; Kenneth Maxwell, 'The Generation of the 1790s and the Idea of Luso-Brazilian Empire', in Dauril Alden, ed., *Colonial Roots of Modern*

Brazil (Berkeley, CA, 1973), pp. 107–44. Jovellanos is cited in José Alvarez Junco, *Mater Dolorosa: La idea de España en el Siglo XIX* (Madrid, 2001), pp. 120–1.

19. Brian Hamnett, *La política española en una época revolucionaria, 1790–1820* (Mexico City, 1985), pp. 57–67; Valentim Alexandre, *Os Sentidos do Império: Questão Nacional e Questão colonial na Crise do Antigo Regime Português* (Lisbon, 1993).

20. François-Xavier Guerra and Annick Lempérière, 'Introducción', in Guerra and Lempérière, eds, *Los espacios públicos en Iberoamérica. Ambigüedades y problemas, siglos XVIII–XIX* (Mexico City, 1998), pp. 5–21; Victor Uribe-Uran, 'The Birth of a Public Sphere in Latin America During the Age of Revolution', *Comparative Studies in Society and History* 42 (2000), 425–57; Kirsten Schultz, *A Tropical Versailles: Empire, Monarchy and the Portuguese Royal Court in Rio de Janeiro, 1808–1821* (New York, 2001).

21. *El Argos Americano*, 18 November 1811; Hamnett, *La política española*, pp. 73–101; Jaime E. Rodríguez O., *The Independence of Spanish America* (Cambridge, 1998), pp. 82–91.

22. Michael P. Costeloe, 'Spain and the Latin American Wars of Independence: The Free Trade Controversy', *Hispanic American Historical Review* 61 (1981), 209–34; Adelman, *Sovereignty and Revolution*, pp. 238–46.

23. Rodríguez, *The Independence of Spanish America*, ch. 3; Adelman, *Sovereignty and Revolution*, ch. 5; Roderick Barman, *Brazil: The Forging of a Nation, 1798–1852* (Stanford, CA, 1988), pp. 43–55.

24. Arno J. Mayer, *The Persistence of the Old Regime: Europe to the Great War* (New York, 1981).

25. Schultz, *A Tropical Versailles*; José da Silva Lisboa, *Refutação das declamacões contra o commercio inglez extrahida de escritores eminentes* (Rio de Janeiro, 1810), p. iv.

26. Peter Blanchard, 'The Slave Soldiers of Spanish South America: From Independence to Abolition', in Christopher Leslie Brown and Philip D. Morgan, eds, *Arming Slaves: From Classical Times to the Modern Age* (New Haven, CT, 2006), pp. 261–6; Marixa Lasso, *Myths of Harmony: Race and Republicanism During the Age of Revolution, Colombia 1795–1831* (Pittsburgh, 2007); Peter Guardino, *Time of Liberty: Popular Political Culture in Oaxaca, 1750–1850* (Durham, NC, 2005); Ronald Fraser, *Napoleon's Cursed War: Popular Resistance in the Spanish Peninsular War* (London, 2008), p. 469.

27. Lucía Sala de Touron, Nelson de la Torre and Julio C. Rodríguez, *Artigas y su revolución agraria, 1811–1820* (Montevideo, 1967), pp. 114–53; Simón Bolívar, 'The Angostura Address', in *El Libertador: Selected Writings of Simón Bolívar*, ed. David Bushnell (New York, 2001), p. 52.

28. John Charles Chasteen, *Americanos: Latin America's Struggle for Independence* (New York, 2008); Margaret Woodward, 'The Spanish Army and the Loss of America, 1810–1824', *Hispanic American Historical Review*

48 (1968), 586–90; John Lynch, *The Spanish American Revolutions, 1808–1826* (New York, 1986), pp. 212–14; Timothy E. Anna, *Spain and the Loss of America* (Lincoln, NB, 1983).

29. *Gazeta do Rio de Janeiro*, 6 August 1822; Isabel Lustosa, *Insultos impressos: A guerra dos jornalistas na independência, 1821–1823* (São Paulo, 2000); Barman, *Brazil*, pp. 70–1; Márcia Regina Berbel, *A Nação como artefato: Deputados do Brasil nas Cortes Portuguesas, 1821–1822* (São Paulo, 1999).
30. Albert O. Hirschman, *Shifting Involvements: Private Interest and Public Action* (Princeton, NJ, 2002), pp. 4–5.
31. Bayly, *The Birth of the Modern World*, p. 83.
32. José Carlos Chiaramonte, 'Modificaciones del Pacto Imperial', in Antonio Annino, Luis Castro Leiva and François-Xavier Guerra, eds, *De los imperios a las naciones: Iberoamérica* (Zaragoza, 1994), esp. pp. 108–11; José Murilho de Carvalho, *A construção da ordem* (Rio de Janeiro, 1996).

Chapter 5: The Caribbean in the Age of Revolution

1. Sidney Mintz, 'The Caribbean as a Socio-Cultural Area', *Cahiers d'Histoire Mondiale* 9 (1966), 916–41. In this chapter, I follow Mintz in defining the Caribbean as the West Indies, Bahamas, Guianas, and Belize.
2. David Geggus, 'The Haitian Revolution in Atlantic Perspective', in Philip D. Morgan and Nicholas Canny, eds, *The Atlantic World c.1450–c.1820* (Oxford, forthcoming).
3. If antislavery and democratic politics had a shared origin in libertarian ideology, they did not always share the same supporters or follow the same chronology. The French Revolution gave only belated and hesitant support to antislavery; the American Revolution, even less. The French and Haitian Revolutions set back abolitionism in England by a decade, because of the conservative reaction they caused.
4. France lost to Britain: St Kitts (1713); Grenada and the officially neutral islands of St Vincent and Dominica (1763); Tobago and St Lucia (1803). Britain also took Trinidad from Spain (1797) and much of the Guianas from the Netherlands (1803).
5. The above figures involve extrapolation and guesswork using many sources; by far the best is Stanley L. Engerman and Barry W. Higman, 'The Demographic Structure of the Caribbean Slave Societies in the Eighteenth and Nineteenth Centuries', in Franklin W. Knight, ed., *General History of the Caribbean*, III: *The Slave Societies of the Caribbean* (London, 1997), pp. 45–104.
6. Data from David Eltis et al., *The Trans-Atlantic Slave Trade Database* (http://www.slavevoyages.org/tast/index.faces), accessed 1 June 2009.
7. The emancipation act of 4 February 1794 could not be promulgated in Martinique and St Lucia, because they were occupied by British forces.
8. Calculations derived from David Geggus, 'The Caribbean' (Spanish figures adjusted) and 'The French Caribbean', in Paul Finkelman and

Joseph C. Miller, eds, *The Macmillan Encyclopedia of World Slavery* (New York, 1998), pp. 149, 160.

9. Figures from Barry Higman, *Slave Populations of the British Caribbean, 1807–1834* (Baltimore, 1984), p. 3. As deaths generally outnumbered births in Caribbean slave populations, they depended on the slave trade to grow.

10. Moreover, although the Haitian Revolution closed the largest slave market in the Americas (accounting for some 40 per cent of the Africans shipped to the Americas 1786–90), slave imports to the Caribbean fell by less than 20 per cent in the 1790s from their peak level in the 1780s. In the following decade abolition reduced them to only one-third of their peak level.

11. In Jamaica by 56 per cent and in British Guiana by 43 per cent between the years 1830–2 and 1839–41. These were the last years of slavery and the first years of 'full freedom' following a forced labour 'apprenticeship' period. Data from Noël Deerr, *The History of Sugar*, 2 vols (London, 1949–50), I, pp. 198, 203. British Guiana's decline was short-lived, unlike those of Haiti and Jamaica.

12. David Eltis, 'The Slave Economies of the Caribbean: Structure, Performance, Evolution and Significance', in Knight, ed., *General History of the Caribbean*, III, pp. 111–23; David Geggus, 'Slavery, War, and Revolution in the Greater Caribbean', in David Barry Gaspar and Geggus, eds, *A Turbulent Time: The French Revolution and the Greater Caribbean* (Bloomington, IN, 1997), pp. 28–9.

13. West Indian output is detailed in David Watts, *The West Indies: Patterns of Development, Culture and Environmental Change since 1492* (Cambridge, 1987), p. 288; British Guiana's, in Deerr, *History of Sugar*, I, p. 203.

14. J. R. Ward, *Poverty and Progress in the Caribbean, 1800–1960* (London, 1985), p. 27.

15. Data in Francisco Pérez de la Riva, *El Café: Historia de su cultivo y explotación en Cuba* (Havana, 1944), p. 51; James Leyburn, *The Haitian People* (New Haven, CT, 1966), p. 320; Orlando Patterson, *The Sociology of Slavery* (London, 1967), pp. 294–5.

16. Manuel Moreno Fraginals, *El ingenio: Complejo económico social cubano del azúcar*, 3 vols (Havana, 1978), II, pp. 160, 162, 168, 173; Geggus, 'Slavery, War, and Revolution', 29; David Geggus, 'Indigo and Slavery in Saint Domingue', in Verene A. Shepherd, ed., *Slavery Without Sugar: Diversity in Caribbean Economy and Society since the 17th Century* (Gainesville, 2002), pp. 19–35.

17. Lowell Ragatz, *The Fall of the Planter Class in the British Caribbean, 1763–1833* (Washington, DC, 1928), pp. 340, 370; Alex van Stipriaan, *Surinaams Contrast: Roofbouw en Overleven in een Caraïbische Plantagekolonie, 1750–1863* (Leiden, 1993), p. 265.

18. Ragatz, *Fall of the Planter Class*; Eric Williams, *Capitalism and Slavery* (1944; London, 1964).

19. Elected assemblies with an advisory function were granted to Guadeloupe and Martinique in 1787.

242

Notes

20. Of course, a definition of the Caribbean that includes its southern 'rimland', an alternative to the one used here, produces a rather different result. This broader definition has generally received only lipservice from scholars. It is invoked in the preface to the relevant volume of the UNESCO *General History of the Caribbean* (III, p. vi) but ignored by all the volume's contributors. An expanded variant of it is employed in Gaspar and Geggus, *A Turbulent Time*.

21. Geggus, 'Slavery, War, and Revolution', 5–20.

22. Edward Cox, *Free Coloreds in the Slave Societies of St Kitts and Grenada, 1763–1833* (Knoxville, TN, 1984), pp. 96–110; Jerome Handler, *The Unappropriated People: Freedmen in the Slave Society of Barbados* (Baltimore, 1974), ch. 4; Gad Heuman, *Between Black and White: Race, Politics and the Free Coloreds in Jamaica, 1792–1865* (Oxford, 1981), chs 2, 4; Ghislaine Ornème, 'Identité et combat assimilationniste des libres de couleur de la Martinique de 1789 à 1833', in Marcel Dorigny, ed., *Esclavage, résistances et abolitions* (Paris, 1999), pp. 295–304; Neville Hall, *Slave Society in the Danish West Indies* (Mona, 1992), pp. 169–77.

23. A more apt term is 'racial harmony' according to Marixa Lasso, 'Race, War, and Nation in Caribbean Gran Colombia: Cartagena, 1810–1832', *American Historical Review* 111 (2006), 336.

24. Williams, *Capitalism and Slavery*; David B. Davis, *The Problem of Slavery in Western Culture* (Ithaca, NY, 1966); Davis, *The Problem of Slavery in the Age of Revolution, 1770–1823* (Ithaca, NY, 1975); Seymour Drescher, *Econocide: British Slavery in the Era of Abolition* (Pittsburgh, 1977); Drescher, *Capitalism and Antislavery: British Mobilization in Comparative Perspective* (New York, 1986). Christopher L. Brown's *Moral Capital: Foundations of British Abolitionism* (Chapel Hill, NC, 2006) combines Drescher's stress on mobilization with Williams's emphasis on the American Revolution as a watershed, and employs the concept of 'moral capital' in a manner reminiscent of Davis's use of 'hegemony'.

25. Michèle Duchet, *Anthropologie et histoire au siècle des Lumières* (Paris, 1971), ch. 3.

26. Gelien Matthews, *Caribbean Slave Revolts and the British Abolitionist Movement* (Baton Rouge, LA, 2006). For British abolitionists who earlier defended slaves' right to rebellion, see David Geggus, 'British Opinion and the Emergence of Haiti, 1791–1805', in James Walvin, ed., *Slavery and British Society, 1776–1848* (London, 1982), pp. 127–8, 145–6.

27. Michel Craton, *Testing the Chains: Resistance to Slavery in the British West Indies* (London, 1982), minimizes antislavery's influence on these rebellions and depicts the rebellions as having only a negative impact on abolitionism.

28. Robin Blackburn, *The Overthrow of Colonial Slavery, 1776–1848* (London, 1988), pp. 526–9, quotation on p. 527; Robin Blackburn, 'The Force of Example', in David Geggus, ed., *The Impact of the Haitian Revolution in the Atlantic World* (Columbia, SC, 2001), pp. 15–20.

29. Drescher, *Econocide*, pp. 168–9; Drescher, *Capitalism and Antislavery*, pp. 96–9, 105–6.

30. Geggus, 'British Opinion', p. 130; David Geggus, 'The Influence of the Haitian Revolution on Blacks in Latin America and the Caribbean', in Nancy Naro, ed., *Blacks, Coloureds and National Identity in Nineteenth-Century Latin America* (London, 2003), p. 47.
31. Only Spanish Louisiana suspended the import of slaves from Africa as a security measure, and only temporarily: Paul Lachance, 'The Politics of Fear: French Louisianians and the Slave Trade', *Plantation Society in the Americas* 1 (1979), 162–97.
32. David Geggus, 'Haiti and the Abolitionists: Opinion, Propaganda and International Politics in Britain and France, 1804–1838', in David Richardson, ed., *Abolition and its Aftermath: The Historical Context, 1790–1916* (London, 1985), p. 116.
33. Roger Anstey, *The Atlantic Slave Trade and British Abolition, 1769–1810* (London, 1975), pp. 321–402; Drescher, *Capitalism and Antislavery*, pp. 96–9, 105–6.
34. Matthews, *Caribbean Slave Revolts*, pp. 160–4; Drescher, *Capitalism and Antislavery*, pp. 108–9. More recently, Drescher has argued that the non-violent tactics employed by the insurgent slaves in the Demerara rebellion in 1823 elicited an empathy in Britain that boosted the abolitionist movement: Seymour Drescher, 'Civilizing Insurgency: Two Variants of Slave Revolts in the Age of Revolution', in Drescher and Pieter C. Emmer, eds, *Who Abolished Slavery? Slave Revolts and Abolitionism* (New York, 2010).
35. Davis, *Problem of Slavery in the Age of Revolution,* pp. 117, 440; Blackburn, *Overthrow of Colonial Slavery*, p. 145.
36. Léon Deschamps, *Les colonies pendant la Révolution. La Constituante et la Réforme coloniale* (Paris, 1898), p. vi.
37. Jules Saintoyant, *La colonisation française pendant la Révolution* (Paris, 1930); C. L. R. James, *The Black Jacobins: Toussaint L'Ouverture and the San Domingo Revolution* (New York, 1938); Aimé Césaire, *Toussaint-Louverture: La Révolution française et le problème colonial* (Paris, 1960).
38. Yves Benot, *La Révolution française et la fin des colonies* (Paris, 1988); Blackburn, *Overthrow of Colonial Slavery.* A sampling of the works listed in *Historical Abstracts* suggests that, of the past half-century's publications on the Haitian Revolution, some 40 per cent appeared in the past decade, and one-quarter in just the past five years.
39. However, nearly 10 per cent of the general *cahiers de doléances* mentioned slavery or the slave trade.
40. Laurent Dubois, *Avengers of the New World: The Story of the Haitian Revolution* (Cambridge, 2004), p. 3; Dubois, *A Colony of Citizens: Revolution and Slave Emancipation in the French Caribbean, 1787–1804* (Chapel Hill, NC, 2004), pp. 2–7.
41. *Archives parlementaires de 1789 à 1860*, ed. Jérôme Mavidal (Paris, 1862), XXXI, p. 442.
42. Benot, *Révolution*, pp. 75, 86–7, 187 (violence), 200–4, 217; Blackburn, *Overthrow*, p. 223; James, *Black Jacobins*, pp. 75–7, 120, 139; Florence

Gauthier, *Triomphe et mort du droit naturel en révolution* (Paris, 1992); Jean Daniel Piquet, *L'émancipation des noirs dans la Révolution française (1789–1795)* (Paris, 2002), esp. pp. 257, 266.

43. Jean Jaurès, *Histoire socialiste, 1789–1900* (Paris, 1924), I, p. 574.

44. Seymour Drescher, 'The Ending of the Slave Trade and Evolution of European Scientific Racism', *Social Science History* 14 (1990), 415–50.

45. Jeremy Popkin, 'The French Revolution's Other Island', in David Geggus and Norman Fiering, eds, *The World of the Haitian Revolution* (Bloomington, IN, 2009), pp. 199–222, provides an incisive overview.

46. David Geggus, *Haitian Revolutionary Studies* (Bloomington, IN, 2003), ch. 5; Geggus, 'Saint-Domingue on the Eve of Revolution', in *World of the Haitian Revolution*, pp. 3–20.

47. John Garrigus, *Before Haiti* (New York, 2006); Garrigus, 'Opportunist or Patriot? Julien Raimond (1744–1801) and the Haitian Revolution', *Slavery and Abolition* 28 (2007), 1–21.

48. Gabriel Debien, *Les colons de Saint-Domingue et la Révolution française: essai sur le Club Massiac* (Paris, 1953); Charles Frostin, 'L'Histoire de l'esprit autonomiste colon à Saint-Domingue aux XVIIe et XVIIIe siècles' (Thèse de doctorat d'état, Université de Paris I, 1972).

49. David Geggus, 'Racial Equality, Slavery, and Colonial Secession, during the Constituent Assembly', *American Historical Review* 94 (1989), 1290–308.

50. Eugene Genovese, *From Rebellion to Revolution: Afro-American Slave Revolts in the Making of the Modern World* (Baton Rouge, LA, 1979); Sibylle Fischer, *Modernity Disavowed: Haiti and the Cultures of Slavery in the Age of Revolution* (Durham, NC, 2004); Hilary Beckles, 'The Two Hundred Years War', *Jamaica Historical Review* 13 (1982), 1–10.

51. R. R. Palmer, *The Age of the Democratic Revolution: A Political History of Europe and America, 1760–1800*, 2 vols (Princeton, NJ, 1959–64); Jacques Godechot, *France and the Atlantic Revolution of the Eighteenth Century, 1770–1799*, trans. Herbert H. Rowen (London, 1965). Godechot and Palmer make brief, scattered references to the revolution but do not make clear whether they thought it belonged in their club of revolutions 'of the West'. The closest indication we have is Palmer's comment regarding the late 1790s, 'Toussaint Louverture seemed almost to be succeeding in founding a free republic of a kind that some European republicans of 1798, though hardly those of the United States, might accept as akin to their own': Palmer, *Age of the Democratic Revolution*, II, p. 338.

52. David Geggus, 'Print Culture and the Haitian Revolution: The Written and the Spoken Word', *Proceedings of the American Antiquarian Society* 116, 2 (October 2006), 297–314.

53. David Geggus, 'Toussaint Louverture et l'abolition de l'esclavage à Saint-Domingue', in Liliane Chauleau , ed., *Les abolitions dans les Amériques* (Fort de France, 2001), pp. 109–16.

54. Laurent Dubois, 'An Enslaved Enlightenment: Rethinking the

Intellectual History of the French Atlantic', *Social History* 31 (2006), 12; Michel-Rolph Trouillot, *Silencing the Past* (Boston, 1995), p. 89; Drescher and Emmer, eds, *Who Abolished Slavery?*

55. Geggus, 'Slavery, War, and Revolution', 7–12.
56. Geggus, *Haitian Revolutionary Studies*, pp. 125–9, 197–8.
57. Thomas Madiou, *Histoire d'Haïti* (1847–8; Port-au-Prince, 1989–91), I, pp. 431–2.
58. Robin Blackburn, 'Haiti, Slavery, and the Age of the Democratic Revolution', *William and Mary Quarterly* 3rd ser., 63 (2006), 643–73.
59. Blackburn, *Overthrow of Colonial Slavery*, p. 194; Dubois, 'Enslaved Enlightenment', 11–12; Geggus 'Print Culture', 91–2.
60. Dubois, 'Enslaved Enlightenment', 11–12; Dubois, *Colony of Citizens*, pp. 2–3. Curiously, he also attributes the March 1792 decree of racial equality to 'the Republic' (*Colony of Citizens*, p. 113), although it was passed under the monarchy.
61. Archivo General de Simancas, Guerra Moderna 7157, Barthélemy to Thomas, 24 October 1793, is a bizarre example.
62. Dubois, *Colony of Citizens*, pp. 5, 7 and passim.
63. See Claude Moïse, *Constitutions et luttes de pouvoir en Haïti (1804–1987)* (Port-au-Prince, 1997), pp. 35–59. In the elections for the 1806 constitutional convention, Christophe instructed his military commanders, 'I hardly need tell you to assist the people's choice with your knowledge, by pointing out to them, as needs be, those persons who are worthy of public confidence.'
64. Hubert Cole, *King Christophe of Haiti* (London, 1967); *The Armorial of Haiti: Symbols of Nobility in the Reign of Henry Christophe*, ed. Clive Cheesman (London, 2007).
65. David Nicholls, *From Dessalines to Duvalier: Race, Colour and National Independence in Haiti* (Cambridge, 1979), pp. 57–60.
66. Strangely, while the ex-slave leaders rejected any attempt to export their abolitionism, it was the free-born Alexandre Pétion who sought to internationalize Haiti's revolution in assisting Bolívar in 1816 and Miranda in 1806, and participating (albeit accidentally) in an uprising in Curaçao in 1799. Toussaint Louverture in 1799 betrayed an attempt by French agents to raise Jamaican slaves – an ironic clash between the French and Haitian Revolutions – and Christophe similarly denounced a supposed plot by his enemy Pétion. See Geggus, 'Slavery, War, and Revolution', p. 15.
67. David Armitage, *The Declaration of Independence: A Global History* (Cambridge, MA, 2007), pp. 114–15.
68. The most comprehensive account remains Madiou, *Histoire d'Haïti*, III, pp. 159–79. Since the start of the revolution, the colonists had treated rebellious non-whites with the utmost brutality, and in the war of independence, the French army had openly used genocidal tactics.
69. Madiou, *Histoire d'Haïti*, II, pp. 179–83, 274–5. This provision was omitted from Christophe's two constitutions, but included in all others down to

1918. The omission is surprising, as Christophe is regarded as more militantly nationalist than Pétion. He was more uncompromising in negotiations with the French about gaining recognition of Haitian independence, but he also made greater efforts to obtain European assistance.
70. John Lynch, *The Spanish American Revolutions, 1808–1826* (London, 1973), pp. 202–3.
71. Leslie Manigat, *Evolution et révolutions* (Port-au-Prince, 2007), pp. 88, 96.
72. Moreover, although Simón Bolívar mentioned Haiti in his correspondence usually as a site of anarchy and tyranny, in 1826 the increasingly disillusioned Liberator praised the republic's system of life presidency with the right to name a successor as a source of stability. See *Selected Writings of Bolívar*, ed. Harold A. Bierck (New York, 1951), pp. 140, 229, 267–8, 307–8, 499, 599, 624.

Chapter 6: The Dynamics of History in Africa and the Atlantic 'Age of Revolutions'

1. R. R. Palmer, *The Age of the Democratic Revolution: A Political History of Europe and America, 1760–1800*, 2 vols (Princeton, NJ, 1959–64).
2. William R. McNeill, *The Rise of the West: A History of the Human Community* (Chicago, 1963); Immanuel Wallerstein, *The Modern World System* (New York, 1974); Eric R. Wolf, *Europe and the People without History* (Berkeley, CA, 1982); C. A. Bayly, *Imperial Meridian: The British Empire and the World, 1780–1830* (London, 1989); Bayly, *The Birth of the Modern World, 1780–1914: Global Connections and Comparisons* (Oxford, 2004); Joseph C. Miller, 'Beyond Blacks, Bondage, and Blame: Why a Multi-centric World History Needs Africa', *Historically Speaking* 5, 2 (2004), 7–31.
3. Joseph C. Miller, 'History and Africa/Africa and History', *American Historical Review* 104 (1999), 1–32; Miller, 'Life Begins at Fifty: African Studies Enters its Second Half Century', *African Studies Review* 50 (2007), 1–35.
4. Compare John K. Thornton, *Africa and Africans in the Making of the Atlantic World, 1500–1680*, 2nd edn (Cambridge, 1998); Herbert S. Klein, *The Atlantic Slave Trade* (Cambridge, 1999).
5. Joseph C. Miller, 'A Theme in Variations: A Historical Schema of Slaving in the Atlantic and Indian Ocean Regions', in Gwyn Campbell, ed., 'The Structure of Slavery in Indian Ocean Africa and Asia', *Slavery and Abolition* 24, 2 (2003), 169–94.
6. Or, in one of the most thoughtful and comprehensive treatments, 'baroque to modern': Robin Blackburn, *The Making of New World Slavery: From the Baroque to the Modern, 1492–1800* (London, 1997).
7. In effect, I am here adding Africa to Bayly's *Imperial Meridian*.
8. See studies in Michael L. Bush, ed., *Serfdom and Slavery: Studies in Legal Bondage* (London, 1996).

9. Lauren Benton, 'Legal Spaces of Empire: Piracy and the Origins of Ocean Regionalism', *Comparative Studies in Society and History* (2005), 700–24.
10. This synoptic focus on mercantile sources of financing monarchy in Europe does not pause to consider the Spanish New World territories, famously financed by mining silver and subcontracting its commercial aspects to foreign merchants, until a new dynasty in Spain very belatedly attempted the so-called 'Bourbon reforms', part of the Iberian experience of the Atlantic 'Age of Revolution'. The Portuguese counterpart came with English removal of the ruling house from Lisbon to Rio de Janeiro in 1807 to escape Napoleon's armies in Iberia.
11. Pernille Røge, '"La clef de commerce" – The Changing Role of Africa in France's Atlantic Empire ca. 1760–1797', in Allan Potofsky, ed., 'New Perspectives on the Atlantic', *History of European Ideas* 34, 4 (2008), 431–43.
12. Joseph C. Miller, 'The Slave Trade', in Jacob Ernest Cooke, gen. ed., *Encyclopedia of the North American Colonies*, 2 vols (New York, 1993), II, pp. 45–66.
13. Barbara L. Solow, 'Capitalism and Slavery in the Exceedingly Long Run', *Journal of Interdisciplinary History* 17 (1987), 711–37.
14. Not 'imperial' in the integrated sense developed in the nineteenth century, in ways that space limitations prevent me from developing here.
15. Philip Gould, *Barbarous Traffic: Commerce and Anti-Slavery in the Eighteenth-Century Atlantic World* (Cambridge, MA, 2003).
16. Orlando Patterson's famed definition of slavery as 'social death' depends on the premise of modern civic-style 'social' recognition or recognizability: Patterson, *Slavery and Social Death: A Comparative Study* (Cambridge, MA, 1982).
17. For an alternative statement, Jan Vansina, 'Pathways of Political Development in Equatorial Africa and Neo-evolutionary Theory', in Susan Keech McIntosh, ed., *Beyond Chiefdoms: Pathways to Complexity in Africa* (New York, 1999), pp. 166–72.
18. Susan Keech and Roderick J. McIntosh, 'Finding West Africa's Oldest City', *National Geographic*, 162, 3 (September 1982), 396–418; Susan Keech McIntosh, 'Urbanism in Sub-Saharan Africa', in Joseph O. Vogel, ed., *Encyclopedia of Precolonial Africa: Archaeology, History, Languages, and Environments* (Walnut Creek, CA, 1997), pp. 461–72; Roderick J. McIntosh, *Ancient Middle Niger: Urbanism and the Self-organizing Landscape* (New York, 2005).
19. Credit extended south of the desert from Mediterranean cities has been documented: Michael Brett, 'Ifriqiya as a Market for Saharan Trade from the Tenth to the Twelfth Century A.D.', *Journal of African History* 10 (1969), 347–64.
20. Compare Philip D. Curtin, *Cross-Cultural Trade in World History* (Cambridge, 1984).
21. George E. Brooks Jr, *Landlords and Strangers: Ecology, Society and Trade in Western Africa, 1000–1630* (Boulder, CO, 1994).

22. Paul E. Lovejoy and Toyin Falola, eds, *Pawnship, Slavery, and Colonialism in Africa*, expanded edn (New Brunswick, NJ, 2003); Claude Meillassoux, 'The Role of Slavery in the Economic and Social History of Sahelo-Sudanic Africa', in Joseph E. Inikori, ed., *Forced Migration: The Impact of the Export Slave Trade on African Societies* (London, 1981), pp. 74–99, usefully distinguishes mercantile strategies, but in a more structural vein than the historical dynamics emphasized here.

23. I am limiting the examples of this tendency, recurrent in every part of Africa, to examples in touch with the maritime commercial economies surrounding the continent.

24. Compare Joseph C. Miller, *Way of Death: Merchant Capitalism and the Angolan Slave Trade, 1730–1830* (Madison, WI, 1988), esp. part I.

25. Thornton, *Africa and Africans*, has depicted Africa's engagement with the European 'Atlantic' in terms not inconsistent with the accents argued here, though with emphases on rather different aspects of the similarities.

26. David M. Anderson and Richard Rathbone, eds, *Africa's Urban Past* (Oxford, 2000).

27. The literature on the 'canoe houses of the Niger Delta' is classic; for recent treatments, David Northrup, *Trade without Rulers: Pre-colonial Economic Development in South-Eastern Nigeria* (Oxford, 1978), and Ralph A. Austen and Jonathan Derrick, *Middlemen of the Cameroons Rivers: the Duala and their Hinterland, c. 1600–c. 1960* (New York, 1999). For the Congo River basin, Jan Vansina, *Paths in the Rainforests: Toward a History of Political Tradition in Equatorial Africa* (Madison, WI, 1990); Robert W. Harms, *River of Wealth, River of Sorrow: The Central Zaire Basin in the Era of the Slave and Ivory Trade, 1500–1891* (New Haven, CT, 1981); Harms, *Games against Nature: An Eco-cultural History of the Nunu of Equatorial Africa* (New York, 1987).

28. The so-called Swahili towns of Africa's northern Indian Ocean coast are the best known examples, often treated as highly commercialized; however, John Middleton, 'Merchants: An Essay in Historical Ethnography', *Journal of the Royal Anthropological Institute* 9 (2003), 509–26, shows the extent to which Africans converted the 'coins' minted in towns along the Swahili coast, deeply embedded as they were in the commercial culture of the Indian Ocean, into distinctive and durable tokens of personal relationships, more characteristic of a communal ethos than of a mercantile economy.

29. See Elizabeth Isichei, *Voices of the Poor in Africa* (Rochester, NY, 2002), chs 2–6; Robert Martin Baum, *Shrines of the Slave Trade: Diola Religion and Society in Precolonial Senegambia* (New York, 1999); Rosalind Shaw, *The Dangers of Temne Divination: Ritual Memories of the Slave Trade in West Africa* (Chicago, 2002).

30. Ernst van den Boogart, 'The Trade between Western Africa and the Atlantic World, 1600–90: Estimates of Trends in Composition and Value', *Journal of African History* 33 (1992), 369–85; David Eltis, 'The Relative

Importance of Slaves and Commodities in the Atlantic Trade of Seventeenth-century Africa', *Journal of African History* 35 (1994), 237–49.
31. John K. Thornton, *The Kingdom of Kongo: Civil War and Transition, 1641–1718* (Madison, WI, 1983).
32. Joseph C. Miller, 'Kings, Lists, and History in Kasanje', *History in Africa* 6 (1979), 51–96; Jan Vansina, 'Ambaca Society and the Slave Trade, c.1760–1845', *Journal of African History* 46 (2005), 1–27.
33. Robin C. C. Law, *The Oyo Empire, c.1600–c.1836: A West African Imperialism in the Era of the Atlantic Slave Trade* (Oxford, 1977).
34. Robin Law, 'Francisco Felix de Souza in West Africa, 1820–1849', in José C. Curto and Paul E. Lovejoy, eds, *Enslaving Connections: Changing Cultures of Africa and Brazil during the Era of Slavery* (Amherst, NY, 2003), pp. 187–211; Law, *Ouidah: The Social History of a West African Slaving 'Port', 1727–1892* (Athens, GA, 2004).
35. Jay Alan Coughtry, *The Notorious Triangle: Rhode Island and the African Slave Trade, 1700–1807* (Philadelphia, 1981); Charles Rappleye, *Sons of Providence: The Brown Brothers, the Slave Trade, and the American Revolution* (New York, 2006).
36. Joseph C. Miller, 'A Marginal Institution on the Margin of the Atlantic System: The Portuguese Southern Atlantic Slave Trade in the Eighteenth Century', in Barbara Solow, ed., *Slavery and the Rise of the Atlantic System* (Cambridge, 1991), pp. 120–50.
37. Paul E. Lovejoy and David Richardson, 'Trust, Pawnship, and Atlantic History: The Institutional Foundations of the Old Calabar Slave Trade', *American Historical Review* 104 (1999), 333–55; Lovejoy and Richardson, 'The Business of Slaving: Pawnship in Western Africa, c.1600–1810', *Journal of African History* 41 (2001), 67–89; Lovejoy and Richardson, '"This Horrid Hole": Royal Authority, Commerce and Credit at Bonny, 1690–1840', *Journal of African History* 45 (2004), 363–92; Lovejoy and Richardson, 'African Agency and the Liverpool Slave Trade', in David Richardson, Suzanne Schwarz and Anthony Tibbles, eds, *Liverpool and Transatlantic Slavery* (Liverpool, 2007), pp. 43–65.
38. For recent insight into this epistemology, see E. J. Alagoa, 'Historiography: Oral', in John Middleton and Joseph C. Miller, eds, *New Encyclopedia of Africa*, 5 vols (Farmington Hills, MI, 2007), II, pp. 565–8.
39. I have found very provocative Jeremy Adelman, 'An Age of Imperial Revolutions', *American Historical Review* 113 (2008), 319–40, and Adelman, 'Iberian Passages: Continuity and Change in the South Atlantic', ch. 4 in this volume, for the evidence he offers of the contradictoriness of change envisaged in essentially structural abstractions of 'empire' and 'democratic' civic polities.
40. As highlighted in Michael A. Gomez, *Exchanging Our Country Marks: The Transformation of African Identities in the Colonial and Antebellum South* (Chapel Hill, NC, 1998).
41. Along these lines, Stephanie Smallwood, *Saltwater Slavery: A Middle Passage from Africa to American Diaspora* (Cambridge, MA, 2007). Also

Joseph C. Miller, 'Retention, Re-Invention, and Remembering: Restoring Identities through Enslavement in Africa and Under Slavery in Brazil', in Curto and Lovejoy, eds, *Enslaving Connections*, pp. 81–121.
42. For the closest approximations to this definition, see Igor Kopytoff and Suzanne Miers, 'Introduction', in Miers and Kopytoff, eds, *Slavery in Africa: Historical and Anthropological Perspectives* (Madison, WI, 1977); Kopytoff, 'Slavery', *Annual Review of Anthropology* 11 (1982), 207–30.

Chapter 7: Playing Muslim: Bonaparte's Army of the Orient and Euro-Muslim Creolization

1. Isabel P. B. Feo Rodrigues, 'Islands of Sexuality: Theories and Histories of Creolization in Cape Verde', *International Journal of African Historical Studies* 36, 1, special issue, *Colonial Encounters between Africa and Portugal* (2003), 83–103; for an argument about the difference between creolization and hybridity and the reasons for which the latter has gained greater currency in interdisciplinary work, see Deborah A. Kapchan and Pauline Turner Strong, 'Theorizing the Hybrid', *Journal of American Folklore* 112, 445, special issue, *Theorizing the Hybrid* (Summer 1999), 239–53.
2. Lionel Caplan, 'Creole World, Purist Rhetoric: Anglo-Indian Cultural Debates in Colonial and Contemporary Madras', *Journal of the Royal Anthropological Institute* 1 (1995), 743–62.
3. Mattison Mines, 'Courts of Law and Styles of Self in Eighteenth-century Madras: From Hybrid to Colonial Self', *Modern Asian Studies* 35 (2001), 56.
4. Ibid.
5. C. A. Bayly, *The Birth of the Modern World, 1780–1914: Global Connections and Comparisons* (Oxford, 2004), pp. 45, 76–106.
6. Jane Hathaway, *The Politics of Households in Ottoman Egypt: The Rise of the Qazdaglis* (Cambridge, 2002).
7. Juan Cole, *Napoleon's Egypt: Invading the Middle East* (New York, 2007).
8. 'Abd al-Rahman Al-Jabarti, *Ta'rikh Muddath al-faransis bi misr*, ed. Abd al-Rahim A. Abd al-Rahim (Cairo, 2000), pp. 33–41. Another translation is Shmuel Moreh, *Napoleon in Egypt: Al-Jabarti's Chronicle of the French Occupation, 1798* (Princeton, NJ, 1995), pp. 24–7.
9. 'Abd al-Rahman al-Jabarti, *Muzhir al-taqdis bi dhihab dawlat al-faransis* (Cairo, 1969), pp. 36–9.
10. Isma'il al-Khashshab, *Ta'rikh al-musalsal fi hawadith al-Zaman wa waqa'i' al-Diwan (1800–1801)*, ed. Mohammad Afifi and André Raymond (Cairo, 2003).
11. Pierre Amédée Jaubert/brother, 20 Messidor 6/8 July 1798, in *Copies of Original Letters from the Army of General Bonaparte in Egypt, intercepted by the fleet under the command of Admiral Lord Nelson. Part the first. With an English translation*, 9th edn (London, 1798), p. 31.
12. Nicolas-Philibert Desvernois, *Mémoires du Général Baron Desvernois*, ed. Albert Dufourcq (Paris, 1898), p. 135.

13. Napoléon Bonaparte, *Correspondence de Napoléon I*, 32 vols (Paris, 1858–70), IV, p. 420, no. 3148.

14. Jean Gabriel de Niello-Sargy, *Mémoires secrets et inédits, pour servir à l'histoire contemporaine*, ed. Alphonse de Beauchamp, 2 vols (Paris, 1825), I, p. 308.

15. Joseph-Marie Moiret, *Mémoires sur l'expédition d'Egypte* (Paris, 1984), pp. 64–5.

16. Moiret, *Mémoires*, p. 80.

17. François Bernoyer, *Avec Bonaparte en Egypte et en Syrie, 1798–1800: Dix-neuf lettres inédites*, ed. Christian Tortel (Abbeville, 1976), pp. 72, 76.

18. 'Abd al-Rahman al-Jabarti, *'Aja'ib al-Athar fi al-Tarajim wa al-Akhbar*, 2nd edn, 4 vols (Bulaq, 1904), II, pp. 106–7; for the nudity of dervishes see Victor Cousin, *Fragments Philosophiques*, 2nd edn, 2 vols (Paris, 1838), II, p. 391, citing a letter of the Diwan to Menou.

19. Al-Jabarti, *Muzhir*, pp. 103, 105; al-Jabarti, *'Aja'ib*, III, pp. 39–40.

20. Michael Winter, *Egyptian Society under Ottoman Rule, 1517–1798* (London, 1992), p. 74; al-Jabarti, *'Aja'ib*, II, pp. 17–19.

21. Bernoyer, *Avec Bonaparte en Égypte et en Syrie*, pp. 128–30.

22. Niello-Sargy, *Mémoires secrets*, I, pp. 340–3.

23. General Jean-Pierre Doguereau, *Journal de l'expedition d'Egypte*, ed. Clément de la Jonquière (Paris, 1904), p. 266.

24. Rebecca Joubin, 'Islam and Arabs through the Eyes of the *Encyclopédie*: The "Other" as a Case of French Cultural Self-Criticism', *International Journal of Middle East Studies* 32 (2000), 198.

25. Abdullah al-Sharqawi, *Tuhfat al-Nazirin fiman waliya misr min al-Muluk wa al-Salatin*, ed. Rihab Abd al-Hamid al-Qari (Cairo, 1996), pp. 122–3.

26. Averröes, *On the Harmony of Religion and Philosophy: A Translation, with Introduction and Notes of Ibn Rushd's Kitāb fasl al-maqāl*, trans. George F. Hourani (London, 1961); for Abbasid Baghdad, see Hugh Kennedy, *When Baghdad Ruled the Muslim World:The Rise and Fall of Islam's Greatest Dynasty* (Cambridge, MA, 2005).

27. Peter Gran, *The Islamic Roots of Capitalism: Egypt, 1760–1840* (Austin, TX, 1979), chs 2, 3; Juan Cole, 'Rifa'ah al-Tahtawi and the Revival of Practical Philosophy: An Examination of Neo-classicism in his "The Paths of Egyptian Minds in the Joys of Modern Manners"' (MA Thesis, American University in Cairo, 1978), ch. 1.

Chapter 8: Imperial Revolutions and Global Repercussions: South Asia and the World, c.1750–1850

I am very grateful to Peter Holquist, Lynn Hunt, Maya Jasanoff, Peter Marshall, Philip Stern, Eric Tagliacozzo and especially to David Armitage and Sanjay Subrahmanyam for advice about different aspects of this chapter.

1. Eric Hobsbawm, *The Age of Revolution, 1789–1848* (London, 1962), p. 4.

2. Ibid., p. 33
3. Ibid., p. 26.
4. Ibid.
5. Ibid.
6. David Washbrook, 'India in the Early Modern World Economy: Modes of Production, Reproduction and Exchange', *Journal of Global History* 2 (2007), 89.
7. Hobsbawm, *Age of Revolution*, p. 54. For a recent treatment of Roy's political thought, situating it within a broader global 'moment' of constitutional liberalism, see C. A. Bayly, 'Rammohan Roy and the Advent of Constitutional Liberalism in India, 1800–30', *Modern Intellectual History* 4 (2007), 25–41.
8. Hobsbawm, *Age of Revolution*, p. 139.
9. C. A. Bayly, *The Birth of the Modern World, 1780–1914: Global Connections and Comparisons* (Oxford, 2004), p. 1.
10. Ibid., pp. 86, 89. For another formulation of a connected 'Eurasian revolution', in which a 'long equilibrium of cultures and continents was swept away' by 'a series of forced entries or forcible overthrows', see John Darwin, *After Tamerlane: The Rise and Fall of Global Empire* (London, 2007), pp. 160–210.
11. For an earlier formulation of this Asian context for European imperialism, emphasizing the new threats to land empires posed by 'tribal breakouts' of nomadic groups from the frontiers of settled agriculture, see C. A. Bayly, *Imperial Meridian: The British Empire and the World 1780–1830* (London, 1989). For the significance of Nadir Shah, see Sanjay Subrahmanyam, *Penumbral Visions: Making Polities in Early Modern South India* (New Delhi, 2001), p. 15.
12. For a fine-grained account of this process in Bengal, see P. J. Marshall, *Bengal: The British Bridgehead: Eastern India, 1740–1828* (Cambridge, 1987).
13. Jeremy Adelman, 'The Age of Imperial Revolutions', *American Historical Review* 113 (2008), 319–40. While adapting Adelman's suggestive concept, I do not attempt any sustained comparison here between imperial trajectories in the Atlantic world and in Asia. Nonetheless, his reframing of Atlantic revolutions, less as the collapse of defunct empires and the rise of new nations, and more as an extended crisis within imperial forms of sovereignty, involving a 'prolonged effort to reassemble the practices of sovereignty under empire' (p. 337), appears to offer interesting possibilities for further comparative analyses.
14. Sudipta Sen, *A Distant Sovereignty: Nationalism, Imperialism and the Origins of British India* (New York, 2002), p. xiii.
15. For an emphasis on the recharging of British imperial nationalism during the French wars, see Bayly, *Imperial Meridian*.
16. For an emphasis on the importance of European maritime strength in enabling territorial conquests, see D. A. Washbrook, 'From Comparative Sociology to Global History: Britain and India in the Prehistory of

Modernity', *Journal of the Economic and Social History of the Orient*, 40 (1997), 410–43.
17. See, for example, William Watts, *Memoirs of the Revolution in Bengal* (London, 1760).
18. Burke's Speech on Fox's East India Bill (1 December 1783), reprinted in Edmund Burke, *On Empire, Liberty and Reform: Speeches and Letters*, ed. David Bromwich (New Haven, CT, 2000), pp. 298–9.
19. For a discussion of contemporary uses of this term see F. Lehman, 'The Eighteenth Century Transition in India: Responses of Some Bihar Intellectuals' (PhD dissertation, University of Wisconsin, 1967), p. 18. For a later use of the term by critics of modernizing Muslim states in the nineteenth century, see Amira K. Bennison, 'Muslim Universalism and Western Globalization', in A. G. Hopkins, ed., *Globalization in World History* (London, 2002), p. 92.
20. For surveys of contemporary Indian treatments of European conquests, see Sanjay Subrahmanyam, *Penumbral Visions*, ch. 1, and Kumkum Chatterjee, 'History as Self-Representation: The Recasting of a Political Tradition in Bengal and Bihar', *Modern Asian Studies* 32 (1998), 913–48.
21. From the Tuzak-i-Walajah, cited by Subrahmanyam, *Penumbral Visions*, p. 202.
22. Ghulam Husain Khan Tabataba'i, *A Translation of the Sëir Mutaqherin; or View of Modern Times*, trans. Haji Mustafa, 3 vols (Calcutta, 1789–90), III, p. 161.
23. Ibid., III, p. 27.
24. P. J. Marshall, *A Free though Conquering People: Britain and Asia in the Eighteenth Century* (London, 1981).
25. For extended discussions of Burke's views, see Robert Travers, *Ideology and Empire in Eighteenth Century India: The British in Bengal* (Cambridge, 2007), pp. 217–23, and P. J. Marshall, 'Edmund Burke and India', in Rudrangshu Mukherjee and Lakshmi Subramanian, eds, *Politics and Trade in the Indian Ocean World: Essays in Honor of Ashin Das Gupta* (New Delhi, 1998), pp. 250–69.
26. David Bromwich, 'Introduction', in Burke, *On Empire, Liberty and Reform*, ed. Bromwich, p. 17.
27. Hastings to George Vansittart, 5 March 1777, British Library, Additional Manuscripts 48,370 fo. 41v.
28. For a longer explication of British views of the Mughal constitution, see Travers, *Ideology and Empire*. And for a suggestion of certain broad overlaps between conceptions of imperial virtue and corruption in different parts of early modern Eurasia, especially the impulse to defend 'ancient traditions of community and the honor of the land' from new forms of commercialism and militarism, see Bayly, *Birth of the Modern World*, pp. 288–9.
29. Travers, *Ideology and Empire*, ch. 6. As Jon E. Wilson has recently emphasized, high imperial complacency coexisted with severe anxiety among isolated British officials scattered across remote districts, as they struggled

to apply general administrative regulations in particular circumstances. See Jon E. Wilson, *The Domination of Strangers: Modern Governance in Eastern India, 1780–1835* (Basingstoke, 2008).

30. Kenneth Balhatchet, *Race, Sex and Class under the Raj: Imperial Attitudes and Policies and Their Critics* (London, 1980). For a recent argument that more 'scientific' conceptions of racial difference, combining notions of culture, religion, and biology, were being articulated in the late eighteenth and early nineteenth centuries, see Shruti Kapila, 'Race Matters. Orientalism and Religion in India and Beyond *c*.1770–1880', *Modern Asian Studies* 41 (2007), 471–513. Compare this with David Washbrook, 'South India 1770–1840: The Colonial Transition', *Modern Asian Studies* 38 (2004), 479–516, who suggests that British racial sensibilities in South India were cut across by cross-cutting class hierarchies and elite social interactions. 'The binary oppositions and strict racial hierarchies', he suggests, 'characteristic of late nineteenth century "colonialism", were a very long time reaching South India, if they ever did' (p. 486).

31. Thomas R. Trautmann, *Aryans and British India* (Berkeley, CA, 1997); Tony Ballantyne, *Orientalism and Race: Aryanism in the British Empire* (Basingstoke, 2002).

32. For the links between British legal regimes and Hindu social reformism in early nineteenth-century Bengal, see Wilson, *Domination of Strangers*, ch. 6.

33. For important works along these lines, see Muzaffar Alam, *The Crisis of Empire in Mughal North India: Awadh and the Punjab 1707–48* (Delhi, 1986); and André Wink, *Land and Sovereignty in India: Agrarian Society and Politics under the Eighteenth Century Maratha Svarajya* (Cambridge, 1986).

34. Eric Stokes, 'The First Century of British Colonial Rule in India. Social Revolution or Social Stagnation?', *Past and Present* 58 (February 1973), 136–60. For a more elaborate synthesis, emphasizing the themes of continuity and Indian agency, but also pointing to new processes of 'peasantization' and 'traditionalization' under the colonial regime, see C. A. Bayly, *Indian Society and the Making of the British Empire* (Cambridge, 1998).

35. For collections of representative articles from these debates, see Seema Alavi, ed., *The Eighteenth Century in India* (New Delhi, 2002), and P. J. Marshall, ed., *The Eighteenth Century in Indian History: Evolution or Revolution?* (New Delhi, 2003).

36. Frank Perlin, 'State Formation Reconsidered', in Perlin, *The Invisible City: Monetary, Administrative and Popular Infrastructure in Asia and Europe 1500–1900* (Aldershot, 1993), pp. 15–90.

37. For fine recent examples of this kind of new political history, see Sanjay Subrahmanyam, *Penumbral Visions*, and Prachi Deshpande, *Creative Pasts: Historical Memory and Identity in Western India 1700–1960* (New Delhi, 2007).

38. Subrahmanyam, *Penumbral Visions*, pp. 20–1.

39. Perlin, 'State Formation Reconsidered', p. 39.

40. For caste, see Susan Bayly, *Caste, Society and Politics in India from the Eighteenth Century to the Modern Age* (Cambridge, 1999), and Nicholas B.

Dirks, *Castes of Mind: Colonialism and the Making of Modern India* (Princeton, NJ, 2001); for historical narrative, see Velcheru Narayana Rao, David Shulman and Sanjay Subrahmanyam, eds, *Textures of Time: Writing History in South India 1600–1800* (Delhi, 2001); and for corporate groups and urban history, see C. A. Bayly, *Rulers, Townsmen and Bazaars: North Indian Society in the Age of British Expansion, 1770–1870* (Cambridge, 1983).

41. For a subtle reading of new forms of temporality produced within a 'modern' colonial state as a 'future-oriented project of state-formation', see Wilson, *Domination of Strangers*, p. 14.

42. Deshpande, *Creative Pasts*.

43. Norbert Peabody, *Hindu Kingship and Polity in Precolonial India* (Cambridge, 2002).

44. Perlin, 'State Formation Reconsidered', pp. 88–90.

45. See, for example, David Washbrook, 'Economic Depression and the Making of "Traditional" Society in Colonial India', *Transactions of the Royal Historical Society* 6th ser. 3 (1993), 237–63.

46. Frank Perlin, *Unbroken Landscape: Commodity, Category, Sign and Identity; Their Production as Myth and Knowledge from 1500* (Aldershot, 1994), p. 80.

47. Jon E. Wilson, 'Early Colonial India Beyond Empire', *The Historical Journal* 50 (2007), 951–70.

48. See in particular the two volumes of Sanjay Subrahmanyam, *Explorations in Connected History: Mughals and Franks* (Delhi, 2005), and *Explorations in Connected History: From the Tagus to the Ganges* (Delhi, 2005).

49. John Maynard Keynes, 'Economic Possibilities for Our Grandchildren' (1930), in Keynes, *Essays in Persuasion*, in *Collected Writings of John Maynard Keynes*, 30 vols (London, 1971), IX, pp. 323–4.

50. For a summary and critique of what he calls 'Europe-centered stories' of modern economic development, see Kenneth Pomeranz, *The Great Divergence: China, Europe and the Making of the Modern World Economy* (Princeton, NJ, 2000), pp. 10–17.

51. For two especially rich versions of such an approach , see Pomeranz, ibid., and David Washbrook, 'From Comparative Sociology to Global History'.

52. Jan de Vries, 'The Industrious Revolution and the Industrial Revolution', *Journal of Economic History* 54 (1994), 249–70.

53. P. K. O'Brien, 'Inseparable Connections: Trade, Economy, Fiscal State and the Expansion of Empire, 1688–1815', in P. J. Marshall, ed., *The Oxford History of the British Empire*, II: *The Eighteenth Century* (Oxford, 1998), pp. 53–77; Boyd Hilton, *A Mad, Bad and Dangerous People? England, 1783–1846* (Oxford, 2006), p. 4. The classic work on the rise of the 'fiscal-military state' remains John Brewer, *The Sinews of Power: War, Money and the English State 1688–1783* (London, 1989). For the influential argument that the economic underpinnings of British imperialism from the late seventeenth century onwards rested on an alliance of

landed and commercial elites, termed 'gentlemanly capitalism', see P. J. Cain and A. G. Hopkins, *British Imperialism, 1688–2000*, 2nd edn (New York, 2001).

54. For detailed statistical analyses of imperial trades, see Jacob Price, 'The Imperial Economy, 1700–1776', in Marshall, ed., *Oxford History of the British Empire*, II, pp. 78–105. Marshall notes that 'trade statistics show that Asia was a major source of imports, although always a smaller one than the West Indies, throughout the eighteenth century, but that as a destination for exports it lagged far behind North America, the gap actually widening by the end of the century'. Marshall, 'Britain without America – A Second Empire?', in Marshall, ed., *Oxford History of the British Empire*, II, p. 577.

55. O'Brien, 'Inseparable Connections'; Pomeranz, *The Great Divergence*, pp. 20–1.

56. These interconnections are emphasized by J. R. Ward, 'The Industrial Revolution and British Imperialism, 1750–1850', *Economic History Review* new ser. 47 (1994), 44–65, who argues that the East India Company's military expansionism from the 1780s onwards was enabled not only by capturing local Indian resources, but also by tapping into networks of trade and credit which themselves depended on the growing wealth of an industrializing metropolis.

57. Marshall writes that by the end of the eighteenth century tea was 'rivalling sugar as the most valuable import' to Britain. 'Tea was by far the most valuable commodity in which the East India Company dealt, and the duties levied on it provided the government with 6 or 7% of its total revenue': Marshall, 'Britain without America', p. 582.

58. Pomeranz, *The Great Divergence*, pp. 192–3.

59. H. V. Bowen, *Revenue and Reform: The Indian Problem in British Politics, 1757–1773* (Cambridge, 1999); Holden Furber, *John Company at Work: A Study of European Expansion in the Late Eighteenth Century* (Cambridge, MA, 1948).

60. Hilton, *A Mad, Bad and Dangerous People*.

61. Javier Cuenca Esteban, 'The British Balance of Payments, 1772–1820: India Transfers and War Finance', *Economic History Review* new ser. 54 (2001), 58–86.

62. Huw Bowen, *The Business of Empire: The East India Company and Imperial Britain, 1756–1833* (Cambridge, 2006), pp. 260–95.

63. Kenneth Pomeranz and Steven Topik, *The World that Trade Created: Society, Culture and the World Economy*, 2nd edn (New York, 2006), pp. 91–3.

64. For estimates of mortality rates, see P. J. Marshall, *East Indian Fortunes. The British in Bengal in the Eighteenth Century* (Oxford, 1976), pp. 218–19.

65. For India and the British question, see Bowen, *Business of Empire*, p. 275, and Linda Colley, *Britons: Forging the Nation 1707–1837* (New Haven, CT, 1992), pp. 127–9.

66. Philip Harling, *The Waning of the Old Corruption: The Politics of Economical*

Reform in Britain, 1779–1846 (Oxford, 1996), p. 39; Lucy Sutherland, *The East India Company in Eighteenth Century Politics* (Oxford, 1952), pp. 411–13.
67. H. V. Bowen, 'British India 1765–1813: The Metropolitan Context', in Marshall, ed., *Oxford History of the British Empire*, II, pp. 530–1.
68. For the idea of the 'garrison state', see Douglas Peers, *Between Mars and Mammon: Colonial Armies and the Garrison State in India 1819–35* (London, 1995).
69. Bayly, *Imperial Meridian*; Hilton, *Mad, Bad and Dangerous People?*
70. Martha McLaren, 'From Analysis to Prescription: Scottish Concepts of Asiatic Despotism in Early Nineteenth Century British India', *International History Review* 15 (1993), 469–501.
71. Miles Taylor, 'Queen Victoria and India, 1837–61', *Victorian Studies* 46 (2004), 264–75. For a longer discussion of elite British notions of social hierarchy in relation to imperial governance, see David Cannadine, *Ornamentalism: How the British Saw their Empire* (Oxford, 2001).
72. For a good survey of changing gender relations in Britain, emphasizing the intersections between domestic and imperial histories, see Susan Kingsley Kent, *Gender and Power in Britain, 1640–1990* (London, 1999).
73. Lata Mani, *Contentious Traditions: The Debate over Sati in Colonial India* (Berkeley, CA, 1998).
74. Durba Ghosh, *Sex and the Family in Colonial India: The Making of Empire* (Cambridge, 2006).
75. Miles Taylor, 'Joseph Hume and the Reformation of India, 1819–33', in Glenn Burgess and Matthew Festenstein, eds, *English Radicalism 1550–1850* (Cambridge, 2007), pp. 293–4, and the same author's 'Empire and Parliamentary Reform: The 1832 Reform Act Revisited', in Arthur Burns and Joanna Innes, eds, *Rethinking the Age of Reform: Britain 1780–1850* (Cambridge, 2003), pp. 295–311.
76. The classic study is Eric Stokes, *The English Utilitarians in India* (Oxford, 1959; repr. New Delhi, 1982); see also Thomas R. Metcalf, *Ideologies of the Raj* (Cambridge, 1994).
77. Bayly, 'Rammohan Roy and the Advent of Constitutional Liberalism in India'.
78. Jennifer Pitts, *A Turn to Empire: The Rise of Imperial Liberalism in Britain and France* (Princeton, NJ, 2005). For an emphasis on the durability of Whiggish evolutionism in nineteenth-century Britain, see Peter Mandler, *The English National Character: The History of an Idea from Edmund Burke to Tony Blair* (New Haven, CT, 2007).
79. Marshall, *Bengal: The British Bridgehead*.
80. For a longer history of the Company as an early modern form of state, see Philip J. Stern, '"One Body Corporate and Politick": The Growth of the East India Company State in the Later Seventeenth Century' (PhD dissertation, Columbia University, 2004).
81. For Hastings's Tibetan connection, see Kate Teltscher, *The High Road to China: George Bogle, The Panchen Lama, and the First British Expedition to*

Tibet (New York, 2006); and for his Middle Eastern interests, see Edward Ingram, *In Defence of British India: Great Britain and the Middle East, 1775–1842* (London, 1984), p. 21.

82. Alan Frost, *The Global Reach of Empire 1764–1815* (Carlton, Victoria, 2006).

83. Ministerial reticence about territorial conquests in India is emphasized in P. J. Marshall, 'British Expansion in India: A Historical Revision', *History* 60 (1975), 19–43.

84. Sugata Bose, *A Hundred Horizons: The Indian Ocean in the Age of Global Empire* (Cambridge, MA, 2006), pp. 36–71.

85. Ibid., and Thomas R. Metcalf, *Imperial Connections: India in the Indian Ocean Arena, 1860–1920* (Berkeley, CA, 2007).

86. For Tipu's embassy, see Jean-Marie Lafont, *Indika: Essays in Indo-French Relations* (New Delhi, 2000), and for the wider context of Anglo-French imperial conflict, Robert Tombs and Isabella Tombs, *That Sweet Enemy: The French and the British from the Sun King to the Present* (New York, 2007).

87. Cited in Tombs and Tombs, *That Sweet Enemy*, p. 227.

88. Maya Jasanoff, *Edge of Empire: Lives, Culture and Conquest in the East 1750–1850* (New York, 2005); Juan Cole, *Napoleon's Egypt: Invading the Middle East* (New York, 2007).

89. Tombs and Tombs, *That Sweet Enemy*, p. 239; Lafont, *Indika*, pp. 209–10.

90. Alex Marshall, *The Russian General Staff and Asia, 1800–1917* (Oxford, 2006), p. 12.

91. For a discussion of these different views, see Roderick McGrew, *Paul I of Russia, 1754–1801* (Oxford, 1992), p. 316.

92. Cited in Cole, *Napoleon's Egypt*, p. 13

93. Marshall, *Russian General Staff and Asia*, p. 36.

94. Malcolm Yapp, *Strategies of British India: Britain, Iran and Afghanistan, 1798–1850* (Oxford, 1980).

95. Michael Greenberg, *British Trade and the Opening of China, 1800–42* (Cambridge, 1951); Pomeranz and Topik, *The World that Trade Created*, pp. 90–4. But see the argument of Pomeranz in this volume that imperial China's major challenges in this period were mainly internally generated.

96. For problems of structural dependency, see Washbrook, 'India in the Early Modern World Economy'; and for the long build-up of an English East India Company polity in Asia, well before the conquests of the mid-eighteenth century, see Philip J. Stern, '"A Politie of Civill and Military Power": Political Thought and the Late Seventeenth Century Foundations of the East India Company State', *Journal of British Studies* 47 (2008), 253–83.

97. For a collection of essays emphasizing the layered character of phases of globalization, from 'archaic' to 'proto-modern' to modern and post-modern, see Hopkins, ed., *Globalization in World History*.

98. Washbrook, 'India in the Early Modern World Economy', p. 90.

99. Tirthankar Roy focuses on the creative adaption and survival of arti-
    sanal manufacturing in *Traditional Industry in the Economy of Colonial
    India* (Cambridge, 1999).
100. Prasannan Parthasarathi, *The Transition to a Colonial Economy: Weavers,
    Peasants and Kings in South India* (Cambridge, 2001); see also Hameeda
    Hossain, *The Company Weavers of Bengal: The East India Company and the
    Organization of Textile Production in Bengal, 1750–1813* (Delhi, 1988).
101. Other European traders also provided an important vehicle for remit-
    tances back to Europe of British private fortunes made in India. See
    Marshall, *Bengal: The British Bridgehead*, pp. 105–6.
102. Washbrook, 'South India 1770–1840', p. 508, and Washbrook, 'The Two
    Faces of Colonialism: India 1818–1860', in Andrew Porter, ed., *The
    Oxford History of the British Empire, III: The Nineteenth Century* (Oxford,
    1999), pp. 395–421.
103. Bayly, *Birth of the Modern World*, p. 35.
104. C. A. Bayly, 'The Age of Hiatus: The North Indian Economy and
    Society, 1830–50', in Asiya Siddiqi, ed., *Trade and Finance in Colonial
    India, 1750–1860* (Delhi 1995), pp. 218–49, and K. N. Chaudhuri,
    'India's Foreign Trade and the Cessation of the East India Company's
    Trading Activities, 1828–40', in ibid., pp. 290–320.
105. Anthony Webster, *The Richest East India Merchant: The Life and Business
    of John Palmer of Calcutta, 1767–1836* (Woodbridge, 2007). The follow-
    ing two paragraphs are based on Webster's account.
106. Bose, *A Hundred Horizons*, p. 74; Rajat K. Ray, 'Asian Capital in the Age
    of European Domination: The Rise of the Bazaar, 1800–1914', *Modern
    Asian Studies* 29 (1995), 449–554.
107. Claude Markovits, *The Global World of Indian Merchants, 1750–1947:
    Traders of Sind from Bukhara to Panama* (Cambridge, 2000).
108. Bennison, 'Muslim Universalism and Western Globalization'.
109. Tim Harper, 'Empire, Diaspora and the Languages of Globalism,
    1850–1914', in Hopkins, ed., *Globalization in World History*, p. 145. For
    a fine recent treatment of the Hadhrami diaspora, which, as the author
    notes, predated the Portuguese and outlasted the British Empire in the
    Indian Ocean, see Engseng Ho, *The Graves of Tarim: Genealogy and
    Mobility Across the Indian Ocean* (Berkeley, CA, 2006).
110. For the Awadh case, see Michael H. Fisher, *A Clash of Cultures: Awadh,
    the British and the Mughals* (Delhi, 1987), and Juan Cole, *Roots of North
    Indian Shi'ism in Iran and Iraq* (Berkeley, CA, 1989).
111. Bose, *A Hundred Horizons*, p. 65.
112. Thomas R. Metcalf, *An Imperial Vision: Indian Architecture and Britain's
    Raj* (Oxford, 2002). Bernard S. Cohn, 'Representing Authority in
    Victorian India', in Eric Hobsbawm and Terence Ranger, eds, *The
    Invention of Tradition* (Cambridge, 1983), pp. 165–209.
113. Juan Cole, 'Iranian Culture in South Asia, 1500–1900', in Nikki Keddie
    and Rudi Matthee, eds, *Iran and the Surrounding World: Interactions in
    Culture and Cultural Politics* (Washington, DC, 2002), pp. 15–16.

114. Mahomad Tavakoli-Targhi, *Refashioning Iran: Orientalism, Occidentalism and Historioraphy* (New York, 2001), pp. 18–34.
115. Cole, 'Iranian Culture', pp. 30–1.
116. Edward Ingram, *Britain's Persian Connection 1798–1828: Prelude to the Great Game in Asia* (Oxford, 1993).
117. Cited in Elmer Cutts, 'The Background to Macaulay's Minute', *American Historical Review* 58 (1953), 829.
118. Marshall, *Bengal: The British Bridgehead*, p. 115.
119. Thomas Munro, *Liberty of the Press in India: A Minute Written by Thomas Munro, 35 Years Ago* (London, 1857), pp. 3, 4, 7.
120. Washbrook, 'South India: 1770–1840', p. 510.
121. For 'expatriate nationalism' and 'competing universalisms', see Bose, *A Hundred Horizons*, especially chs 5 and 7; for the importance of 'circulation' and mobility as a theme in South Asian history, despite colonial attempts to 'demobilize' circulatory regimes, see Claude Markovits, Jacques Pouchepadass and Sanjay Subrahmanyam, eds, *Society and Circulation: Mobile People and Itinerant Cultures in South Asia, 1750–1950* (New Delhi, 2003).
122. For a recent treatment emphasizing these themes, see Durba Ghosh and Dane Kennedy, eds, *Decentring Empire: Britain, India and the Transcolonial World* (Hyderabad, 2006).

Chapter 9: Revolutionary Europe and the Destruction of Java's Old Order, 1808–1830

1. John Hoffman, 'A Foreign Investment: Indies Malay to 1901', *Indonesia* 27 (1979), 65–92.
2. Simon Schama, *Patriots and Liberators: Revolution in the Netherlands, 1780–1813* (London, 1977), pp. 342–3.
3. Peter Carey, *The Power of Prophecy: Prince Dipanagara and the End of an Old Order in Java (1825–1830)* (Leiden, 2007), p. 166; H. W. Daendels, *Staat der Nederlandsche Oostindische bezittingen, onder het bestuur van den Gouverneur-Generaal Herman Willem Daendels, ridder, luitenant-generaal &c. in de jaren 1808–1811* ('s-Gravenhage, 1814), p. 94.
4. Carey, *Power of Prophecy*, pp. 171, 309–10.
5. *De Opkomst van het Nederlandsch Gezag in Oost-Indië: verzameling van onuitgegeven stukken uit het oud-koloniaal archief*, ed. J. K. J. de Jonge and M. L. van Deventer, 18 vols ('s-Gravenhage, 1888), XIII, p. 128.
6. When he succeeded as sultan, the Crown Prince (the future Sultan Hamengkubuwana III, reigned 1812–14) continued his custom of serving European-style food including wheat bread and butter, foods normally eaten only by Europeans at this time, during court entertainments: *The British in Java: A Javanese Account, 1812–1816*, ed. Peter Carey (Oxford, 1992), p. 467 n. 320.
7. Carey, *Power of Prophecy*, p. 180.
8. Ibid., p. 199.

Notes 261

9. V. J. H. Houben, *Kraton and Kumpeni: Surakarta and Yogyakarta 1830–1870* (Leiden, 1994), pp. 81–2; Ricklefs, *Mangkubumi*, pp. 274–6; *The British in Java*, ed. Carey, p. 467 n. 321.
10. Carey, *Power of Prophecy*, p. 200.
11. Ibid., p. 215
12. Raffles's letters to various Indonesian rulers from Melaka are described in Ahmat bin Adam, 'A Descriptive Account of the Malay Letters sent by Thomas Stamford Raffles in Malacca in 1810 and 1811 to the Various Rulers of the Indigenous States of the Malay Archipelago' (MA thesis, Department of History, School of Oriental and African Studies, 1971). See also Carey, *Power of Prophecy*, p. 280.
13. C. A. Bayly, *Imperial Meridian: The British Empire and the World, 1780–1830* (London, 1989).
14. John Bastin, *The Native Policies of Sir Stamford Raffles in Java and Sumatra: An Economic Interpretation* (Oxford, 1957), p. xx.
15. Carey, *Power of Prophecy*, p. 283 n. 91.
16. Ibid., p. 285.
17. Ibid., p. 340.
18. Ibid., p. 347.
19. Ibid., p. 377.
20. Ibid., p. 383.
21. The late Dutch legal historian G. J. ('Han') Resink (1911–97) defined 'government law' as a mixture of Javanese customary law (*adat*) and Dutch colonial law, the latter being described by Raffles as 'the laws of the Dutch States General and the statutes passed in Holland and Batavia with particular application to Java': ibid., p. 385 n. 103.
22. Ibid., p. 254 n. 205.
23. Carey, *British in Java*, pp. 90, 241. The British confiscation of all the *kris* of the senior Yogyakarta officials and princes would certainly have been experienced as a form of unmanning given the special symbolic importance of the *kris* in Javanese culture, where the weapon can represent the presence of a male owner at a wedding.
24. P. J. F. Louw, *De Java-Oorlog van 1825–30*, 6 vols ('s-Gravenhage and Batavia, 1897), II, pp. 685–7.
25. Quoted in Carey, *Power of Prophecy*, p. 389.
26. Ibid., pp. 834–9.
27. Arsip Nasional Republik Indonesia (henceforth ANRI), Solo Brieven (henceforth S.Br.) 170, J. I. van Sevenhoven, H. MacGillivray and A. H. Smissaert (Commissarissen belast met het onderzoek in de regering der tolpoorten, de administratie der vogelnestjes en het oprigten eenen landraad in de Residentiën Soerakarta en Jogjokarta', henceforth 'Commissioners') (Yogyakarta/Surakarta) to G. A. G. Ph. van der Capellen (Batavia/Bogor), 24 October 1824.
28. This detail was pointed out by Van Sevenhoven's colleague as commissioner, Hendrik Mauritz MacGillivray, who served as Acting Resident of Surakarta (1823–4) just before Van Sevenhoven's one-year incumbency

(1824–5); see MvK 4132, MacGillivray, 'Nota omtrent den staat der Javasche vorstenlanden, de thans bestaande onlusten en de middelen welke tot herstel en verzekering der rust kunnen worden aangewend' (henceforth MacGillivray, 'Nota'), Surakarta, 13 May 1826. MacGillivray's report was later published: C. E. van Kesteren, 'Waarschuwingen vóór den Java-oorlog', *De Indische Gids* 14, 2 (1892), 973–96.

29. KITLV H 503,Van Sevenhoven,'Aanteekeningen', p. 77;AvJ, G.A. G. Ph. van der Capellen (Batavia/Bogor) to A. H. Smissaert (Yogyakarta), 9 May 1824.

30. MvK 4132, MacGillivray, 'Nota', 13 May 1826, gives the following figures for the value of goods stolen from the *bandar* in the period 1817–24: 1817: *f.* 2,278; 1818: *f.* 3,005; 1819: *f.* 2,442; 1820: *f.* 4,240; 1821: *f.* 8,791; 1822: *f.* 15,623; 1823: *f.* 15,660; 1824: *f.* 32,100 (estimate).

31. Archief Nationaal (The Hague) H. M. de Kock private collection (henceforth dK) 197, A. H. Smissaert (Yogyakarta) to H. M. de Kock (Surakarta), 30 July 1825. On the situation in the eastern *mancanagara*, see further Peter Carey 'Changing Javanese Perceptions of the Chinese Communities in Central Java, 1755–1825', *Indonesia* 37 (1984), 1–2.

32. Soeripto, *Ontwikkelingsgang der vorstenlandsche wetboeken* (Leiden, 1929), pp. 88, 268; *The Archive of Yogyakarta, I: Documents Relating to Politics and Internal Court Affairs*, ed. Peter Carey (Oxford, 1980), pp. 126–8, 130 n. 1.

33. *Babad Dipanagara: An Account of the Outbreak of the Java War (1825–30)*, ed. Peter Carey (Kuala Lumpur, 1981), p. 243 n. 36.

34. S.Br.170, Commissioners (Yogyakarta/Surakarta) to G.A. G. Ph. van der Capellen (Batavia/Bogor), 24 October 1824.

35. Archief Nationaal (The Hague), G. J. Schneither private collection 92, Pieter le Clercq,'Algemeen verslag der Residentie Kadoe over het jaar 1824', 30 May 1825. The *bandar* along the Brantas and Madiun rivers were also abolished in December 1823, KITLV H 395, Chevallier, 'Rapport', 13 June 1824. On the importance of river networks in east Java for trade, see Thomas Stamford Raffles, *History of Java*, 2 vols (London, 1817), I, p. 196.

36. S.Br.170, Commissioners (Yogyakarta/Surakarta) to G.A. G. Ph. van der Capellen (Batavia/Bogor), 24 October 1824.

37. MvK 4132, MacGillivray, 'Nota', 13 May 1826. See further Louw, *De Java-oorlog van 1825–30*, I, p. 13; P. H. van der Kemp,'Dipanegara, eene geschiedkundige Hamlettype', *Bijdragen tot de Taal-, Land- en Volkenkunde* 46 (1896), 386.

38. The Commissioners' remarks about the 'good-natured and peaceful Javanese', who were liable to run amok if aroused, constitute a classic expression of the widespread and self-deluding Dutch colonial view of '*De Javaan als het zachste volk ter aarde*' (the Javanese as the gentlest people in the world). See further Peter Carey and Vincent Houben, 'Spirited Srikandhis and Sly Sumbadras: The Social, Political and Economic Role of Women in the Central Javanese Courts in the 18th and Early 19th

Centuries', in Elsbeth Locher-Scholten and Anke Niehof, eds, *Indonesian Women in Focus: Past and Present Notions* (Dordrecht, 1987), pp. 12–42.

39. S.Br.170, Commissioners (Yogyakarta/Surakarta) to G.A. G. Ph. van der Capellen (Batavia/Bogor), 24 October 1824.

40. P. H. van der Kemp, ed., 'Brieven van den Gouverneur-Generaal Van der Capellen over Dipanagara's opstand zoomede eene wederlegging van den Minister Elout', *Bijdragen tot de Taal-, Land- en Volkenkunde* 46 (1896), pp. 44–5.

41. Dj.Br.59, Gan Hiang Sing (Bantul) to A. H. Smissaert (Yogyakarta), 9 November 1824.

42. KITLV H 395, Chevallier, 'Rapport', 15 June 1824.

43. Ibid.

44. Ibid.

45. S.Br. 170, Commissioners (Yogyakarta/Surakarta) to G.A. G. Ph. van der Capellen (Batavia/Bogor), 24 October 1824. The expression in the Dutch original was '*linie van douanen*'. The Javanese phrase was '*bangsa bandar*'.

46. S.Br. 122, H. G. Nahuys van Burgst (Yogyakarta) to G.A. G. Ph. van der Capellen (Batavia/Bogor), 29 September 1822.

47. India Office Library, Mackenzie Private collection 21 part 10, Lt H. G. Jourdan, 'Report on Japan and Wirosobo', 28 April 1813, 361.

48. Carey, 'Changing Javanese Perceptions', 17 n. 76; Ong Tae Hae, *The Chinaman Abroad: Or a Desultory Account of the Malayan Archipelago, Particularly of Java*, ed. and trans. W. H. Medhurst (Shanghai, 1849), p. 13.

49. KITLV H 503, Van Sevenhoven, 'Aanteekeningen', pp. 135–6.

50. J. J. Hasselman, 'Nota omtrent de opium-pacht op Java en Madoera', *Handelingen en Geschriften van het Indisch Genootschap* 5 (1858), 18–37.

51. J. J. Wiselius, *De opium in Nederlandsch- en Britsch-Indië, economisch, critisch, historisch* (The Hague, 1886), p. 6.

52. James Rush, *Opium to Java: Revenue Farming and Chinese Enterprise in Colonial Indonesia, 1860–1910* (Jakarta, 2007), pp. 26–30.

53. Raffles, *History*, I, pp. 102–3.

54. KITLV H 503, Van Sevenhoven. 'Aanteekeningen', p. 73.

55. Ibid., pp. 79-80.

56. Carey, 'Changing Javanese perceptions', p. 35 n. 160.

57. R. A. Kern, 'Uit oude beschieden (geschiedenis van de afdeeling Patjitan in de eerste helft der 19e eeuw) met bijlage', *Tijdschrift van het Binnenlands Bestuur* 34 (1908), 163.

58. Rush, *Opium to Java*, p. 34.

59. Carey, *Power of Prophecy*, p. 610.

60. Ibid., p. 480.

61. Universiteits Bibliotheek Leiden, Bibliotheca Publica Latina 616 Portfolio 9 part 3, H. G. Nahuys van Burgst, 'Onlusten op Java' (Maastricht, 1826).

62. Carey, *Power of Prophecy*, pp. 342–3.

Chapter 10: Their Own Path to Crisis? Social Change, State-building and the Limits of Qing Expansion, c.1770–1840

1. The empire's majority ethnic group, with over 90 per cent of the total population.
2. See Daniel Headrick, *The Tools of Empire: Technology and European Imperialism in the Nineteenth Century* (New York, 1981), pp. 17–57.
3. See, for instance, William Lavely and R. Bin Wong, 'Revising the Malthusian Narrative: The Comparative Study of Population Dynamics in Late Imperial China', *Journal of Asian Studies* 57 (1998), 714–48; Kenneth Pomeranz, *The Great Divergence: China, Europe, and the Making of the Modern World Economy* (Princeton, NJ, 2000).
4. For a general discussion, see Pomeranz, *Great Divergence*; Pomeranz, 'Beyond the East–West Binary: Resituating Development Paths in the Eighteenth-century World', *Journal of Asian Studies* 61 (2002), 539–90; and Pomeranz, 'Standards of Living in Rural and Urban China: Preliminary Estimates for the Mid Eighteenth and Early Twentieth Centuries' (paper for Panel 77 of International Economic History Association Conference, Helsinki, 2006); Debin Ma, 'Modern Economic Growth in the Lower Yangzi in 1911–1937: A Quantitative, Historical, and Institutional Analysis' (Discussion paper 2004-06-002, Foundation for Advanced Studies on International Development, Tokyo, 2004), p. 6; Jan Luiten Van Zanden, 'Estimating Early Modern Economic Growth' (Working Paper, International Institute of Social History, University of Utrecht, 2004, available at http://www.iisg.nl/research/jvz-estimating.pdf, accessed 17 December 2007), pp. 22–3; Robert C. Allen, 'Mr Lockyer Meets the Index Number Problem: The Standard of Living in Canton and London in 1704'; Allen, 'Agricultural Productivity and Rural Incomes in England and the Yangzi Delta, ca. 1620–1820' (2005) (both available at http://www.economics.ox.ac.uk/Members/robert.allen/default.htm). For market integration, see Wolfgang Koller and Carol Shiue, 'Markets in China and Europe on the Eve of the Industrial Revolution' (NBER Working paper 10778, September 2004).
5. On real wages, see Robert C. Allen, Jean-Pascal Bassino, Debin Ma, Christine Moll-Murata and Jan Luiten Van Zanden, 'Wages, Prices and Living Standards in China, Japan, and Europe, 1738–1925' (http://www.econ.yale.edu/seminars/echist/eh06-07/Ma040407.pdf); for more discussion and data on the earnings of tenants versus proletarians, see Pomeranz, 'Standards of Living'.
6. For some eighteenth-century data see Li Wenzhi and Jiang Taixin, *Zhongguo dizhu zhi jingji lun* (*An Economic Discourse on China's Landlord System*) (Beijing, 2005), pp. 303, 310. For twentieth-century data see John L. Buck, *Land Utilization in China* (1937; New York, 1964), especially p. 293. Joseph Esherick, 'Number Games: A Note on Land Distribution in Pre-Revolutionary China', *Modern China* 7 (1981), 387–412, finds many problems with Buck, but does not change the general northern and

southern patterns. For specific regions see Robert Marks, *Revolution in South China: Peasants and the Making of History in Haifeng County, 1570–1930* (Madison, WI, 1984), p. 44, and Chen Hanseng, *Landlord and Peasant in China: A Study of the Agrarian Crisis in South China* (New York, 1936), p. 19, on the far south; Philip Huang, *The Peasant Family and Rural Development in the Lower Yangzi Region, 1350–1988* (Stanford, CA, 1990), p. 103, on the Lower Yangzi; Jing Su and Luo Lun, *Qing dai Shandong jingying dizhu jingnji yanjiu* (1958; Jinan, 1986), pp. 34–5, and Philip Huang, *The Peasant Economy and Social Change in North China* (Stanford, CA, 1985), p. 103, on the North China plain. The south-west may have had unusually high tenancy rates for a poor region, and unusually harsh terms; by the early twentieth century, its land distribution (along with that of Manchuria, which had few settlers until the late nineteenth century) was the most unequal in the country. See, for example, Madeleine Zelin, 'The Rights of Tenants in Mid-Qing Sichuan', *Journal of Asian Studies* 45 (1986) 499–526, and Wu Tingyu et al., eds, *Xian dai Zhongguo nong cun jing ji de yan bian* (Changchun, 1993), p. 150.

7. There is a vast literature on this phenomenon. Kenneth Pomeranz, 'Land Markets in Late Imperial and Republican China', *Continuity and Change* 22 (2008), 1–50, gives my own views, and includes a partial bibliography.

8. For an overview of the period, see Timothy Brook, *The Confusions of Pleasure: Commerce and Culture in Ming China* (Berkeley, CA, 1998). For land rights in particular, see Yang Guozhen, *Ming Qing tudi qiyue yanjiu* (Beijing, 1988), pp. 8–43.

9. See Pomeranz, 'Land Markets', for a summary.

10. Sifa Xingzhengbu, *Zhongguo min shang shi xiguan diaocha lu* (Originally compiled 1912; published Nanjing, 1930; reprinted Taibei, 1969). Pomeranz, 'Land Markets', 107–8, briefly describes the survey.

11. Pomeranz, 'Land Markets', 136–8, and accompanying notes (especially 147 n. 142), provides a summary. See also Yang, *Ming Qing tudi*, Li and Jiang, *Zhongguo dizhu*.

12. For data from the eighteenth-century Lower Yangzi, see Li and Jiang, *Zhongguo dizhu*, p. 291; Han Hengyu, 'Shilun Qingdai qianqi diannong yongdianquan de youlai ji qi xingzhi' ('An Introductory Discussion of the Origins and Nature of Tenants' Rights of Permanent Tenancy During the First Half of the Qing Dynasty'), *Qingshi luncong* 1 (1979), 38, 45; for the twentieth century, see Kathryn Bernhardt, *Rents, Taxes, and Peasant Resistance: The Lower Yangzi Region, 1840–1950* (Stanford, CA, 1992), p. 220. See also Li Wenzhi, *Ming Qing shidai fengjian tudi guanxi de songjie (The Loosening of Feudal Land Relationships in the Ming-Qing period)* (Beijing, 1993), p. 98; for Fujian and Taiwan see Chen Qiukun, *Qingdai Taiwan tu zhu diquan: guanliao, Handian yu an lishe ren de tudi bianqian* (Taibei, 1997), p. 161. All told, a secure tenant probably earned about 70 per cent of what a smallholder with a similar sized plot earned.

13. R. Bin Wong, *China Transformed: Historical Change and the Limits of European Experience* (Ithaca, NY, 1997), pp. 135–6.

14. Liu Cuirong, 'Demographic Constraint and Family Structure in Traditional Chinese Lineages, ca. 1200–1900', in Stevan Harrell, ed., *Chinese Historical Microdemography* (Berkeley, CA, 1995), p. 130, suggests 3.7 per cent.

15. James Lee and Cameron Campbell, *Fate and Fortune in Rural China: Social Organization and Population Behavior in Liaoning, 1774–1873* (Cambridge, 1997), pp. 58–83; James Lee and Wang Feng, *One Quarter of Humanity: Malthusian Mythologies and Chinese Realities* (Cambridge, MA, 1999), pp. 47–51.

16. Lee and Wang, *One Quarter of Humanity*, p. 50.

17. Elizabeth Perry, *Rebels and Revolutionaries in North China, 1845–1945* (Stanford, CA, 1980), p. 51.

18. For how some 'bare sticks' created unconventional marriages (with two men, one usually disabled, and one woman), see Matthew Sommer, 'Making Sex Work: Polyandry as a Survival Strategy in Qing Dynasty China', in Bryna Goodman and Wendy Larson, eds, *Gender in Motion: Divisions of Labor and Cultural Change in Late Imperial and Modern China* (Lanham, MD, 2005), pp. 29–54.

19. Charles Tilly, 'Demographic Origins of the European Proletariat', in David Levine, ed., *Proletarianization and Family History* (Orlando, FL, 1984), pp. 39–44.

20. See, for instance, James Millward, *Beyond the Pass: Economy, Ethnicity, and Empire in Qing Central Asia, 1759–1864* (Stanford, CA, 1998), pp. 206–7, 226, for the Qing preferring that not only soldiers but merchants on the Xinjiang frontier not bring their families; David Ownby, *Brotherhoods and Secret Societies in Early and Mid-Qing China: The Formation of a Tradition* (Stanford, CA, 1996), p. 13, for the Qing attempt to keep men from bringing their families to Taiwan.

21. On wages in China see Allen et al., ' Wages, Prices, and Living Standards', pp. 51–2; on the earnings of tenants versus proletarians, see Pomeranz, 'Living Standards'.

22. G. William Skinner, 'Regional Urbanization in Nineteenth Century China', in G. William Skinner, ed., *The City in Late Imperial China* (Stanford, CA, 1977), p. 226.

23. Li Bozhong, 'Cong "fufu bing zuo" dao "nan geng nu zhi"' ('From "Husband and Wife Work Together" to "Man Ploughs, Woman Weaves"'), *Zhongguo jingji shi yanjiu* 11 (1996), 99–107.

24. See, for instance, Kenneth Pomeranz, 'Women's Work and the Economics of Respectability', in Goodman and Larson, eds, *Gender in Motion*, pp. 234–9.

25. Susan Mann, 'Household Handicrafts and State Policy in Qing Times', in Jane Kate Leonard and John Watt, eds, *To Achieve Security and Wealth: The Qing State and the Economy* (Ithaca, NY, 1992), pp. 75–96; Francesca Bray, *Technology and Gender: Fabrics of Power in Late Imperial China* (Berkeley, CA, 1997), pp. 242–72.

26. Mann, 'Household Handicrafts', pp. 84–91.

27. Debin Ma, 'Modern Economic Growth', p. 6.

28. Allen et al., 'Wages, Prices, and Living Standards', pp. 51–2.
29. Pomeranz, 'Land Markets', 132; Anne Osborne, 'Property, Taxes, and State Protection of Rights', in Madeleine Zelin, Johnathan Ocko and Robert Gardella, eds, *Contract and Property in Early Modern China* (Stanford, CA, 2004), pp. 122–32.
30. Lee and Wang, *One Quarter of Humanity*, pp. 115–18.
31. Wang Yeh-chien, *Land Taxation in Imperial China, 1750–1911* (Cambridge, MA, 1973), pp. 84–109; Wong, *China Transformed*, pp. 118–22.
32. See, for example, Kenneth Pomeranz, *The Making of a Hinterland: State, Society, and Economy in Inland North China, 1853–1937* (Berkeley, CA, 1993), pp. 128–32, 154–6; Lillian Li, *Fighting Famine in North China: State, Market, and Environmental Decline, 1690s–1990s* (Stanford, CA, 2007), pp. 38–73; Wong, *China Transformed*, pp. 113–18; Susan Naquin and Evelyn Rawski, *Chinese Society in the Eighteenth Century* (New Haven, CT, 1987), p. 24; Sun Xiaofen, *Qingdai qianqi de yimin zhen (Migration to Sichuan in the First Half of the Qing Dynasty)* (Chengdu, 1997), pp. 30–4.
33. In addition to changes in Western science, at least north-west European handicrafts were more likely to be clustered in specialized districts and staffed by full-time workers fully detached from agriculture; these conditions encouraged information exchange, as did the journeyman system. See, for instance, Saito Osamu, *Puroto-Kōgyōka no jidai: Seiō to Nihon no hikakushi (The Age of Proto-Industrialization: A Comparative History of Western Europe and Japan)* (Tokyo, 1985); Markus Cerman and Sheilagh Ogilvie, eds, *European Proto-Industrialization* (Cambridge, 1996); S. R. Epstein and Maarten Prak, eds, *Guilds, Innovation, and the European Economy, 1400–1800* (Cambridge, 2008).
34. Pomeranz, *Great Divergence*, pp. 63–4, 225–6; Li Bozhong, *Jiangnan de zaoqi gongyehua (The Early Industrialization of the Yangzi Delta Region)* (Beijing, 2000), pp. 272–342.
35. Pomeranz, *Great Divergence*, pp. 62–5.
36. Data from Allen, 'Mr Lockyer Meets the Index Number Problem', pp. 6, 17. These numbers may differ from true averages, but not enough to affect the point being made here about the extremely high relative cost of fuel.
37. Wang Yeh-chien, 'Food Supply and Grain Prices in the Yangtze Delta in the Eighteenth Century', in *The Second Conference on Modern Chinese History* (Taibei, 1989), p. 429; Pomeranz, *Great Divergence*, pp. 34–5; Xu Dixin and Wu Chengming, *Zhongguo zibenzhuyi de mengya (The Sprouts of Capitalism in China)* (Beijing, 1985), pp. 272, 277.
38. Pomeranz, *Great Divergence*, pp. 323–6.
39. Ibid., pp. 244–6, 288, and accompanying notes.
40. Lillian Li, *Fighting Famine in North China*, pp. 38–73, 250–82.
41. Peter Perdue, *Exhausting the Earth: State and Peasant in Hunan, 1500–1850* (Cambridge, MA, 1987); Anne Osborne, 'The Local Politics

of Land Reclamation in the Lower Yangzi Highlands', *Late Imperial China* 15 (1994), 1–46.

42. Hakka are considered to be Han Chinese, but they constitute a fairly clearly marked subgroup with a different dialect and very little intermarriage with other Han. See Sow-Theng Leong, *Migration and Ethnicity in Chinese History: Hakkas, Pengmin, and Their Neighbors*, ed. Tim Wright (Stanford, CA, 1997).

43. This account of the origins of the White Lotus owes much to Wang Wensheng, 'White Lotus Rebels and South China Pirates: Social Crises and Political Changes in the Qing Empire, 1796–1810' (PhD dissertation, University of California, Irvine, 2008), pp. 70–148. See also Blaine Gaustad, 'Religious Sectarianism and the State in Mid-Qing China: Background to the White Lotus Uprising of 1796–1804' (PhD dissertation, University of California, Berkeley, 1994).

44. Ke Zhiming, *Fan tou jia: Qingdai Taiwan zuqun zhengzhi yu shufan diquan* (*Aboriginal Leaders: Ethnic Policy and the Land Rights of 'Cooked' Aborigines in Qing Dynasty Taiwan*) (Taibei, 2001), especially pp. 237–75; John Shepherd, *Statecraft and Political Economy on the Taiwan Frontier, 1600–1800* (Stanford, CA, 1993), pp. 308–62.

45. Millward, *Beyond the Pass*, pp. 219–25.

46. Compare David Atwill, *The Chinese Sultanate: Islam, Ethnicity and the Panthay Rebellion in Southwest China, 1856–1873* (Stanford, CA, 2006), pp. 48–83. For roughly parallel phenomena in Shaanxi, see Jonathan Lipman, *Familiar Strangers: A History of Muslims in Northwest China* (Seattle, 1997), pp. 103–15, 119.

47. See, for instance, Ownby, *Brotherhoods and Secret Societies in Early and Mid-Qing China*, pp. 29–54, 187–8, on the Lin Shuangwen Rebellion on Taiwan.

48. Lee and Wang, *One Quarter of Humanity*, p. 118.

49. Ping-ti Ho, *Studies on the Population of China, 1368–1953* (Cambridge, 1959), pp. 145–8.

50. On staff sizes see Bradly W. Reed, *Talons and Teeth: County Clerks and Runners in the Qing Dynasty* (Stanford, CA, 2000), pp. 45–51, 144–9. Reed's late nineteenth-century numbers are undoubtedly higher than averages for our period would be. There were 1,303 local governments for all of China in the mid to late Qing, governing a population of roughly 400,000,000. See Ch'u t'ung-tsu, *Local Government Under the Ch'ing* (Stanford, CA, 1962), p. 3.

51. A classic example is Susan Mann Jones and Philip Kuhn, 'Dynastic Decline and the Roots of Rebellion', in John K. Fairbank, ed., *The Cambridge History of China*, X.1 (Cambridge, 1978), pp. 110–13. For one of many surveys of 'gentry' activities in relation to local government, see Ch'u, *Local Government*, pp. 168–92.

52. See, for instance, Tsing Yuan, 'Urban Riots and Disturbances', in Jonathan Spence and John E. Wills Jr, eds, *From Ming to Ch'ing: Conquest, Region, and Continuity in Seventeenth-century China* (New Haven, CT, 1979), pp. 277–320; Atwill, *Chinese Sultanate*, pp. 67–9.

53. C. K. Yang , 'Some Preliminary Statistical Patterns of Mass Actions in Nineteenth-century China', in Frederic Wakeman Jr and Carolyn Grant, eds, *Conflict and Control in Late Imperial China* (Berkeley, CA, 1975), pp. 186–7.

54. See, for instance, Charles Tilly, 'Town and Country in Revolution', in John Wilson Lewis, ed., *Peasant Rebellion and Communist Revolution in Asia* (Stanford, CA, 1974), pp. 271–302, esp. pp. 288–91.

55. For Fujian, see Melissa Macauley, *Social Power and Legal Culture: Litigation Masters in Late Imperial China* (Stanford, CA, 1998), pp. 274–5. For some comparisons, see, for example, David Fryson, 'Blows and Scratches, Swords and Guns: Violence Between Men as Material Reality and Lived Experience in Early Nineteenth Century Lower Canada', paper presented at the annual meeting of the Canadian Historical Association, Sherbrooke, 1999 (http://www.hst.ulaval.ca/profs/dfyson/Violence. htm), accessed 23 March 2007, citing data for England, France, Canada, and the United States.

56. Thomas Gottschaung and Diana Lary, *Swallows and Settlers: The Great Migration from North China to Manchuria* (Ann Arbor, MI, 2000), p. 2.

57. Randall Dodgen, 'Hydraulic Evolution and Dynastic Decline: the Yellow River Conservancy, 1796–1855', *Late Imperial China* 12 (1991), 36–63; Lillian Li, *Fighting Famine in North China*, pp. 38–73, 250–66.

58. Chang Hsin-pao, *Commissioner Lin and the Opium War* (New York, 1970), pp. 19, 21, 34–5. All figures are very rough estimates. See also Jonathan Spence, 'Opium Smoking in Ch'ing China', in Wakeman and Grant, eds, *Conflict and Control in Late Imperial China*, pp. 148–54.

59. See generally David Bello, *Opium and the Limits of Empire: Drug Prohibition in the Chinese Interior, 1729–1850* (Cambridge, MA, 2005).

60. Chang, *Commissioner Lin*, pp. 36–46; Peng Zeyi, 'Yapian Zhan hou shinianjian yin gui qianjian bodong xia de Zhongguo jingji yu jieji guanxi' ('The Chinese Economy and Class Relations under the Impact of Trends towards Expensive Silver and Cheap Copper Cash in the Decade after the Opium War'), *Lishi yanjiu* 6 (1961), 40–68. For a contrary view, see Man-houng Lin, *China Upside Down: Currency, Society, and Ideologies, 1808–1856* (Cambridge, MA, 2006), pp. 72–114.

61. Compare, for instance, John Richards, *The Mughal Empire* (Cambridge, 1993), p. 86; Thomas Smith, *The Agrarian Origins of Modern Japan* (Stanford, CA, 1959), p. 160. See P. H. H. Vries, 'Governing Growth: A Comparative Analysis of the Role of the State in the Rise of the West', *Journal of World History* 13 (2002), 97 n. 92, for references to other estimates.

62. See, for example, Charles Tilly, *Coercion, Capital, and European States, AD 990–1992* (Malden, MA, 1992), pp. 122–6.

63. Millward, *Beyond the Pass*, pp. 225–35.

64. Fredric Wakeman Jr, 'Drury's Occupation of Macao and China's Response to Early Modern Imperialism', *East Asian History* 28 (2004), 27–34; Wang, 'White Lotus Rebels and South China Pirates', pp. 492–508.

65. Perdue, *China Marches West*, pp. 165, 409, 429–57.

66. Hostetler, *Qing Colonial Enterprise*; Perdue, *China Marches West*.

67. For Yongzheng era ambitions, see William Rowe, *Saving the World: Chen Hongmou and Elite Consciousness in Eighteenth Century China* (Stanford, CA, 2001), pp. 427–37, and Charles Patterson Giersch, *Asian Borderlands: The Transformation of Qing China's Yunnan Frontier* (Cambridge, MA, 2006), pp. 43–63; for the retreat, see Donald Sutton, 'Violence and Ethnicity on a Qing Colonial Frontier: Customary and Statutory Law in the Eighteenth-century Miao Pale', *Modern Asian Studies* 37 (2003), 71–7, who dates it to the accession of Qianlong in 1736, and Giersch, *Asian Borderlands*, pp. 111–22, who dates it significantly later.

68. James Millward, 'Coming onto the Map: Western Regions, Geography and Cartographic Nomenclature in the Making of Chinese Empire in Xinjiang', *Late Imperial China* 20 (1999), 61–98.

69. I discuss some of these briefly, and in comparative perspective, in Kenneth Pomeranz, 'Imperialism, Development, and "Civilizing" Missions, Past and Present', *Daedalus* 134 (April 2005), 34–8. See also Millward, 'Coming onto the Map'; Kuhn and Mann Jones, 'Dynastic Decline', pp. 156–60.

70. Bernhardt, *Rents, Taxes, and Peasant Resistance*, pp. 44–6.

71. Wang Yeh-chien, *Land Taxation*, p. 127; Dwight Perkins, 'Government as an Obstacle to Industrialization: The Case of Nineteenth-Century China', *Journal of Economic History* 27 (1967), 487, using late nineteenth-century data. By that time, revenue had probably tripled since the mid-eighteenth century, and population perhaps doubled.

72. Meaning those that belonged to the state rather than the imperial family – though the distinction was often blurry and became more so with time.

73. Evelyn Rawski, 'The Qing Formation and the Early Modern Period', in Lynn Struve, ed., *The Qing Formation in World-Historical Time* (Cambridge, MA, 2004), p. 214; Wang, *Land Taxation*, p. 80.

74. On flood control costs see Dodgen, 'Hydraulic Evolution and Dynastic Decline'; Dodgen, *Controlling the Dragon: Confucian Engineers and the Yellow River in Late Imperial China* (Honolulu, 2001); Li, *Fighting Famine in North China*, pp. 38–73. On stipends for bannermen, see Mark Elliott, *The Manchu Way: The Eight Banners and Ethnic Identity in Late Imperial China* (Stanford, CA, 2001), pp. 306–12, esp. p. 311.

75. Thomas Metzger, *The Internal Organization of the Chinese Bureaucracy* (Cambridge, MA, 1973), pp. 53–4, 58–61, 78–9, 291–3.

76. For a similar phenomenon of British propagandists railing against mercantilist measures (in this case in South Asia) not unlike those they engaged in at home, see C. A. Bayly *Imperial Meridian: The British Empire and the World, 1780–1830* (London, 1989), pp. 69–73.

77. Paul van Dyke, *The Canton Trade: Life and Enterprise on the China Coast, 1700–1845* (Hong Kong, 2005), pp. 95–115, 119.

78. Wang Yeh-chien, *Land Taxation*, p. 9.

79. Han Seunghyun, 'Re-inventing Local Tradition: Politics, Culture, and

Identity in Early Nineteenth-century Suzhou' (PhD dissertation, Harvard University, 2005).
80. Wong, *China Transformed*, p. 155; see also Rawski, 'Qing Formation', p. 214.
81. Sevket Pamuk, 'The Evolution of Financial Institutions in the Ottoman Empire, 1600–1914', *Financial History Review* 11 (2004), 18–19, indicates an increase from about 2–3 per cent of GDP in the eighteenth century to 5–6 per cent by the mid-nineteenth.
82. Gabriel Ardant, 'Financial Policy and Economic Infrastructure of Modern States and Nations', in Charles Tilly, ed., *The Formation of National States in Western Europe* (Princeton, NJ, 1975), p. 221.
83. Vries, 'Governing Growth', p. 95, and accompanying notes.
84. Central government silver revenues rose almost eightfold between 1850 and the fall of the dynasty in 1911, and quadrupled again by 1937. Even in gold that is more than a tripling by 1911, and almost a further doubling by 1937. The increase after 1901 was much larger still, because provincial and local revenues, which were trivial until the twentieth century, made up about 60 per cent of central government expenditures in 1936; that makes *total* government revenues in gold about ten times what they had been in 1850. The data come from scattered sources too numerous to list here, but principally Wei Guangqi, 'Qingdai houqi zhongyang jiquan caizheng tizhi de wajie' ('The Collapse of the Central Authority over the Fiscal System in the Late Qing Period'), *Jindai shi yanjiu* 1 (1986), 207–30, and Arthur N. Young, *China's Nation-building Effort, 1927–1937: The Financial and Economic Record* (Stanford, CA, 1971), esp. pp. 71, 435. Conversions to gold made using 'The Price of Gold, 1257–2007' (http://www.measuringworth.org/gold/), accessed 1 June 2009.
85. Wang Wensheng, 'White Lotus Rebels and South Coast Pirates', pp. 236–368. See esp. p. 302, noting that the three years of ineffective campaigning prior to Jiaqing's reforms cost more than the six years that followed.
86. Tilly, *Coercion, Capital, and European States*, pp. 103–26, 185–6.
87. A similar point is made with respect to events in 1730s China by Pierre Etienne Will in his review essay on Beatrice S. Bartlett, *Monarchs and Ministers: The Grand Council in Mid-Ch'ing China, 1723–1820* (1991), *Harvard Journal of Asiatic Studies* 54 (1994), 320–2.
88. Wong, *China Transformed*, pp. 113–16, 119–22.
89. Susan Mann, *Local Merchants and the Chinese Bureaucracy* (Stanford, CA, 1987), pp. 94–199; Wong, *China Transformed*, pp. 155–6; Wei Guangqi, 'Qingdai houqi'.
90. Pomeranz, *Making of a Hinterland*, pp. 138–52, 154–64, 201–11, 267–76.
91. On the expansion of sub-bureaucracies, see Reed, *Talons and Teeth*, pp. 45–61, 144–9. Exactly how relations between the state and local elites changed remains one of the most complex questions in nineteenth-century Chinese history; one influential formulation is Philip Kuhn,

Rebellion and Its Enemies in Late Imperial China: Militarization and Social Structure, 1796–1864 (Cambridge, MA, 1970).

The Age of Revolutions in Global Context: An Afterword

I have considered some of the issues I raise here in more detail in C. A. Bayly, 'An End to Revolution: "Reform" and "Reaction" in the Colonial World 1780–1830', in Richard Bessel, Nicholas Guyatt and Jane Rendall, eds, *War, Empire and Slavery, 1770–1830* (Basingstoke, forthcoming). I am grateful to the participants in this volume and in the preceding conference at the University of York for their insights.

1. I am grateful to Professor Crossley for elucidating this. See Pamela Crossley, *A Translucent Mirror: History and Identity in Qing Imperial Ideology* (Berkeley, CA, 1999).
2. John Brewer, *The Sinews of Power: War, Money, and the English State, 1688–1783* (London, 1989).
3. T. C. W. Blanning and Peter Warde, eds, *Reform in Great Britain and Germany 1750–1850* (Oxford, 1999); compare Blanning, *The French Revolution in Germany: Occupation and Resistance in the Rhineland 1792–1802* (Oxford, 1983).
4. Frederick Cooper, *Colonialism in Question: Theory, Knowledge, History* (Berkeley, CA, 2005).
5. David Armitage, *The Declaration of Independence: A Global History* (Cambridge, MA, 2007).
6. J. G. A Pocock, *The Machiavellian Moment: Florentine Political Thought and the Atlantic Republican Tradition*, 2nd edn (Princeton, NJ, 2003).
7. C. A. Bayly, 'Rammohan Roy and the Advent of Constitutional Liberalism in India', *Modern Intellectual History* 4 (2007), 25–41.
8. On which see the essays in C. A. Bayly and Eugenio Biagini, eds, *Giuseppe Mazzini and the Globalization of Democratic Nationalism, 1830–1920* (Oxford, 2008).
9. Christopher Leslie Brown, *Moral Capital: Foundations of British Abolitionism* (Chapel Hill, NC, 2006).
10. Philip A. Kuhn, *Soulstealers: The Chinese Sorcery Scare of 1768* (Cambridge, MA, 1990).

Further Reading

Introduction: The Age of Revolutions in Global Context, *c*.1760–1840 – Global Causation, Connection, and Comparison

The classic studies of the Age of Revolutions remain R. R. Palmer, *The Age of the Democratic Revolution: A Political History of Europe and America, 1760–1800*, 2 vols (Princeton, NJ, 1959–64), and Eric Hobsbawm, *The Age of Revolution, 1789–1848* (London, 1962). Neither engaged much with the broader literature on revolutions in world history but they can be usefully read alongside such important later works as Theda Skocpol, *States and Social Revolutions: A Comparative Analysis of France, Russia, and China* (Cambridge, 1979), Jack A. Goldstone, *Revolution and Rebellion in the Early Modern World* (Berkeley, CA, 1991), and Reinhart Koselleck, 'Historical Criteria of the Modern Concept of Revolution', in Koselleck, *Futures Past: On the Semantics of Historical Time*, trans. Keith Tribe (Cambridge, MA, 1985), pp. 39–54.

Joel Mokyr, *The Lever of Riches: Technological Creativity and Economic Progress* (New York, 1990), provides a useful overview of economic changes in the period. The more specific question of the 'Industrial Revolution' is discussed in Pat Hudson, *The Industrial Revolution* (London, 1992). Important perspectives from the history of science can be found in Lissa L. Roberts, Simon Schaffer and Peter Dear, eds, *The Mindful Hand: Inquiry and Invention from the Late Renaissance to Early Industrialization* (Amsterdam, 2007). Richard H. Grove, *Green Imperialism: Colonial Expansion, Tropical Island Edens, and the Origins of Environmentalism, 1600–1860* (Cambridge, 1995), is a pioneering work on ecology and empire in the period. Martin J. S. Rudwick, *Bursting the Limits of Time: The Reconstruction of Geohistory in the Age of Revolution* (Chicago, 2005), and Chenxi Tang, *The Geographic Imagination of Modernity: Geography, Literature, and Philosophy in German Romanticism* (Stanford, CA, 2008), explore changing conceptions of time and space.

In recent years, comparative studies of the Age of Revolutions in Europe and America have been mostly the province of cultural historians: see, for example, Colin Jones and Dror Wahrman, eds, *The Age of Cultural Revolutions, 1750–1850* (Berkeley, CA, 2002) and Leora Auslander, *Cultural Revolutions: Everyday Life and Politics in Britain, North America, and France* (Berkeley, CA, 2009). However, for a recent political synthesis in critical dialogue with Palmer, see Wim Klooster, *Revolutions in the Atlantic World: A Comparative History* (New York, 2009) and for novel perspectives on intellectual history, see Manuela Albertone and Antonino De Francesco, eds, *Rethinking the Atlantic World: Europe and America in the Age of Democratic Revolutions* (Basingstoke, 2009).

There have been various efforts to expand the analytical frameworks for considering the American, French, and Latin American revolutions in our period. The most profound are Franco Venturi, *The End of the Old Regime in Europe, 1768–1776: The First Crisis*, trans. R. Burr Litchfield (Princeton, NJ, 1989), and Venturi, *The End of the Old Regime in Europe, 1776–1789*, trans. Litchfield, 2 vols (Princeton, NJ, 1991). On the American Revolution, see, for example, David Brion Davis, *Revolutions: Reflections on American Equality and Foreign Liberations* (Cambridge, MA, 1990), Eliga H. Gould and Peter S. Onuf, eds, *Empire and Nation: The American Revolution in the Atlantic World* (Baltimore, 2005), P. J. Marshall, *The Making and Unmaking of Empires: Britain, India, and America* c.1750–1783 (Oxford, 2005), and David Armitage, *The Declaration of Independence: A Global History* (Cambridge, MA, 2007). On the French Revolution, see R. R. Palmer, *The World of the French Revolution* (New York, 1971), Joseph Klaits and Michael H. Haltzel, eds, *The Global Ramifications of the French Revolution* (Cambridge, 1994), two synthetic studies by Bailey Stone, *The Genesis of the French Revolution: A Global-Historical Perspective* (Cambridge, 1994) and *Reinterpreting the French Revolution: A Global-Historical Perspective* (Cambridge, 2002), and Juan Cole, *Napoleon's Egypt: Invading the Middle East* (New York, 2007). And on Iberian America in this period, see Lester D. Langley, *The Americas in the Age of Revolution, 1750–1850* (New Haven, CT, 1996), Jaime E. Rodríguez O., *The Independence of Spanish America* (Cambridge, 1998), Jeremy Adelman, *Sovereignty and Revolution in the Iberian Atlantic* (Princeton, NJ, 2006), and, especially, Adelman, 'An Age of Imperial Revolutions', *American Historical Review* 113 (2008), 319–40. Important starting points for integrating the Haitian Revolution into the Age of Revolutions are C. L. R. James, *The Black Jacobins: Toussaint L'Ouverture and the San Domingo Revolution*, 2nd edn (New York, 1963), and Robin Blackburn, 'Haiti, Slavery, and the Age of Democratic Revolution', *William and Mary Quarterly* 3rd ser. 63 (2006), 643–74. For comparisons among the American revolutions see 'AHR Forum: Revolutions in the Americas', *American Historical Review* 105 (2000), 92–152.

For the Middle East, Thomas Naff and Roger Owen, eds, *Studies in Eighteenth-century Islamic History* (Carbondale, IL, 1977), remains important, while Donald Quataert, *The Ottoman Empire, 1700–1922*, 2nd edn (Cambridge, 2005), considers Ottoman developments. For South Asia, see the important if controversial work of André Wink, *Land and Sovereignty in India: Agrarian Society and Politics under the Eighteenth-century Maratha Svarā jya* (Cambridge, 1986), as well as Jamal Malik, ed., *Perspectives of Mutual Encounters in South Asian History, 1760–1860* (Leiden, 2000). For useful comparative perspectives on Asia, see Leonard Blussé and Femme S. Gaastra, eds, *On the Eighteenth Century as a Category of Asian History: Van Leur in Retrospect* (Aldershot, 1998), and Jack A. Goldstone, 'Neither Late Imperial nor Early Modern: Efflorescences and the Qing Formation in World History', in Lynn A. Struve, ed., *The Qing Formation in World-Historical Time* (Cambridge, MA, 2004), pp. 242–302. In a global context, the classic work on 'European expansion' from a military-fiscal perspective remains that of Geoffrey Parker, *The Military Revolution: Military Innovation and the Rise of the West, 1500–1800*, 2nd edn (Cambridge, 1996).

The most illuminating attempts so far to place the Age of Revolutions in a wider global context are C. A. Bayly, *The Birth of the Modern World, 1780–1914: Global Connections and Comparisons* (Oxford, 2004), ch. 3, 'Converging Revolutions, 1780–1820', and John Darwin, *After Tamerlane: The Rise and Fall of Global Empire* (London, 2007), ch. 4, 'The Eurasian Revolution'. Also indispensable are C. A. Bayly, *Imperial Meridian: The British Empire and the World, 1780–1830* (London, 1989), and Bayly, 'The First Age of Global Imperialism, *c.*1760–1830', *Journal of Imperial and Commonwealth History* 26 (1998), 28–47. More recent works also see the decades on either side of 1800 as pivotal for the global economy and the fortunes of empires: for example, Kenneth Pomeranz, *The Great Divergence: China, Europe, and the Making of the Modern World Economy* (Princeton, NJ, 2000), Alan Frost, *The Global Reach of Empire: Britain's Maritime Expansion in the Indian and Pacific Oceans, 1764–1815* (Carlton, Victoria, 2003), Maya Jasanoff, *Edge of Empire: Lives, Culture, and Conquest in the East, 1750–1850* (New York, 2005), Jennifer Pitts, *A Turn to Empire: The Rise of Imperial Liberalism in Britain and France* (Princeton, NJ, 2005), Leonard Blussé, *Visible Cities: Canton, Nagasaki, and Batavia and the Coming of the Americans* (Cambridge, MA, 2008), Lisa Ford, *Settler Sovereignty: Jurisdiction and Indigenous People in America and Australia, 1788–1836* (Cambridge, MA, 2010), and Richard Bessel, Nicholas Guyatt and Jane Rendall, eds, *War, Empire and Slavery, 1770–1830* (Basingstoke, forthcoming).

Chapter 1: Sparks from the Altar of '76: International Repercussions and Reconsiderations of the American Revolution

The classic work on the global influence of the American Revolution, published several decades before Atlantic basin studies came into vogue, is R. R. Palmer, *The Age of the Democratic Revolution: A Political History of Europe and America, 1760–1800*, 2 vols (Princeton, NJ, 1959–64). Among books inspired by Palmer are Michael Durey, *Transatlantic Radicals and the Early American Republic* (Lawrence, KS, 1997), Andrew Jackson O'Shaughnessy, *An Empire Divided: The American Revolution and the British Caribbean* (Philadelphia, 2000), Lester D. Langley, *The Americas in the Age of Revolution, 1750–1850* (New Haven, CT, 1996), and David Armitage, *The Declaration of Independence: A Global History* (Cambridge, MA, 2007). Important recent books have spatially and temporally extended Palmer's Age of the Democratic Revolution. The most comprehensive and important are C. A. Bayly, *The Birth of the Modern World, 1780–1914: Global Connections and Comparisons* (Oxford, 2004), and P. J. Marshall, *The Making and Unmaking of Empires: Britain, India, and America, c.1750–1783* (Oxford, 2005).

How African Americans and Afro-Britons carried revolutionary ideology outside the new United States or influenced Europeans in extending universalistic concepts of freedom to the emancipation of serfs are explored in

Simon Schama, *Rough Crossings: Britain, the Slaves, and the American Revolution* (New York, 2006), Cassandra Pybus, *Epic Journeys of Freedom: Runaway Slaves of the American Revolution and Their Global Quest for Liberty* (Boston, 2006), Vincent Carretta, *Equiano the African: Biography of a Self-made Man* (Athens, GA, 2005), *Unchained Voices: An Anthology of Black Authors in the English-speaking World of the Eighteenth Century*, ed. Carretta (Lexington, KY, 1996), and Gary B. Nash and Graham Russell Gao Hodges, *Friends of Liberty: Thomas Jefferson, Tadeusz Kosciuszko, and Agrippa Hull: Three Patriots, Two Revolutions, and a Tragic Betrayal in the New Nation* (New York, 2008).

Chapter 2: The French Revolution in Global Context

New work on the French slave colonies during the French Revolution is appearing at a rapid rate. For an excellent introduction, see Laurent Dubois, *Avengers of the New World: The Story of the Haitian Revolution* (Cambridge, MA, 2004). A more focused and even more recent overview can be found in Miranda Frances Spieler, 'The Legal Structure of Colonial Rule during the French Revolution', *William and Mary Quarterly* 3rd ser. 66 (2009), 365–408. Although the influence of the French Revolution on the rest of Europe, the United States, and the Middle East has long been recognized, the European and Middle Eastern impact has not drawn as much as attention of late as the influence on slavery and the slave colonies. Some reflections on the long-term resonance of the French Revolution, including in twentieth-century Turkey, can be found in Carolina Armenteros, Tim Blanning, Isabel DiVanna and Dawn Dodds, eds, *Historicising the French Revolution* (Newcastle upon Tyne, 2008). Despite the flurry of recent research, much can be gained still from reading R. R. Palmer, *The Age of the Democratic Revolution: A Political History of Europe and America, 1760–1800*, 2 vols (Princeton, NJ, 1959–64). Palmer was the first to develop a coherent interwoven narrative of the events unfolding on both sides of the Atlantic Ocean.

Chapter 3: Revolutionary Exiles: The American Loyalist and French Émigré Diasporas

Within the vast historiographies of the American and French Revolutions, the literature on loyalist refugees and émigrés constitutes a decidedly small subfield. Ernest Daudet, *Histoire de l'émigration pendant la révolution française* (Paris, 1904–7), still stands out as a classic account of the emigration. The best overview of the emigration in English remains Donald Greer's *The Incidence of the Emigration During the French Revolution* (Cambridge, MA, 1951). Kirsty Carpenter, *Refugees of the French Revolution: Émigrés in London, 1789–1802* (Basingstoke, 1999), offers a splendid investigation of the émigré experience in Britain. Emigration to other parts of Europe is helpfully surveyed in Kirsty Carpenter and Philip Mansel, eds, *The French Émigrés in Europe and the Struggle Against Revolution, 1789–1814* (London, 1999). For émigrés in the

United States, Frances Sergeant Childs, *French Refugee Life in the United States, 1790–1800* (Baltimore, 1940), provides a useful if somewhat outdated touchstone; for more recent reflections see R. Darrell Meadows, 'Engineering Exile: Social Networks and the French Atlantic Community, 1789–1809', *French Historical Studies* 23 (2000), 67–102. The question of compensation for émigrés has been exhaustively treated by André Gain, *La Restauration et les biens des émigrés: la législation concernant les biens nationaux de seconde origine et son application dans l'Est de la France (1814–1832)* (Nancy, 1928); and by Almut Franke, *Le Milliard des émigrés: die Entschädigung der Emigranten im Frankreich der Restauration (1814–1830)* (Bochum, 1999).

Most of the foundational American scholarship on loyalism – such as Bernard Bailyn, *The Ordeal of Thomas Hutchinson* (Cambridge, MA, 1974), and Robert M. Calhoon, *The Loyalists in Revolutionary America* (New York, 1973) – explores loyalist intellectual and social history before and during the war. There is as yet no global history of the loyalist diaspora, but several works investigate the loyalist emigration in specific parts of the British Empire. Canada as a site of exodus has generated by far the most attention, and the best recent studies include Ann Gorman Condon, *The Loyalist Dream for New Brunswick: The Envy of the American States* (Fredericton, 1984), Norman J. Knowles, *Inventing the Loyalists: The Ontario Loyalist Tradition and the Creation of Usable Pasts* (Toronto, 1997), Neil MacKinnon, *This Unfriendly Soil: The Loyalist Experience in Nova Scotia, 1783–1791* (Kingston, 1986), and Janice Potter-MacKinnon, *While the Women Only Wept: Loyalist Refugee Women* (Montreal and Kingston, 1993). For loyalist refugees in Britain, see Mary Beth Norton, *The British-Americans: The Loyalist Exiles in England, 1774–1789* (Boston, 1972). For the Caribbean and Bahamas, see Wilbur H. Siebert, *The Legacy of the American Revolution to the West Indies and Bahamas* (Columbus, OH, 1913), and Gail Saunders, *Bahamian Loyalists and Their Slaves* (London, 1983). Mohawk loyalism has been most recently addressed by Alan Taylor, *The Divided Ground: Indians, Settlers, and the Northern Borderland of the American Revolution* (New York, 2006). Two pathbreaking studies of the black loyalist refugees written by James W. St G. Walker, *The Black Loyalists: The Search for a Promised Land in Nova Scotia and Sierra Leone, 1783–1870* (London, 1976), and Ellen Gibson Wilson, *The Loyal Blacks* (New York, 1976), have been supplemented by Cassandra Pybus's innovative *Epic Journeys of Freedom: Runaway Slaves of the American Revolution and Their Global Quest for Liberty* (Boston, 2006), which traces black loyalist trajectories to Sierra Leone and Australia.

In addition to these scholarly works, many of the revolutionary refugees' own memoirs, diaries, and papers have been published. A few representative French émigré memoirs include Duc de la Rochefoucauld-Liancourt, *Journal de voyage en Amérique et d'un séjour à Philadelphie, 1 octobre 1794–18 avril 1795*, ed. Jean Marchand (Baltimore, 1940), Marquise de la Tour du Pin, *Journal d'une femme de cinquante ans, 1778–1815*, ed. Aymar de Liedekerke-Beaufort, 2 vols (Paris, 1913), and Adèle d'Osmond de Boigne, *Mémoires de la comtesse de Boigne, née d'Osmond*, ed. Jean-Claude Berchet, 2 vols (Paris, 1986).

Important editions of American loyalist refugee papers include Samuel Curwen, *The Journal of Samuel Curwen, Loyalist*, ed. Andrew Oliver, 2 vols (Cambridge, MA, 1972), William Smith, *The Diary and Selected Papers, 1784–1793*, ed. L. F. S. Upton, 2 vols (Toronto, 1963–5), and *Winslow Papers, AD 1776–1826*, ed. W. O. Raymond, intr. George Athan Billias (Boston, 1972).

Chapter 4: Iberian Passages: Continuity and Change in the South Atlantic

The study of Iberian empires in the eighteenth century has been undergoing a large-scale renewal in recent years. But it has not altogether lost touch with classic formulations, which tended to emphasize the endurance of archaic patterns. For useful syntheses, see the essays by Dauril Alden, 'Late Colonial Brazil', in Leslie Bethell, ed., *The Cambridge History of Latin America*, II: *Colonial Latin America* (Cambridge, 1984), pp. 601–60, and John Lynch, 'The Origins of Spanish American Independence', in Bethell, ed., *The Cambridge History of Latin America*, III: *From Independence to c.1870* (Cambridge, 1985), pp. 3–50. There is little, however, that compares them explicitly. John Elliott's majestic *Empires of the Atlantic World: Britain and Spain in America, 1492–1830* (New Haven, CT, 2006) compares the Spanish and British empires: see in particular chs 9–12 on the eighteenth century. For closer examination of the trials of reform, see Stanley J. Stein and Barbara H. Stein, *Apogee of Empire: Spain and New Spain in the Age of Charles III* (Baltimore, 2003), Gabriel B. Paquette, *Enlightenment, Governance, and Reform in Spain and its Empire, 1759–1808* (Basingstoke, 2008), and on the Portuguese empire, Kenneth Maxwell, *Conflicts and Conspiracies: Brazil and Portugal, 1750–1808* (New York, 1970).

The 'revolutions' after 1810 have created a veritable mini-industry of books and monographs. The broadest is Jeremy Adelman, *Sovereignty and Revolution in the Iberian Atlantic* (Princeton, NJ, 2006), which casts the process in imperial terms. See also John Chasteen, *Americanos: Latin America's Struggle for Independence* (New York, 2008). Much of the recent debate has focused on Jaime Rodriguez O., *The Independence of Spanish America* (Cambridge, 1998). Among recent interpretations of the Portuguese empire see especially Kirsten Schultz, *Tropical Versailles: Empire, Monarchy, and the Portuguese Royal Court in Rio de Janeiro, 1808–1821* (New York, 2001). Examples of recent efforts to include the stories of slaves and indigenous peoples in the revolutionary process include Peter Blanchard, *Under the Flags of Freedom: Slave Soldiers and the Wars of Independence in Spanish South America* (Pittsburgh, 2008), Marixa Lasso, *Myths of Harmony: Race and Republicanism During the Age of Revolution, Colombia 1795–1831* (Pittsburgh, 2007), and Eric Van Young, *The Other Rebellion: Popular Violence, Ideology and the Mexican Struggle for Independence, 1810–1821* (Stanford, CA, 2001).

Chapter 5: The Caribbean in the Age of Revolution

Important overviews of Caribbean demography and economy in this period are provided in Stanley L. Engerman and Barry W. Higman, 'The Demographic Structure of the Caribbean Slave Societies in the Eighteenth and Nineteenth Centuries', and David Eltis, 'The Slave Economies of the Caribbean: Structure, Performance, Evolution and Significance', in Franklin W. Knight, ed., *General History of the Caribbean*, III (London, 1997), pp. 45–104, 111–23. For the political economy of slavery, see Part 2 of Robin Blackburn, *The Making of New World Slavery: From the Baroque to the Modern, 1492–1800* (London, 1997). Cuba's transformation is charted in Manuel Moreno Fraginals, *The Sugarmill: The Socioeconomic Complex of Sugar in Cuba*, trans. Cedric Belfrage (New York, 1976), Pablo Tornero Tinajero, *Crecimiento económico y transformaciones sociales: Esclavos, hacendados y comerciantes en la Cuba colonial (1760–1840)* (Madrid, 1996), and Allan Kuethe, *Cuba, 1753–1815: Crown, Military, and Society* (Knoxville, TN, 1986). Other valuable local studies include Barry Higman, *Slave Population and Economy in Jamaica, 1807–1834* (Cambridge, 1976), Alex van Stipriaan, *Surinaams Contrast: Roofbouw en Overleven in een Caraïbische Plantagekolonie, 1750–1863* (Leiden, 1993), Frédéric Régent, *La France et ses esclaves: De la colonisation aux abolitions* (Paris, 2007), and Dale Tomich, *Slavery in the Circuit of Sugar: Martinique and the World Economy, 1830–1848* (Baltimore, 1990). The 'decline thesis' advanced in Lowell Ragatz, *The Fall of the Planter Class in the British West Indies, 1763–1834* (Washington, DC, 1928), is dismantled in Seymour Drescher, *Econocide: British Slavery in the Era of Abolition* (Pittsburgh, 1977), and defended in Selwyn Carrington, *The Sugar Industry and the Abolition of the Slave Trade, 1775–1810* (Gainesville, FL, 2002).

Eric Williams, *Capitalism and Slavery* (1944; London, 1964), remains central to discussions of antislavery. Alternative analyses are offered in David B. Davis's *The Problem of Slavery in Western Culture* (Ithaca, NY, 1966) and *The Problem of Slavery in the Age of Revolution, 1770–1823* (Ithaca, NY, 1975), Seymour Drescher's *Capitalism and Antislavery: British Mobilization in Comparative Perspective* (New York, 1986) and *The Mighty Experiment: Free Labor versus Slavery in the British Emancipation* (New York, 2002). Less Anglo-focused are Robin Blackburn, *The Overthrow of Colonial Slavery, 1776–1848* (London, 1988), and Marcel Dorigny, ed., *The Abolitions of Slavery: From Léger-Félicité Sonthonax to Victor Schoelcher, 1793, 1794, 1848* (New York, 2003).

Revolutionary France's impact on the Caribbean is treated in David Barry Gaspar and David Geggus, eds, *A Turbulent Time: The French Revolution and the Greater Caribbean* (Bloomington, IN, 1997). For the colonial question in the French Revolution, see Yves Benot's *La Révolution française et la fin des colonies* (Paris, 1988) and *La démence coloniale sous Napoléon* (Paris, 1992), Jean Daniel Piquet, *L'émancipation des noirs dans la Révolution française (1789–1795)* (Paris, 2002), and Yves Benot and Marcel Dorigny, eds, *Rétablissement de l'esclavage dans les colonies françaises, 1802: Ruptures et continuités de la politique coloniale française, 1800–1830: Aux origines d'Haïti* (Paris, 2003).

Still essential reading on the Haitian Revolution are Thomas Madiou, *Histoire d'Haïti* (1847–8; rpt Port-au-Prince, 1989–91), and Beaubrun Ardouin, *Études sur l'histoire d'Haïti* (1853; rpt Port-au-Prince, 2007). The best modern narrative is Laurent Dubois, *Avengers of the New World: The Story of the Haitian Revolution* (Cambridge, MA, 2004). An older classic is C. L. R. James, *The Black Jacobins: Toussaint L'Ouverture and the San Domingo Revolution* (New York, 1938). Good collections of primary sources include Jacques Thibau, *Le temps de Saint-Domingue* (Paris, 1989), and Jeremy D. Popkin, *Facing Racial Revolution: Eyewitness Accounts of the Haitian Insurrection* (Chicago, 2008). On the revolution in Guadeloupe, see Laurent Dubois, *A Colony of Citizens: Revolution and Slave Emancipation in the French Caribbean, 1787–1804* (Chapel Hill, NC, 2004), and Frédéric Régent, *Esclavage, métissage, liberté: La révolution française en Guadeloupe, 1789–1802* (Paris, 2004). For military matters, see Michael Duffy, *Soldiers, Sugar and Seapower: The British Expeditions to the West Indies and the War against Revolutionary France* (Oxford, 1987), and for repercussions elsewhere, David Geggus, ed., *The Impact of the Haitian Revolution in the Atlantic World* (Columbia, SC, 2001), David Geggus and Norman Fiering, eds, *The World of the Haitian Revolution* (Bloomington, IN, 2009), and Eleázar Córdova-Bello, *La independencia de Haití y su influencia en Hispanoamérica* (Caracas, 1967). Slave resistance elsewhere is analysed in Seymour Drescher and Pieter Emmer, eds, *Who Abolished Slavery? Slave Revolts and Abolitionism* (New York, 2010), Michel Craton, *Testing the Chains: Resistance to Slavery in the British West Indies* (London, 1982), Emilia Viotti da Costa, *Crowns of Glory, Tears of Blood: The Demerara Slave Rebellion of 1823* (New York, 1994), and Matt Childs, *The 1812 Aponte Rebellion in Cuba and the Struggle Against Slavery* (Chapel Hill, NC, 2006).

Chapter 6: The Dynamics of History in Africa and the Atlantic 'Age of Revolutions'

The approach to Africa's past sketched in this chapter will not be found in an integrated form in the current literature on Africa. Existing survey treatments exhibit the projections of modern conceptualizations of 'states', 'stateless societies', and other structural abstractions – including the seventeenth and eighteenth centuries as dominated by 'the Atlantic slave trade' – that this treatment aims to replace with concepts closer to those of the people in Africa engaged with European and other merchants. My own statement of the epistemological principles at stake may be found in Joseph C. Miller, 'Beyond Blacks, Bondage, and Blame: Why a Multi-centric World History Needs Africa', *Historically Speaking* 5, 2 (2004), 7–31, with responses from several world historians. Further statements of these principles in the contexts of the modern historiography of Africa appear in Joseph C. Miller, 'History and Africa/Africa and History', *American Historical Review* 104 (1999), 1–32, and Miller, 'Life Begins at Fifty: African Studies Enters Its Second Half Century', *African Studies Review* 50 (2007), 1–35.

With regard to Africans' positions in the Atlantic world, the present chapter derives from a framework contextualizing Africans' ways in a concentric set of widening historical contexts in Miller, *Way of Death: Merchant Capitalism and the Angolan Slave Trade, 1730–1830* (Madison, WI, 1988). Among the other, and growing numbers of, approaches to locating Africa in Atlantic contexts are John K. Thornton, *Africa and Africans in the Making of the Atlantic World, 1500–1680*, 2nd edn (Cambridge, 1998), which takes account of Africa's differences from early-modern Europe in European terms but emphasizes military, economic, and political similarities (prior to about the end of the seventeenth century), and continuities in cultural terms from Africa into the Americas. Linda M. Heywood and Thornton have recently developed this emphasis on Africa's position in an Atlantic world through cultural continuities in their *Central Africans, Atlantic Creoles, and the Foundation of the Americas, 1585–1660* (Cambridge, 2007).

Africa's 'Atlantic presence' first emerged in the 1930s as a matter of African cultures in the Americas and has generated complex ongoing debates among anthropologists and historians, often phrased in terms of an ill (or multiply) defined notion of 'creolization'. The touchstone for those who emphasize the cultural destructiveness of the slave trade is Sidney Mintz and Richard Price, *An Anthropological Approach to the Afro-American Past* (Philadelphia, 1976), republished as *The Birth of African-American Culture: An Anthropological Perspective* (Boston, 1992). Another – no less contentious – approach to emphasizing transatlantic continuity is through 'ethnicity', referring to the appearance of allegedly African ethnic labels among Africans enslaved in the Americas. Recent and exemplary contributions along these lines include Michael A. Gomez, *Exchanging Our Country Marks: The Transformation of African Identities in the Colonial and Antebellum South* (Chapel Hill, NC, 1998), and Gwendolyn Midlo Hall, *Slavery and African Ethnicities in the Americas: Restoring the Links* (Chapel Hill, NC, 2005). For this author's approach, see my 'Retention, Re-invention, and Remembering: Restoring Identities through Enslavement in Africa and Under Slavery in Brazil', in José C. Curto and Paul E. Lovejoy, eds, *Enslaving Connections: Changing Cultures of Africa and Brazil during the Era of Slavery* (Amherst, NY, 2003), pp. 81–121.

Since the 1970s, Africa has entered Atlantic history largely through its position as the source of the captives taken into slavery in the Americas. The paradigmatic work remains Philip D. Curtin, *The Atlantic Slave Trade: A Census* (Madison, WI, 1969). Forty years of close demographic work on the volume and directions of the maritime trade have culminated in a searchable website detailing nearly 35,000 ships known to have carried slaves into the Atlantic from African shores (see http://www.slavevoyages.org/tast/index.faces). These data, based on an earlier and less-complete version of the database, are summarized in Herbert S. Klein, *The Atlantic Slave Trade* (Cambridge, 1999). One may get a feel for the enhancements in the current database in the collection of papers edited by the two principal coordinators of this massive and extremely careful compilation, David Eltis and David Richardson, eds, *Extending the Frontiers: Essays on the New Transatlantic Slave Trade Database*

(New Haven, CT, 2008). For a radically innovative and provocative sense of what this Middle Passage may have meant to those carried in the holds of these slaving ships, see Stephanie Smallwood, *Saltwater Slavery: A Middle Passage from Africa to the American Diaspora* (Cambridge, MA, 2007).

The terrors of this era in Africa, related to slaving, are now being elucidated in Africans' terms. Among a fast-growing literature see Sandra E. Greene, *Gender, Ethnicity and Social Change on the Upper Slave Coast: A History of the Anlo-Ewe* (Portsmouth, NH, 1996), Robert Martin Baum, *Shrines of the Slave Trade: Diola Religion and Society in Precolonial Senegambia* (Oxford, 1999), Elizabeth Isichei, *Voices of the Poor in Africa* (Rochester, NY, 2002), and Rosalind Shaw, *The Dangers of Temne Divination: Ritual Memories of the Slave Trade in West Africa* (Chicago, 2002). The enabling importance of European commercial capital remains to be explored fully, but see Paul E. Lovejoy and David Richardson, 'Trust, Pawnship, and Atlantic History: The Institutional Foundations of the Old Calabar Slave Trade', *American Historical Review* 104 (1999), 333–55, and their 'African Agency and the Liverpool Slave Trade', in David Richardson, Suzanne Schwarz and Anthony Tibbles, eds, *Liverpool and Transatlantic Slavery* (Liverpool, 2007), pp. 43–65. The political strategies and processes that form the focus of this chapter remain largely obscured by the fascination in the literature with 'kingdoms' and 'empires'. A recent and accessible survey exemplifying the limitations of including Africa in world history by rendering it in pseudo-modern terms is Erik Gilbert and Jonathan T. Reynolds, *Africa in World History from Prehistory to the Present* (Upper Saddle River, NJ, 2004). A comprehensive survey of the recent specialized literature on Africa's 'Atlantic era' is Philip D. Morgan, 'Africa and the Atlantic, *c*.1450 to 1820', in Jack P. Greene and Morgan, eds, *Atlantic History: A Critical Appraisal* (New York, 2009), pp. 223–48.

Chapter 7: Playing Muslim: Bonaparte's Army of the Orient and Euro-Muslim Creolization

More background on modern Egypt can be found in Afaf Lutfi al-Sayyid Marsot, *A History of Egypt: From the Arab Conquest to the Present*, 2nd edn (Cambridge, 2007), and the same author's *Egypt in the Reign of Muhammad Ali* (Cambridge, 1984). See also the relevant chapters in M. W. Daly, ed., *The Cambridge History of Egypt*, II: *Modern Egypt, from 1517 to the End of the Twentieth Century* (Cambridge, 1998). For the Mamluk beys, see Jane Hathaway, *The Politics of Households in Ottoman Egypt: The Rise of the Qazdaglis* (Cambridge, 2002). The French occupation is chronicled in Abd al-Rahman al-Jabarti, *Napoleon in Egypt: Al-Jabarti's Chronicle of the First Seven Months of the French Occupation, 1798*, trans. Shmuel Moreh (Princeton, NJ, 1995) and discussed at greater length in Juan Cole, *Napoleon's Egypt: Invading the Middle East* (New York, 2007).

For late eighteenth-century France as a context for the invasion and occupation of Egypt, see Howard G. Brown, *Ending the French Revolution:*

Violence, Justice, and Repression from the Terror to Napoleon (Charlottesville, VA, 2006). On imperial France and the Near East, see especially L. Carl Brown and Matthew S. Gordon, eds, *Franco-Arab Encounters: Studies in Memory of David C. Gordon* (Beirut, 1996), and Leila Tarazi Fawaz and C. A. Bayly, with Robert Ilbert, eds, *Modernity and Culture: From the Mediterranean to the Indian Ocean* (New York, 2002).

Chapter 8: Imperial Revolutions and Global Repercussions: South Asia and the World, c.1750–1850

Readers will find references to many relevant works in the endnotes to my chapter. Rather than repeating myself, I will mainly list different works here, some of which point to themes that are neglected in my piece. A different approach to South Asia in the Age of Revolutions might have focused more on changing forms of resistance, social protest and violent rebellion. Notable works include Ranajit Guha, *Elementary Aspects of Peasant Insurgency in Colonial India* (Oxford, 1983), Eric Stokes, *The Peasant Armed: The Indian Revolt of 1857* (Oxford, 1986), Ajay Skaria, *Hybrid Histories: Frontiers, Forests and Wildness in Western India* (Delhi, 1999), Willam R. Pinch, *Warrior Ascetics and Indian Empires* (Cambridge, 2006), and C. A. Bayly, 'The British Military-Fiscal State and Indigenous Resistance', in Lawrence Stone, ed., *An Imperial State at War 1689–1815* (London, 1994), pp. 322–54. C. A. Bayly, *Origins of Nationality in South Asia: Patriotism and Ethical Government in the Making of Modern India* (Delhi, 1998), and Rajat Ray, *The Felt Community: Commonalty and Mentality Before the Emergence of Indian Nationalism* (Delhi, 2003), locate the roots of national sentiment in discourses of ethical government and in 'regional patriotisms' forged in the age of imperial revolutions.

For a helpful introduction to the history of the Mughal Empire, see Muzaffar Alam and Sanjay Subrahmanyam, eds, *The Mughal State, 1526–1750* (Delhi, 1998). For South Asia in relation to early modern Indian ocean networks, see K. N. Chaudhuri, *The Trading World of Asia and the English East India Company 1600–1760* (Cambridge, 1978), and Ashin Das Gupta, *India and the Indian Ocean World: Trade and Politics* (Delhi, 2004). For a survey of the rise of British power in India, together with interesting visual materials, see C. A. Bayly, ed., *The Raj: India and the British, 1600–1947* (London, 1990). 'The Colonial Transition: South Asia 1780–1840', was reconsidered in a special issue of *Modern Asian Studies* 38 (2004), edited by Ian J. Barrow and Douglas E. Haynes. Samples from a vast and contentious literature on the economic impact of colonial conquests in South Asia are included in Asiya Siddiqi, ed., *Trade and Finance in Colonial India, 1750–1860* (Delhi, 1995), and G. Balachandran, ed., *India and the World Economy, 1850–1950* (Delhi, 2003). For British India's role within global networks of scientific knowledge, see Richard Drayton, *Nature's Government: Science, Imperial Britain and the 'Improvement' of the World* (New Haven, CT, 2000), Richard H. Grove, *Green Imperialism: Colonial Expansion, Tropical Island Edens, and the Origins of*

Environmentalism, 1600–1860 (Cambridge, 1995), and Kapil Raj, *Relocating Modern Science: Circulation and the Construction of Knowledge in South Asia and Europe* (Basingstoke, 2007).

Too few works have treated the rich subject of intra-European encounters in South Asia, and how conceptions of 'Europeanness' were articulated in the region; notable exceptions include Holden Furber, *Rival Empires of Trade in the Orient* (Minneapolis, 1976), Furber, *Private Fortunes and Company Profits in the India Trade in the Eighteenth Century* (Aldershot, 1997), and Maya Jasanoff, *Edge of Empire: Lives, Culture and Conquest in the East, 1750–1850* (New York, 2005). European observers with ringside seats on the 'imperial revolutions' of South Asia can be studied in *A European Experience of the Mughal Orient: The I'jaz-i Arsalani: Persian Letters (1773–1779) of Antoine-Louis Henri Polier*, ed. Muzaffar Alam and Seema Alavi (Delhi, 2001), *A Man of the Enlightenment in Eighteenth Century India: The Letters of Claude Martin 1766–1800*, ed. Rosie Llewellyn-Jones (Delhi, 2003), and Linda Colley, *The Ordeal of Elizabeth Marsh: A Woman in World History* (London, 2007). For Indian travellers and travel writers in this period see Muzaffar Alam and Sanjay Subrahmanyam, *Indo-Persian Travels in the Age of Discoveries 1400–1800* (Cambridge, 2007), Michael Fisher, *Counterflows to Colonialism: Indian Travellers and Settlers in Britain* (Delhi, 2004), and Tapan Raychaudhuri, *Europe Reconsidered: Perceptions of the West in Nineteenth Century Bengal*, 2nd edn (Delhi, 2002). Increasing numbers of Indians were coerced into travelling overseas as convicts, slaves, or indentured labourers: for convicts, see Clare Anderson, 'Sepoys, Servants and Settlers: Convict Transportation in the Indian Ocean, 1787–1945', in Frank Dikotter and Ian Brown, eds, *Cultures of Confinement: A History of the Prison in Africa, Asia and Latin America* (London, 2007), pp. 185–220; on slavery, see Indrani Chatterjee and Richard Maxwell Eaton, eds, *Slavery and South Asian History* (Bloomington, IN, 2006).

An important strand of recent research is rethinking the place of South Asia within global intellectual history, moving away from conventional emphases on the diffusion or imposition of 'colonizing ideas' from Europe: see the special issue of *Comparative Studies of South Asia, Africa and the Middle East* 24 (2004), on 'Forms of Knowledge in Early Modern South Asia', edited by Sheldon Pollock; a special edition of *Modern Intellectual History* 4 (2007), on 'An Intellectual History for India', edited by Shruti Kapila; Jon E. Wilson, *The Domination of Strangers: Modern Governance in Eastern India* (Basingstoke, 2008); and Michael S. Dodson, *Orientalism, Empire and National Culture: India 1770–1870* (Basingstoke, 2007).

Chapter 9: Revolutionary Europe and the Destruction of Java's Old Order, 1808–1830

For further reading on the process of cultural and mystic synthesis between Islam and Javanese society exemplified by the life of Prince Diponegoro (1785–1855), see M. C. Ricklefs, *Mystic Synthesis in Java: A History of*

Islamization from the Fourteenth to the Early Nineteenth Centuries (Norwalk, CT, 2006), Ricklefs, *Polarising Javanese Society: Islamic and Other Visions (c. 1893–1930)* (Singapore, 2007), and Peter Carey, *The Power of Prophecy: Prince Dipanagara and the End of an Old Order in Java, 1785–1855* (Leiden, 2007). The wider global effects of the colonial 'tsunami' wrought by the twin industrial and political revolutions of late eighteenth-century Europe can best be explored in C. A. Bayly, *Imperial Meridian: The British Empire and the World, 1780–1830* (London, 1989), Bayly, *The Birth of the Modern World, 1780–1914: Global Connections and Comparisons* (Oxford, 2004), and Kenneth Pomeranz, *The Great Divergence: China, Europe and the Making of the Modern World Economy* (Princeton, NJ, 2000). For comparative studies of the transitions from mestizo 'cultural' fusion between Europe and Asia and the 'high' colonial period, see William Dalrymple, *White Mughals: Love and Betrayal in Eighteenth-century India* (London, 2002), Jean Gelman Taylor, *The Social World of Batavia: European and Eurasian in Dutch Asia* (Madison, WI, 1983), and Ulbe Bosma and Remko Raben, *Being 'Dutch' in the Indies: A History of Creolization and Empire, 1500–1920* (Singapore, 2008).

On the role of the Chinese in Java, see Peter Carey, 'Changing Javanese Perceptions of the Chinese in Central Java, 1755–1825', *Indonesia* 37 (1984), 1–48, and the fascinating memoir of a schoolteacher from Fujien province who lived on the north coast of Java in the mid-eighteenth century: Ong Tae-Hae [Wang Dahai], *The Chinaman Abroad: Or a Desultory Account of the Malayan Archipelago*, ed. and trans. W. H. Medhurst (Shanghai, 1849), available online at http://digital.library.cornell.edu/cgi/t/text/text-idx?c=sea;idno=sea056. James Rush, *Opium to Java: Revenue Farming and Chinese Enterprise in Colonial Indonesia, 1860–1910* (Ithaca, NY, 1990), has important information on the origins of the colonial opium farm. M. C. Ricklefs, *Jogjakarta under Sultan Mangkubumi, 1749–1792: A History of the Division of Java* (Oxford, 1974), ch. IX, explores the Javanese understanding of the role of the pre-nineteenth century Dutch in Java and the political division of the island. For a masterly overview of the traditional Javanese administration, see Soemarsaid Moertono, *State and Statecraft in Old Java: A Study of the Later Mataram Period, 16th to 19th Century* (Ithaca, NY, 1968). John Bastin's two monographs on the period of the British administration (1811–16), *Raffles' Ideas on the Land Rent System and the Mackenzie Land Tenure Commission* ('s-Gravenhage, 1954) and *The Native Policies of Sir Stamford Raffles in Java and Sumatra* (Oxford, 1957), are still useful. Vincent Houben, *Kraton and Kumpeni: Surakarta and Yogyakarta 1830–1870* (Leiden, 1994), covers the immediate aftermath of the Java War on the basis of both Dutch and Javanese sources.

Chapter 10: Their Own Path to Crisis? Social Change, State-building and the Limits of Qing Expansion, c.1770–1840

On the White Lotus, see Barend Ter Haar, *The White Lotus Teaching in Chinese Religious History* (Honolulu, 1999); on their largest uprising, see Blaine

Gaustad, 'Religious Sectarianism and the State in Mid-Qing China: Background to the White Lotus Uprising of 1796–1804' (PhD dissertation, University of California, Berkeley, 1994). A very provocative discussion of Qing reactions to the White Lotus and subsequent reforms is Wang Wensheng, 'White Lotus Rebels and South China Pirates: Social Crises and Political Changes in the Qing Empire, 1796–1810' (PhD dissertation, University of California, Irvine, 2008). A detailed account of another, smaller, White Lotus uprising in our period is Susan Naquin, *Millenarian Rebellion in China: The Eight Trigrams Uprising of 1813* (New Haven, CT, 1976). Military affairs during this period have been understudied, but Philip Kuhn, *Rebellion and Its Enemies in Late Imperial China: Militarization and Social Structure, 1796–1864* (Cambridge, MA, 1970), is a landmark study of the relationships among local militia, Qing armies, state policy, and the transformation of the rural elite.

There are many good case studies of Qing policy on frontiers and ethnic minorities, but no single synthetic work. On Taiwan, see John Shepherd, *Statecraft and Political Economy on the Taiwan Frontier, 1600–1800* (Stanford, CA, 1993). On the Miao, see Donald Sutton, 'Violence and Ethnicity on a Qing Colonial Frontier: Customary and Statutory Law in the Eighteenth-century Miao Pale', *Modern Asian Studies* 37 (2003), 41–80. For Yunnan, see David Atwill, *The Chinese Sultanate: Islam, Ethnicity, and the Panthay Rebellion in Southwest China, 1856–1873* (Stanford, CA, 2005); though focused on a later period, its background chapters have much to say about ours. For the north-west, see James Millward, *Beyond the Pass: Economy, Ethnicity, and Empire in Qing Central Asia, 1759–1864* (Stanford, CA, 1998), and Peter Perdue, *China Marches West: The Qing Conquest of Central Eurasia* (Cambridge, MA, 2005); Perdue's work mostly covers an earlier period, but is extraordinarily rich. Joseph Fletcher, 'Ch'ing Inner Asia c.1800', in John K. Fairbank, ed., *The Cambridge History of China*, X.1 (Cambridge, 1978), pp. 35–106, remains a very useful general survey. The Qing rulers belonged to an ethnic minority themselves, and Manchu studies have boomed in the past twenty years. Two important works with different viewpoints are Pamela Crossley, *A Translucent Mirror: History and Identity in Qing Imperial Ideology* (Berkeley, CA, 1999), and Mark Elliott, *The Manchu Way: The Eight Banners and Ethnic Identity in Late Imperial China* (Stanford, CA, 2001).

This chapter's analysis of Qing political economy is developed further in Kenneth Pomeranz, 'Chinese Development in Long-run Perspective', *Proceedings of the American Philosophical Society* 152 (2008), 83–100; a book-length version is in progress. On Qing economic and political ideas, see R. Bin Wong, *China Transformed: Historical Change and the Limits of European Experience* (Ithaca, NY, 1997), and Pierre Etienne Will, 'Discussions about the Market-place and the Market Principle in Eighteenth-Century Guangdong', *Zhongguo haiyang fazhan shilun wenji* 7 (Taibei, 1989), pp. 323–89. The best English treatment of taxation remains Wang Yeh-chien, *Land Taxation in Imperial China, 1750–1911* (Cambridge, MA, 1973), though there is important later work in Chinese. On trends, see Robert Marks, *Tigers, Rice, Silk,* and Silt: *Environment and Economy in Late Imperial South China* (Cambridge, 1997), Peter Perdue, *Exhausting the Earth: State and Peasant in Hunan, 1500–1850* (Cambridge, MA, 1987), Anne Osborne, 'The Local Politics of Land Reclamation in the Lower Yangzi Highlands', *Late Imperial China* 15 (1994), 1–46, and, for a grand historical sweep, Mark Elvin, *The Retreat of the Elephants: An Environmental History of China* (New Haven, CT, 2004). The issue is placed in a global framework by Kenneth Pomeranz, *The Great Divergence: China, Europe, and the Making of a Modern World Economy* (Princeton, NJ, 2000). On Qing attempts to stabilize both ecology and society in the pre-Taiping period, see Randall Dodgen, *Controlling the Dragon: Confucian Engineers and the Yellow River in Late Imperial China* (Honolulu, 2001), Pierre-Etienne Will and R. Bin Wong, *Nourish the People: The State Civilian Granary System in China, 1650–1850* (Ann Arbor, MI, 1991), Lillian Li, *Fighting Famine in North China: State, Market, and Environmental Decline, 1690s–1990s* (Stanford, CA, 2007), and the sources noted above.

The defining works on the Qing monarchy generally emphasize the period slightly before ours. For how government worked at its most effective, see Beatrice Bartlett, *Monarchs and Ministers: The Grand Council in Mid-Ch'ing China, 1723–1820* (Berkeley, CA, 1991); a revealing and beautifully written case study from the early part of that era is Jonathan Spence, *Treason by the Book* (New York, 2001). Philip Kuhn, *Soulstealers: The Chinese Sorcery Scare of 1768* (Cambridge, MA, 1990), uses another case study to illuminate later, more troubled, emperor–bureaucrat relationships. William Rowe, *Saving the World: Chen Hongmou and Elite Consciousness in Eighteenth-century China* (Stanford, CA, 2001), looks at administration and ideology through a biography of one of the era's most important officials. Wang Wensheng's analyses of post-1796 reform, noted above, build on two important inquiries into why Qing statecraft became much less effective by the end of our period (while partly dissenting from their pessimism). James Polachek, *The Inner Opium War* (Cambridge, MA, 1992), argues that the increasing influence of elite literati networks helped to produce disastrous policies. Susan Mann Jones and Philip Kuhn, 'Dynastic Decline and the Roots of Rebellion', in Fairbank, ed., *Cambridge History of China*, X.1, pp. 107–62, is a remarkably broad-ranging overview of how the mid-nineteenth century turned disastrous; though subsequent research has modified many of its details, it remains essential for anyone interested in this period.

Index

abolitionism
  and the Caribbean 88–91
  dominant Europe-centred narratives
    on 88
  influence of Haitian Revolution on
    27, 41, 86, 89, 90, 91
Adams, John xiii, 7, 8, 14, 40–1
Adelman, Jeremy xxii, 56, 59, 146
Africa xviii, 101–24, 210
  and Atlantic commercialization/
    commerce 101, 102, 105,
    114–19, 121–2, 124
  commodities traded with Europeans
    115
  'communal ethos' 101, 105, 111,
    112–13, 114, 117, 118, 119, 123,
    124
  development of major trading
    networks 116
  early trade in 111
  emergence of warrior polities
    117–18
  European commercial investment in
    108
  financing of African merchants by
    European credit 117–18, 119,
    120, 123
  gold sources 108, 115
  historical dynamics of commercial
    capital in 110–14
  historical dynamics of debt 119–20
  increase in competitive individuation
    and violence 116–17
  parallels with Europe 121–4
  populist uprisings 117
  slavery 108, 110, 117–18, 119, 121,
    124
  and Soninke traders 111–12, 116
'Age of Revolutions'
  origin of term xii–xiii

Algeria 210
Aliens Act (1793) 48, 49
Allen, Richard 9
American loyalists 37–58
  absence of in United States
    historiography 39
  black 41, 46, 47, 57
  in Britain 55
  British relief programme for 46–7
  comparison with French émigrés
    50–7
  destination of migrants 46, 47
  impact of in new settings 47
  indemnification for property losses
    46–7
  migration of and numbers involved
    38–9, 41, 42, 46
  parallels and differences between
    French émigrés and 50–1
  persecution of and legislation against
    42–3
  reasons for migrating 42
  response to measures against 43
  role played in reconfiguration of
    imperial government in Canada
    47, 53
  similarities with Saint Domingue
    émigrés 51–2
  stereotyping of 39
American Revolution xii, xiii, xv,
  xxix, 1–9, 37, 51, 211
  contrast between French Revolution
    and 38, 51
  impact of on British Empire 52–3,
    56
  international impact of 2–3
  migration of American loyalists see
    American loyalists
  Palmer's view of 1
  perception of as civil war 39

American Revolution – *continued*
reasons for muted resonance in
Atlantic world and beyond
4–5
and slavery issue 3, 4–19
spread of key elements of ideology of
1
American War of Independence 2–3
Americas 62, 81, 106, 108
map 67
slave trade 66
unrest in 1780s 64
see also individual countries
Amiens, Peace of (1802) 50, 68, 169
Anderson, Benedict 35
Anglo-Dutch War, Fourth (1780–4)
168
Anglo-Mysore War (1787–9) 178
Arblay, general Alexandre d' 49
Aristotle 139, 140
Armistead, James 10–11
Armitage, David xii, 31, 98, 213
*The Declaration of Independence: A
Global History* 2
*The Ideological Origins of the British
Empire* 28–9
Arnold, Benedict 37, 47
Artigas, José 78
Atlantic commerce/commercialization
and Africa 101, 102, 105, 114–19,
121–2, 124
Auckland, George Eden, 1st earl of
156
Aurangzeb, Emperor 146
Averröes (Ibn Rushd) 139
Avicenna (Ibn Sina) 139
Azimabad xiii

Bahamas
settlement of American loyalists
47
Bailyn, Bernard 41–2
al-Bakri, Sheikh 'Ali 134–5
Balkans xxviii
Bancroft, Edward 17

'bare sticks' 192
Batavian Legion 172
Batavian Republic 21, 168
Batsányi, István
'On the Changes in France' xxiii
Bayly, C. A. xix, 30, 31, 33, 34, 35, 61,
126, 157–8, 176, 209
The Birth of the Modern World 3–4,
145–6
Bazin, Louis xvi
Beaumetz, Bon Albert de 49
Beaumont, Élie de 8
Beccaria, Cesare 31
Belgrano, Manuel 69
Benezet, Anthony 7, 9
Bengal xvi, 146, 158, 211
conquest of by East India Company
xii–xiii, 145, 147, 149
Benot, Yves 92, 93
La Révolution française 23
Bentham, Jeremy 6
Benton, Lauren 61
Bernier, François xv, xvi
Bernoyer, François 134, 143
Biassou, Georges 97
black loyalists 41, 46, 47, 57
Blackburn, Robin 26, 27, 89, 92, 93,
96, 97
Blanning, T. C. W. 212
Bogle, George 160
Boigne, Adèle d'Osmond de 49
Bolívar, Simón 27, 75, 78–9, 99
Bonaparte, Joseph xxx
Bonaparte, Louis 169
Bonaparte, Napoleon *see* Napoleon
'Book of Negroes, The' 46
Bose, Sugata 159, 163
Bosnia xxvii
Botany Bay 53
Bowen, Huw 155
Boxer Rebellion (1898–1901) xxxii
Brazil 64, 66, 71, 74, 76–7, 78, 80, 86,
107
Brewer, John 211
'brig men' 113

Brissot de Warville, Jacques Pierre   16
Britain
  abolition of slavery in colonies (1833)
    84, 85, 91
  abolition of slave trade (1807)   19,
    212
  American loyalists in and relief
    programme for   46–7, 55
  and American Revolution   2
  cotton industry   144
  French émigrés in   48–9, 52, 54,
    55–6
  and India *see* India
  industrialization   144
  invasion and occupation of Java
    (1811–16)   56, 167, 169, 175,
    176–80, 187
  sponsoring of émigré landing at
    Quiberon (1795)   48
  support of French Catholic priests
    55
  trade with Asia   154
British Empire   52, 56–7, 147,
  210–11
  expansion of   56
  impact of American Revolution on
    52–3, 56
  impact of French wars on   56
Brown, Christopher L.   215
Buffon, Georges Louis Leclerc, comte
  de   12
Burke, Edmund   25, 32, 55, 147, 148
Burlamaqui, Jean-Jacques   31
Burma   162, 189, 215
Burney, Charles   55
Burney, Fanny (Madame d'Arblay)   49,
  55

Cádiz, constitution of (1810)   213
Calcutta   162
Camus, Albert   210
Canada
  black loyalists in   47, 53
Carey, Peter   xxvi, 167
Caribbean   xviii–xix, 83–100

and abolitionism   88–91
colonial rule   83–4, 99
decline in economic and geopolitical
  importance   85–6, 100
decline in slave population   86
free coloured activism   87, 88, 93,
  94
impact of abolition of legal racial
  discrimination in colonies
  87–8
influence of events in on French
  politics   28
map   90
revolutionary change   86–7
and slavery   27, 28, 83, 84–5, 88–91,
  100
sugar production   85, 86
see also Haitian Revolution; Saint
  Domingue
Cartwright, John   7
Castlereagh, Robert Stewart, viscount
  78
Catherine II the Great, Empress   xvii,
  212
Catholics
  targeting of in Britain   55
  see also non-juring priests
causation   xix, xxix–xxx
Césaire, Aimé   92
Ceylon   211, 213, 216
Chapelain, Jean   xv–xvi
Charles IV, King of Spain   xxx
Charles X, King of France (Comte
  d'Artois)   44, 48, 50
Chastellux, François Jean, marquis de
  12
Chevallier, Pierre Frederic Henri   184
China   xxvi, 160
  map   198–9
  see also Qing empire
Chinese, in Java   180–6
Christophe, Henry   97, 98
Civil Constitution of the Clergy (1790)
  42, 44
civil war(s)

African 116
American 216
American and French Revolutions as 38, 39, 51
English 42
Spanish American 60, 70–1, 81–2
Clarkson, Thomas 16
Clive, Robert xiii, xvi, 187
Coatsworth, John H. 2
Cobb, Richard 40
Cole, Juan xxvi, 125, 159, 164
Colwill, Elizabeth 26, 28
commercialization
 Africa and Atlantic 101, 102, 105, 114–19, 121–2, 124
 history of process xviii, 101, 105–10
Committee for the Affairs of East Indian Trade and Colonies 168
Committee of Public Safety 49
'communal ethos', African 101, 105, 111, 112–13, 114, 117, 118, 119, 123, 124
Compagnie des Indes 29, 159
comparison xxiii, xxxi, 152, 165–6, 203–8
Condorcet, Jean-Antoine-Nicolas de Caritat, marquis de 8, 12, 13, 16, 28
 Reflections on Negro Slavery 8
Constant, Benjamin 214
Constitutional Act (1791) 53
Constitutional Convention (US) 9–10
constitutionalism 60, 61
constitutions xii, 213–14
Continental Friends of Liberty 6
Cortés, Hernán 107
Cosway, Maria 15–16
Cosway, Richard 16
Council of the Indies (Spanish) 66
Coutinho, José Joaquim da Cunha Azeredo 69
Craton, Michael 89
creolization, French-Muslim xxvii, 125–42
crisis, model of xix, xxii

see also General Crisis, World Crisis
Crossley, Pamela 211
Crouzet, François xxv
Cuba 27, 84, 85, 86
Cugoano, Ottobah 16
 Thoughts and Sentiments on the Evil of Slavery 16
cultural factors xxv

Daendels, Willem 167, 169, 172–6, 178, 187
Danton, Georges 29
Darwin, John xix
Davis, David Brion 15, 88
Day, Thomas 7, 8
Declaration of Independence, US (1776) 4, 6, 17, 21, 213
Declaration of Independence, Haitian (1804) 98
Declaration of the Rights of Man and Citizen (1789) 22, 31, 36, 94–5
decolonization xii, 83
Démeunier, Jean Nicolas 15
Deschamps, Léon 91
Deshpande, Prachi 151
Dessalines, Jean-Jacques 97, 98
Desvernois, Nicolas Philibert, baron 131
Diponegoro, Pangéran 170, 171–2, 180, 187
divine-right monarchy 129
Doguereau, Jean-Pierre 138
Dominican Republic (Santo Domingo) 84
Douglass, Frederick 19
Drake, Francis 62
Drescher, Seymour 88, 89, 91, 93
dress
 and French Revolution 34–5
Dubois, Laurent 28, 93, 97
Duchet, Michèle 88
Dundas, Henry, 1st viscount Melville 158
Dunmore, John Murray, 4th earl of 6
Durkheim, Emile 34
Dutch *see* Holland

Dutch East India Company (VOC) 167, 168
Dutch West India Company 107

East Asia xxvi
East India Company xiii, 49, 148, 153, 162, 211
American loyalists in army of 47
closer supervision of under India Act 53
conquest and rule of Bengal xii–xiii, 145, 147, 149
dismantling of commercial monopoly 156
extension of operations 158–9
as major pillar in London stock market 154–5
reform of 157
war with Burma (1825–6) 162
see also Dutch East India Company
East Indies 169
economic
and political xxiv–xxv
Egypt xxvi, 125–43, 211
attitudes towards Islam by French officers and civilians 141–2
condemnation of Islam by militant partisans 133–4
condemnation of Sufis by al-Jabarti 135–7
conquest of by Napoleon 21, 125, 128, 159
criticism of Sufi spectacles by Bernoyer 134–5, 137
Greek theology in Islamic debate 139–40, 143
invasion of by Britain 56
Mahdist revolt against French 137–8
Napoleon's Islam policy 126, 128–32, 138, 141, 142
Ottoman rule 127
sharing of cynicism about Sufi practices between Bernoyer and elite Egyptians 135–7, 143
émigrés *see* French émigrés

Engelhard, Nicolaus 174
Engels, Friedrich xxiv
England *see* Britain
Equiano, Olaudah 16
Esteban, Javier Cuenca 155
Étang, Antoine de l' 49
'Eurasian Revolution' xix
Europe 104, 105–10
domination of xvii, 144, 145–6

Fabre d'Eglantine, Philippe François Nazaire 29
Fatih, Sayyid Badawi ibn 136
Ferdinand VII, King 71, 72, 76, 77–8
firearms
in private hands in China 201–2
First World War xxviii
Flügel, J. C. 34
Founding Fathers, American 5, 6
France 107, 159
abolition of slavery (1794) 21, 26, 92–3
conquest of Algeria 210
and India 159
revenues 205
Franklin, Benjamin 7–10
Free African Society 9
free trade imperialism 215
French colonies 21, 23, 28–9, 36
influence of events in on French Revolution 28–9
and slavery 23–4
see also Saint Domingue
French émigrés 37–58
amnesty given to and return to France 50
in Britain 48–9, 52, 54, 55–6
composition 41
depiction of in historiography 39–40
emigration to India 49
geographical distribution of Third Estate emigration 45
measures taken against 44–5
French émigrés – *continued*

migration of and numbers involved
38–9, 41, 45
monitoring of activities in European
states 48
pace of migration 43–4
parallels and differences with
American loyalists 50–7
property claims 50
reasons for migration 42
sheltering of in foreign states 47–8
in United States 49
and women 45
French Revolution xii, xiii, xvii, xxiii,
20–36, 51
Burke on 25
commercialization of politics 32–3
connections to the broader world
20–2
contrast between American
Revolution and 38, 51
and Declaration of the Rights of
Man and Citizen 22, 31, 36,
94–5
and dress 34–5
as experienced in Afro-Asia 126
expulsion of non-juring priests 44,
49, 55
and Haitian Revolution 3, 22,
26–7, 28, 91–9, 100
and Indies Company 29
influence of events in French
colonies on 28–30
internalist accounts 20, 22–4, 32, 52
international influence of xxx, 25
migration of French émigrés *see*
French émigrés
neglect of colonial dimension of
23–4
politicization of daily life 32, 33
and rights of free blacks 28
rivalry with Britain as cause 24, 29
role of global framework in
precipitating 30
September massacres 44, 54
sources for the Rights of Man 31–2

Friend of the People, The 20
Friends of Liberty 18
Frost, Alan 158
Fujian 197, 200
Furet, François xxxii, 34
Interpreting the French Revolution 23

Galib, Sheyh xxviii
Garrigus, John 28
Garrison, William Lloyd 12
Gauthier, Florence 26, 93
Geggus, David xviii–xix, xxii, 22, 28,
83
General Crisis xix, xxii
Genovese, Eugene 95, 97
global history xiv
global 'turn', in historical studies
33–4, 36, 209
globalization xiv, 145, 158, 161, 164–5
Godechot, Jacques xvi
France and the Atlantic Revolution
95
gold, African 107, 115
Gold Coast 108, 115, 116, 117
Goldstone, Jack xxv
Gordon Riots (1780) 55
Gordon, William 11
'Great Masculine Renunciation' 34
Greek learning
and Islam 139–40
Grégoire, Henri, abbé 12, 28
Grenada 87
'Grito de Ipiranga' (1822) 80
Grotius, Hugo 31
Guadeloupe 28
Guiana 49
Guizhou 189
gunpowder revolution 106
Gusmão, Alexandre de 63

Habermas, Jürgen 215
Habsburgs xxvii, 107
Haitian Revolution (1791–1804) xvii,
4, 23, 25, 26–8, 85, 86, 10
Haitian Revolution – *continued*

and French Revolution 3, 22, 26–7, 28, 91–9, 100
influence on abolitionism 27, 41, 86, 89, 90, 91
lack of impact of American Revolution on 3
and United States 27
Haiti xv, 22, 98–9, 212
Declaration of Independence (1804) 98
massacre of French colonists 98
US recognition 3
see also Saint Domingue
Hamilton, Alexander 49
Han Chinese 189, 195
Hanover, House of xxx
Harper, Tim 163
Hartley, David 8, 9
Hasan al-Kafrawi, Sheikh 137
Hastings, Warren 25, 53, 149, 158
Havana, Masonic plots in 87
Heber, Reginald 215
Hegel, G. W. F. xviii
Hemings, Sally 17
Hidalgo Revolt (1810) 74
Hilton, Boyd 155, 157
Hobsbawm, Eric xix, xxiv
The Age of Revolution xvii–xviii, 144–5
Ho Chi Minh 21–2
Holland
French occupation of 56
and Java War 170
rule in Java 167, 168, 169, 170, 172–6
war with Britain (1780–3) 168
Hong Kong 159
human rights 31–2, 38, 214
Hunan 189
Hunt, Lynn xxx, 50, 52, 212
Husayn (grandson of Muhammad) 135
Hutchinson, Thomas 43
hybrid legitimacy 61
Hyder Ali 159

Hyderabad, Nizam of 56, 162

Iberian empires 59–82
defensive positions of 62–3
demise and reasons 76–80
driving out of French 75
erupting of civil wars 75
flourishing of trade within 68
impact of Revolutionary Wars 68–9, 71
internal discord within 75–80
linking of interests of metropole with colonies 68–9
militarization of politics 80
Napoleon's campaign against and response to occupation 71–5, 210
and property 70
reconstruction strategies after French occupation 76–8
reforms and provoking of unrest 63–5
and slave trade 65–6
sources of friction in colonies 73–5
steps taken to preserve regimes under attack from Napoleon 72–3
trade reforms 63–4
and Treaty of Tordesillas 62
Ibrahim Bey 127–8
ideology xxv
'imperial revolutions'
age of xxii, 56
and state formation in South Asia 144–52
Indemnity Bill (1825) 50
independence 31
India xii, 21, 56, 144–52, 187, 213, 216
Anglo-French conflict in southern 147
bankruptcy of agency houses in Calcutta 162–3
British rule and expansion in 145, 147, 149, 150, 163–4

India – *continued*
  decline of Mughal empire 146, 147,
    149–50
  decline in textile exports 161
  demand for imperial reform 157–8
  East India Company's conquest of
    Bengal xii–xiii, 145, 147, 149
  effect of colonial governance 151–2
  emigration of American loyalists to
    47
  and France 159
  global repercussions of British
    conquest of 153
  influence on British domestic and
    political affairs 155–7
  invasion of by Cossacks (1801) 160
  and opium trade 201
  Persian connection 164
  poor Britons serving in British forces
    in 155–6
  presence of French émigrés in 49
  role of in British trade and value of
    to Britain 154–5
India Act (1784) 53, 156
Indian Ocean 146
Indian Rebellion (1857–8) xiii, xxxii,
  145
indigo 86
individualism 108–9
Indochina 216
Indonesia 171, 188
  independence from Dutch (1945)
    170, 172
  see also Java
Industrial Revolution xii, xvii, xxiv,
  144
infanticide
  China and selective 191–2
Iran xvi, 211
Ireland 55, 210
Irish rebellion (1798) 210
Islam
  engagement with Greek learning
    139–40
  five pillars of 130–1

and Java 170, 171–2
and Napoleon's policy in Egypt
  126, 128–32, 138, 141, 142
and Qing empire 202

al-Jabarti, 'Abd al-Rahman 129–30,
  131, 132, 134–6, 140, 141, 142
al-Jabarti, Hasan 140
Jacobins 38
Jahangir (Mughal emperor) 202
Jamaica 85
  'Christmas Rebellion' (1831) 3, 91
  slave rebellion (1776) 3
  slavery 27
  sugar and coffee production 86
James, C. L. R. 92
  The Black Jacobins 26, 28
Janissaries 127, 211
Japan xxvi, xxxi, 216
Jasanoff, Maya xxvi, 37, 159
Jaubert, Pierre Amedée 131
Jaurès, Jean 23, 93
Java xxvi, 56, 167–88
  British invasion and occupation
    (1811–16) 56, 159, 167, 169,
    175, 176–80, 187
  Chinese in 180–6
  and Diponegoro 170, 171–2, 180,
    187
  divisions at courts during Dutch rule
    173–4
  and Dutch East India Company
    167
  Dutch occupation (1794–5) 168
  Edict on Ceremonial and Etiquette
    (1808) 182–3
  Franco-Dutch regime of Daendels
    (1808–11) 167, 168, 169, 170,
    172–6, 178, 187
  impact of 1812 treaties on 178–9
  and Islam 170, 171–2
  legal reforms under Raffles 178–9
  looting of Yogyakarta *kraton* by
    British 177–8, 179–80
  and opium retail trade 185–6

Java – *continued*
  pre-1808 history 168–9
  tiger and buffalo fights 175–6
  tollgates (*bandar*) and impact of
    180–4, 185
Java War (1825–30) 169–70, 171, 179,
    180, 186
Jay, John 7
Jean-François (Haitian general) 97
Jefferson, Thomas 2, 7
  and Maria Cosway 15–16
  and Haitian Revolution 27
  Notes on the State of Virginia 17
  and slavery 12–15, 18, 19
João VI, Prince 75
Jones, Absalom 9
Jones, Sir William 164
José I, King 64
Joubin, Rebecca 138
Jovellanos, Gaspar Melchor de 71

al-Kabir, Yusuf Bey 137
'Kew Letters' 168
Keynes, John Maynard 153–4
Knox, Henry 49
Kokandis 189, 195
Koselleck, Reinhart xv
Kuhn, Philip
  Soulstealers 216

La Marche, Jean François de 54
La Rochefoucault-Liancourt, François-
    Alexandre-Frédéric, duc de 12,
    49
Lafayette, Marie Joseph Paul Yves Roch
    Gilbert Du Motier, marquis de
    10–11, 12, 14–15, 16, 18, 28, 38
Langley, Lester
  The Americas in the Age of Revolution
    2
Latin America 1, 2, 25, 56, 61, 99
Law, John 29
Lear, Tobias 12
Lee, Richard Henry 7
Levant Company 153

Lib Sing 184
Lind, John
  Three Letters to Dr Price 6
Loango 116, 118
Louis XVI, King of France xxvii, 44,
    96
Louis XVIII (Comte de Provence) 48
Louis-Philippe, King of France 50,
    159
Louisiana 4, 21, 27
Louverture, Toussaint 92, 96, 97, 98
Loyalist Associations 56
Loyalist Claims Commission 47, 55
loyalists, American *see* American loyalists
loyalty oaths 43, 44
Luanda 66, 116, 117, 118

Macartney, George, 1st earl Macartney
    160
Macaulay, Thomas Babington 165
MacGillivray, Mauritz 183
Madiou, Thomas 96
Madison, James 14, 18, 61
Mahdi 137–8, 142
Mahmud II, Sultan xvi
Malesherbes, Chrétien Guillaume de
    Lamoignon de 8
Malthus, Thomas xxiv
Manchuria 194, 200
Manigat, Leslie 99
Marat, Jean-Paul 20
Marathas 147, 151
Markovits, Claude 163
Marshall, P. J. 52
  The Making and Unmaking of Empires
    2
Martinique 95
Marx, Karl 33
al-Masiri, Sheikh 131
Matthews, Gelien 89
Mauritius 176
Mayo, Joseph 11, 17
Mecca xxviii
Medina xxviii
Merapi, Mount (Java) 169

merchant capitalists
  Iberian empires 64–5, 66, 67, 68,
    69, 70, 77
merchant guilds 64
Metcalf, Thomas 159
Mexico 65, 73–4, 81
Miller, Joseph C. xviii, 101, 210
Millikan, Max xvii
Mines, Mattison 126
Ming empire xxii
Minto, Gilbert Elliot, 1st earl of 177,
    187
Mintz, Sidney 83
Mirabeau, Honoré Gabriel Riqueti,
    comte de 28
Miranda, Francisco de 56
Mississippi Bubble 29
Mohawk Indians 41
Moiret, Joseph-Marie 132, 133
monarchical rule 105–6, 108, 109
Monroe, James 27
Montesquieu, Charles de Secondat,
    baron de 61
More, Hannah 55
Morillo, general Pablo 77
Mughal Empire xv, xxix, 146–7, 209
  decline of 146, 147, 149–50
  invasion of by Nadir Shah (1738–9)
    146
Munro, Sir Thomas 165
Muntinghe, Harman Warner 187
Murad Bey 127–8
Muslims 111, 125 *see also* Islam
Mustafa, Haji xvi
Mustafa IV, Sultan xvi, xxvii
Mysore 21, 56, 211

Nadir Shah xiii, xvi, 146
Naples 21
Napoleon xxi, 21, 27, 33, 50, 57, 71,
    92
  attempt to re-establish slavery in
    Caribbean 26, 29, 85
  conquest and occupation of Egypt
    21, 125, 128, 159

Continental Blockade 215
  and Iberian campaign 71–5, 210
  and India 159
  Islam policy 126, 128–31, 138, 141,
    142
Napoleonic wars 59, 169
Nash, Gary B. xv, 1
nation-state 215
National Assembly, French 92
National Convention, French 21
'national honour', concept of 53
nationalism xii, 35
New Brunswick 47
newspapers 215–16
Ngabèhi, Pangéran 179
Nicholls, David 98
Niello-Sargy, Jean-Gabriel de 137
non-juring priests 44, 49, 50, 55
North Briton, The 32
Nova Scotia 47, 53

O'Brien, Patrick 154
Olavide, Pablo de 62
opium trade 160, 162, 201
  in Java 185–6
Opium War (1839–42) xii, 162, 189,
    216
Oswald, Richard 8, 9
Othello (slave) 8
Ottoman Empire xxvii–xviii, 21, 56,
    107, 127, 131–2, 146, 209
  Islamic law courts 132
  Janissary infantry 127
  survival of and reasons xxviii–xxix,
    211
Ouidah 119

Pacific Ocean xxiii
Páez, José Antonio 78
Paine, Thomas xiii, xvi, 1–2, 6, 19, 38,
    214
  Common Sense 1–2
  'Letters To the Citizens of the United
    States' 19
Palmer, John 162–3

Palmer, R. R.   17, 20, 23
    The Age of the Democratic Revolution
        xvi–xvii, xviii, 95
Paris, Treaty of (1783)   46
Parthasarathi, Prasannan   161
Paul I, Tsar   160
pawns, slaves as   112
Pax Britannica   xxiv–xxv
Peabody, Norbert   151–2
Pedro I, Regent of Brazil   80
Pellerin, Jean-Charles   33
Pennsylvania Abolition Society   10
Pepperell, Sir William   54
Perlin, Frank   150–1, 152
Persian language   164
Pétion, Alexandre   27, 98–9
Philadelphia   9
Philippines   213
Piar, Manuel   78
Piattoli, Scipione   16
Pichegru, general Jean-Charles   168
Pindaris   215
Piquet, Jean-Daniel   93
Pitt, William, the Elder   211
Pitt the Younger, William   55, 156, 158
Place, Lionel   126, 141
Plassey, Battle of (1757)   xiii
Pocock, J. G. A.   213
Polish revolution (1794)   23
political outcomes
    and economic outcomes   xxiv–xxv
political thought   212–13
Pombal, Sebastião José de Carvalho e
    Melo, marquês de   64
Pombo, José Ignacio de   69
Pomeranz, Kenneth   xxiv, xxvi, 154,
        162, 189, 211, 216
Popkin, Jeremy   26
Portugal/Portuguese Empire   59
    commercial system   63
    internal discord   79–80
    resistance to reforms   64
    response to Napoleon's campaign
        against   71
    see also Iberian empires

Price, Dr Richard   5–6, 7, 8, 13
    Observations on the American Revolution
        5–6, 6–7
Protestantism, millenarian   202
Prussia
    and French émigrés   48
public sphere   216
Puerto Rico   84
Pufendorf, Samuel   31
Punjab   147, 159, 211, 214

Qing empire   189–208, 211, 214, 216
    absence of foreign threats and urban
        uprisings   197
    defeat of in Opium War   189
    foreign trade   200
    frontiers   195–6
    influence of foreign ideas   202
    Jahangir's invasion (1826)   202
    land and tenancy   190–1
    migration   193
    obstacles to industrial growth
        193–4
    and opium trade   201
    political and demographic
        reinforcement   191–2
    proliferation of firearms in private
        hands   201–2
    rebellions   189, 195–6, 200
    reforms   206
    regional differences   193
    revenue-raising   203–6
    road towards crisis   193–4
    rural unrest   197
    successes   207
    wage labourers   190
    and White Lotus Rebellion   189,
        195, 204, 206, 207
Quebec   47, 53
Quiberon Bay, Battle of (1795)   48

Raffles, Sir Thomas Stamford   167,
        169, 176, 177, 178, 185, 187
Ragatz, Lowell   86
Raimond, Julien   26, 94, 95

Rainsford, Marcus 28
Rajput kingship 151–2
Ramayana xxviii
Ranjit Singh 147, 159, 211
al-Rashid, Harun 139
Ray, Rajat Kanta 163
Raynal, Guillaume-Thomas-François,
  abbé xvi, 8, 12–13, 15
  Histoire des deux Indes 28
  republicanism xv, xxxii, 56
Restoration, French 40
Réveillon Riot (1789) (Paris) xxvii
revolution, concept and meaning of
  xiv–xvi
revolutions, European (1848) 216
Revolutionary Wars 53, 56, 68, 169
Richelieu, Armand-Emmanuel du
  Plessis, duc de 48
rights 214, 215 *see also* human rights
Rio de Janeiro 64, 66, 71, 72, 73,
  76–7, 79
River Plate 56, 75
Robespierre, Maximilian de 49–50
Rodrigues, Feo 125
Rome, Treaty of (2006) 213
Rostow, W. W. xvii
Rothschild, Emma 29
Rousseau, Jean-Jacques xxii, 34
  Émile xiii
Roy, Rammohan 145, 158, 213, 214
Rush, Benjamin 7, 9
Russia xxvii, xxxi, 212
  Cossack invasion of India 160
  Russian Revolution (1917) xxxii

Safavid empire 146, 209
Saint-Denys, Jucherau de
  Révolutions de Constantinople xvi
Saint Domingue (later Haiti) 83, 86–7
  coffee production 85
  émigrés 49, 51–2
  free coloured population 28, 94, 95,
    97
  independence of 97, 98
  slave population 26, 66

slave resistance in 93–4
slave uprising (1791) 21, 23, 26,
  95–7
wealth of 26
white settler autonomism 93, 94
see also Haitian Revolution
Saint-Just 49–50
St Vincent 87
Saintoyant, Jules 92
Sanger, Abner 43
Santo Domingo 83–4
Schama, Simon
  Citizens 23
Schmitt, Carl 60
Schultz, Kirsten 76
Scottish Association of the Friends of
  the People 20
Sedition Act (1798) 49
Selim III, Sultan xxvii–xxviii, xvi, 128
Sen, Sudipta 147
Senegambia 108, 116
September Massacres (1792) 44, 54
Serbia xxvii
Seven Years War (1756–63) xiii, xxx, 4,
  24, 209, 216
Sharp, Granville 7, 13
al-Sharqawi, Sheikh 'Abdullah 139,
  140, 141
Sheikha 134–5
Shovlin, John 29
Sierra Leone 13, 47, 53, 54, 57
Sikh movements 214
Silva Lisboa, José da 77
silver 107, 201
Silverman, Kaja 35
Singapore 159
Siraj-ud-daula xiii
Skocpol, Theda 24
slave trade xii, 114, 212
  abolition of in Britain (1807) 19,
    212
  abolition of in United States (1807)
    17
  and Iberian empires 65–6
slave-soldiery 127

slavery   65–6
    abolition of in British colonies
        (1833)   83, 84, 85, 91
    abolition of by France (1794)   21,
        26, 92–3
    and Africa   108, 110, 117–18, 119,
        121, 124
    and American Revolution   3, 4–19
    and Caribbean   27, 28, 83, 84–5,
        88–91, 100
    Cugoano's attack on   16
    and Franklin   7–10
    and French colonies   23–4
    growth of in American South   19
    and Haitian Revolution *see* Haitian
        Revolution
    and Jefferson   12–17, 18, 19
    and Lafayette   10–11, 12, 18
    Napoleon's efforts to re-establish in
        Caribbean   26, 29, 85
    population   66
    settlement of slaves in Sierra Leone
        plan   13, 47
    uprising in Saint Domingue (1791)
        21, 23, 26, 95–7
    and Washington   10, 11–12
Smith, Adam   34
Société des Amis des Noirs   16–17, 28
Société des Colons Américains   93
Society for the Abolition of the Slave
    Trade   53
Soninke   111–12, 116
Sons of Liberty   42
Sonthonax, Léger-Félicité   96, 97
Sousa, Francisco Felix de   119
South Asia
    global connections of   161–6
    imperial repercussions   153–60
    imperial revolutions and early
        modern state formation in
        144–52
    see also India
South-east Asia   xxvi, xxxi *see also* Java
Souza Coutinho, Rodrigo de   71, 72,
    75, 77

sovereignty   59–61, 109, 213
Spain/Spanish Empire   25, 59, 62, 107
    demise and reasons   76–9
    internal discord   77–9
    reforms and unrest provoked by
        64–5
    response to Napoleon's campaign
        against   71–2
    and Revolutionary Wars   68
    and slave trade   66
    trade boom   65
    see also Iberian empires
Spanish America   xv, xxvi, 27, 73, 75,
    81–2
Spanish West Indies   84, 99
Spanish-American revolutions   xiii
standard of living, divergences in
    xxiv
state   210
    early formation of in South Asia
        144–52
statehood   61
Stokes, Eric   150
Stone, Bailey   24
Subrahmanyam, Sanjay   xii, 150
Sufis   134
Suleiman the Magnificent   132

Tabataba'i, Ghulam Husain Khan   xiii,
    xvi, 148
Taiping Rebellion (1851–64)   xiii,
    xxxii, 202, 205, 207–8, 214–15
Taiwan
    Lin Shuangwen rebellion   189, 195,
        196
Talleyrand, Charles-Maurice de, prince
    de Bénévent   37–8, 49, 140
Tamerlane   xiii, xv
Taylor, Miles   157
Tenmei Famine (1782–7)   xxvi
Thailand   211
Thompson, E. P.   39, 40
Thornton, Henry   54
Tibet   160, 189
Tilly, Charles   61, 206

Tipu Sultan of Mysore   21, 56, 147,
    178, 211
Tiradentes revolt (1789)   64
Tocqueville, Alexis de   23–4, 33
    Democracy in America   24
    *The Old Regime and the French
        Revolution*   23
Todd, James   152
Tokugawa Ieharu   xxvi
tollgates (*bandar*)   180–4, 185
Tordesillas, Treaty of (1494)   62
Torres, Camilo   74
Travers, Robert   xvii, xxxi, 144, 214
Trouillot, Michel-Rolphe   26
Túpac Amaru revolt (1780)   64
Turgot, Anne-Robert-Jacques, baron de
    l'Aulne   8

ulema (Muslim clergy)   132–3, 142
Union of Britain and Ireland (1801)
    210
United States
    abolition of slave trade   17
    French émigrés in   49
    and French Revolution   20
    and Haitian Revolution   27
    slave population   26
    see also American Revolution
Uruguay   78
Utrecht, Treaty of (1713)   62

van Braam, Jacob Andries   175
van Burgst, Huibert Gerard Nahuys
    184, 186
van den Bosch, Governor-general
    Johannes   170
van der Capellen, Governor-general
    Godert   169, 183, 185
van Hogendorp, Willem   180
van Sevenhoven, Jan Isäak   181, 182,
    183, 185, 186
Vaughan, Benjamin   8, 9
Venezuela   84
Victoria, Queen   157

Vienna, Treaty of (1815)   167
Vietnam   21, 189
Virginia   14, 15, 85
Vodou   94
Volney, Constantin-François   12
Voltaire   xxxii, 8

Wahhabis   xxviii, 211, 214
War of the Spanish Succession
    (1701–14)   xxii, 62
warrior-kings   122
Washbrook, David   145, 161, 165
Washington, George   7, 38
    and slavery   10, 11–12
Watson, Brook   54
Weber, Max   34, 60
Webster, Anthony   162
Wellesley, Henry, 1st baron Cowley
    77–8
Wellesley, Richard, 1st marquess
    Wellesley   156, 178
West, Benjamin   55
White Lotus Rebellion (1796–1805)
    189, 195, 204, 205, 206, 207, 214
Wiencek, Henry   11, 12
Wilberforce, William   13, 54, 57–8, 212
Wilkes, John   32
Williams, Eric   86, 88
Wilmot Committee   54
Wilmot, John Eardley   47, 54, 55
Wilson, Jon E.   152
Windward Isles   87
women
    and clothing   34
    as French émigrés   45
    selling of in China   191
Wong, R. Bin   207
Woolman, John   7
World Crisis   xxiii, xix, 58
Wythe, George   15

Yeh-chen, Wang   205
Yogyakarta   177–8, 179–80, 187
Yunnan, rebellion (1817–18)   195

CPSIA information can be obtained
at www.ICGtesting.com
Printed in the USA
FSHW021254260319
56690FS